Advanced Plastic Forming Processes: Theory, Experiments and Numerical Simulations

Advanced Plastic Forming Processes: Theory, Experiments and Numerical Simulations

Guest Editor

Gaochao Yu

MDPI

Basel • Beijing • Wuhan • Barcelona • Belgrade • Novi Sad • Cluj • Manchester

Guest Editor
Gaochao Yu
School of Mechanical
Engineering
Yanshan University
Qinhuangdao
China

Editorial Office
MDPI AG
Grosspeteranlage 5
4052 Basel, Switzerland

This is a reprint of the Special Issue, published open access by the journal *Metals* (ISSN 2075-4701), freely accessible at: https://www.mdpi.com/journal/metals/special_issues/40F8NXQUP1.

For citation purposes, cite each article independently as indicated on the article page online and as indicated below:

Lastname, A.A.; Lastname, B.B. Article Title. *Journal Name* **Year**, *Volume Number*, Page Range.

ISBN 978-3-7258-6948-0 (Hbk)
ISBN 978-3-7258-6949-7 (PDF)
https://doi.org/10.3390/books978-3-7258-6949-7

Contents

About the Editor

Gaochao Yu

Gaochao Yu is an Associate Professor in the Department of Plastic Forming Engineering, School of Mechanical Engineering, Yanshan University, whose research interests include sheet and tube metal forming and intelligent manufacturing systems. He has made significant contributions to the fundamental theories and engineering technologies of longitudinal submerged arc welded pipe forming and straightening processes. His work includes the refinement of elastic springback theory for small curvature plane bending and the proposal and experimental validation of the unified curvature theorem for reciprocating bending. He has developed several innovative forming processes, specialized equipment, and intelligent control strategies, with successful applications in aerospace, oil and gas pipeline, and power equipment industries. His research has established distinctive strengths in pipeline equipment manufacturing and intelligent forming control.

metals

MDPI

Editorial

Advanced Plastic Forming Processes: Theory, Experiments and Numerical Simulations

Gaochao Yu

School of Mechanical Engineering, Yanshan University, Qinhuangdao 066004, China; gch_yu@ysu.edu.cn

1. Introduction and Scope

Plastic-forming technologies represent an essential component of advanced manufacturing, as they enable not only the fabrication of components with complex geometries but also the simultaneous achievement of excellent comprehensive in-service performance [1]. The rapid development of major engineering equipment in aerospace, aviation, high-speed rail, and nuclear power industries has posed significant challenges to the fundamental theories of plastic forming, advanced forming processes, the accuracy of process simulations, and the control of characteristic component dimensions.

Springback is a key factor that affects the forming accuracy of metal profiles, and its reliable prediction requires an accurate constitutive model [2]. The degradation behavior of the elastic modulus and its nonlinear response [3–6], plastic hardening behavior [7,8], Bauschinger effect [9], and strength-differential effect [10,11] are critical factors that limit the springback prediction accuracy. By embedding accurate constitutive models into finite element simulation software, high-precision prediction of bending springback in metal sheets and tubes has been achieved [12–14]. In recent years, with the rapid development of the microforming process, the theory of plastic forming has evolved from the macroscopic to the microscopic scale [15–17].

For materials with poor deformability and structures with difficult forming, the field-assisted plastic-forming process can improve the mechanical properties of the materials, unlock the forming potential of the materials and enhance the forming limit. A series of new field-assisted plastic-forming processes has been developed, such as impact hydraulic forming [18,19], electric-assisted forming [20–22], thermal-assisted forming [23,24], low-temperature forming [25,26], viscous pressure bulging [27], and electromagnetic forming [28–31]. The proposal and development of these advanced plastic-forming processes have provided new technical approaches for the high-precision forming of complex components.

2. Contributions

This Special Issue features 11 original contributions in the advanced plastic-forming field, covering topics such as ultrasonic vibration-assisted forming, hydraulic forming, electromagnetic forming, forging processes, bar straightening, stiffened plates for anti-buckling structural design, and composite material structure design.

Li et al. (contribution 1) investigated ultrasonic vibration-assisted superplastic forming of amorphous alloys, demonstrating that the introduction of ultrasonic vibration significantly reduces the flow stress of the amorphous alloy and thereby enhances its plastic deformation capability. Numerical simulations revealed that ultrasonic vibration induces periodic interfacial separation between the indenter and the specimen, leading to the cyclic disappearance of frictional forces. In addition, ultrasonic vibration effectively decreases the apparent viscosity of the amorphous alloy, thereby improving its material filling ability.

Liu et al. (contribution 2) investigated the influence of forming process parameters on the dimensional accuracy of multilayer metal bellow hydroforming. Process parameter optimization was carried out using response surface methodology in conjunction with a genetic algorithm. The bellows formed under the optimized conditions were demonstrated to satisfy the dimensional tolerances specified by the EJMA standard.

Jia et al. (contribution 3) investigated the effects of inclination angle, roll reduction, straightening speed, and roll gap on the straightening quality of 20CrMnTi bars during the eleven cross-roll straightening process.

Lancanova et al. (contribution 4) investigated the influence of geometric configurations on the buckling load-carrying capacity and structural stability of stiffened plates, demonstrating that an appropriate distribution of stiffener height and plate thickness can significantly enhance buckling resistance.

Alves et al. (contribution 5) employed constructal design coupled with exhaustive search to optimize the geometry of transverse hat-stiffeners in steel plates under bending. The optimized configuration achieved a substantial reduction in deflection and demonstrated superior structural performance over longitudinal stiffeners under equivalent material volume.

Zhang et al. (contribution 6) investigated the effects of pass number and die channel angle in equal channel angular pressing (ECAP) on the microstructure, mechanical properties, and corrosion resistance of the nano-MgO/Mg–Zn–Ca composite material. By optimizing ECAP processing parameters, a synergistic enhancement of strength, ductility, and corrosion resistance in the composite material was achieved.

Dou et al. (contribution 7) investigated the influence of electrically assisted forming parameters on the mechanical behavior and springback of 7075-T6 aluminum alloy. Electrically assisted three-point bending tests revealed that increasing current density effectively reduces the springback angle.

Wang et al. (contribution 8) investigates the effects of electric pulse treatment on the interfacial properties of roll-bonded Cu/304 stainless steel composite thin strips, revealing that electric pulses promote interfacial diffusion and metallurgical bonding, thereby rapidly enhancing interfacial strength as an alternative to conventional annealing.

Wang et al. (contribution 9) analyzes the multi-physical field coupling behavior in electro-controlled permanent magnet blank holder processes. A coupled electromagnetic–thermal model considering magnetic losses is established, revealing the influence of magnetic degradation on blank holding force stability and forming accuracy.

Niu et al. (contribution 10) studied near-net shape forging of large marine crank throws through numerical simulation and experiments. Metal flow behavior and defect evolution were clarified, enabling improved forming accuracy and material utilization for large-scale marine crank components.

Yan et al. (contribution 11) investigated the influence of asymmetric roll bending forces on metal deformation and strip shape in cold rolling using a three-dimensional elastic–plastic finite element model. The results clarify the linear regulation mechanisms of thickness, crown, edge drop, and flatness, providing guidance for controlling asymmetric strip shape defects.

3. Conclusions and Outlook

This Special Issue highlights recent advances in plastic forming through the integration of novel forming techniques, multi-physical field assistance, and advanced numerical modeling. The collected studies demonstrate that auxiliary fields, such as ultrasonic

https://doi.org/10.3390/met16020203

vibration, electric current, and electromagnetic control, effectively improve formability, dimensional accuracy, and interfacial or structural performance. Meanwhile, simulation-based optimization methods and refined constitutive models enable accurate prediction and efficient control of complex deformation behaviors. Future research is expected to further emphasize multi-field coupling mechanisms, intelligent optimization strategies, and precision plastic-forming process.

Funding: This work was supported by National Natural Science Foundation of China [grant number 52375389], the Science Research Project of Hebei Education Department [grant number BJK2023103], and the S&T Program of Hebei [grant number 226Z1802G].

Acknowledgments: I thank all authors for their high-quality contributions and the anonymous reviewers for their rigorous assessments. I am grateful to the *Metals* Editorial Office for professional support throughout the peer review process.

Conflicts of Interest: The author declares no conflicts of interest.

List of Contributions:

1. Li, H.; Liu, J.; Shen, C.; Li, C. An Ultrasonic Vibration-Assisted Superplastic Forming Method for Zr-Based Bulk Amorphous Alloys: Experiment and Simulation. *Metals* **2025**, *15*, 1299.
2. Liu, J.; Li, L.; Liu, J.; Li, L. Optimization of Multilayer Metal Bellow Hydroforming Process with Response Surface Method and Genetic Algorithm. *Metals* **2025**, *15*, 1046.
3. Jia, S.; Bao, L.; Wang, S.; Meng, Q.; Zhao, J.; Zhai, R. Optimization of Eleven Cross-Roll Straightening Process for 20CrMnTi Bars Based on Combined Hardening Model. *Metals* **2025**, *15*, 908.
4. Lançanova, A.F.; Vieira, R.L.; dos Santos, E.D.; Rocha, L.A.O.; da Silveira, T.; Lima, J.P.S.; Estrada, E.d.S.D.; Isoldi, L.A. Constructal Design and Numerical Simulation Applied to Geometric Evaluation of Stiffened Steel Plates Subjected to Elasto-Plastic Buckling Under Biaxial Compressive Loading. *Metals* **2025**, *15*, 879.
5. Alves, M.A.; Rodrigues, E.M.; Rocha, L.A.O.; dos Santos, E.D.; Almeida, W.R.; Isoldi, L.A. Numerical and Geometrical Evaluation of Steel Plates with Transverse Hat-Stiffeners Under Bending. *Metals* **2025**, *15*, 647.
6. Zhang, X.; Han, J.; Tian, J.; Zhu, L.; Zhang, P.; Wang, Y.; Jiang, Z. The Effects of Pass Number and Die Channel Angle of Equal Channel Angular Pressing on Innovative Magnesium Composite Material. *Metals* **2025**, *15*, 349.
7. Dou, S.; Liu, Z.; Li, Z.; Shi, H.; Zhou, K.; Xia, J. Mechanical Properties of 7075-T6 Aluminum Alloy in Electrically Assisted Forming. *Metals* **2025**, *15*, 117.
8. Wang, Z.; Niu, X.; Wang, M.; Yang, Y.; He, D.; Du, W. Effect of Electric Pulse Treatment on the Interfacial Properties of Copper/304 Stainless Steel Composite Thin Strips Fabricated by Roll Bonding. *Metals* **2025**, *15*, 112.
9. Wang, Z.; Meng, L.; Yu, G.; Ji, X. Multi-Physical Field Coupling Analysis of Electro-Controlled Permanent Magnet Blank Holder Processes Considering Thermal Magnetic Losses. *Metals* **2025**, *15*, 39.
10. Niu, L.; Zhang, Q.; Zhang, Y.; Wang, J.; Luo, W.; Liu, D.; Ma, T.; Velay, X. Study on Near-Net Shape Forging of Large Marine Crank Throws. *Metals* **2025**, *15*, 14.
11. Yan, Z.; Pan, S.; Tang, Y.; Cao, W. Theoretical Study of Asymmetric Bending Force on Metal Deformation in Cold Rolling. *Metals* **2024**, *14*, 1168.

References

1. Lin, Z.; Huang, Q.; Yuan, S.; Zhao, G.; Hua, L.; Yi, Y.; Zhan, M.; Li, S.; Liu, W.; Wang, B.; et al. Major breakthrough and progress in metal forming technology and equipment of China in the last 30 years. *J. Plast. Eng.* **2024**, *31*, 2–45.
2. Yoshida, F.; Uemori, T. A model of large-strain cyclic plasticity and its application to springback simulation. *Int. J. Mech. Sci.* **2003**, *45*, 1687–1702. [CrossRef]
3. Yoshida, F.; Amaishi, T. Model for description of nonlinear unloading-reloading stress-strain response with special reference to plastic-strain dependent chord modulus. *Int. J. Plast.* **2020**, *130*, 102708. [CrossRef]

https://doi.org/10.3390/met16020203

4. Chang, Y.; Wang, N.; Wang, B.T.; Li, X.D.; Wang, C.Y.; Zhao, K.M.; Dong, H. Prediction of bending springback of the medium-Mn steel considering elastic modulus attenuation. *J. Manuf. Process.* **2021**, *67*, 345–355. [CrossRef]
5. Ghaei, A.; Green, D.E.; Aryanpour, A. Springback simulation of advanced high strength steels considering nonlinear elastic unloading-reloading behavior. *Mater. Des.* **2015**, *88*, 461–470. [CrossRef]
6. Yoshida, F. Description of elastic-plastic stress-strain transition in cyclic plasticity and its effect on springback prediction. *Int. J. Mater. Form.* **2022**, *15*, 12. [CrossRef]
7. Zhong, Y.-L.; Wang, Y.-B.; Xiang, Y.; Li, G.-Q. Constitutive model for cyclic behavior of mild steel under various strain amplitudes. *J. Constr. Steel Res.* **2022**, *196*, 107396. [CrossRef]
8. Meng, Q.D.; Zhao, J.; Mu, Z.K.; Zhai, R.X.; Yu, G.C. Springback prediction of multiple reciprocating bending based on different hardening models. *J. Manuf. Process.* **2022**, *76*, 251–263. [CrossRef]
9. Meng, Q.; Zhai, R.; Zhang, Y.; Fu, P.; Zhao, J. Analysis of springback for multiple bending considering nonlinear unloading-reloading behavior, stress inheritance and Bauschinger effect. *J. Mater. Process. Technol.* **2022**, *307*, 117657. [CrossRef]
10. Maeda, T.; Noma, N.; Kuwabara, T.; Barlat, F.; Korkolis, Y.P. Measurement of the strength differential effect of DP980 steel sheet and experimental validation using pure bending test. *J. Mater. Process. Technol.* **2018**, *256*, 247–253. [CrossRef]
11. Lee, S.Y.; Yoon, S.Y.; Kim, J.H.; Oh, K.S. Evaluation of loading-path-dependent constitutive models for springback prediction in martensitic steel forming. *Int. J. Mech. Sci.* **2023**, *251*, 108317. [CrossRef]
12. Zhai, R.X.; Ding, X.H.; Yu, S.M.; Wang, C.G. Stretch bending and springback of profile in the loading method of prebending and tension. *Int. J. Mech. Sci.* **2018**, *144*, 746–764. [CrossRef]
13. Zhao, J.; Zhai, R.X.; Qian, Z.P.; Ma, R. A study on springback of profile plane stretch-bending in the loading method of pretension and moment. *Int. J. Mech. Sci.* **2013**, *75*, 45–54. [CrossRef]
14. Ma, J.; Welo, T. Analytical springback assessment in flexible stretch bending of complex shapes. *Int. J. Mach. Tools Manuf.* **2021**, *160*, 103653. [CrossRef]
15. Wang, H.; Zhang, P.; Wang, C.J.; Zhu, Q.; Chen, G. Evolution of geometrically necessary dislocations in a thin sheet of pure copper and the influence on the springback in micro-bending. *J. Manuf. Process.* **2025**, *141*, 1650–1661. [CrossRef]
16. Yan, B.Y.; Meng, B.; Zhu, Y.; Wang, Y.H.; Wan, M. A global springback compensation method for manufacturing metallic seal ring with complex cross-section and submillimeter precision. *J. Mater. Process. Technol.* **2024**, *331*, 118498. [CrossRef]
17. Zhang, R.; Xu, Z.T.; Peng, L.F.; Fu, M. Multi-scale modelling of the heterogeneous grain deformation in ultra-thin sheets. *Int. J. Mech. Sci.* **2025**, *304*, 110690. [CrossRef]
18. Li, H.; Xie, S.R.; Zhang, S.H.; Chen, S.F.; Song, H.W.; Xu, Y.; Pokrovsky, A.I.; Khina, B.B. Spring-back behaviors of Ti-6Al-4V sheet under effect of strain rate. *Int. J. Mech. Sci.* **2023**, *260*, 108646. [CrossRef]
19. Xia, L.L.; Xu, Y.; Xie, W.L.; Li, J.; Liu, X.F.; Pokrovsky, A.I.; Zhang, S.H. A novel strategy for reducing sheet springback by coupled with high strain rate and shear deformation via impact hydroforming. *J. Manuf. Process.* **2024**, *132*, 392–403. [CrossRef]
20. Niu, Z.L.; Yue, Z.M.; Xia, Z.C.; Liu, W.J.; Zhang, S.; Xu, A.J. A generalized electro-thermo-mechanical framework for electrically assisted tube forming: Case study on TA18 titanium alloy. *J. Mater. Process. Technol.* **2025**, *343*, 118974. [CrossRef]
21. Xiao, A.; Yan, Z.Q.; Huang, C.Q.; Yu, Z.X.; Wang, S.P.; Cui, X.H. Reduction of springback of Ti6Al4V alloy by high-density and instantaneous pulsed current. *Mat. Sci. Eng. A-Struct.* **2023**, *877*, 145188. [CrossRef]
22. Li, C.Z.; Xu, Z.T.; Peng, L.F.; Lai, X.M. An electric-pulse-assisted stamping process towards springback suppression and precision fabrication of micro channels. *Int. J. Mech. Sci.* **2022**, *218*, 107081. [CrossRef]
23. Li, W.N.; Attallah, M.M.; Essa, K. Heat-assisted incremental sheet forming for high-strength materials—A review. *Int. J. Adv. Manuf. Technol.* **2023**, *124*, 2011–2036. [CrossRef]
24. Fu, K.N.; Zhao, Z.W.; Peng, H.L.; Zheng, K.L.; Yuan, S.J. Manufacturing of ultra-thin large titanium alloy tube using the novel hot gas pressure-bending process. *J. Mater. Process. Technol.* **2024**, *326*, 118358. [CrossRef]
25. Wu, F.X.; Fan, X.B.; Yang, G.; Chen, X.S.; Yuan, S.J. Dimensional change and springback of spherical shell in cryogenic forming. *Int. J. Mech. Sci.* **2024**, *284*, 109757. [CrossRef]
26. Fan, X.B.; Wang, Q.L.; Wu, F.X.; Wang, X.G. Cryogenic springback of 2219-W aluminum alloy sheet through V-shaped bending. *Trans. Nonferr. Met. Soc. China* **2024**, *34*, 3185–3193. [CrossRef]
27. Feng, Y.K.; Wang, Z.J. Characterizing springback stress behavior in VPB by experimental-numerical hybrid method. *Int. J. Mech. Sci.* **2022**, *224*, 107321. [CrossRef]
28. Li, C.X.; Xu, X.F.; Ouyang, S.W.; Du, L.M.; Zhang, W.; Zhu, X.H.; Han, X.T.; Cao, Q.L.; Li, L. Improving forming accuracy of variable-diameter tube by electromagnetic forming using segmented coil. *Int. J. Adv. Manuf. Technol.* **2024**, *132*, 4829–4840. [CrossRef]
29. Du, Z.H.; Han, Y.B.; Han, D.; Zhang, H.B.; Mao, X.B.; Zhang, Z.; Cui, X.H. Effect of heat treatment and electromagnetic forming on springback and related properties of 7075 aluminum alloy sheet. *J. Braz. Soc. Mech. Sci.* **2024**, *46*, 707. [CrossRef]

https://doi.org/10.3390/met16020203

30. Du, Z.H.; Yan, Z.Q.; Cui, X.H.; Chen, B.G.; Yu, H.L.; Qiu, D.Y.; Xia, W.Z.; Deng, Z.S. Springback control and large skin manufacturing by high-speed vibration using electromagnetic forming. *J. Mater. Process. Technol.* **2022**, *299*, 117340. [CrossRef]
31. Ghaffari, H.; Alimirzaloo, V.; Farhadi, S. Improvement of electromagnetic calibration of springback in bent sheet metals using a novel tool coil. *J. Manuf. Process.* **2024**, *117*, 111–124. [CrossRef]

https://doi.org/10.3390/met16020203

metals

MDPI

Article

An Ultrasonic Vibration-Assisted Superplastic Forming Method for Zr-Based Bulk Amorphous Alloys: Experiment and Simulation

Hui Li [1], Jinfu Liu [1], Chenpu Shen [1] and Canhua Li [2,*]

[1] School of Intelligent Control, Changzhou Vocational Institute of Industry Technology, Changzhou 213164, China; lihui1992aq@163.com (H.L.); liujinfu@mail.ustc.edu.cn (J.L.); 13776642940@163.com (C.S.)

[2] School of Metallurgical Engineering, Anhui University of Technology, Ma'anshan 243002, China

* Correspondence: licanhua1979@163.com

Abstract: The processing of bulk amorphous alloys is typically realized through superplastic deformation in the supercooled liquid region, and current research efforts predominantly focus on enhancing formability by optimizing processing parameters such as temperature and duration. However, excessive temperatures or prolonged exposure times can induce crystallization, which severely compromises the mechanical and functional properties of the alloy. This study presents the design of an ultrasonic vibration (UV)-assisted metal hot-forming apparatus that integrates an ultrasonic vibration field into the superplastic flow deformation of amorphous alloys. High-temperature compression experiments were conducted on $Zr_{55}Cu_{30}Al_{10}Ni_5$ amorphous alloy, and finite element simulations were performed to model the experimental process. Results show that ultrasonic vibration reduces the flow stress of the amorphous alloy, thereby enhancing its superplastic deformation capability. Simulation analysis reveals that surface effects arise from periodic interface separation between the pressure plate and the specimen caused by ultrasonic vibration, leading to a cyclic disappearance of friction forces, which manifest macroscopically as a reduction in effective friction. On the other hand, vibration introduces additional strain rates. Since the undercooled liquid of amorphous alloys exhibits non-Newtonian fluid behavior characterized by shear-thinning, ultrasonic vibration assistance can effectively reduce the apparent viscosity, thereby improving their filling capacity.

Keywords: amorphous alloys; ultrasonic vibration; rheological forming ability; volume effects; surface effects

1. Introduction

Amorphous alloys exhibit long-range disorder and short-range order in three-dimensional space due to the insufficient time for atomic rearrangement during rapid solidification of the liquid metal [1]. Owing to their metastable structure, these alloys demonstrate exceptional properties such as high strength, high hardness, excellent corrosion and wear resistance, and superior soft magnetic characteristics, making them highly attractive for diverse applications. As a result, they are widely regarded as promising advanced structural and functional materials. With continuous advancements in fabrication technologies, representative systems—including Zr-based, Fe-based, Pd-based, and Ti-based alloys—have progressively achieved commercialization. For instance, the Zr-based amorphous alloy surgical scissors developed by Liquidmetal Technologies (Lake

Forest, CA, USA) offer a service life exceeding five times that of conventional stainless-steel instruments, while also significantly reducing postoperative infection rates [2]. Fe-based amorphous alloys, characterized by high magnetic permeability and low core loss, have been employed as soft magnetic materials to replace silicon steel in transformers, achieving up to a 30% reduction in no-load losses [3]. Furthermore, amorphous alloy motors show great potential in new energy vehicles, enabling high torque output at low starting currents, maintaining stable torque at high speeds, and improving energy efficiency under high-speed operation. Additionally, Zeiss (Oberkochen, Germany) utilizes Pd-based amorphous alloys in the fabrication of X-ray lens mounts, markedly enhancing imaging stability under high-energy radiation conditions [4].

Bulk amorphous alloys exhibit high strength and hardness at room temperature, making them highly resistant to conventional mechanical machining. However, upon heating to the supercooled liquid region, their viscosity decreases dramatically, enabling pronounced superplastic behavior. Leveraging this low-viscosity flow capability allows for highly precise near-net-shape forming, offering a promising solution for the fabrication of micro-scale components in advanced technological fields such as biomedical devices, aerospace systems, and micro-electromechanical systems (MEMS) [5–8]. Savaedi et al. [9] reviewed research on the superplastic forming of amorphous alloys and found that the strain rate sensitivity coefficient approaches unity ($m \approx 1$) in the supercooled liquid region, indicating Newtonian flow behavior during thermal forming. While increasing temperature reduces viscosity and enhances formability, excessively high temperatures risk inducing crystallization. Liu et al. [10] systematically investigated the rheological behavior of two amorphous alloys, $Zr_{61}Cu_{25}Al_{12}Ti_{2}$ and $Zr_{52.5}Cu_{17.9}Ni_{14.6}Al_{10}Ti_{5}$, under uniaxial compression in the supercooled liquid region by using a thermomechanical simulator and established the boundary conditions for the transition from Newtonian to non-Newtonian flow, as well as constructed deformation maps accordingly. Yang et al. [11] studied the rheological behavior of the high-entropy amorphous alloy $Ti_{20}Zr_{20}Hf_{20}Be_{20}(Cu_{10}Ni_{10})$ in the supercooled liquid region and observed a transition from Newtonian to non-Newtonian behavior with decreasing temperature and increasing strain rate. Based on these findings, they optimized the superplastic deformation process parameters. Li et al. [12] constructed both heat treatment diagrams and thermoplastic forming maps for the $(Zr_{0.6336}Cu_{0.1452}Ni_{0.1012}Al_{0.12})_{99.4}Y_{0.6}$ amorphous alloy and established its Time–Temperature–Transformation (TTT) curve, providing a theoretical foundation for selecting appropriate time and temperature conditions during thermal forming. In the supercooled liquid region, the viscosity of amorphous alloys is significantly higher than that of oxide glasses. This elevated viscosity imparts greater resistance to flow, making amorphous alloys more challenging to form compared to conventional glass materials. To achieve enhanced formability, current research primarily relies on elevating the forming temperature to reduce the viscosity of the supercooled liquid; however, this approach increases the risk of crystallization. Therefore, alternative strategies are needed to improve the formability of amorphous alloys without compromising thermal stability.

Introducing ultrasonic vibration into metal plastic forming processes can effectively reduce forming forces, enhance material ductility, decrease friction between the blank and die, and improve the surface quality of formed parts. Lou et al. [13] investigated ultrasonic-assisted micro-extrusion of pure copper and found that flow stress, friction coefficient, and microhardness decreased with increasing vibration amplitude, while surface quality improved correspondingly. Xie et al. [14,15] conducted ultrasonic vibration compression experiments on 6063 aluminum alloy and observed that the upper surface in contact with the tool head exhibited significantly better surface quality, hardness, and anti-friction performance compared to the lower surface, which was attributed to ultrasonic energy attenuation during wave propagation. Furthermore, based on the Johnson–Cook model, they established a constitutive model for 6063 aluminum alloy under ultrasonic vibration at room temperature and quantitatively analyzed the effects of amplitude and frequency on yield strength, strain hardening coefficient, and strain hardening exponent. Wan et al. [16–18] systematically explored the coupling mechanisms of volume, surface, and size effects in multi-mode ultrasonic-assisted micro-extrusion of T2 red copper. They developed a stress–strain constitutive relationship model for micro-forward extrusion and demonstrated that multi-mode ultrasonic vibration enhances metal geometric filling capacity, enabling the fabrication of micro-flange components with high dimensional accuracy and superior mechanical performance. Zhang et al. [19] studied the anisotropic and heterogeneous acoustic plasticity behavior of α-Ti through ultrasonic-assisted compression experiments, microstructural characterization, and full-field crystal plasticity simulations. By analyzing ultrasonic activation of multiple slip and twinning systems and grain-scale deformation mechanisms, they elucidated the underlying mechanisms of acoustic plasticity in α-Ti.

This paper proposes to introduce ultrasonic vibration into the rheological forming of amorphous alloys, designs an experimental scheme for ultrasonic vibration-assisted thermoplastic forming, conducts experimental research on the compression performance of Zr-based amorphous alloys under different frequencies and amplitudes of ultrasonic vibration, and performs finite element simulation of the deformation process, analyzes the surface effect and stress superposition under the action of vibration and discusses the influence of ultrasonic vibration on the rheological forming performance of amorphous alloys.

2. Materials and Methods

The experimental setup for ultrasonic vibration-assisted forming of amorphous alloy thermoplastics primarily consists of a material testing machine and an ultrasonic vibration system, as illustrated in Figure 1. The experiments are conducted using a Zwick material testing machine (ZwickRoell, Ulm, Germany) equipped with an environmental chamber. The ultrasonic vibration system is mounted onto the testing machine via a connecting bracket. The environmental chamber enables heating of the amorphous billet to the supercooled liquid region. The material testing machine is responsible for load application as well as load and displacement measurement. The ultrasonic vibration system has a maximum output power of 2 kW, operates at a resonant frequency of 20 kHz, and achieves a maximum output amplitude of up to 10 μm. The output amplitude can be precisely adjusted by varying the input power.

The experimental material was $Zr_{55}Cu_{30}Al_{10}Ni_5$ bulk amorphous alloy, with a glass transition temperature of 420 °C and a crystallization onset temperature of 501 °C [20]. The alloy was first fabricated into rods with a diameter of 3 mm via copper mold suction casting. These rods were subsequently machined into cylindrical specimens of ϕ2.8 mm × 2.6 mm, and both end faces were carefully polished to ensure surface parallelism.

Uniaxial compression experiments were conducted on the specimens under quasi-static loading conditions using the ultrasonic vibration-assisted amorphous alloy thermoplastic forming setup. The top platen was loaded at a constant speed of 10 μm/s, and the experiments were performed at a temperature of 452 °C. Prior to testing, lubricant was applied to both ends of each specimen, which was then positioned centrally on the bottom platen. The specimen was heated to the target temperature and held for 1 min to ensure thermal equilibrium before deformation. After reaching a predetermined preload, ultrasonic vibration was activated and maintained until the specified ultimate load was achieved. Subsequently, the test was terminated, and the specimen was removed. The entire experimental process was completed within 7 min to prevent crystallization of the amorphous alloy. Detailed experimental parameters are summarized in Table 1.

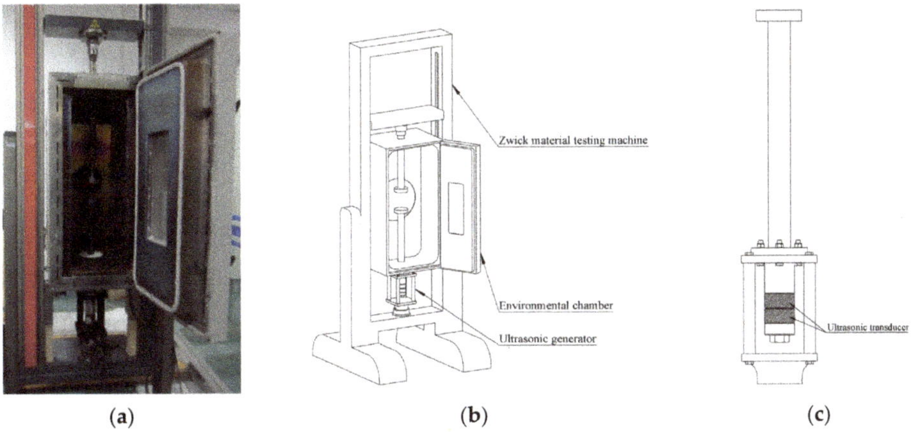

Figure 1. Experimental scheme: (**a**) Test setup; (**b**) 3D model of test setup; (**c**) Ultrasonic generator.

Table 1. Materials and experimental parameters.

Materials	$Zr_{55}Cu_{30}Al_{10}Ni_5$
Specimen size (mm)	ϕ 2.8 × 2.6
Lubricant	Graphite colloid
Loading speed (μm/s)	10
Experimental temperature (°C)	452
Ultimate load (N)	1300
Input amplitude (μm)	4.5, 6, 7.5, 9
Input frequency (kHz)	19, 20

The deformed specimens were examined using a deep-focus microscope to analyze morphological changes, followed by X-ray diffraction (XRD) analysis to confirm the preservation of the amorphous phase structure. Prior to testing, the specimen surfaces were polished to ensure surface integrity. XRD analysis was performed using a Shimadzu XRD-7000S (SHIMADZU, Kyoto City, Japan) X-ray diffractometer, with a scanning range of 20° to 80° and a scan rate of 0.5° per minute. The complete experimental procedure is illustrated in Figure 2.

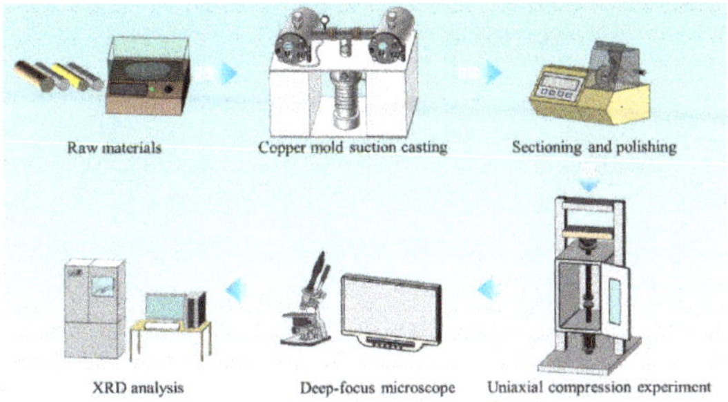

Figure 2. Schematic of the experimental procedure.

To investigate the evolution of stress and strain during the ultrasonic vibration-assisted process, finite element simulations of the compression behavior of bulk amorphous alloys under various vibration amplitudes were conducted using ABAQUS (Abaqus CAE 2019). The material was modeled as elastic–plastic, with the constitutive relationship defined by experimentally obtained stress–strain curves at different strain rates from uniaxial compression tests. Axisymmetric elements were employed to improve computational efficiency without compromising accuracy. Ultrasonic vibration was applied to the lower platen, at a frequency of 20 kHz and an amplitude of 4.5 μm, the time-dependent displacement of the lower platen was expressed as $X_{lower}(t) = a \cdot \sin(2\pi f \cdot t) = 4.5 \times 10^{-6} \cdot \sin(1.256 \times 10^{5} \cdot t)$. Differentiating this expression with respect to time yielded the velocity function $v_{lower}(t) = 2\pi af \cdot \cos(2\pi f \cdot t) = 0.5652 \cdot \cos(1.256 \times 10^{5} \cdot t)$. In Abaqus, ultrasonic vibration boundary conditions of lower platen were implemented through a periodic amplitude profile of the velocity function in the Amplitude module, and the velocity of upper platen was set to 10 μm/s.

3. Results

After the compression experiments, specimens deformed under different ultrasonic vibration frequencies and amplitudes, but at the same temperature, ultimate load, and loading speed were obtained, as shown in Figure 3. Under constant ultimate load conditions, the diameter of the deformed specimen serves as an indicator of its superplastic forming capability [21]. The measured diameters without vibration and under various vibration parameters are summarized in Table 2. Upon application of ultrasonic excitation, the diameters of all deformed specimens increased significantly. At an input amplitude of 9 μm, the deformation diameter increased from 3.80 mm to 4.24 mm, representing an 11% increase compared to the non-vibration condition. This demonstrates that ultrasonic vibration effectively enhances the superplastic flow and formability of amorphous alloys. The deformation diameter exhibits a clear dependence on vibration amplitude, increasing with higher input amplitudes, whereas the influence of frequency is less pronounced.

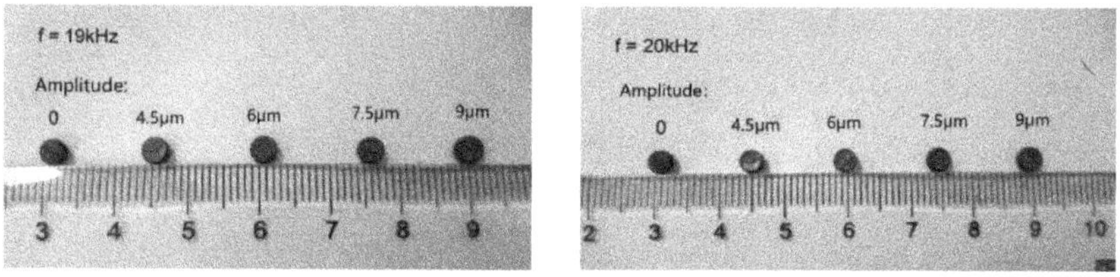

(**a**) (**b**)

Figure 3. Specimens after deformation: (**a**) f = 19 kHz; (**b**) f = 20 kHz.

The true stress–strain curve of the $Zr_{55}Cu_{30}Al_{10}Ni_5$ bulk amorphous alloy under compressive deformation can be derived from the experimental load–displacement data, as shown in Figure 4. The black curve represents the true stress–strain behavior without ultrasonic vibration (UV). When the true strain reaches 0.1, the material transitions from the elastic deformation stage to the steady-state rheological stage, and no stress overshoot is observed—this absence is attributed to the relatively high deformation temperature. Compared with constant strain rate conditions, the true stress–strain curve obtained under constant compression speed exhibits an upward trend due to non-uniform strain distribution. Upon application of ultrasonic vibration, the sample is no longer subjected to pure uniaxial compression; the introduction of ultrasonic energy reduces the flow stress of the amorphous alloy, leading to a phenomenon known as vibration-induced softening. Nevertheless, the overall trend of the curve remains consistent with that under constant load conditions, and neither stress overshoot nor stress undershoot—typically associated with rapid strain rate changes—is induced [22]. The sample avoids localized shear fracture and sustains uniform plastic deformation, which is attributed to the high-frequency, low-amplitude nature of ultrasonic vibration.

Table 2. Diameter of specimens after deformation.

Input Frequency (kHz)	Input Amplitude (μm)	Diameter After Deformation (mm)
19	0	3.80
	4.5	3.86
	6	3.92
	7.5	3.96
	9	4.24
20	0	3.80
	4.5	3.84
	6	3.94
	7.5	4.04
	9	4.24

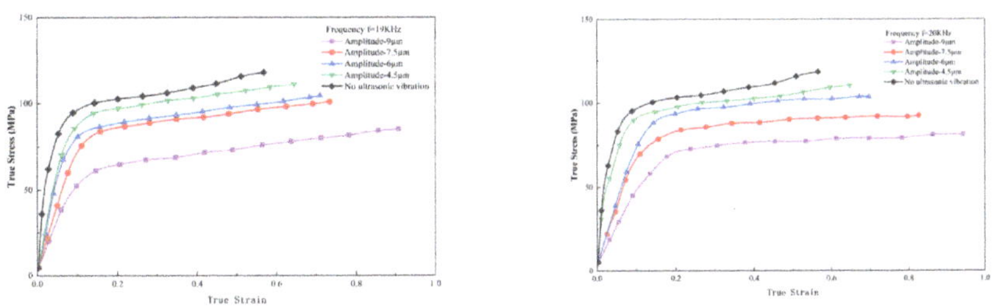

(**a**) (**b**)

Figure 4. True stress–strain curves of $Zr_{55}Cu_{30}Al_{10}Ni_5$ bulk amorphous alloy under different ultrasonic amplitudes and frequencies: (**a**) f = 19 kHz; (**b**) f = 20 kHz.

Figure 5 presents the rheological stress curves as a function of vibration frequency and amplitude. Since the strain rate varies during deformation, the true stress values at a true strain of 0.4 are selected for comparison. As shown in the figure, the vibration-induced softening effect exhibits a pronounced dependence on vibration amplitude. With increasing amplitude, the rheological stress decreases significantly; specifically, when the amplitude reaches 9 μm, the stress is reduced by approximately 30% relative to the constant load condition. In contrast, the influence of frequency on rheological stress is less evident, which may be attributed to the limited range of frequency variation in the experiments.

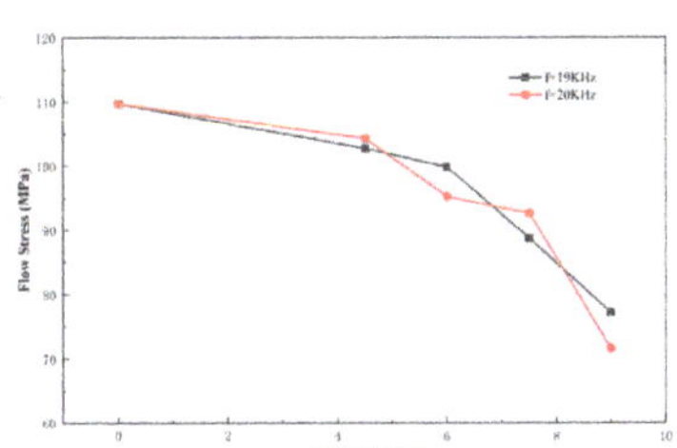

Figure 5. Rheological stress curves as a function of vibration amplitudes and frequencies.

The two specimens exhibiting the longest deformation duration and largest deformation extent were selected for XRD analysis, along with a specimen deformed without vibration. These correspond to specimens subjected to vibration parameters of f = 20 kHz, a = 90% (9 μm) and f = 19 kHz, a = 90% (9 μm), respectively. As shown in Figure 6, the XRD patterns of all three specimens display distinct diffuse amorphous halos and absence of sharp Bragg diffraction peaks associated with crystalline grains, indicating that the samples retain a fully amorphous structure after deformation. The amorphous envelopes in the diffraction patterns are consistently located at $2\theta = 38^{\circ}$, demonstrating that ultrasonic vibration does not induce significant alterations to the amorphous phase structure.

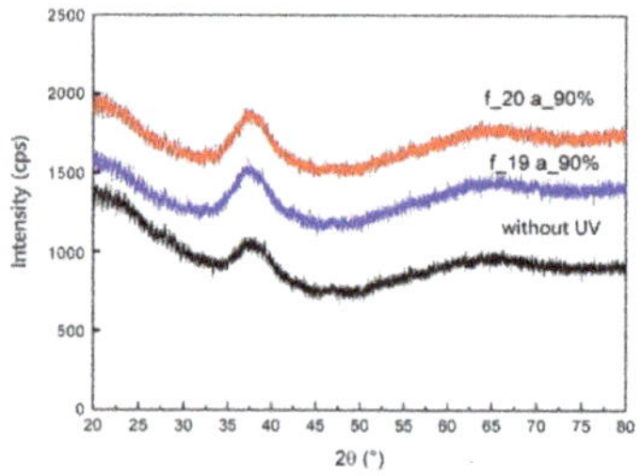

Figure 6. XRD pattern of deformed specimens.

4. Discussion

The reduction in flow stress during plastic deformation of metals induced by ultrasonic vibration is generally attributed to two primary mechanisms: the volume effect and the surface effect. The volume effect involves two aspects: thermal softening resulting from the absorption of ultrasonic energy during metal forming, and stress superposition based on phenomenological mechanical principles. The surface effect refers to the influence of ultrasonic vibration on the frictional interaction between the specimen and the die. Unlike crystalline materials, amorphous alloys possess a homogeneous structure devoid of grain boundaries and dislocations—key sites for ultrasonic energy dissipation. As reported in literature [23], high-frequency vibrations exceeding 300 kHz can disrupt the glassy structure of amorphous alloys, whereas low-frequency vibrations do not produce such effects, suggesting that amorphous alloys exhibit negligible absorption of low-frequency ultrasound. Therefore, this study primarily focuses on the stress superposition and surface effects induced by ultrasonic vibration. Finite element simulations are employed to effectively capture the evolution of the stress–strain field and interfacial friction forces.

The compression processes without ultrasonic vibration and with different ultrasonic amplitudes were simulated and analyzed separately. The simulated load–displacement curves were compared with experimental data, as shown in Figure 7. In the absence of ultrasonic vibration, the simulation results closely matched the experimental data, validating the rationality of the numerical model. When an ultrasonic vibration with an amplitude of 4.5 μm was applied, the reaction force on the upper platen extracted from Abaqus exhibited an oscillating sawtooth pattern. By taking the peak values for curve fitting, the simulation still captured a trend consistent with the experimental results.

Figure 8a shows the stress distribution contour of the deformed specimen at a true strain of 0.4 without vibration, where the specimen has already reached the steady-state flow stage. A friction coefficient of 0.3 is applied between the pressure plates and the specimen. The specimen exhibits a typical symmetric drum-shaped profile, induced by interfacial friction between the specimen and the pressure plates. The magnitude of the friction force directly influences the radius of the top and bottom surfaces after deformation. After applying ultrasonic vibration with an amplitude of 4.5 μm, the deformation pattern changes, as shown in Figure 8b. Notably, the specimen no longer maintains a symmetric shape. The radius of the bottom surface (1.78 mm) exceeds that of the top surface

(1.60 mm) and also surpasses the radius observed without vibration (1.55 mm), indicating that ultrasonic vibration reduces friction, with a more pronounced effect on the bottom interface, resulting in lower friction force there compared to the top. A similar deformation asymmetry is observed when the friction coefficients are reduced, as illustrated in Figure 8c.

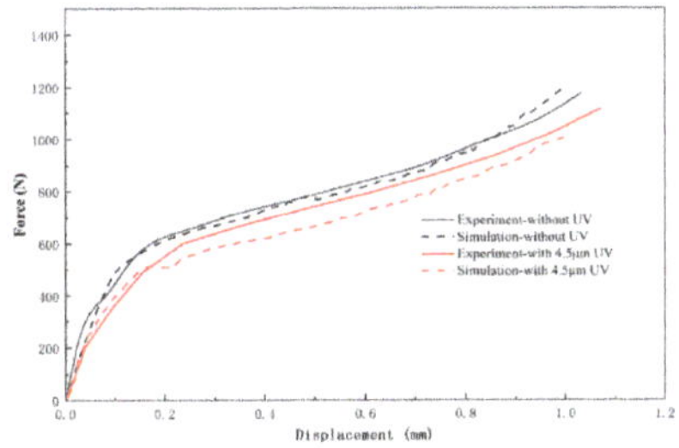

Figure 7. Comparison of experimental and simulated load–displacement curves.

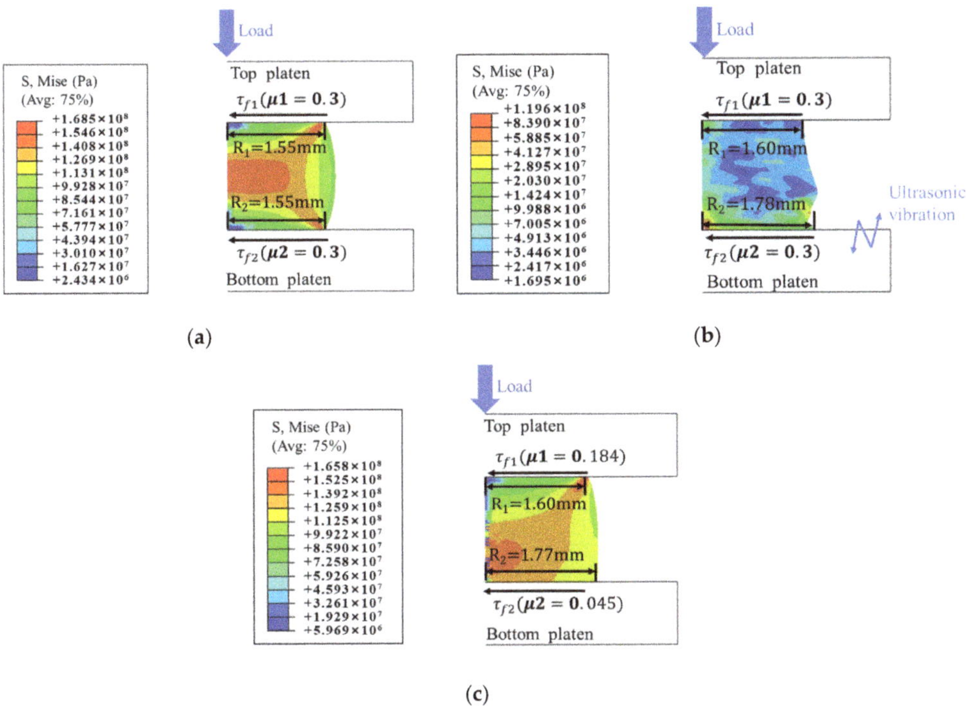

Figure 8. Stress distribution contour after deformation: (**a**) Without vibration. (**b**) With 4.5 μm ultrasonic vibration. (**c**) With lower coefficient of friction.

The friction force curves on the top and bottom surfaces of the specimen during the deformation process are extracted and presented in Figure 9. Without ultrasonic vibration, the friction forces on both surfaces are equal and remain approximately constant at around 250 N after reaching the steady-state rheological stage. Upon application of ultrasonic vibration, the friction forces exhibit an oscillating sawtooth pattern, with peak amplitudes significantly lower than those observed without vibration. Specifically, the peak friction force on the top surface is approximately 200 N, representing a reduction of about 20%, while that on the bottom surface is approximately 50 N, corresponding to a reduction of nearly 80%.

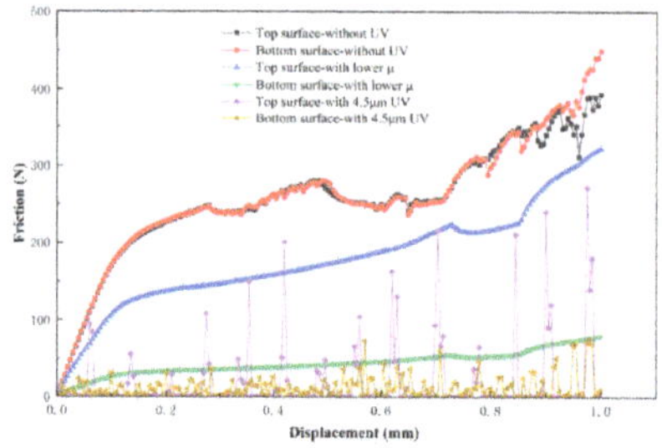

Figure 9. Friction force curves on the upper and lower surfaces of the specimen.

In the process of ultrasonic vibration-assisted compression, the displacement–time curves of the top and bottom pressing plates are shown in Figure 10. Since the peak ultrasonic velocity of the lower pressing plate reaches 5.65×10^5 μm/s, far exceeding the top pressing plate's speed of 10 μm/s, the distance between the two plates decreases only during approximately the first quarter of each ultrasonic vibration period, during which compressive deformation of the specimen occurs, and its height reduces from the initial value H_0 to H_{min}. For the remainder of the period, the distance between the plates exceeds H_{min}, leading to separation between the pressing plates and the specimen, thereby causing intermittent friction loss. This friction force is generated and dissipated periodically, and, on a macroscopic level, it manifests as improved friction conditions.

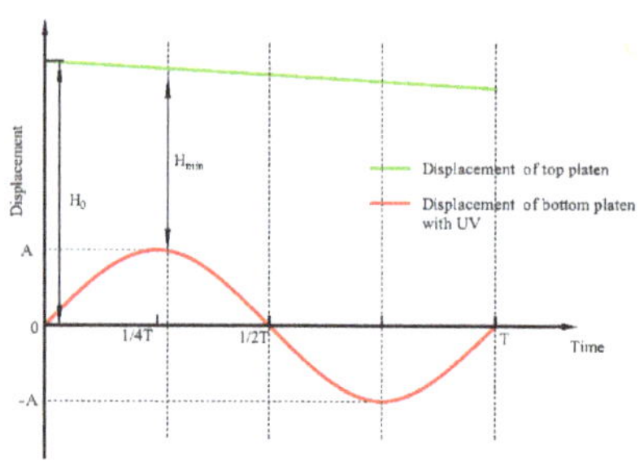

Figure 10. Displacement–time curve of top and bottom pressure plates.

Figure 11 shows the surface morphology of the deformed specimens. Under the constant load mode, the specimen surface accurately replicates the surface topography of the die. After applying ultrasonic vibration, the surface quality deteriorates significantly, with large concave pits forming on the specimen surface. Figure 12 presents the three-dimensional surface morphology reconstructed by a deep-focus microscope. In the constant load mode, the specimen surface is smooth. With small vibration amplitudes, localized concavity appears on the surface while the edges remain smooth. At high amplitudes, even the edges become uneven and lose their smoothness. Traditionally, it has been believed that the surface effect of ultrasonic vibration improves the surface quality of formed parts. However, the findings of this study contradict this conventional view. The discrepancy arises because previous studies were primarily based on cold forming processes of solid metals, whereas in the case of amorphous alloy forming in the supercooled liquid region, the material viscosity is significantly lower than that of solid metals. Ultrasonic vibration induces intermittent separation at the interface between the specimen and the die, followed by repeated impact of the die on the specimen surface. In solid metal forming, this can promote lubricant infiltration and enhance surface finish. In contrast, for amorphous supercooled liquid, the extremely low viscosity and the potential for viscous welding lead to surface damage rather than improvement. The observed concave pits may result from air entrapment during interfacial separation.

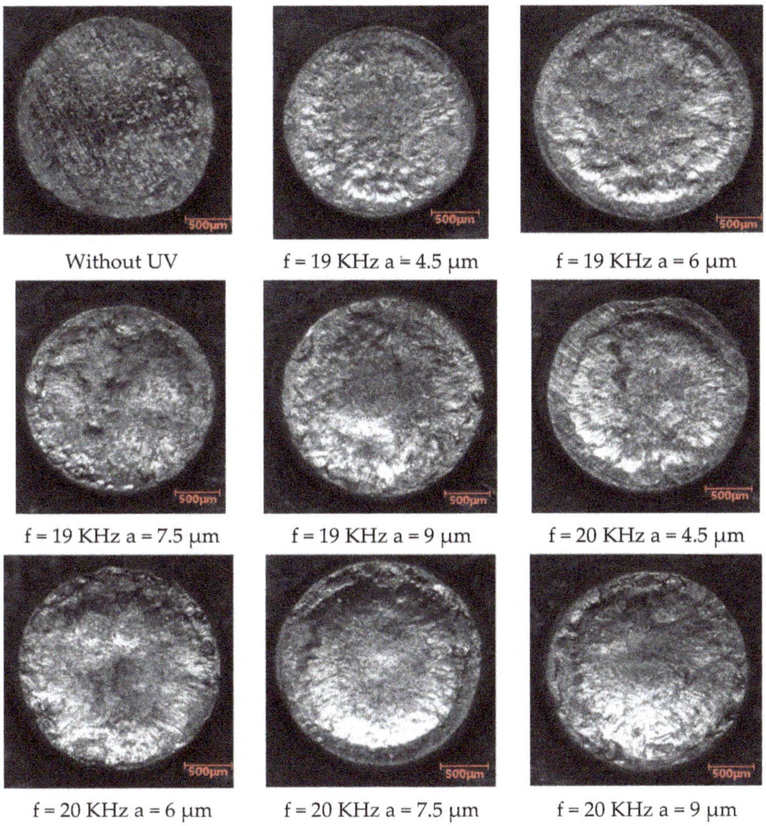

Figure 11. Surface morphology of the specimens after deformation.

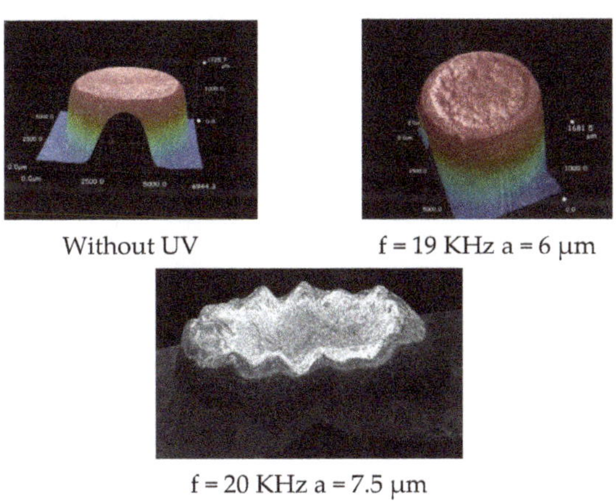

Figure 12. Surface morphology by deep-focus microscope.

To eliminate the influence of surface effects and investigate stress superposition during the ultrasonic vibration process, a frictionless contact condition was applied between the specimen and the pressure plate in the simulation analysis. The stress and strain distributions are shown in Figure 13.

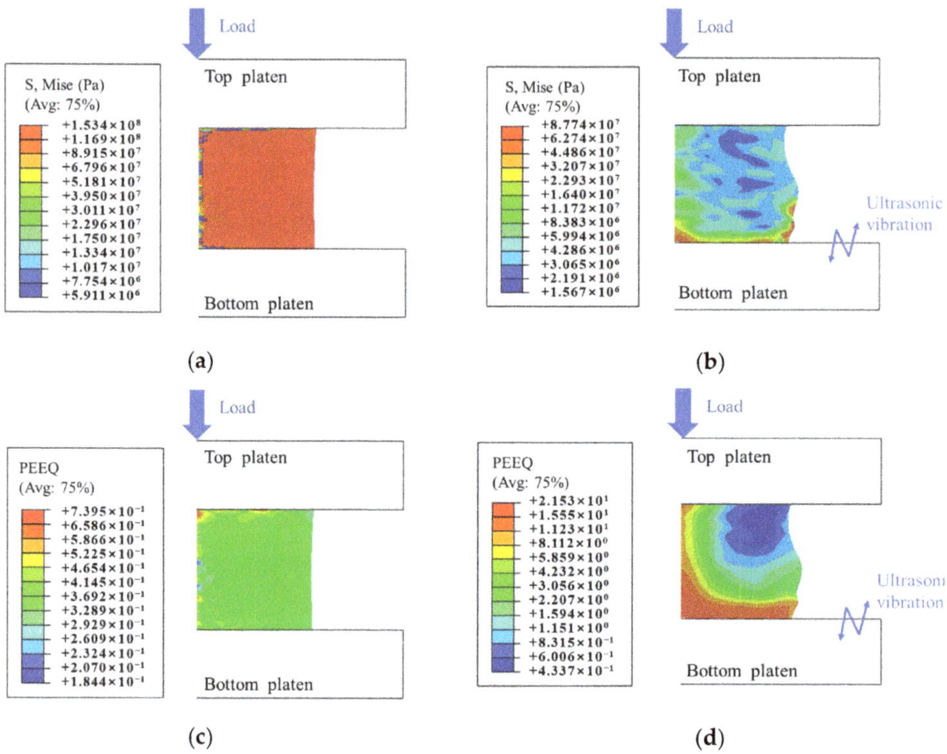

Figure 13. Stress and strain distribution contour without friction: (**a**) Stress distribution contour without UV. (**b**) Stress distribution contour with 4.5 μm UV. (**c**) Strain distribution contour without UV. (**d**) Strain distribution contour with 4.5 μm UV.

When no vibration was applied, in the absence of friction, the specimen exhibited an ideal state of uniform deformation, with stress and strain evenly distributed. After applying ultrasonic vibration, the stress distribution became non-uniform. Since the vibration was applied to the bottom plate, stress concentration occurred at the bottom of the specimen. Stress data along the horizontal and vertical centerlines of the specimen were extracted, as shown in Figure 14a. Ultrasonic vibration resulted in a significant reduction in the Mise stress within the specimen, which explains the observed decrease in deformation load. From the equivalent plastic strain distribution, it can be observed that strain concentration developed at both the bottom and the center of the specimen after ultrasonic vibration was applied. Due to this non-uniform strain distribution, the specimen shape became distorted. Strain data along the same centerlines were also extracted, as shown in Figure 14b. Ultrasonic vibration was observed to increase plastic strain in strain-concentrated regions such as the specimen bottom and central axis, with the maximum plastic strain reaching 40.4 times the value observed without vibration.

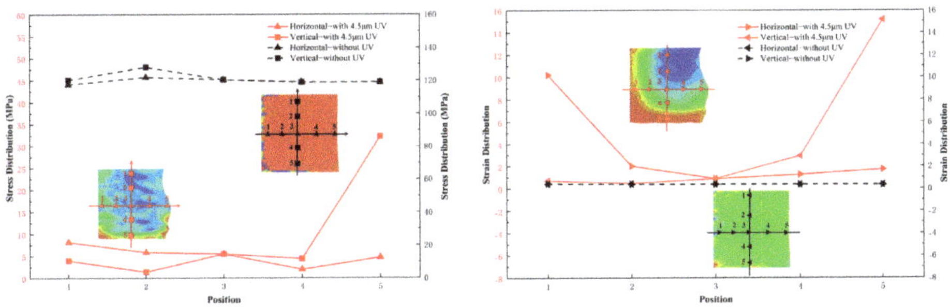

(**a**) (**b**)

Figure 14. Comparison of Stress and Strain: (**a**) Stress comparison. (**b**) Strain comparison.

The strain rate data was derived from the plastic strain. As illustrated in Figure 15, the application of ultrasonic vibration leads to a general increase in strain rate by more than a factor of two. At localized regions such as the specimen's bottom and center areas, the enhancement can reach up to 40-fold.

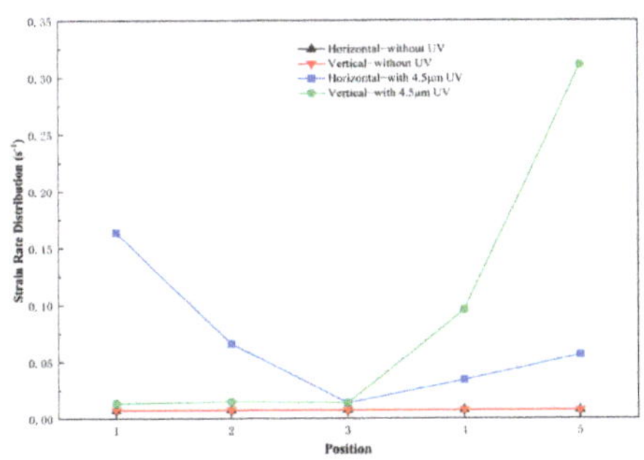

Figure 15. Comparison of strain rate.

According to previous studies, supercooled liquid of amorphous alloys exhibits non-Newtonian fluid behavior at high strain rates, characterized by a stress sensitivity coefficient $m < 1$ and shear-thinning characteristics, wherein the material's viscosity decreases with increasing of strain rate.

Assuming that the amorphous alloy undergoes viscous flow during rheological deformation in the supercooled liquid region—characterized by a Reynolds number approximately zero and no-slip boundary conditions at the flow channel interface—the micro-forming capability of the alloy under these conditions can be described by the Hagen–Poiseuille equation:

$$p = 32v\eta L/d^2, \tag{1}$$

Here, p denotes the pressure required for a fluid with rheological viscosity η to flow at velocity v through a channel of thickness d and length L. The maximum processing time of amorphous alloys is governed by their crystallization kinetics and is denoted as t_{max}. Substituting $v = L/t_{max}$ into Equation (1) yields the maximum filling length [18]:

$$L = \sqrt{\frac{pt_{max}d^2}{32\eta}}, \tag{2}$$

As indicated by Equation (2), reducing the apparent viscosity at a given temperature can improve the formability of amorphous alloys. The apparent viscosity of the supercooled liquid state of amorphous alloys is:

$$\eta = \frac{\sigma}{3\dot{\varepsilon}}, \quad (3)$$

In the equation, σ denotes the flow stress and $\dot{\varepsilon}$ represents the strain rate. During the compression process, experimental data of rheological stress and strain rate at a true strain of 0.4 were used to calculate apparent viscosity. The calculated results are presented in Figure 16.

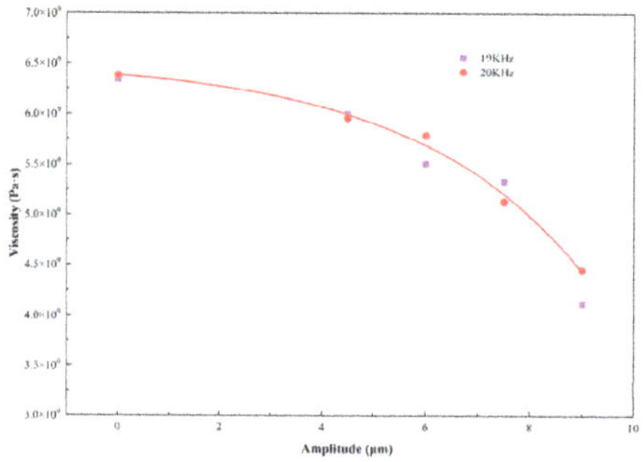

Figure 16. Viscosity as a function of input amplitudes and frequencies.

As shown in Figure 16, ultrasonic vibration reduces the apparent viscosity of the supercooled liquid of amorphous alloys, thereby improving their superplastic formability. At a fixed frequency, the viscosity decreases exponentially with increasing input amplitude. Based on experimental data, the empirical relationship between viscosity η and input amplitude A is fitted as $\eta = 6.511 \times 10^9 – 1.265 \times 10^8\ e^{0.311a}$. In contrast, viscosity exhibits negligible variation with frequency.

5. Conclusions

This study introduces ultrasonic vibration into the superplastic flow forming process of amorphous alloys, designs an experimental setup for ultrasonic vibration-assisted thermoplastic forming, conducts compression deformation experiments, and performs numerical simulations to analyze the deformation behavior, leading to the following conclusions:

(1) The experimental results demonstrate that applying ultrasonic vibration during the deformation of amorphous alloys leads to a reduction in rheological stress with increasing input amplitude. At an amplitude of 9 μm, the rheological stress is reduced by 30% relative to the conventional loading condition. Under an ultimate load of 1300 N, the maximum sample deformation increases by 11%, confirming that ultrasonic vibration assistance enhances the superplastic formability of amorphous alloys.

(2) The finite element simulation results indicate that ultrasonic vibration induces periodic separation at the interface between the pressure plate and the sample, leading to a corresponding periodic disappearance of friction force. Macroscopically, this manifests as a reduction in effective friction. However, due to the low viscosity of the supercooled liquid and the occurrence of viscous welding, the vibration adversely affects the surface morphology of the sample, thereby degrading its surface quality.

(3) Ultrasonic vibration leads to a significant reduction in the principal stress and an increase in plastic strain within the sample. Given that the supercooled liquid of amorphous alloys exhibits non-Newtonian fluid behavior, the introduction of ultrasonic vibration generates an additional strain rate, which reduces the material's

viscosity and consequently enhances its filling capability. An empirical relationship describing the apparent viscosity as a function of amplitude is expressed as $\eta = 6.511 \times 10^9 - 1.265 \times 10^8\, e^{0.311a}$.

This study provides novel insights and effective methodologies for the development of superplastic forming processes of amorphous alloys while establishing a robust theoretical foundation to support the expansion of their industrial applications.

Author Contributions: Conceptualization, H.L.; methodology, H.L.; software, H.L.; validation, H.L. and C.S.; formal analysis, H.L. and C.S.; investigation, H.L. and C.S.; resources, H.L. and C.S.; data curation, H.L.; writing—original draft preparation, H.L.; writing—review and editing, J.L. and C.L.; visualization, C.L.; supervision, J.L. and C.L.; project administration, J.L. and C.L.; funding acquisition, J.L. and H.L. All authors have read and agreed to the published version of the manuscript.

Funding: This research was funded by Natural Science Foundation of Jiangsu Province, grant number BK20220241, 2024 Jiangsu Provincial "Qinglan Project" Outstanding Young Key Teacher Program, Jiangsu Higher Education Teaching Reform Research Project grant number 2025JGYB033, Changzhou Applied Basic Research Program, grant number CJ20220181, and Research Project on Higher Vocational Education of Changzhou University, grant number CDGZ202530.

Data Availability Statement: The original contributions presented in this study are included in the article. Further inquiries can be directed to the corresponding author.

Acknowledgments: We thank Canhua Li for his technical support and helpful discussions. We also acknowledge Changzhou Vocational Institute of Industry Technology for its financial support. Finally, we appreciate the constructive comments from colleagues during the preparation of this manuscript.

Conflicts of Interest: The authors declare no conflicts of interest.

References

1. Sohrabi, S.; Fu, J.N.; Li, L.Y.; Zhang, Y.; Li, X.; Sun, F.; Ma, J.; Wang, W.H. Manufacturing of Metallic Glass Components: Processes, Structures and Properties. *Prog. Mater. Sci.* **2024**, *144*, 101283. [CrossRef]
2. Schroers, J. Processing of Bulk Metallic Glass. *Adv. Mater.* **2010**, *22*, 1566–1597. [CrossRef]
3. Najgebauer, M.; Chwastek, K.; Szczyglowski, J. Energy Efficient Distribution Transformers. *Prz. Elektrotechniczny* **2011**, *2*, 111–114.
4. He, F.; Zhi, J.Y.; He, Z.J.; Tian, Y.L.; Zhao, Z.Y.; Xie, J.L. Preparation of Low Thermal Expansion Transparent LAS Glass-ceramics via Simplified Heat-treatment Method. *Ceram. Int.* **2024**, *50*, 41654–41663. [CrossRef]
5. Kim, W.J.; Ma, D.S.; Jeong, H.G. Superplastic Flow in a $Zr_{65}Al_{10}Ni_{10}Cu_{15}$ Metallic Glass Crystallized during Deformation in a Supercooled Liquid Region. *Scr. Mater.* **2003**, *49*, 1067–1073. [CrossRef]
6. Wang, G.; Shen, J.; Sun, J.F.; Huang, Y.J.; Zou, J.; Lu, Z.P.; Stachurski, Z.H.; Zhou, B.D. Super Plasticity and Superplastic Forming Ability of a Zr-Ti-Ni-Cu-Be Bulk Metallic Glass in the Supercooled Liquid Region. *J. Non-Cryst. Solids* **2005**, *351*, 209–217. [CrossRef]
7. Gong, P.; Wang, S.B.; Liu, Z.; Chen, W.; Li, N.; Wang, X.Y.; Yao, K.F. Lightweight Ti-Based Bulk Metallic Glasses with Superior Thermo plastic Formability. *Intermetallics* **2018**, *98*, 54–59. [CrossRef]
8. Song, S.M.; Liao, Y.C.; Li, T.H.; Lee, C.K.; Tasi, P.H.; Jang, J.S.C.; Huang, J.C. Thermoplastic Deformation Behavior of a Fe-Based Bulk Metallic Glass within the Supercooled Liquid Region. *J. Mater. Res. Technol.* **2019**, *8*, 1907–1914. [CrossRef]
9. Savaedi, Z.; Motallebi, R.; Mirzadeh, H.; Malekan, M. Superplasticity of Bulk Metallic Glasses (BMGs): A review. *J. Non-Cryst. Solids* **2022**, *583*, 121503. [CrossRef]
10. Liu, S.S.; Hou, C.N.; Wang, E.G.; Peng, J. Plastic Rheological Behaviors of $Zr_{61}Cu_{25}Al_{12}Ti_2$ and $Zr_{52.5}Cu_{17.9}Ni_{14.6}Al_{10}Ti_5$ Amorphous Alloys in the Supercooled Liquid Region. *Acta Metall. Sin.* **2022**, *58*, 807–815.
11. Yang, K.; Fan, X.H.; Li, B.; Li, Y.L.; Wang, X. Optimisation of Superplastic Processing Parameters for a TiZrHfBeCuNi High Entropy Bulk Metallic Glass in the Supercooled Liquid Region. *J. Mater. Res. Technol.* **2022**, *24*, 1911–1921. [CrossRef]
12. Li, J.L.; Li, C.Y.; Wang, S.P.; Wang, H.B.; Kou, S.Z. Thermal Processing Map and Thermoplastic Forming Map of Zr-Based Bulk Metallic Glass in the Super cooled Liquid Region. *J. Non-Cryst. Solids* **2021**, *570*, 121008. [CrossRef]
13. Lou, Y.; He, J.S.; Chen, H.; Long, M. Effects of Vibration Amplitude and Relative Grain Size on the Rheological Behavior of Copper during Ultrasonic-assisted Microextrusion. *Int. J. Adv. Manuf. Technol.* **2017**, *89*, 2421–2433. [CrossRef]
14. Xie, Z.D.; Guan, Y.J.; Zhu, L.H.; Zhai, J.Q.; Lin, J.; Yu, X.H. Investigations on the Surface Effect of Ultrasonic Vibration-assisted 6063 Aluminum Alloy Ring Upsetting. *Int. J. Adv. Manuf. Technol.* **2018**, *96*, 4407–4421. [CrossRef]

15. Xie, Z.D.; Guan, Y.J.; Zhu, L.H.; Zhai, J.Q.; Lin, J.; Yu, X.H. Constitutive Model of 6063 Aluminum Alloy under the Ultrasonic Vibration Upsetting Based on Johnson-Cook Model. *Ultrasonics* **2019**, *96*, 1–9. [CrossRef]
16. Wan, W.Q.; Ying, Z.D.; Han, G.C.; Yang, M.; Hu, J.T.; Liu, F.C.; Xun, L.H.; Bai, W.; Chen, H. Mechanical Properties and Microstructure Evolution of T2 Copper in Multimodal Ultrasonic Vibration Assisted Micro-compression. *J. Mater. Sci. Technol.* **2025**, *208*, 152–163. [CrossRef]
17. Wan, W.Q.; Han, G.C.; Liu, F.C.; Yang, M.; Hu, J.T.; Liu, F.C.; Xun, L.H.; Bai, W.; Chen, H. Surface and Volume Effects in Multimodal Ultrasonic Vibration Assisted Micro-extrusion Forming: Experiments and Modelling. *J. Mater. Process. Technol.* **2023**, *322*, 118185. [CrossRef]
18. Han, G.C.; Wan, W.Q.; Zhang, Z.C.; Xu, L.H.; Liu, F.C.; Zhang, H.O. Experimental Investigation into Effects of Different Ultrasonic Vibration Modes in Micro-extrusion Process. *J. Manuf. Process.* **2021**, *67*, 427–437. [CrossRef]
19. Zhang, H.D.; Deng, L.; Hao, Y.; Li, C.; Tang, X.F.; Gong, P.; Zhang, M.; Jin, J.S.; Wang, X.Y. Anisotropic and Heterogeneous Acoustoplasticity of α-Ti during Ultrasonic Vibration Assisted Compression: Modeling and Experiments. *Int. J. Plast.* **2024**, *173*, 103886. [CrossRef]
20. Wu, X.; Li, J.J.; Zheng, Z.Z.; Liu, L.; Li, L. Micro-back-extrusion of a Bulk Metallic Glass. *Scr. Mater.* **2010**, *63*, 469–472. [CrossRef]
21. Schroers, J. On the Formability of Bulk Metallic Glass in Its Supercooled Liquid State. *Acta Mater.* **2008**, *56*, 471–478. [CrossRef]
22. Lu, J.; Ravichandran, G.; Johnson, W.L. Deformation Behavior of the $Zr_{41.2}Ti_{13.8}Cu_{12.5}Ni_{10}Be_{22.5}$ Bulk Metallic Glass ver a Wide Range of Strain-rates and Temperatures. *Acta Mater.* **2003**, *51*, 3429–3443. [CrossRef]
23. Ichitsubo, T.; Kai, S.; Ogi, H.; Hiraoet, M.; Tanaka, K. Elastic and Anelastic Behavior of $Zr_{55}Al_{10}Ni_{5}Cu_{30}$ Bulk Metallic Glass around the Glass Transition Temperature under Ultrasonic Excitation. *Scr. Mater.* **2003**, *49*, 267–271. [CrossRef]

metals

MDPI

Article

Optimization of Multilayer Metal Bellow Hydroforming Process with Response Surface Method and Genetic Algorithm

Jing Liu [1,*], Liang Li [2], Jian Liu [1] and Lanyun Li [1]

[1] School of Materials Science and Engineering, Xi'an Shiyou University, Xi'an 710065, China; liujian199503@126.com (J.L.); lanyunli@xsyu.edu.cn (L.L.)
[2] Aerosun-Tola Expansion Joint Co., Ltd., Nanjing 211153, China; kgll2007@163.com
* Correspondence: jingliu@xsyu.edu.cn

Abstract: In this paper, an optimization strategy for the hydroforming process of bellows is proposed, based on finite element analysis, design of experiments, response surface methodology, and genetic algorithms. A numerical model of the bellows hydroforming process is developed using the finite element simulation code ABAQUS and validated experimentally. A combination of experimental design, numerical simulations, and regression analysis is employed to establish the mathematical models relating the objectives to the design variables. An analysis of variance (ANOVA) is conducted to evaluate the significance of each individual factor on the response variable. The main and interaction effects of the process parameters on the outer diameter and convolution pitch are illustrated and discussed. Furthermore, the response surface methodology and a Pareto-based multi-objective genetic algorithm (MOGA) are applied to determine optimal solutions within the given optimization criteria. The optimized results show good agreement with the experimental data, demonstrating that the optimization methodology is reliable.

Keywords: hydroforming; bellows; optimization; response surface methodology; genetic algorithm

1. Introduction

Metal bellows are a kind of thin-walled shell of revolution with a corrugated profile along the meridian. They are widely used in various fields, such as piping systems, power systems, micro-electromechanical and automotive industries, owing to their exceptional ability to compensate for thermal expansion, contraction, and mechanical vibrations during operation [1–3]. Bellows can be classified into single-layer and multilayer structures based on their construction. Compared to single-layer bellows, multilayer bellows (see Figure 1) demonstrate higher pressure resistance, enhanced flexibility and improved fatigue life. These advantages make them ideal for extreme service environments, such as reactor coolant pump seals and liquid rocket engine propellant lines. To meet increasing requirements of high performance and low cost, the hydroforming process has become an advanced and preferred technique for forming multilayer bellows over recent decades [4].

A typical bellows hydroforming process, as illustrated in Figure 2 [5], consists of four main stages:

- During the initial stage, the tube is positioned with both ends sealed, and a series of annular fin dies are fitted equally spaced along its outer surface.
- In the bulging stage, the tube is slightly expanded under internal pressure and secured between the annular fin dies.
- Throughout the folding stage, the tube is shaped into a bellows profile through the combined application of internal pressure and axial compression.

- Finally, during the unloading stage, springback occurs as the internal pressure and axial force are released.

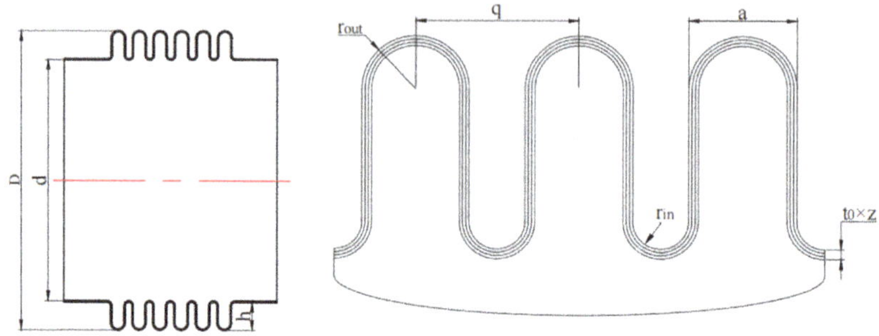

Figure 1. Sketch of the three-layered U-shaped bellow.

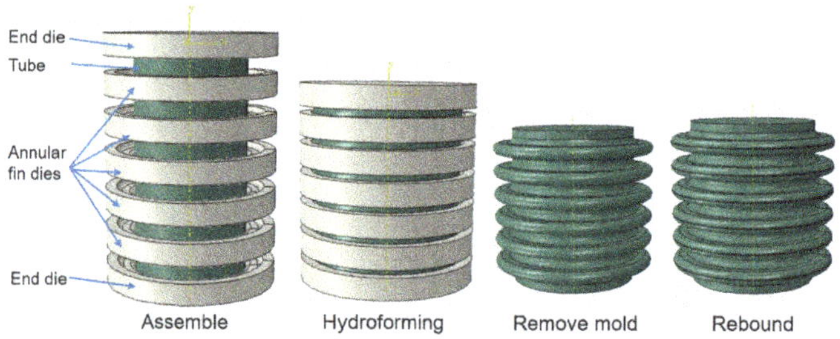

Figure 2. The hydroforming process of the bellow. Reprinted from Ref. [5].

In bellows hydroforming process, defects such as excessive thinning, cracking and insufficient bulging are likely to occur if the process and die parameters are not properly designed. These challenges are especially critical in multilayer bellows, where interlayer slippage during forming intensifies geometric nonlinearity. This will lead to material flows difficulty and stress concentration, thereby increasing the susceptibility to defects such as wrinkling and cracking. To produce defect-free multilayer bellows with precise dimensional accuracy, a proper optimization of both process parameters and die geometry is necessary.

Many researchers have studied the bellows hydroforming process and investigated the influence of process parameters on the product by experiments and finite element (FE) simulations. Faraji et al. [6–8] demonstrated that the formed U-shaped bellows are sensitive to internal pressure, axial movement, and die stoke. Lee [9] identified die spacing as the dominant factor affecting the final profile of the U-shaped bellow. Yuan et al. [10] investigated the reinforced S-shaped bellows hydroforming by FE simulation and concluded that internal pressure has the most significant influence on the forming results. These studies collectively indicate that internal pressure and die spacing are the primary influencing factors in the hydroforming of both U-shaped and S-shaped bellows. Several studies have further investigated the profile evolution and springback behaviour of bellows during hydroforming. Liu et al. [11] studied the springback characteristics of single- and bi-layered bellows and observed that the intended U-shaped profile deformed into a tongue-like shape after springback. To compensate for this effect and achieve the desired U-shaped bellows, Liu et al. [12] suggested that the fin die should be designed with a water-drop-shaped profile to account for springback.

To obtain a bellow with the desired shape, both process and die parameters must be taken into account. It remains challenging to derive a universal approach or parameter combination from the existing literature, where studies often focus solely on either process parameters or die parameters. Thus, an optimization algorithm is necessary. Thus, an optimization algorithm is necessary. Typically, optimization approaches such as response surface method (RSM), radial basis function (RBF), kriging (KRG), artificial neural network (ANN) and support vector regression (SVR) are widely adopted for parameter optimization in hydroforming coupled with finite element analysis (FEA). Alaswad et al. [13] studied the effects of loading paths on the hydroforming of a bi-layer T-shaped tube using FE simulation and RSM. The prediction formulas of the formed bellow profile, including convolution height, wall thinning, and wrinkling height were established. A similar methodology was also employed by Raut et al. [14] and Chen et al. [15] to optimize loading paths. The Taguchi method and RSM were applied by Rajaeea et al. [16] and Feng et al. [17] to optimize the process parameters in the hydroforming of stepped tubes and Y-shape tubes, respectively. Additionally, Abbassi et al. [18] adopted an ANN approach coupled with FE simulation for loading path optimization.

Determining the optimal process and die parameters in bellows hydroforming constitutes a multi-objective problem (MOP) involving objectives such as convolution height, pitch, and wall thickness [19]. Several researchers have addressed this using a multi-objective genetic algorithm (MOGA), for its ability to optimize multiple dependent objectives simultaneously in a single run. Bahloul et al. [20] developed an integrated approach combining FE simulation, RSM, and a MOGA to optimize forming process parameters. Sharma et al. [21] utilized artificial neural networks (ANN) and genetic algorithms (GA) for the optimization of tube-to-tubesheet joint forming processes. Han and Kim [22] employed ANN along with a Pareto-based genetic algorithm to enhance the multistage deep drawing process. Darabi et al. [23] adopted both full-factorial and GA methods to identify the optimal combination of bilayer materials that achieve both high formability and minimal weight. Despite these advances, limited research has been conducted on the multi-objective optimization of both process and die parameters specifically in the context of bellows hydroforming.

In this study, a multi-objective optimization framework integrating FE simulation, design of experiments, response surface methodology, and genetic algorithm is proposed for the hydroforming process of bellows. The primary contribution of this work lies in the establishment of an efficient and integrated virtual optimization system specifically designed for bellows hydroforming. This system effectively combines Box–Behnken experimental design with analysis of variance (ANOVA)-based model validation and MOGA optimization. In contrast to prior research that has largely focused on conventional tube hydroforming, this study addresses the distinctive forming mechanisms and process characteristics of metal bellows, thereby enhancing both optimization accuracy and computational efficiency. The paper is structured as follows: Section 2 presents the development of the FE model for the bellows hydroforming process. Section 3 describes the DOE approach and formulates the multi-objective optimization problem. Section 4 details the development of the RSM models, evaluates their significance and reliability using ANOVA, and identifies the optimal solution through MOGA. Experimental validation of the optimization results is also presented.

2. FE Modelling

In this study, a three-layered U-shaped Incoloy 825 bellow is selected. The schematic and dimensions of the bellow are shown in Figure 1 and Table 1. The FE model is developed using ABAQUS software (ABAQUS 6.10) and illustrated in Figure 3. The key modelling techniques are summarized as follows:

- According to the symmetric character of the bellow, a 2D axisymmetric model is used.
- Due to large deformation and dynamic contact, the explicit algorithm is suitable and adopted for the bulging and folding stages, while the implicit algorithm is employed for the springback stage.
- Determination of the internal pressure. The internal pressure p is calculated by Equation (1).

$$p = \frac{2zt\sigma_b}{d} \tag{1}$$

where z is the number of layers, t is the initial tube thickness, σ_b is the ultimate tensile strength, and d is the inner diameter.

Table 1. Specification of the bellow.

Parameters	Values
Outer diameter, D (mm)	106
Inner diameter, d (mm)	85
Convolution height, h (mm)	9.6
Convolution pitch, q (mm)	6.9
Convolution width, a (mm)	4.3
Radius of crest, r_{out}(mm)	2.15
Radius of trough, r_{in}(mm)	1.3
Wall thickness of each layer, t_0(mm)	0.3
Number of layers, z	3

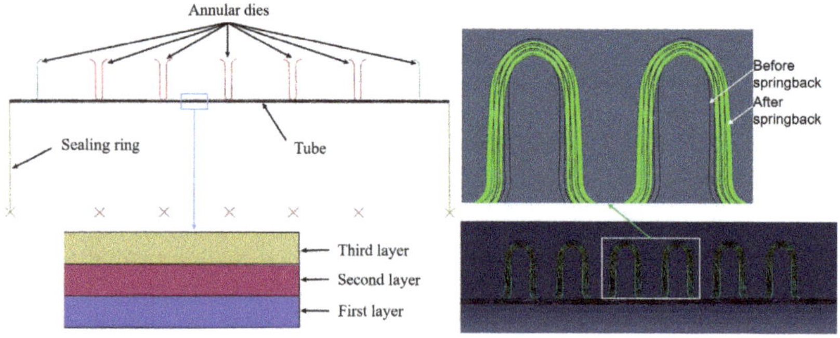

Figure 3. FE model of the three-layered bellow hydroforming process.

- Determination of the developed length of a single convolution. The developed length of a single convolution L_0 refers to the length of a complete bellows segment when flattened along its neutral layer. Numerically, it equals the sum of the arc lengths of the crest and trough, plus the lengths of the two straight sections between the crest and trough. The expression for L_0 is given as follows:

$$L_0 = D - d + (\pi - 2)(r_{out} + r_{in}) - 2t \tag{2}$$

where D is the outer diameter, r_{out} is the radius of crest, and r_{in} is the radius of trough.

- Determination of spacer block height. In hydroforming, adjacent annular dies are separated by spacer blocks with a height of H_d, and the calculation formula for H_d is as follows:

$$H_d = L_0 - H_m \tag{3}$$

where H_m is the annular die thickness and equals to convolution pitch, as shown in Figure 4.

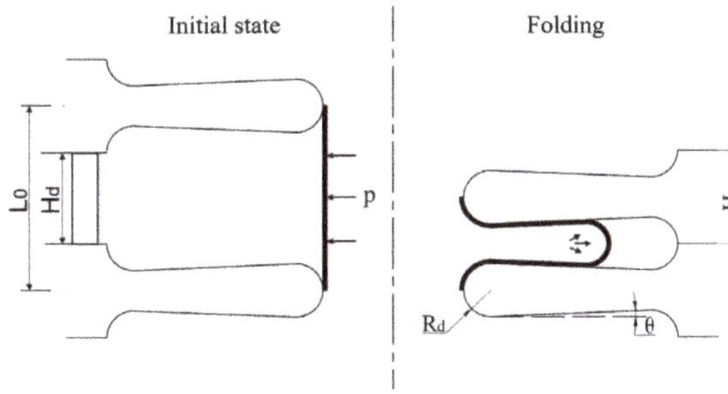

Figure 4. Process and die parameters in bellow hydroforming.

- During the bulging stage, the internal pressure increases uniformly from 0 to the specified value; during the folding stage, the internal pressure remains constant. The loading path is shown in Figure 5.

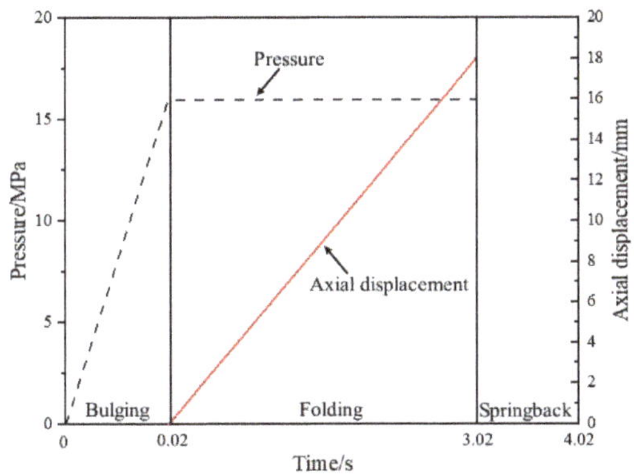

Figure 5. Loading path schematic in bellow hydroforming.

- The movement of the dies are controlled by displacement constraints. During the bulging stage, all dies remain stationary. In the folding stage, while one end die is fixed, the opposite end die and the middle dies move axially at a constant velocity until complete closure is achieved (shown in Figure 5).
- The contact between the tube, die, and every two adjacent layers are described with the surface-to-surface contact algorithm. The Coulomb friction coefficients are set as 0.1 for tube-die interfaces and 0.3 for tube-tube contact surfaces.
- The tubes are meshed with the four-node bilinear axisymmetric quadrilateral element (CAX4R), while two-node linear axisymmetric rigidity element RAX2 is used in meshing the rigid dies.
- In the springback model, the workpiece is imported into the Part module. Meanwhile, a predefined field is created in the initial step to import the stress field.

The true stress–strain curves of the Incoloy825 sheet are obtained by uniaxial tensile test. The flow stress is approximated by the Swift law presented in Equation (4) and the mechanical properties are shown in Table 2.

$$\overline{\sigma} = K(\overline{\varepsilon} + \varepsilon_0)^n \tag{4}$$

where K is the strength coefficient, n is the hardening exponent, and ε_0 is the strain constant.

Table 2. Mechanical properties of the tube material.

Parameters	Values
Young's modulus, E (GPa)	206
Poisson's ratio, v	0.3
Density, ρ (kg/m^3)	7850
Yield strength, σ_s (MPa)	241
Ultimate strength, σ_b (MPa)	659
Elongation percentage, e (%)	32
Strength coefficient, K (MPa)	1779.21
Strain hardening exponent, n	0.51
Strain constant, ε_0	0.061
Normal anisotropic exponent, r	0.68

3. Optimization Scheme

An optimization method is presented and illustrated in Figure 6, comprising the following steps:

Step 1: Select the design variables and optimization objectives.
Step 2: Design virtual experiments using the Box–Behnken Design (BBD) method.
Step 3: Perform numerical simulations according to the BBD matrix and extract the resulting sample data.
Step 4: Establish a RSM based on the sample data.
Step 5: Evaluate the accuracy and reliability of the RSM through ANOVA.
Step 6: determine the optimal solution by applying the MOGA.

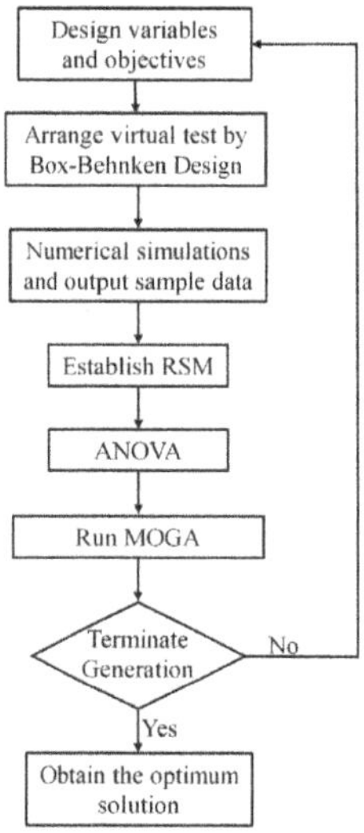

Figure 6. Flowchart of the optimization scheme.

3.1. Design of Variables and Objectives

In the bellows hydroforming process, as illustrated in Figures 2 and 4, the internal pressure (p), die angle (θ), die fillet radius (R_d) and die thickness (H_m) are the dominant parameters influencing the formed bellows profile. The upper bound of the internal pressure is determined based on Equation (1), while the lower bound is set to 60% of the calculated pressure. The design of the die angle, fillet radius, and thickness primarily accounts for the effect of springback. After springback, the cross-section of the bellows changes from U-shaped to a tongue-shaped profile, accompanied by an increase in both the convolution pitch and the valley radius. Therefore, compensatory adjustments are incorporated into the die design. Based on empirical experience combined with simulation results, the die angle is set within 0° to 4°, the die fillet radius is selected between 60% and 100% of the trough radius, and the die thickness is chosen in the range of 75% to 100% of the convolution pitch. The specific ranges of the parameters are provided in Table 3.

Table 3. Ranges of variables in optimization.

Variables	θ (°)	R_d (mm)	H_m (mm)	p (MPa)
Range	[0, 4]	[0.78, 1.3]	[5.16, 6.9]	[8.38, 13.96]

The convolution height (relates to the outer diameter) is a paramount installation dimension, while the pitch is the key geometric determinant for performance metrics like compensation capacity, as per standards such as the Standards of the Expansion Joint Manufacture Association (EJMA). During hydroforming, these two parameters are directly defined and constrained by the die geometry, making their variation a direct indicator of process stability and repeatability. Therefore, the outer diameter (D) and the convolution pitch (q) are selected as the response parameters in this study. Due to springback after unloading, which results in a decrease in outer diameter and an increase in convolution pitch, the outer diameter and convolution pitch of the bellows are measured after springback.

According to EJMA standard [24], the manufacturing tolerances for convolution height and convolution pitch of the bellows are specified as ± 0.79 mm (corresponding to $D = 106 \pm 1.58$ mm) and ± 1.59 mm (corresponding to $q = 6.9 \pm 1.59$ mm), respectively.

3.2. Design of Experiments

The BBD was adopted for virtual simulation experiments of bellows. This design offers efficient estimation of second-order effects while avoiding extreme experimental points, thereby improving numerical stability. Compared to full factorial designs, BBD requires significantly fewer experimental runs while maintaining comparable resolution. In contrast to space-filling designs such as Sobol or Latin Hypercube, BBD is more suitable for building explicit quadratic response surface models. This makes it particularly ideal for multi-parameter optimization studies. In this study, a four-factor, three-level BBD was employed, with the levels of each factor set at −1, 0, and 1. The design variables and their corresponding levels are summarized in Table 4. All statistical analyses and response surface plots were performed using MATLAB software (MATLAB R2016b). A total of 29 numerical simulations were conducted, all of which results in formed bellows free from defects such as wrinkling or rupture. The outer diameter (D) is determined by measuring the radial distance from the peak of the outermost convolution to the tube centerline, while the convolution pitch (q) is obtained from the axial distance between adjacent peaks of the outermost corrugations. The measured results are presented in Table 5.

Table 4. The levels of factors for numerical simulations.

Variables	Description	−1	0	1
θ (°)	Die angle	0	2	4
R_d (mm)	Die fillet radius	0.78	1.04	1.30
H_m (mm)	Die thickness	5.16	6.03	6.90
p (MPa)	Internal pressure	8.38	11.17	13.96

Table 5. Design matrix with coded independent design variables and numerical results.

Number	θ (°)	R_d (mm)	H_m (mm)	p (MPa)	D (mm)	q (mm)
1	2	1.30	6.03	8.38	105.23	7.16
2	2	1.04	6.03	11.17	105.50	7.17
3	2	1.04	6.03	11.17	105.50	7.17
4	2	1.04	6.03	11.17	105.50	7.17
5	2	0.78	5.16	11.17	105.23	7.16
6	0	1.30	6.03	11.17	105.75	7.14
7	4	1.30	6.03	11.17	105.25	7.29
8	0	1.04	5.16	11.17	106.26	5.99
9	2	1.04	5.16	8.38	105.63	6.15
10	4	1.04	6.90	11.17	104.75	8.34
11	0	1.04	6.03	8.38	105.43	7.21
12	2	1.04	6.03	11.17	105.50	7.17
13	2	0.78	6.03	13.96	105.96	6.67
14	4	1.04	6.03	8.38	104.97	7.35
15	2	1.30	6.03	13.96	105.91	7.17
16	0	0.78	6.03	11.17	105.56	7.46
17	2	1.04	6.90	8.38	104.64	7.88
18	2	1.04	6.03	11.17	105.50	7.17
19	4	0.78	6.03	11.17	105.20	7.31
20	2	1.30	6.90	11.17	105.02	8.32
21	2	1.04	6.90	13.96	105.39	7.90
22	4	1.04	6.03	13.96	105.80	7.03
23	2	0.78	6.03	8.38	105.08	7.33
24	0	1.04	6.03	13.96	106.22	6.67
25	2	1.30	5.16	11.17	106.12	5.78
26	2	0.78	6.90	11.17	105.04	7.98
27	4	1.04	5.16	11.17	105.69	6.07
28	2	1.04	5.16	13.96	106.36	6.01
29	0	1.04	6.90	11.17	105.32	7.93

3.3. Establishment of RSM

In the paper, the second-order polynomial response surface model is used to approximately describe the objective function. This form of model is widely used in modelling metal forming processes due to its ability to capture both main and interaction effects between process variables. A second-order model is preferred over a first-order model to account for potential mild nonlinearities that are commonly present in hydroforming processes. Moreover, the second-order model offers improved predictive capability while maintaining computational efficiency, providing a balanced approach between model accuracy and complexity. The second-order regression polynomial equation is as follows:

$$y = F(x) = \beta_0 + \sum \beta_i x_i + \sum \beta_{ii} x_{ii}^2 + \sum \beta_{ij} x_i x_j + \varepsilon \tag{5}$$

where β are polynomial coefficients; ε is minor error; x_i and x_j are the design variables, and y is the response value.

Equation (5) can be expressed in matrix expression as follows:

$$\mathbf{Y} = \mathbf{X}\beta + \varepsilon \tag{6}$$

where

$$\mathbf{Y} = \begin{bmatrix} y_1 \\ y_2 \\ \vdots \\ y_n \end{bmatrix}, \mathbf{X} = \begin{bmatrix} 1 & x_{11} & x_{12} & \cdots & x_{1m} \\ 1 & x_{21} & x_{22} & \cdots & x_{2m} \\ \vdots & \vdots & \vdots & \ddots & \vdots \\ 1 & x_{n1} & x_{n2} & \cdots & x_{nm} \end{bmatrix}, \beta = \begin{bmatrix} \beta_1 \\ \beta_2 \\ \vdots \\ \beta_n \end{bmatrix}, \varepsilon = \begin{bmatrix} \varepsilon_1 \\ \varepsilon_2 \\ \vdots \\ \varepsilon_n \end{bmatrix} \quad (7)$$

in which **Y** is the response vector, **X** is the matrix of the independent variables, β is the vector of the unknown coefficients and ε is the random error vector of the approximation.

3.4. Optimization Using MOGA

In actual forming processes, multiple forming criteria must be met. However, it is challenging to directly determine suitable process parameters. The Pareto-based multi-objective genetic algorithm (MOGA) provides an effective approach for identifying optimized solutions. In multi-objective optimization, the Pareto front represents the optimal trade-off between competing objectives. In a typical two-objective optimization problem, each design objective is represented along a coordinate axis, with the optimization goal being the simultaneous minimization of both objectives. Due to inherent conflicts between the objectives, simultaneous minimization is generally unattainable—optimization of one objective inevitably leads to suboptimal performance in the other. As defined previously, Pareto-optimal solutions represent compromise solutions within the feasible design space that optimally balance these competing objectives [25].

The objective is to determine the optimal combination of forming variables such that the resulting bellow profile, including outer diameter and convolution pitch, conforms as closely as possible to the designed geometry. This optimization problem can be formulated as a constrained nonlinear programming task expressed in the following form:

Minimize

$$F(x) = (f_1(x_1), f_2(x_2), \ldots, f_j(x_i)),\ j = 1, 2, \ldots, m \quad (8)$$

Subject to

$$\begin{gathered} b_i^{lower} \le x_i \le b_i^{upper},\ i = 1, 2, \ldots, n \\ g_k(x_i) \le 0,\ k = 1, 2, \ldots, p \end{gathered} \quad (9)$$

where x_i is the ith design variable; b_i^{lower} and b_i^{upper} represent the lower and upper boundaries of x_i, respectively; $f_j(x_i)$ is the jth objective function of x_i and $g_k(x_i)$ is the kth constraint function of x_i.

The optimization procedure of MOGA comprises the following steps [20]:

Step 1: Coding. The design variables, represented in real-valued form, are converted into binary numbers.

Step 2: Fitting. The objective function is constructed using MOGA subject to the constraints given in Equation (10).

$$\begin{gathered} 0 \le \theta \le 4(^\circ) \\ 0.78 \le R_d \le 1.3(mm) \\ 5.16 \le H_m \le 6.9(mm) \\ 8.38 \le p \le 13.96(mm) \end{gathered} \quad (10)$$

Step 3: Evaluating. The fitness of each individual is evaluated against the objective functions. The Pareto ranking method is applied to assign fitness values.

Step 4: Grouping. According to the sorting order of the fit value, all the two adjacent individuals are paired into one group.

Step 5: Crossover and mutation. Within each group, crossover and mutation are car-ried out. The child individuals are generated to replace the parent individuals.

Step 6: Assembling. The newly generated individuals and the original individuals are combined into one group.
Step 7: Re-evaluating. Similarly to step 3, the Pareto ranking method is reapplied to determine fitness values with a different objective function.
Step 8: Selecting. The top half of individuals with higher fitness values are selected as the preferred solutions.
Step 9: Judging. The termination condition is checked. If met, the MOGA process ends; otherwise, the algorithm returns to Step 4.

4. Results and Discussion

4.1. Factorial Analysis

To evaluate the influence of various factors on the outer diameter (D) and the convolution pitch (q), the main effects of the factors are presented in Figure 7. As shown in Figure 7a, the outer diameter decreases markedly with an increase in die angle (θ) and die thickness (H_m), while it increases significantly with higher internal pressure (p). in contrast, the effect of the die fillet radius (R_d) on the outer diameter is relatively minor. From Figure 7b, it can be observed that the convolution pitch is sensitive to die thickness (H_m), showing a monotonically increasing trend. Other process parameters exhibit negligible influence on the convolution pitch.

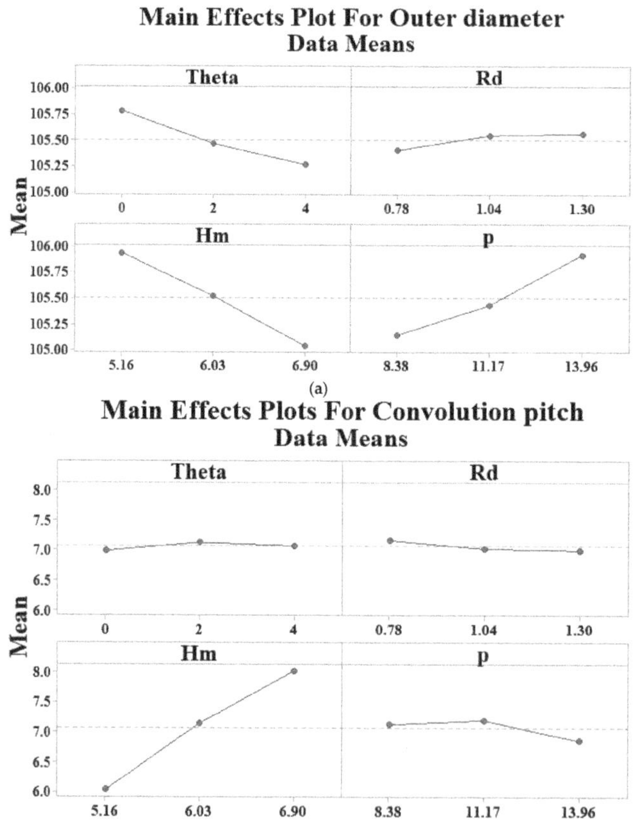

Figure 7. The main effects of four factors on (**a**) Outer diameter; (**b**) Convolution pitch.

The interaction plots for the two responses, outer diameter (D) and convolution pitch (q), are presented in Figure 8. From the interaction plot related to the outer diameter (Figure 8a), it can be observed that the response is significantly influenced by die thickness and internal pressure. The nonparallel lines in the interaction plot between die fillet radius and die thickness indicate a notable interaction effect between these two variables. The largest outer diameter occurs at the maximum die fillet radius and the minimum die thickness. Figure 8b shows the interaction diagram for the convolution pitch. The convolution pitch is strongly affected by die thickness, showing an increasing trend. A combination of greater die thickness and larger die fillet radius leads to a significant increase in convolution pitch. The interaction between die fillet radius and die thickness is also relatively significant. In contrast, the interaction of internal pressure with the other factors exerts negligible effects.

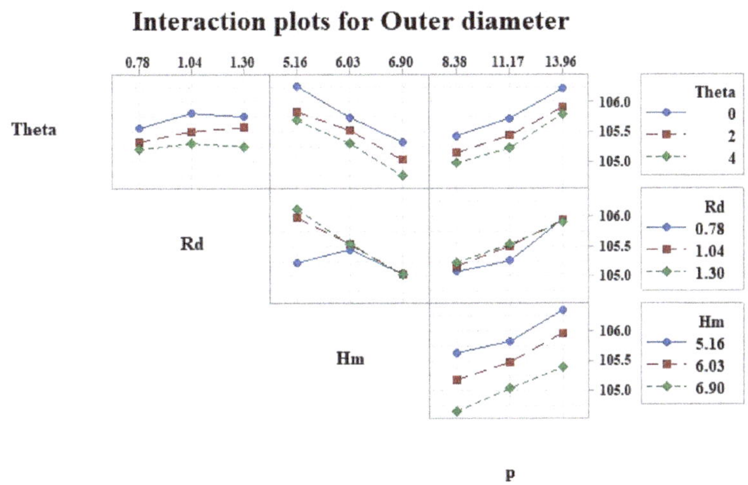

(a)

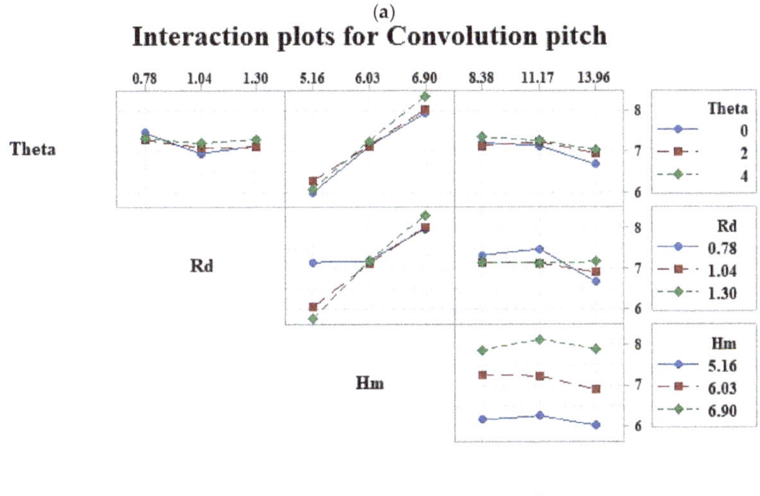

(b)

Figure 8. The interaction effects of four factors on (**a**) Outer diameter; (**b**) Convolution pitch.

4.2. Complete Quadratic Models

Response surface models for the outer diameter and convolution pitch are developed based on the design variables. Complete quadratic polynomial regression models are established for both the outer diameter and convolution pitch, incorporating all constant, linear, interaction, and quadratic terms, as follows:

$$\begin{aligned} D = &+96.982 - 0.103 \times \theta + 9.613 \times R_d + 1.501 \times H_m - 0.050 \times p - 0.067 \times \theta \times R_d \\ &+2.153 \times 10^{-15} \times \theta \times H_m + 1.792 \times 10^{-3} \times \theta \times p - 1.006 \times R_d \times H_m - 0.069 \times R_d \times p \\ &+2.060 \times 10^{-3} \times H_m \times p + 8.229 \times 10^{-3} \times \theta^2 - 1.085 \times R_d^2 - 0.080 \times H_m^2 + 0.011 \times p^2 \end{aligned} \quad (11)$$

$$\begin{aligned} q = &+16.124 - 0.503 \times \theta - 18.387 \times R_d - 0.638 \times H_m + 0.037 \times p + 0.142 \times \theta \times R_d \\ &+0.047 \times \theta \times H_m + 9.937 \times 10^{-3} \times \theta \times p + 1.898 \times R_d \times H_m + 0.231 \times R_d \times p \\ &+0.017 \times H_m \times p + 1.469 \times 10^{-4} \times \theta^2 + 1.801 \times R_d^2 - 0.045 \times H_m^2 - 0.020 \times p^2 \end{aligned} \quad (12)$$

The statistical technique of ANOVA is utilized to evaluate the fitness of the models and to identify the main effects of design variables. The total sum of squares SS_T is expressed as follows:

$$SS_T = \sum_{i=1}^{k}\sum_{j=1}^{n}\left(y_{ij} - \overline{y}\right)^2 \quad (13)$$

where n is the number of replicates within each of k factor levels, y_{ij} is the jth forming result within factor level I, and $\overline{y}$ is the mean value of the forming results.

The SS_T is a combination of the sum of squares due to error SS_E and the sum of squares due to factors SS_A, given by

$$SS_E = \sum_{i=1}^{k}\sum_{j=1}^{n}\left(y_{ij} - \overline{y_i}\right)^2 \quad (14)$$

$$SS_A = SS_T - SS_E = \sum_{i=1}^{k} n_i\left(\overline{y_i} - \overline{y}\right)^2 \quad (15)$$

where n_i is the number of the tests of the i-th factor, $\overline{y_i}$ is the mean of results with factor level i.

The mean square (SS_m) is obtained by dividing the SS_A by its associated degrees of freedom (DOF). The F value for each parameter is the mean square of each independent variable divided by the mean square of the residuals. The p-value is the marginal significance level within the hypothesis testing that represents the probability of occurrence of the given event.

The ANOVA results of the outer diameter and the convolution pitch are listed in Tables 6 and 7, respectively. It can be observed that the "Model p-values" of the outer diameter and the convolution pitch are below 0.0001, indicating that the two models are highly significant. Additionally, terms with p-value greater than 0.05 are considered statistically insignificant. In the case of outer diameter, the significant model terms are θ, R_d, H_m, p and the interaction R_d*H_m. Similarly, for the convolution pitch, H_m, p, and the interaction R_d*H_m are identified as significant terms, as shown in Table 7.

Table 6. ANOVA for outer diameter.

Source	Sum of Squares	Dof	Mean Square	F Value	p-Value	Significance
Model	5.18	14	0.37	28.94	<0.0001	**
θ	0.69	1	0.69	54.09	<0.0001	**
R_d	0.12	1	0.12	9.55	0.0080	**

Table 6. *Cont.*

Source	Sum of Squares	Dof	Mean Square	*F* Value	*p*-Value	Significance
H_m	2.19	1	2.19	171.63	<0.0001	**
p	1.81	1	1.81	141.62	<0.0001	**
θ^*R_d	0.0049	1	0.0049	0.38	0.5457	
θ^*H_m	0	1	0	0	1	
θ^*p	0.0004	1	0.0004	0.031	0.8621	
$R_d^*H_m$	0.21	1	0.21	16.20	0.0013	**
R_d^*p	0.01	1	0.01	0.78	0.3913	
H_m^*p	0.0001	1	0.0001	0.0078	0.9308	
θ^2	0.007	1	0.007	0.55	0.4706	
R_d^2	0.035	1	0.035	2.73	0.1207	
H_m^2	0.024	1	0.024	1.88	0.1921	
p^2	0.047	1	0.047	3.7	0.0749	
Residual	0.18	14	0.013			
Cor Total	5.36	28				

If $p < 0.01$, mark ** on the significance item; if $p < 0.05$, mark *.

Table 7. ANOVA for convolution pitch.

Source	Sum of Squares	Dof	Mean Square	F Value	*p*-Value	Significance
Model	12.06	14	0.86	25.05	<0.0001	**
θ	0.084	1	0.084	2.45	0.1399	
R_d	0.092	1	0.092	2.67	0.1244	
H_m	10.43	1	10.43	303.36	<0.0001	**
p	0.22	1	0.22	6.35	0.0245	*
θ^*R_d	0.022	1	0.022	0.63	0.4405	
θ^*H_m	0.027	1	0.027	0.79	0.3888	
θ^*p	0.012	1	0.012	0.36	0.5593	
$R_d^*H_m$	0.74	1	0.74	21.45	0.0004	**
R_d^*p	0.11	1	0.11	3.25	0.0928	
H_m^*p	0.0066	1	0.0066	0.19	0.6670	
θ^2	2×10^{-6}	1	2×10^{-6}	6.5×10^{-6}	0.9937	
R_d^2	0.096	1	0.096	2.80	0.1166	
H_m^2	0.00764	1	0.00764	0.22	0.6445	
p^2	0.16	1	0.16	4.56	0.0508	
Residual	0.48	14	0.034			
Cor Total	12.54	28				

If $p < 0.01$, mark ** on the significance item; if $p < 0.05$, mark *.

4.3. Reduced Quadratic Models

The second-order polynomial response surface model, as shown in Equation (5), is fitted by the stepwise regression analysis. which is employed to eliminate statistically non-significant terms. Subsequently, based on the identified significant factors, the second-order polynomial models for the outer diameter and the convolution pitch are presented in Equations (16) and (17), respectively.

$$D = +100.457 - 0.12 \times \theta + 6.437 \times R_d + 0.551 \times H_m + 0.139 \times p - 1.004 \times R_d \times H_m \quad (16)$$

$$q = +1.222 + 1.116 \times H_m - 0.048 \times p - 0.042 \times R_d \times H_m \quad (17)$$

The ANOVA results for the outer diameter and the convolution pitch are presented in Tables 8 and 9. These results indicate that the response surface models (Equations (16) and (17)) are statistically reasonable.

Table 8. Summary of ANOVA for outer diameter.

Parameter	Value
Standard Deviation	0.12
Mean Value	105.49
C. V. %	0.11
PRESS	0.83
R-squared	0.9377
Adj R-squared	0.9242
Pred R-squared	0.8442
Adeq precision	29.78

Table 9. Summary of ANOVA for convolution pitch.

Parameter	Value
Standard Deviation	0.21
Mean Value	7.14
C. V. %	2.95
PRESS	2.00
R-squared	0.9153
Adj R-squared	0.9012
Pred R-squared	0.8401
Adeq precision	31.172

The distributions of residual error of the regression equations (Equations (16) and (17)) are shown in Figure 9. The relationship between the predicted values and the actual ones are illustrated in Figure 10. Both Figures 9 and 10 indicate that the predicted response values are in good agreement with the actual values. Thus, the second-order response model is suitable for predicting the formed shape in this study.

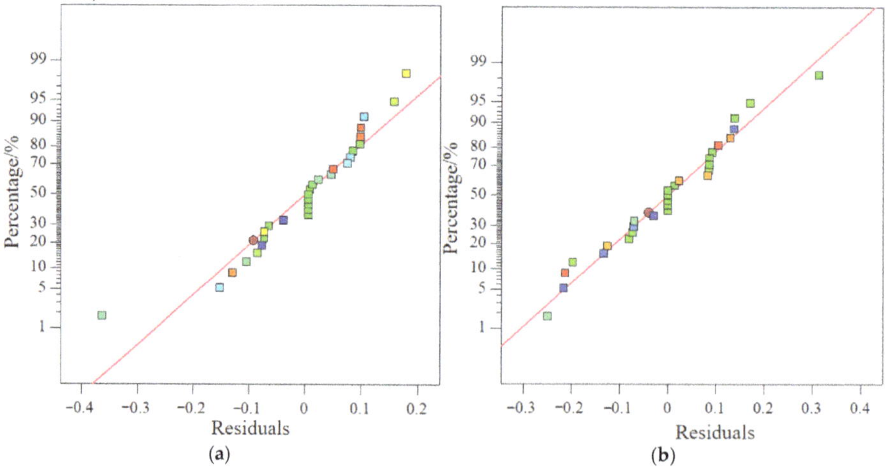

Figure 9. Residual distribution: (**a**) Outer diameter; (**b**) Convolution pitch.

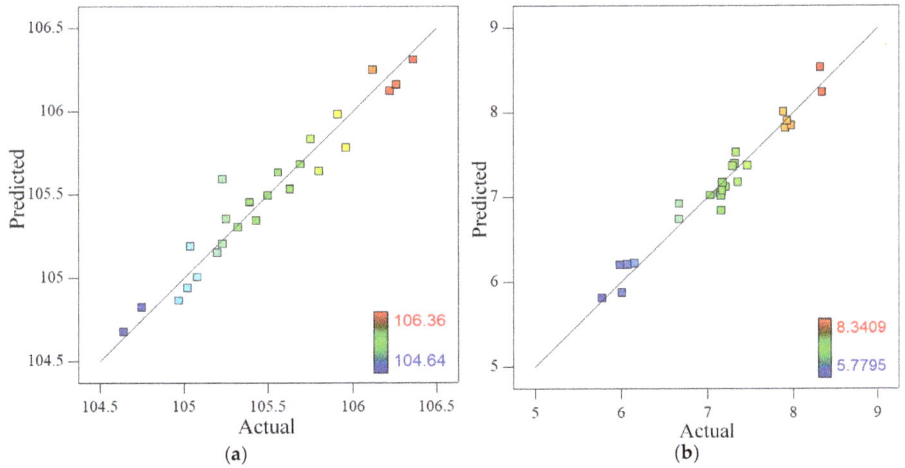

Figure 10. Relationship between predicted value and actual value: (**a**) Outer diameter; (**b**) Convolution pitch.

4.4. Response Surface Analysis

To intuitively reflect the relationship between forming quality and process parameters described by Equations (14) and (15), three-dimensional response surface of the outer diameter and convolution pitch are presented in Figures 11a and 11b, respectively. For this analysis, the die angle (θ) is set to 2°, as the corrugation shape is found to be close to a U-shape in the study by Chen et al. [26].

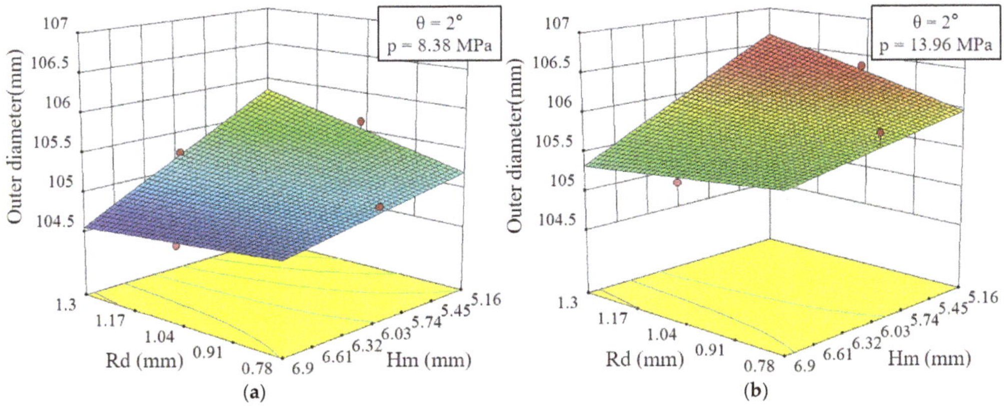

Figure 11. Outer diameter results given in form of second-order response surfaces and contours plots of two variables: (**a**) p = 8.38 MPa; (**b**) p = 13.96 MPa.

The influence of die fillet radius (R_d) and die thickness (H_m) on the outer diameter is evaluated at internal pressure (p) values of 8.38 MPa and 13.96 MPa, as shown in Figures 11a and 11b, respectively. It can be observed that the outer diameter increases with an increase in die fillet radius (R_d) and a decrease in die thickness (H_m). Furthermore, a comparison of the two response surfaces indicates that the outer diameter is significantly influenced by the internal pressure (p). The maximum outer diameter occurs at a die fillet radius R_d = 1.3 mm and die thickness H_m = 5.16 mm.

The influence of die fillet radius (R_d) and die thickness (H_m) on convolution pitch was evaluated at internal pressure (p) values of 8.38 MPa and 13.96 MPa, as illustrated in Figures 12a and 12b, respectively. It can be observed that the convolution pitch increases with increasing die thickness (H_m) and decreasing die fillet radius (R_d). Furthermore, the convolution pitch is more significantly influenced by changes in die thickness than by die fillet radius. The maximum convolution pitch occurs at a die fillet radius R_d = 1.3 mm and die thickness H_m = 6.9 mm.

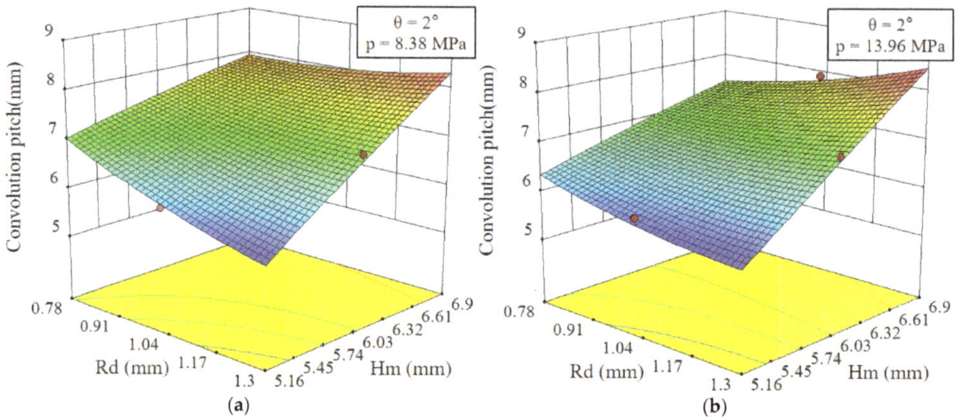

Figure 12. Convolution pitch results given in form of second-order response surfaces and contours plots of two variables. (**a**) p = 8.38 MPa; (**b**) p = 13.96 MPa.

4.5. Multi-Objective Optimization

Four process parameters, namely, die angle (θ), die fillet radius (R_d), die thickness (H_m) and internal pressure (p), were chosen as the design variables, while the outer diameter (D) and convolution pitch (q) were selected as the optimization objectives. According to the EJMA standard, one objective is to achieve a convolution diameter within a tolerance of ±1.58 mm, and the other is to maintain the convolution pitch within ±1.59 mm, as specified in Figure 1 and Table 1. Based on the preceding analysis, the optimization process for bellows hydroforming can be formulated as follows:

Minimize

$$\begin{aligned} F_1 &= D_m(\theta, R_d, H_m, p) - 106 \\ F_2 &= q_m(\theta, R_d, H_m, p) - 6.9 \end{aligned} \tag{18}$$

Subject to

$$\begin{gathered} 0 \le \theta \le 4(^\circ) \\ 0.78 \le R_d \le 1.3(mm) \\ 5.16 \le H_m \le 6.9(mm) \\ 8.38 \le p \le 13.96(mm) \end{gathered} \tag{19}$$

In this study, a MOGA-based optimization framework was developed in MATLAB to systematically identify combinations of design variables that satisfy the optimization objectives. The termination criterion is set at 200 generations, a value determined through preliminary convergence tests. These tests indicate that the Pareto front has stabilized beyond this point, with additional generations yielding no significant improvement in solution diversity or accuracy. Following 200 generations of MOGA iteration based on the RSM, the Pareto-optimal solutions for all objectives are plotted in Figure 13, where each point represents a Pareto-optimal solution. To verify the reliability of the optimization method proposed in this study, the design variables corresponding to point A (θ = 1.98°,

R_d = 1.28 mm, H_m = 6.90 mm, p = 11.03 MPa) are selected for the experimental validation and FE analysis. However, to accommodate practical process constraints, the die angle (θ), the die fillet radius (R_d), the die thickness (H_m), and the internal pressure (p) are adjusted to 2°, 1.3 mm, 6.9 mm, and 11 MPa, respectively.

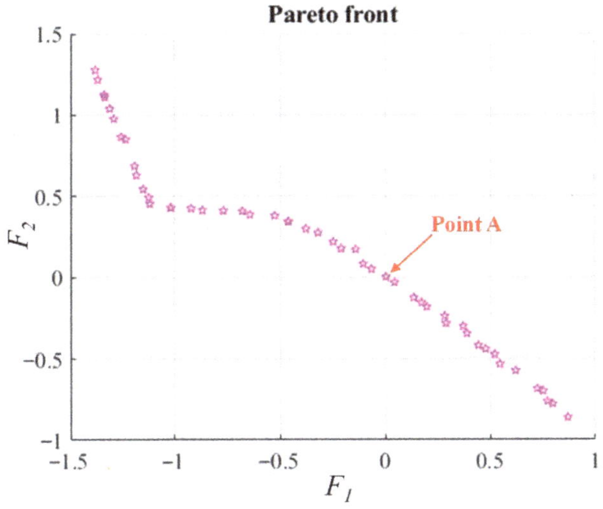

Figure 13. Pareto-optimal combinations of outer diameter and convolution pitch.

The hydroforming process is performed using the apparatus (Aerosun-Tola Expansion Joint Co., Ltd., Nanjing, China) illustrated in Figure 14a. The bellow manufactured under the optimal conditions is shown in Figure 14b. A comparison between the optimized and experimental results under the same optimum conditions is provided in Table 10. For the outer diameter, the optimized result is 106 mm, while the experimental value is 105.95 mm, resulting in a discrepancy of 0.04%. For the convolution pitch, the optimized result is 6.9 mm compared to the experimental value of 8.08 mm, yielding a discrepancy of 17.1%. Notably, both the outer diameter and convolution pitch of the manufactured bellows conform to the manufacturing tolerances specified in the EJMA standards [24]. The 17% error in convolution pitch prediction is primarily caused by the following factors: Accurate convolution pitch prediction is highly sensitive to springback estimation. The bellows' elastic nature and axial compliance cause highly nonlinear springback behaviour. Additionally, the multi-layer structure introduces greater complexity during forming, leading to intricate deformation mechanisms and challenges in springback prediction. Measurement uncertainties further amplify the discrepancies. Determining convolution pitch requires identifying the centerlines of multiple consecutive crests or troughs, which is sensitive to minor local variations. These variations accumulate and magnify errors in pitch measurement.

To enhance model accuracy, future work will focus on several improvements. Anisotropic constitutive models and kinematic hardening models will be employed to simulate sheet metal behaviour more accurately under complex loading conditions. The springback behaviour of multi-layer bellows will be systematically investigated and compensated through die design modifications or loading path adjustments.

The proposed optimization methodology integrating FE simulation, RSM, GA, and Pareto frontier is also appliable for U-shaped bellows with varying dimensions and materials. However, for bellows with complex cross-sections (e.g., S/Ω-shape), the multiple curvature zones lead to asymmetric material flow during hydroforming and multi-axial springback coupling effects, significantly increasing the complexity of forming prediction and springback control. Therefore, compared with the process optimization of U-shaped bellows, the current method needs to further consider the influence of multi-stage pressure loading and the precision of the mould cavity on the profile and wall thickness uniformity of the bellows in the process optimization for S/Ω-shaped bellows. This will be the key focus area for subsequent research.

(a) (b)

Figure 14. Experimental setup and formed part: (**a**) The hydroforming setup; (**b**) The formed bellow.

Table 10. Optimized and experimental results.

Source of the Result	Outer Diameter (mm)	Convolution Pitch (mm)
Optimization	106	6.9
Experiment	105.95	8.08

5. Conclusions

In this article, an optimization method consisting of FEM, RSM, and MOGA is proposed for the hydroforming process of bellows. The following main conclusions are drawn:

(1) The outer diameter is primarily influenced by the internal pressure (p), die angle (θ), die thickness (H_m), and die fillet radius (R_d), whereas the convolution pitch is mainly controlled by the die thickness (H_m). An increase in internal pressure (p) enlarges the outer diameter, similarly, a reduction in either the die angle (θ) or die thickness (H_m) also results in a larger outer diameter. In contrast, the convolution pitch increases with greater die thickness (H_m). It is also noteworthy that the interaction between die thickness (H_m) and die fillet radius (R_d) significantly affects both the outer diameter and the convolution pitch.

(2) Two second-order polynomial equations for predicting the outer diameter and convolution pitch are established using the RSM. The reliability of these equations is verified through the R^2-test and ANOVA. Furthermore, the effects of design variable and their interactions in the U-shaped bellows hydroforming are analyzed. The outer diameter reaches its maximum at a die fillet radius (R_d) of 1.3 mm and a die thickness (H_m) of 5.16 mm. Similarly, the convolution pitch is maximized at R_d = 1.3 mm and H_m = 6.9 mm.

(3) An MOGA-based optimization framework is developed to identify optimal combinations of design variables that meet the optimization objectives. A set of Pareto-optimal solutions is derived. The optimized results are experimentally verified. The application of the proposed procedure demonstrates its effectiveness in identifying feasible process parameters for manufacturing high-quality, defect-free U-shaped bellows.

Author Contributions: Methodology, J.L. (Jing Liu); Software, J.L. (Jing Liu); Investigation, L.L. (Liang Li) and J.L. (Jian Liu); Writing—original draft, J.L. (Jian Liu); Writing—review and editing, J.L. (Jing Liu), L.L. (Liang Li) and L.L. (Lanyun Li); Visualization, J.L. (Jian Liu); Supervision, J.L. (Jing Liu); Project administration, J.L. (Jing Liu) and L.L. (Liang Li). All authors have read and agreed to the published version of the manuscript.

Funding: The authors would like to thank the funds of the Natural Science Basic Research Plan in Shaanxi Province of China (No. 2025JC-YBMS-473) and the project of Shaanxi Key Laboratory of High-performance Precision Forming Technology and Equipment (SKL-HPFTE) (No. PFTE-2020-KF-02).

Data Availability Statement: The original contributions presented in this study are included in the article. Further inquiries can be directed to the corresponding author.

Conflicts of Interest: Author Liang Li is employed by the Aerosun-Tola Expansion Joint Co., Ltd. The remaining authors declare that the research was conducted in the absence of any commercial or financial relationships that could be construed as a potential conflict of interest.

References

1. Wankhede, S.D.; Gawande, S.H. Design and analysis aspect of metal expansion bellows: A review. *Forces Mech.* **2023**, *13*, 100244. [CrossRef]
2. Ying, X.P.; Yan, J.; Zhang, K.L.; Yang, Z.X.; Cao, H.X.; Bu, Y.F. Study on competition mechanism of deformation modes of U-shaped bellows under internal pressure. *Mar. Struct.* **2023**, *92*, 103497. [CrossRef]
3. Kim, J.; An, Y.H.; Jung, S.M.; Lee, H.K.; Seon, C.; Ha, J.Y.; Lee, J.; Cheon, M.S. Development of double-walled bellows for ITER VUV spectrometer systems. *Fusion Eng. Des.* **2024**, *210*, 114706. [CrossRef]
4. Gao, Y.Y.; Wei, Y.H.; Liu, X.B.; Jia, H.H.; Zhao, W.Y. Stress interaction analysis and mitigation in multi-process bellows manufacturing using continuous finite element simulation. *J. Mater. Process. Technol.* **2025**, *339*, 118826. [CrossRef]
5. Yu, S.; Wan, Z.D.; Lin, J.; Zhou, Z.; Liu, Y.H. Effect of residual stress on the axial buckling behaviour of the hydraulic-formed bellows. *Int. J. Press. Vessels Pip.* **2025**, *215*, 105468. [CrossRef]
6. Faraji, G.; Besharati, M.K.; Mosavi, M.; Kashanizadeh, H. Experimental and finite element analysis of parameters in manufacturing of metal bellows. *Int. J. Adv. Manuf. Technol.* **2008**, *38*, 641–648. [CrossRef]
7. Faraji, G.; Mashhadi, M.M.; Norouzifard, V. Evaluation of effective parameters in metal bellows forming process. *J. Mater. Process. Technol.* **2009**, *209*, 3431–3437. [CrossRef]
8. Faraji, G.; Hashemi, R.; Mosavi, M.M.; Dizaji, A.F.; Norouzifard, V. Hydroforming limits in metal bellows forming process. *Mater. Manuf. Processes.* **2010**, *25*, 1413–1417. [CrossRef]
9. Lee, S.W. Study on the forming parameters of the metal bellows. *J. Mater. Process. Technol.* **2002**, *130*, 47–53. [CrossRef]
10. Yuan, Z.; Huo, S.H.; Ren, J.T.; Han, J.F. Study on the hydroforming technology of reinforced s-shaped bellows. *Int. J. Adv. Manuf. Technol.* **2019**, *103*, 2541–2552. [CrossRef]
11. Liu, J.; Liu, Y.; Li, L.Y.; Li, X. Springback behaviors of bi-layered non-homogeneous bellows in hydroforming. *Int. J. Adv. Manuf. Technol.* **2017**, *93*, 1605–1616. [CrossRef]
12. Liu, J.; Lv, Z.Y.; Liu, Y.; Li, L.Y. Deformation behaviors of four-layered U-shaped metallic bellows in hydroforming. *Chin. J. Aeronaut.* **2020**, *33*, 3479–3494. [CrossRef]
13. Alaswad, A.; Olabi, A.G.; Benyounis, K.Y. Integration of finite element analysis and design of experiments to analyses the geometrical factors in bi-layered tube hydroforming. *Mater. Des.* **2011**, *32*, 838–850. [CrossRef]
14. Raut, S.V.; Ramesh, A.; Arun, A.; Sumesh, C.S. Finite element analysis and optimization of tube hydroforming process. *Mater. today Proc.* **2021**, *46*, 5008–5016. [CrossRef]
15. Chen, M.T.; Xiao, X.T.; Tong, J.H.; Guo, H.; Wen, J.P. Optimization of loading path in hydroforming of parallel double branched tube through response surface methodology. *Adv. Eng. Softw.* **2018**, *115*, 429–438. [CrossRef]
16. Rajaeea, M.; Hosseinipour, S.J.; Aval, H.J. Multi-objective Optimization of HMGF Process Parameters for Manufacturing AA6063 Stepped Tubes using FEM-RSM. *IJE Trans. B Appl.* **2021**, *34*, 1305–1312.
17. Feng, Y.Y.; Jia, Y.; Sun, X.Q.; Chen, G.P.; Luo, Z.A. Optimization of bi-layered Y-shaped tube hydroforming using RSM. *Int. J. Adv. Manuf. Technol.* **2024**, *133*, 521–541. [CrossRef]
18. Abbassi, F.; Ahmad, F.; Gulzar, S.; Belhadj, T.; Karrech, A.; Choi, H.S. Design of T-shaped tube hydroforming using finite element and artificial neural network modeling. *J. Mech. Sci. Technol.* **2020**, *34*, 1129–1138. [CrossRef]
19. Palumbo, G.; Piglionico, V.; Piccininni, A.; Guglielmi, P.; Tricarico, L. Evaluation of the optimal working conditions for the warm sheet Hydroforming taking into account the yielding condition. *Mater. Des.* **2016**, *91*, 411–423. [CrossRef]

20. Bahloul, R.; Arfa, H.; BelHadjSalah, H. A study on optimal design of process parameters in single point incremental forming of sheet metal by combining Box–Behnken design of experiments, response surface methods and genetic algorithms. *Int. J. Adv. Manuf. Technol.* **2014**, *74*, 163–185. [CrossRef]
21. Sharma, S.K.; Mishra, B.K.; Singh, I.V. A multiobjective optimization framework based on FEA, ANN, and NSGA-II to optimize the process parameters of tube-to-tubesheet joint. *Finite Elem. Anal. Des.* **2024**, *241*, 104225. [CrossRef]
22. Han, S.S.; Kim, H.K. Optimum multistage deep drawing process design using artificial neural network-based forming quality evaluation function. *J. Mater. Process. Technol.* **2025**, *341*, 118881. [CrossRef]
23. Darabi, R.; Azodi, H.D.; Jung, D.W. Multi-Objective Optimization of bi-Layer metallic sheet using pareto-based genetic algorithm. *Mater. Sci. Forum* **2018**, *4564*, 276–283. [CrossRef]
24. Expansion Joint Manufacture Association (EJMA) Inc. *Standards of the Expansion Joint Manufacture Association (EJMA) Inc.*, 9th ed.; Expansion Joint Manufacture Association (EJMA) Inc.: Tarrytown, NY, USA, 2009.
25. Liu, W.; Yang, Y.Y. Multi-objective optimization of sheet metal forming process using Pareto-based genetic algorithm. *J. Mater. Process. Technol.* **2008**, *208*, 499–506.
26. Chen, Q.L.; Liu, J.; Lv, Z.Y.; Cui, L. Study on the influence of mold parameters on the wave profile of hydraulically bulged double-layer heterogeneous bellows. *J. Plast. Eng.* **2021**, *28*, 70–78.

metals

MDPI

Article

Optimization of Eleven Cross-Roll Straightening Process for 20CrMnTi Bars Based on Combined Hardening Model

Shangwu Jia [1,2,3,4], Longyi Bao [1,2], Shijie Wang [3,4,5], Qingdang Meng [1,2], Jun Zhao [1,2] and Ruixue Zhai [1,2,*]

1 Key Laboratory of Advanced Forging & Stamping Technology and Science (Yanshan University), Ministry of Education of China, Qinhuangdao 066004, China; jiashangwu@stumail.ysu.edu.cn (S.J.); 15641724367@163.com (L.B.); mengqingdang@ysu.edu.cn (Q.M.); zhaojun@ysu.edu.cn (J.Z.)
2 School of Mechanical Engineering, Yanshan University, Qinhuangdao 066004, China
3 National Key Laboratory of Metal Forming Technology and Heavy Equipment, Xi'an 710000, China; xzswangsj@163.com
4 China National Heavy Machinery Research Institute Co., Ltd., Xi'an 710016, China
5 School of Mechanical Engineering, Xi'an Jiaotong University, Xi'an 710049, China
* Correspondence: zhairuixue@ysu.edu.cn

Abstract: Straightness is one of the important indices to measure the quality of bars; multi-roll straightening is an essential process in bar production. Materials undergo multiple cycles of alternating tensile and compressive loading during multi-roll straightening, subject to the influence of the Bauschinger effect. However, most existing studies have failed to adequately account for the Bauschinger effect, leading to insufficient prediction accuracy of the process. This study establishes an eleven-roll straightening finite element model (FEM) for bars based on the nonlinear combined hardening model. The orthogonal experimental design method is employed to optimize the process parameters. Straightening experiments of 20CrMnTi bars using an eleven-roll straightener were conducted. Based on the FEM, the influence patterns of different process parameters on the straightening results were investigated. The results indicate excellent agreement between the eleven-roll straightening finite element simulation results and the experimental results. Using the optimized parameters, both the simulated and experimental straightness after straightening were within 1‰, with a relative error between them below 8%. The findings of this study can improve the prediction accuracy of the eleven-roll bar straightening process and provide reliable theoretical support and technical reference for the optimization of straightening process parameters.

Keywords: eleven cross-roll straightening process; nonlinear combined hardening model; 20CrMnTi bars; FEM; the orthogonal experimental design; the Bauschinger effect

1. Introduction

The steel industry is crucial to national economic development and national defense. Within this sector, bar products serve as key materials for machinery manufacturing and are extensively utilized. 20CrMnTi bars, renowned for their excellent hardness and wear resistance, are widely employed in the manufacturing of high-precision components. However, in engineering practice, a prevalent issue is straightness deviation exceeding tolerance limits. This problem arises from the coupling effect of uneven residual stresses induced by heat treatment and plastic deformation occurring during the forming process. The straightness of bars directly impacts the installation accuracy, service life, and overall performance of the final products, as well as the processing efficiency and cost of downstream operations. Consequently, the multi-roll straightening process constitutes an essential stage in bar production.

Multi-roll straightening employs various roll arrangement configurations. Common types include five-roll, six-roll, seven-roll, nine-roll, ten-roll, and eleven-roll straighteners. Specifically, the eleven-roll straightener incorporates an additional, smaller stabilizing tail roll compared to the ten-roll design. This tail roll serves to support the bar and restrict post-straightening whipping motion, thereby contributing to improved straightening accuracy. Although multi-roll straightening processes differ in form, their underlying principle remains consistent. By precisely controlling the reduction settings of each inclined roll, the bar is subjected to alternating reverse bending, inducing appropriate elasto-plastic deformation. The rotation of the rolls drives both the rotation and forward advancement of the workpiece. During the straightening process, the bar undergoes a variable-curvature rotary bending deformation. Material experiences multiple cycles of alternating tensile and compressive loading. Consequently, the influence of the Bauschinger effect must be accounted for in research on multi-roll straightening processes.

The Bauschinger effect refers to the phenomenon where, after a material undergoes plastic deformation in one direction, its yield stress upon subsequent reverse loading exhibits a significant reduction. The isotropic hardening model assumes that only the radius of the yield surface changes, while its central position remains fixed. Consequently, this model fails to capture the Bauschinger effect and significantly overestimates the yield strength during reverse loading. To describe the Bauschinger effect, Prager [1] first proposed the linear kinematic hardening model. Subsequently, Ziegler [2] modified Prager's hardening model. The linear kinematic hardening model assumes that the yield surface translates linearly in the direction of the plastic strain. Thus, it can only describe linear hardening behavior and cannot account for nonlinear hardening phenomena. Nonlinear hardening is ubiquitous in materials, particularly when subjected to alternating tensile and compressive loading. Armstrong and Frederick [3] introduced a dynamic recovery term into the linear kinematic hardening model, proposing the renowned A–F back stress evolution law, which can describe nonlinear hardening behavior. Chaboche et al. [4,5] decomposed the back stress into the sum of multiple back stress components, each following the A–F type evolution law. The Chaboche combined hardening model (combining the Chaboche back stress model with the isotropic hardening model) provides an accurate description of the response curves generated under cyclic loading. Its relatively simple formulation has led to its widespread embedding within numerous finite element software packages and broad application. Scholars subsequently made modifications to the Chaboche model [6–8], which, to some extent, improved the fitting accuracy of the model, but at the same time increased the complexity of the model, making it difficult to apply these modified models. Okorokov et al. [9,10] proposed a novel form of kinematic hardening model; this model can accurately describe hysteresis loops under various loading conditions without requiring the superposition of multiple back stresses.

In the research on multi-roll straightening technology, Cui et al. [11] proposed a unique method for designing the main parameters of straighteners, simplifying their design and manufacturing processes, thereby advancing straightening theory and technology. Liu et al. [12] conducted a novel analysis of the roll shape curves for tube and bar straighteners and proposed a universal straightening principle applicable to different profiles using the same straightening roll. Song [13], through research on adjusting the angles of straightening rolls, provided a theoretical basis for straightener setup. Zhu et al. [14] applied the energy method to derive a calculation formula for the flattening reduction, revealing its variation patterns with diameter and wall thickness. Zhao et al. [15] optimized the roll shape curve formula for inclined-roll straighteners, providing a theoretical basis for determining the installation angle and contact line length. Zheng [16] conducted an in-depth study on the straightening process of a 2-2-2-type straightener based on elasto-plastic bending straightening theory. Zhang et al. [17,18] performed a detailed analysis of the flattening issues in tubes during multi-roll straightening. Current research on the cross-roll straightening process often simplifies the rotary bending process to multiple cycles of in-plane reverse bending, neglecting the strain path variation during rotation. Ma et al. [19] derived the relationship between flattening force and flattening displacement using the energy method, enabling control of the ovality in straightened tubes. Ma et al. [20] conducted a theoretical analysis of the eleven-roll inclined-roll straightening process and validated its effectiveness using field data. Li [21] derived a formula for calculating straightening roll service life based on Miner's damage criterion, verifying its rationality through finite element simulation and friction-wear experiments, and analyzed key factors affecting roll life. Yao et al. [22] analyzed the influence of bite conditions, contact stress, and strength conditions on the roll diameter and roll pitch of roller straighteners, concluding that strength conditions are the key factor. Hu et al. [23] addressed issues like traditional straightening processes relying on manual experience and low efficiency by optimizing a BP neural network using the Dung Beetle Optimizer (DBO) algorithm to establish a straightening process prediction model. Results showed this method effectively improves prediction accuracy. Gu et al. [24] reviewed the current state of roller straightening technology, analyzed the influence of straightening strategies and key parameters on post-straightening flatness deviation and residual stress, providing theoretical support for the independent development of large-scale roller straightening equipment.

Mwita et al. [25] conducted numerical predictions of the tensile yield strength and hardness properties of Ti6Al4V alloy subjected to Constrained Bending Straightening (CBS) and Severe Plastic Deformation (SPD) processes. Gruber et al. [26] introduced a control scheme for a leveler employing different load triangles to eliminate straightening residual stresses. Petruska et al. [27] addressed the modeling of round bar cross-roll straightening by proposing a novel finite element formulation. This method, based on an Eulerian description, simulates the flow of elasto-plastic material through a fixed spatial finite element mesh, coupled with a multi-roll straightening machine. Asakawa et al. [28] performed a comprehensive analysis of the bar straightening process through simulation and experimental investigation. They proposed a method for predicting the deflection of bars after straightening. This method proves particularly effective for bars with large initial curvature, but further in-depth analysis and research are still required for bars with smaller initial curvature. Meng et al. [29] conducted an in-depth study on the basic problem of rotational bending springback involved in the cross-roller straightening process and proposed a new analytical method for rotational bending springback considering the strain path. Domitner et al. [30] proposed an experimental method to evaluate the wear of rollers in a multi-cross roller straightening process. Niu et al. [31] proposed a new radial feed-in rotary straightening method to address the planetary roller screw deflection problem and verified the feasibility of the process using numerical simulation and experimental methods.

The main literature comparison results are shown in Table 1. In summary, existing research predominantly employs simplified material models, failing to accurately account for the influence of the Bauschinger effect. This limitation leads to insufficient prediction accuracy for the multi-roll straightening process. To address this, this study establishes an eleven-roll bar straightening finite element model based on a nonlinear combined hardening model. The orthogonal experimental design method is utilized to optimize the process parameters. Straightening experiments on 20CrMnTi bars using an eleven-roll straightener were conducted to validate the reliability of both the numerical simulation results and the optimized process parameters. Leveraging the established eleven-roll straightening

FEM, the influence patterns of various process parameters on the straightening results were systematically investigated. The findings of this research can provide reliable theoretical support and technical reference for the optimization design of the eleven cross-roll straightening process for 20CrMnTi bars.

Table 1. Main literature comparison.

Reference	Hardening Model	Model Accuracy	Roll Config	Key Contribution
[17]	Linear kinematic hardening	Low	Eight cross-roll	Tube ovalization control
[18]	Isotropic hardening	Low	Eight cross-roll	Tube flattening analysis
[19]	Isotropic hardening	Low	Six cross-roll	Optimization of tube flattening displacement
[20]	Bilinear hardening model	Low	Eleven cross-roll	Process analysis
[27]	Linear kinematic hardening	Low	Ten cross-roll	New simulation method
This study	Chaboche combination hardening	High	Eleven cross-roll	Accurate optimization of process parameters

2. Process Parameters

The arrangement of rollers in the eleven cross-roll straightening process for bars is shown in Figure 1. The main working components primarily include the straightening rollers and the front/rear sleeves. The key process parameters for eleven-roll straightening include roll gap, roll reduction, roller inclination angle, and straightening speed. The specific definitions of these parameters are as follows:

(1) Roll gap: Refers to the minimum distance between two rollers.
(2) Roll reduction: Refers to the displacement of the reverse bending roller relative to other rollers in the height direction, as shown in Figure 2. The greater the roll reduction, the greater the degree of deformation.
(3) Roller inclination angle: Refers to the angle between the axes of two rollers.
(4) Straightening speed: Refers to the rotational speed of the straightening rollers.

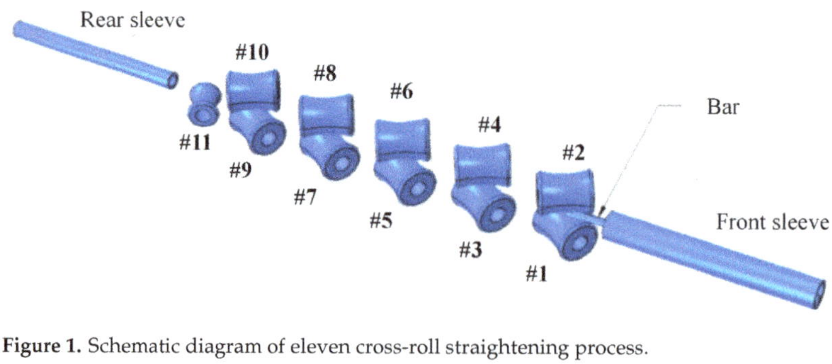

Figure 1. Schematic diagram of eleven cross-roll straightening process.

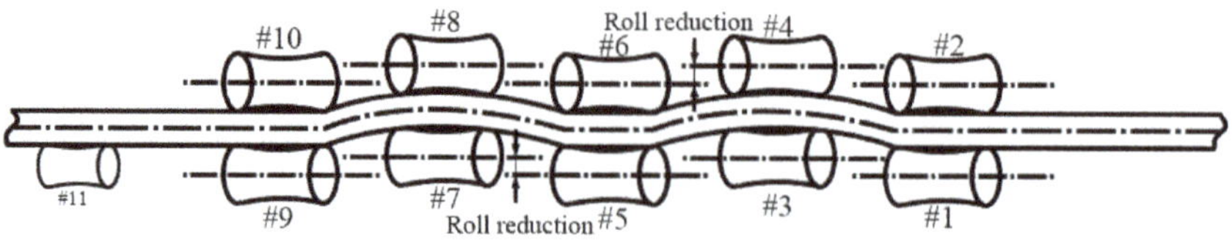

Figure 2. Schematic diagram of roll reduction.

3. Constitutive Model

Considering the balance of accuracy, ease of use, and computational efficiency, the Chaboche combined hardening model with three back stresses was selected for this study.

Based on the von Mises isotropic yield criterion, the yield function for the kinematic hardening model can be expressed as follows:

$$F = \sqrt{\frac{3}{2}(\mathbf{s}_{ij} - \boldsymbol{\alpha}_{ij})(\mathbf{s}_{ij} - \boldsymbol{\alpha}_{ij})} - Y \quad (1)$$

where F is the yield function, $\mathbf{s}_{ij}$ is the deviatoric stress tensor, $\boldsymbol{\alpha}_{ij}$ is the back stress tensor (MPa), i, j are tensor indices, and Y is the yield stress.

The evolution law for back stress is categorized into linear and nonlinear forms. The linear expression is as follows:

$$\mathrm{d}\boldsymbol{\alpha}_{ij} = \frac{2}{3}C\mathrm{d}\varepsilon_{ij}^{p} \quad (2)$$

where C is the parameter for the evolution of back stress.

Armstrong and Frederick [3] introduced a dynamic recovery term into the linear evolution law, proposing the renowned A–F nonlinear back stress evolution law. Its mathematical expression is given by the following equation:

$$\mathrm{d}\boldsymbol{\alpha}_{ij} = \frac{2}{3}C\mathrm{d}\varepsilon_{ij}^{p} - \gamma\boldsymbol{\alpha}_{ij}\mathrm{d}p \quad (3)$$

where γ is the back stress evolution parameters. Compared to the linear kinematic hardening model, the A–F evolution law can accurately describe the nonlinear hardening behavior of materials.

Chaboche [4] proposed an enhanced approach based on the A–F evolution law, representing the back stress as a superposition of multiple components. Each back stress component is assumed to independently follow the A–F evolution law, enabling a more precise description of the material's nonlinear mechanical behavior:

$$\mathrm{d}\boldsymbol{\alpha}_{ij} = \sum_{m=1}^{N} \mathrm{d}\boldsymbol{\alpha}_{ij}^{m} \quad (4)$$

where N is the number of back stress components (in this study, N = 3 is adopted), and $\mathrm{d}\boldsymbol{\alpha}_{ij}^{m}$ is the m-th back stress component.

For the commonly used isotropic hardening model in the form of exponential functions, the expression is as follows:

$$Y = Y_0 + Q[1 - \exp(-bp)] \quad (5)$$

where Y_0 is the initial yield stress (MPa), Q, b is the isotropic hardening parameter, and p is the cumulative plastic strain.

Under uniaxial stress conditions, the back stress evolution law in Equation (3) can be integrated as follows:

$$\alpha_{11}^{m} = \alpha_{11}^{m0}\exp(-\gamma\left|\Delta\varepsilon_{11}^{p}\right|) + \frac{2}{3}\mu\frac{C_m}{\gamma_m}[1 - \exp(-\gamma_m\left|\Delta\varepsilon_{11}^{p}\right|)] \quad (6)$$

where α_{11}^{m0} is the initial value of the back stress at the start of the load cycle, $\Delta\varepsilon_{11}^{p}$ is the change in plastic strain during the loading cycle; μ is the loading direction parameter, where $\mu = \pm 1$ indicates the direction of loading. When $\Delta\varepsilon_{11}^{p}$ is positive, the value is positive, and when $\Delta\varepsilon_{11}^{p}$ is negative, the value is negative.

Then there is the following:

$$\alpha = \sum_{m=1}^{N} \alpha^{m0} \exp(-\gamma_m \left|\Delta\varepsilon_{11}^{p}\right|) + \mu \frac{C_m}{\gamma_m}[1 - \exp(-\gamma_m \left|\Delta\varepsilon_{11}^{p}\right|)] \tag{7}$$

The stress expression for the unidirectional stress state is as follows:

$$\sigma_{11} = \alpha + \mu Y \tag{8}$$

The stress–strain relationship can be expressed using the linear elasticity assumption for the elastic deformation stage as follows:

$$\sigma_{11} = E\varepsilon_{11} \tag{9}$$

where E is the elastic modulus.

4. Materials and Methods

4.1. Material Performance Test

The cyclic test was performed using an Instron 8801 electro-hydraulic servo fatigue testing machine (Hexagon Manufacturing Intelligence, North Kingstown, RI, USA), conducting symmetric cyclic tension–compression tests at room temperature. The specimen specifications are shown in Figure 3. The chemical composition of 20CrMnTi bars is shown in Table 2.

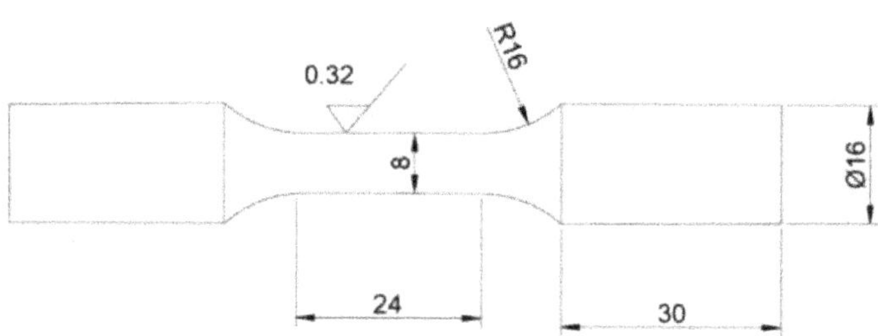

Figure 3. Geometry of cyclic tensile specimens (mm).

Table 2. Chemical composition of 20CrMnTi bars/wt.%.

Material	C	Si	Mn	P	S	Cr	Ti	Ni	Cu	Mo	Fe
20CrMnTi	0.19	0.26	0.96	0.018	0.018	1.14	0.055	0.03	0.02	0.02	Balanced

The test procedure is shown in Figure 4. Figure 4a presents the specimen of 20CrMnTi bars subjected to cyclic loading, Figure 4b shows the cyclic loading process, and Figure 4c displays the Instron 8801 electro-hydraulic servo fatigue testing machine used for the tests. The studied bar eleven cross-roll straightening process belongs to the cold deformation process and is in the medium and low strain rate range. The effect of strain rate is ignored in the study. The loading speed of the testing machine is 0.5 mm/min. Corresponding to the maximum strain during the straightening process, the strain amplitude for the cyclic loading tests was set at 0.03.

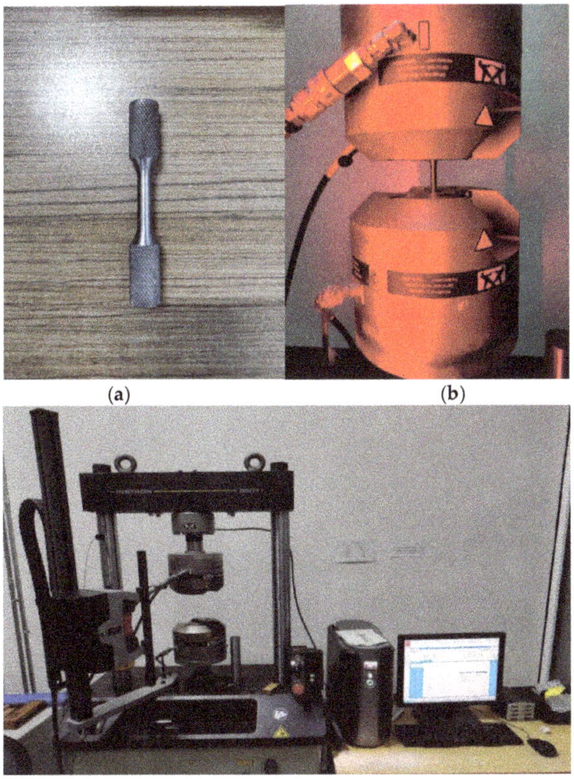

(**a**) (**b**) (**c**)

Figure 4. Cyclic tensile test equipment: (**a**) 20CrMnTi bar specimen; (**b**) cyclic loading process; (**c**) Instron 8801 electro-hydraulic servo fatigue testing machine.

Based on the analytical results of the hardening model under uniaxial stress conditions, the material parameters of the hardening model were fitted using the least squares method. The goal was to minimize the error between the fitted response curve and the experimental response curve. The error expression is as follows:

$$\sigma_{\mathrm{error}} = \sqrt{\frac{\sum_{i=1}^{N_{\mathrm{d}}} (\sigma_{\mathrm{model}} - \sigma_{\mathrm{exp}})^2}{N_{\mathrm{d}}}} \tag{10}$$

where σ_{model} is the fitted stress (MPa), σ_{exp} is the experimental stress (MPa), and N_{d} is the number of data points used in the fitting.

To avoid local optimum solutions during the least squares fitting process, 10,000 sets of initial parameters were randomly generated. The set with the smallest standard deviation of the fitting results was selected as the final optimal parameters. The obtained fitting parameters are listed in Table 3.

During the testing process, strain control was applied with a strain amplitude of ± 0.03, and three stress cycles were performed. The comparison of the fitting results and experimental results of the cyclic response curves is shown in Figure 5. It is evident that the nonlinear combined hardening model provides a good fit for the cyclic response curves, and the model can accurately represent the Bauschinger effect.

Table 3. Material parameters obtained by fitting the nonlinear hardening model.

Parameters	20CrMnTi	Value Range
Y_0/MPa	535	
b	1055	0–10,000
Q/MPa	−324.24	0–10,000
E/GPa	173	
C_1/MPa	451,319.14	0–1,000,000
C_2/MPa	26,005.19	0–300,000
C_3/MPa	2910.56	0–100,000
γ_1	2043.16	0–10,000
γ_2	170.6	0–5000
γ_3	3.07	0–1000

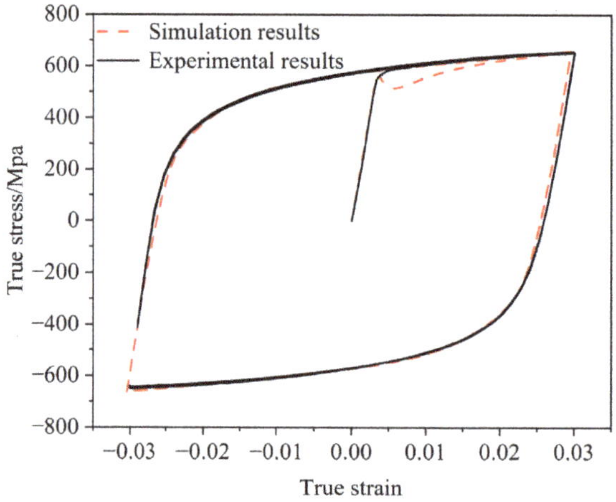

Figure 5. Stress–strain curve of cyclic loading.

4.2. Finite Element Model

Considering the complexity of the straightening machine structure, this study focused on the roller system that directly acts on the bar, excluding non-critical components. The model includes the bar, front and rear sleeves, five pairs of straightening rollers, and the tail roll. Finite element simulations of the eleven-roll straightening process were conducted using the ABAQUS/Explicit module, and the FEM is shown in Figure 6. Since the deformations of the front and rear sleeves and the straightening rollers are minimal during the straightening process, they are assumed to be rigid bodies for computational efficiency. Their mesh type is set as R3D4 with a mesh size of 30 mm for the sleeves and 20 mm for the straightening rollers. The bar is modeled as a deformable body, with material properties as given in Table 3, and its mesh type is set as C3D8R, with 32 nodes along the circumference and 60 nodes along the length. In the contact property formulation, the tangential behavior is modeled using the penalty function. Numerical simulations were performed with friction coefficients of 0.12, 0.15, 0.18, and 0.2. When the friction coefficient was 0.15, the error between the numerical simulation results and the experimental results was the smallest. Therefore, the friction coefficient was taken as 0.15 in the simulation. For normal behavior, a hard contact approach is applied to ensure that the bar is properly constrained by the rollers, preventing unrealistic interpenetration. In terms of boundary conditions, all degrees of freedom for the front and rear sleeves are constrained. A local coordinate system is established for each straightening roller, with the roller axis aligned along the x-axis. All rollers are set as active rollers, and boundary conditions are applied to rotate the rollers along the local x-axis while constraining all other degrees of freedom.

Figure 6. Finite element model of bar eleven-roll straightening.

The connecting-both-ends method is used to calculate the deflection. The connecting both ends method refers to connecting the start and end points of the bar axis, then drawing lines parallel to this connecting line through the highest point and the lowest point. The value measured along the vertical coordinate axis between these two parallel lines represents the deflection value. To obtain the straightness data of the bar in post-processing, a quarter-section of the bar is first swept along the axis to generate a quarter-bar model, and the remaining three-quarters of the bar are modeled similarly. These models are then combined to form a single bar entity. Since the bar has an initial deflection, the axis used for sweeping is a line with initial curvature. In the simulation, the bar is initially stress-free, and the effect of initial residual stress is ignored. The initial deflection of the bar is 40 mm, and the length and diameter of the bar are 5000 mm and 71.8 mm, respectively, as shown in Figure 7. For mesh division, each part is handled separately to ensure the presence of nodes along the bar's axis. The coordinates of all nodes along the axis are extracted to calculate the straightness after straightening. It should be pointed out that due to the existence of half-span straightening blind zones at the head and tail rolls in the multi-cross-roll straightening process, all straightness results in subsequent studies did not calculate the straightening blind zone. The length of the straightening blind zone is 500 mm at the head and tail of the bar, and the straightness is calculated for the middle 4000 mm.

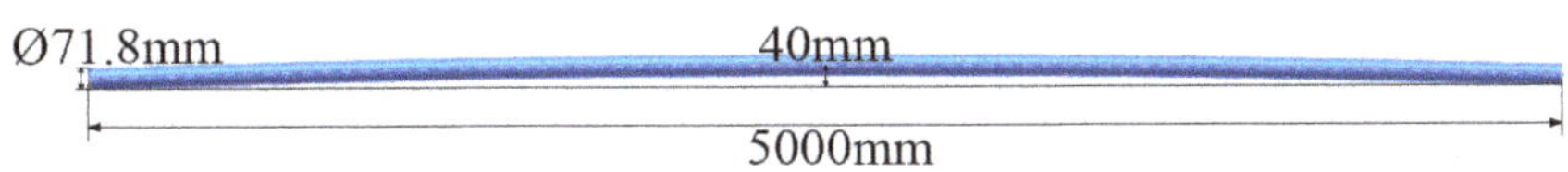

Figure 7. Schematic diagram of the initial bar.

4.3. Eleven Roll Straightening Experiment of Bars

In this study, an eleven-roll straightening machine from Shigang Steel was used for experimental verification. This equipment, developed and manufactured by the China Heavy Machinery Research Institute, is specifically designed for straightening bars with diameters ranging from φ45 mm to φ150 mm. The straightening machine is equipped with a semi-automatic control system, which allows for the adjustment of roll inclination angle, roll gap, and roll reduction to accommodate different bar specifications and materials, ensuring stable and reliable straightening performance. A photo of the straightening machine is shown in Figure 8.

Figure 8. Eleven-roll straightening machine for bars.

Figure 9 presents the flowchart of the experimental straightening process. Initially, the bars to be straightened are bundled and placed on the feeding platform, as shown in Figure 9a. The material is then fed into the front roller channel by a material-feeding machine, as shown in Figure 9b. The bars are conveyed into the straightening machine inlet through the front roller channel, as shown in Figure 9c. At the straightening machine inlet, the bar undergoes gripping and stable straightening, as illustrated in Figure 9d. After straightening, the bars pass through the tail roller and enter the rear roller channel, as shown in Figure 9e. Finally, the material is transferred to the unloading platform by the material-feeding machine, as shown in Figure 9f. In the configuration of the first ten rolls, the first, second, fourth, and fifth pairs are drive rolls, and the third pair is a passive roll. The straightness of the bars after straightening was tested using a combination of feeler gauges and reference gauges, as shown in Figure 10. During experimentation, temperature was not controlled, nor were additional lubrication steps implemented. Process parameters—including roll gap, roll reduction, roller inclination angle, and straightening speed—were controlled to match the settings used in the numerical simulations.

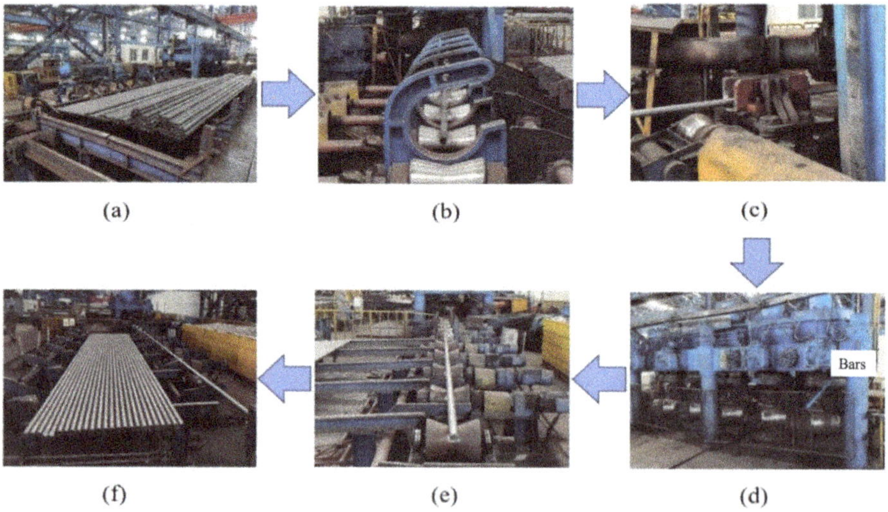

Figure 9. Flow chart of field straightening.

Figure 10. Straightness check after bar straightening.

5. Results and Discussion

5.1. Optimization of Process Parameters

5.1.1. Orthogonal Experimental Scheme

The orthogonal experimental method was employed to optimize the process parameters for the eleven cross-roll straightening process. The factors considered in the experiments include roll inclination angle, roll reduction, straightening speed, and roll gap. The specific levels of these parameters in the orthogonal experiment are shown in Table 4. In order to improve efficiency, the effects of interactions between factors were ignored in the study.

Table 4. Orthogonal test factor level table.

Factor	Parameter	Level 1	Level 2	Level 3	Level 4
A	Angle/°	32	34	36	38
B	Roll reduction/mm	6	8	10	12
C	Straightening speed/(mm/min)	20	40	60	80
D	Roll gap/mm	70.0	70.6	71.2	71.8

The orthogonal experimental design was performed based on a four-factor and four-level model. Simulations were conducted using Abaqus software (Version 2021) to analyze the results, and the optimal combination of process parameters was determined. The orthogonal experimental design and corresponding results are shown in Table 5.

Table 5. Orthogonal test program and results.

Test Number	Factor A	Factor B	Factor C	Factor D	Straightness/‰
1	32°	6 mm	20 m/min	70.0 mm	1.82
2	32°	8 mm	40 m/min	70.6 mm	1.23
3	32°	10 mm	60 m/min	71.2 mm	1.12
4	32°	12 mm	80 m/min	71.8 mm	1.93
5	34°	6 mm	60 m/min	70.6 mm	1.73
6	34°	8 mm	80 m/min	70.0 mm	1.26

Table 5. *Cont.*

Test Number	Factor A	Factor B	Factor C	Factor D	Straightness/‰
7	34°	10 mm	20 m/min	71.8 mm	1.74
8	34°	12 mm	40 m/min	71.2 mm	2.07
9	36°	6 mm	80 m/min	71.2 mm	1.52
10	36°	8 mm	60 m/min	71.8 mm	2.89
11	36°	10 mm	40 m/min	70.0 mm	1.22
12	36°	12 mm	20 m/min	70.6 mm	1.82
13	38°	6 mm	40 m/min	71.8 mm	2.7
14	38°	8 mm	20 m/min	71.2 mm	2.32
15	38°	10 mm	80 m/min	70.6 mm	1.39
16	38°	12 mm	60 m/min	70.0 mm	1.26

5.1.2. Range Analysis of Orthogonal Test Results

The mean value k was used to measure the influence of the four experimental factors at different levels on the straightness of the bar. A range analysis was performed on the orthogonal experimental results of the eleven-roll straightening process, and the range R reflects the impact of changes in factor levels on the experimental outcomes. The larger the value of R, the more significant the effect of that factor on the results. Conversely, a smaller value indicates a less significant effect. The effects of each factor level on bar straightness are shown in Table 6. From Table 6, it can be seen that the most significant factors influencing bar straightness are in the following order: roll gap > roll reduction > straightening speed > roll inclination angle, with roll gap having a much more significant impact compared to the other factors. Roll reduction, straightening speed, and roll inclination angle all have a certain degree of influence on bar straightness.

Table 6. Range analysis of bar straightness.

Range	Factor A	Factor B	Factor C	Factor D
k_1	1.53	1.94	1.93	1.39
k_2	1.70	1.93	1.81	1.54
k_3	1.86	1.37	1.85	1.76
k_4	1.92	1.77	1.43	2.31
R	0.39	0.57	0.5	0.93

5.1.3. Process Analysis of Orthogonal Test and Experimental Verification of Optimal Process Parameters

Based on the range analysis of the orthogonal test, the effects of each factor on the experimental results were studied, and key variables were identified using the range values. The optimal process parameters were selected. By combining the orthogonal table design with data analysis, the effectiveness of various factor combinations was evaluated, thus improving the accuracy and reliability of the experiment and providing a reference for process optimization.

It was found that a larger roll inclination angle can also change the contact angle between the straightening roll and the bar, which in turn affects the direction and effect of the applied force. This variation can lead to an unstable pressure distribution during the straightening process, which may induce different levels of stress on the bar, further affecting the straightening performance. The roll inclination angle directly influences the post-straightening straightness of the bar, and its variation is shown in Figure 11.

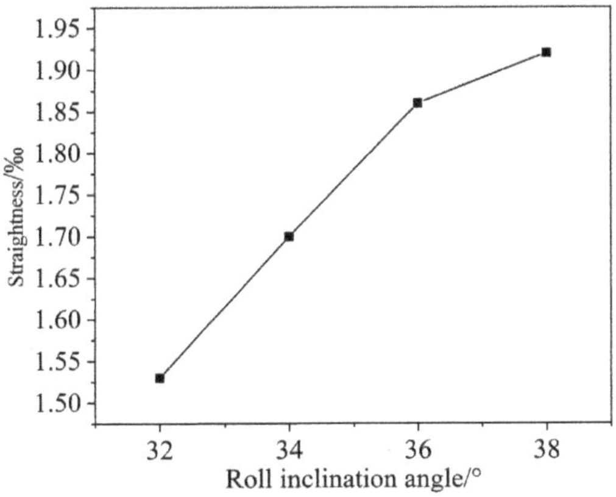

Figure 11. Effect of straightening rollers with different inclination angles on bar straightness.

From Figure 11, it can be observed that when the roll inclination angle is 32°, the post-straightening straightness of the bar is 1.53‰. When the roll inclination angle is increased to 38°, the post-straightening straightness worsens to 1.92‰. As the roll inclination angle increases, the post-straightening straightness decreases. This is because larger angles result in uneven force distribution on the bar during straightening. When the inclination angle is too large, the contact area between the straightening roll and the bar may become concentrated in specific regions, applying higher pressure to those areas while exerting less force on others. As a result, certain areas of the bar experience higher pressures while others receive less, ultimately leading to poorer straightness.

Figure 12 shows the effect of roll reduction on the straightness of the bar. It can be observed that when the roll reduction is 10 mm, the post-straightening straightness is approximately 1.37‰, and when the roll reduction is increased to 12 mm, the straightness is 1.77‰. However, when the roll reduction is 6 mm or 8 mm, the straightness after straightening is worse, indicating that a roll reduction of 10 mm results in the best straightness.

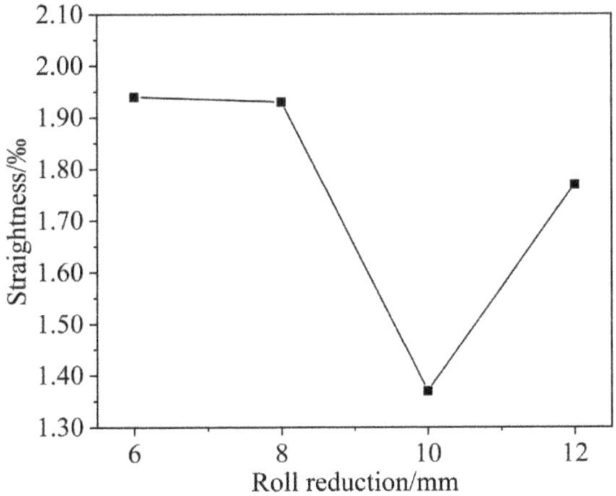

Figure 12. Effect of roll reduction on straightness of bars.

Therefore, in the multi-roll straightening process of the bar, the roll reduction should be controlled within a reasonable range. Excessively large roll reduction can lead to over-bending during straightening, resulting in excessive plastic deformation and potential surface damage, such as scratches or cracks. On the other hand, insufficient roll reduction may fail to adequately remove the original curvature, especially when the material has large internal stresses. In such cases, the straightening process may not fully eliminate the curvature, leading to substandard straightness in the final product.

Figure 13 shows the effect of different roll gap values on the straightness of the bar. From Figure 13, it can be seen that when the roll gap is 70.0 mm, the straightness is 1.39‰. As the roll gap increases, the post-straightening straightness increases. When the roll gap is 71.8 mm, the straightness increases to 2.31‰. When the roll gap is too large, the contact area between the roll and the bar decreases, resulting in uneven pressure distribution. In such cases, certain areas of the bar may not receive enough straightening force, leading to worse straightening results.

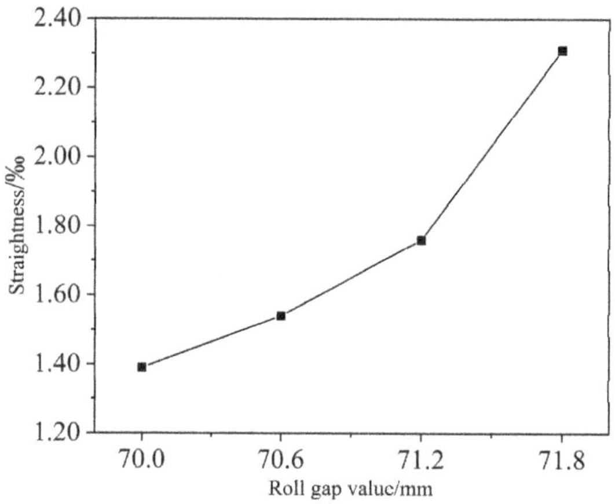

Figure 13. Effect of different roll gap values on bar straightness.

Conversely, an excessively small roll gap can lead to issues such as increased roll wear and higher friction between the roll and the bar, potentially causing surface damage to the bar and affecting its service life. Therefore, to achieve optimal straightness, a reasonable roll gap should be selected in practical production. This range ensures appropriate pressure distribution during the straightening process, preventing both over-straightening and insufficient straightening.

In summary, the optimal process parameters for eleven-roll straightening of bars are A1B3C2D1, where A1 corresponds to a roll inclination angle of 32°, B3 corresponds to a reverse bending displacement of 10 mm, C2 corresponds to a straightening speed of 40 m/min, and D1 corresponds to a roll gap of 70.0 mm. When these optimal parameters were used for straightening, the straightness in numerical simulations was 0.91‰, and the experimental straightness was 0.98‰, with a relative error of 7.6%. This demonstrates the reliability of the numerical simulation results and the optimized process parameters.

5.1.4. Analysis of Variance of Orthogonal Test Results

Range analysis and analysis of variance (ANOVA) can effectively evaluate the influence of various process parameters on the straightening effect, i.e., straightness. Range analysis provides an intuitive demonstration of the influence trends of each factor, but it does not consider the interactions between factors or their statistical significance, thus having certain limitations.

To overcome this issue, ANOVA offers a more precise evaluation method. Table 7 shows the ANOVA table for the orthogonal experiment. ANOVA decomposes the total sum of squares (TSS) into the sum of squares for factors (SS for Factor) and the sum of squares for error (SS for Error). By comparing the mean squares of each part, it can more accurately assess the impact degree of each factor on the straightening effect. A larger mean square for a factor indicates a significant influence of that factor on the straightening effect, while a smaller mean square for error suggests good stability of the experimental data and high reliability of the results.

Table 7. ANOVA of orthogonal test.

Factor	Sum of Squares	Degrees of Freedom	Mean Square	F-Value	*p*-Value
Roll inclination angle	0.334	3	0.111	4.44	0.055
Reverse bending displacement	0.290	3	0.097	3.88	0.052
Straightening speed	0.256	3	0.085	3.40	0.065
Roll gap	0.310	3	0.103	4.12	0.048
Error	0.250	3	0.083		
Total	1.440	15			

As shown in Table 7, the roll gap has a significant effect on the post-straightening straightness of the bars ($p < 0.05$), while the roller inclination angle, roll reduction, and straightening speed have no significant effect ($p > 0.05$). This result is generally consistent with the range analysis of the orthogonal experiment, indicating a high reliability of the conclusions drawn from the orthogonal test.

5.2. Effect of Roll Gap on Straightening Quality

The roll gap refers to the spacing between the upper and lower straightening rolls during the straightening process. It can be adjusted by modifying the position of these rolls. A proper roll gap effectively eliminates deformation and curvature in the material, thereby improving its straightness and dimensional accuracy. An excessively large roll gap may result in insufficient straightening force and incomplete stress release within the material, while an overly small gap could lead to excessive plastic deformation or even material damage. Therefore, the roll gap not only affects the magnitude and distribution of the straightening force but also influences the degree of plastic deformation and the residual stress distribution.

To investigate the influence of roll gap on bar quality, this study selected 20CrMnTi bars with a diameter of 71.8 mm and an initial deflection of 8‰. Four roll gap values (70.0 mm, 70.6 mm, 71.2 mm, and 71.8 mm) were analyzed. All other parameters were set according to the optimal values obtained from orthogonal experiments. Based on the established finite element model, the effects of roll gap on straightening force, residual stress, and final straightness were examined.

5.2.1. Effect of Roll Gap on Straightening Force

Figure 14 illustrates the maximum straightening force under different roll gap values. The results show that as the roll gap increases, the maximum straightening force gradually decreases, indicating a significant effect of roll gap on the straightening force. As the roll gap increases from 70.0 mm to 71.8 mm, the straightening force drops from approximately 8.6×10^5 N to approximately 6.4×10^5 N. Thus, to reduce the straightening force and roller wear while maintaining quality, the roll gap should be set as large as possible within an acceptable range.

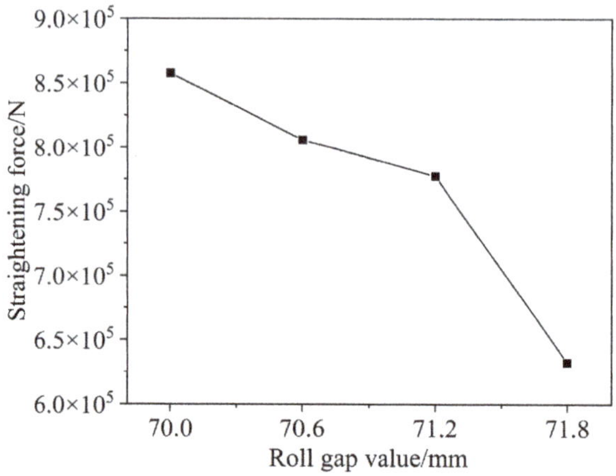

Figure 14. Effect of the size of the roll gap on the straightening force.

5.2.2. Effect of Roll Gap on Residual Stress

Figure 15 displays the residual stress distributions under different roll gaps. The length of the bar in the figure is one span, specifically 1050 mm. It can be observed that increasing the roll gap leads to reduced and more uniformly distributed residual stresses. In practical applications, lower residual stress enhances the stability, deformation resistance, and service life of the bar. Therefore, a reasonably chosen roll gap not only ensures straightening quality but also improves the bar's reliability and performance.

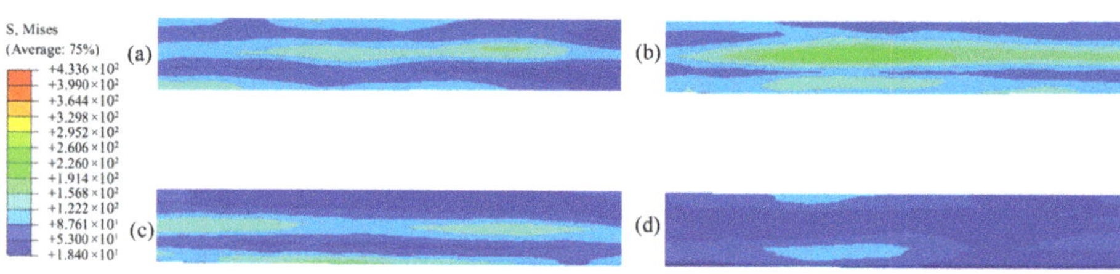

Figure 15. Residual stress distribution at different roll gaps: (**a**) 70.0 mm; (**b**) 70.6 mm; (**c**) 71.2 mm; (**d**) 71.8 mm.

5.2.3. Effect of Roll Gap on Straightness After Straightening

Figure 16 shows the relationship between roll gap and straightness.

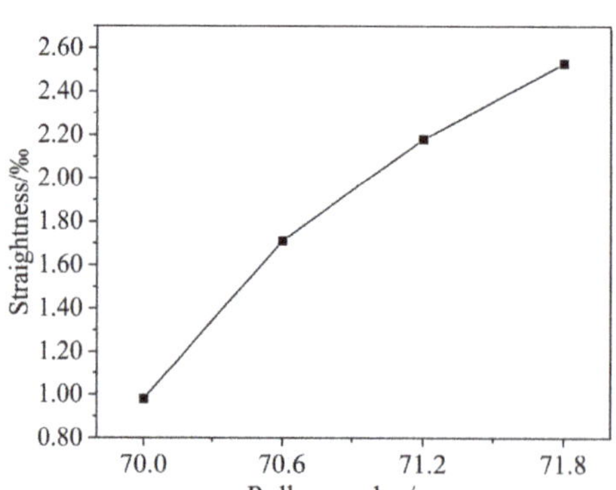

Figure 16. Straightness data of bars after straightening with different roll gap values.

As seen in Figure 16, increasing the roll gap from 70.0 mm to 70.6 mm results in a deterioration of straightness, from 0.98% to 1.72%. Further increases up to 71.8 mm lead to a continued decline in straightness, reaching 2.53%. This trend suggests that excessively large roll gaps reduce the straightening force, making it insufficient to effectively straighten the bar. Thus, a roll gap of 70.0 mm yields the best straightening performance.

5.3. *Effect of Roll Reduction on Straightening Quality*

The roll reduction is a critical process parameter that significantly affects the straightness of the bar. It directly determines the reverse bending curvature within the roller system and thus impacts the final straightness. The roll reduction setting influences not only the straightening outcome but also the distribution of internal stresses within the bar. Therefore, analyzing the influence of roll reduction on straightening quality is essential. The eleven-roll inclined straightener achieves straightening through alternating bending and reverse bending applied by multiple inclined rolls. To investigate the influence of roll reduction on residual stress distribution, four levels of roll reduction (6 mm, 8 mm, 10 mm, and 12 mm) were selected for analysis. All other straightening parameters were set to the optimized values obtained from the orthogonal experiment.

5.3.1. Effect of Roll Reduction on Equivalent Stress After Straightening

During straightening, adjusting the roll reduction can compensate for initial curvature in the bar. However, if not properly controlled, it may lead to over- or under-straightening, generating new residual stresses or failing to fully release existing ones. A small reverse bending amount is generally insufficient to eliminate residual stress caused by the initial curvature, while an excessive reverse bend may induce over-plastic deformation, stress concentration, or even secondary bending, adversely affecting the straightening quality.

Thus, understanding the effect of roll reduction on residual stress is important for process optimization. Roll reduction also influences stress distribution during straightening. To study its effect on peak stress, the stress evolution under different roll reductions was analyzed, as shown in Figure 17.

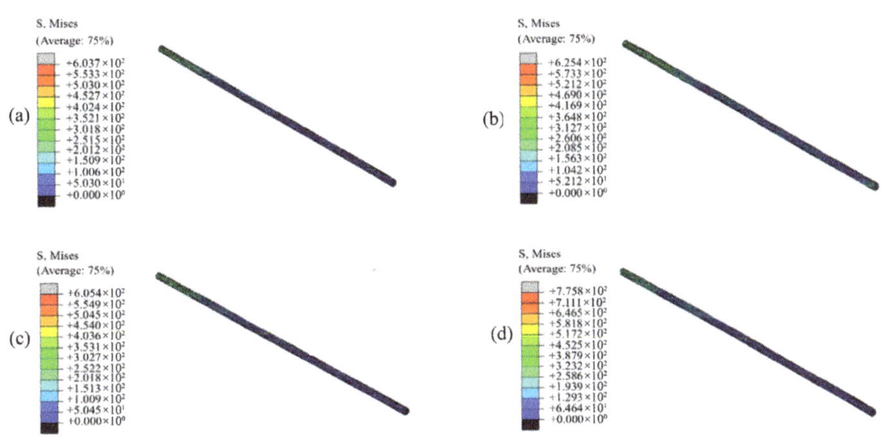

Figure 17. Maximum stresses in bars with different roll reductions: (**a**) roll reduction of 6 mm; (**b**) roll reduction of 8 mm; (**c**) roll reduction of 10 mm; (**d**) roll reduction of 12 mm.

As observed in Figure 17, when the roll reduction is 6 mm, the maximum stress during straightening is approximately 604 MPa. As the roll reduction increases, the maximum stress generally rises. However, at 10 mm, a slight reduction in maximum stress is observed.

This may be due to an optimized distribution of plastic deformation and residual stress, which results in partial stress relief. When the roll reduction increases to 12 mm, the maximum stress reaches approximately 776 MPa, suggesting that while small adjustments can be beneficial, excessive roll reduction degrades the straightening effect.

5.3.2. Effect of Roll Reduction on Straightness After Straightening

Figure 18 shows the effect of different roll reductions on the straightness of the bars after straightening.

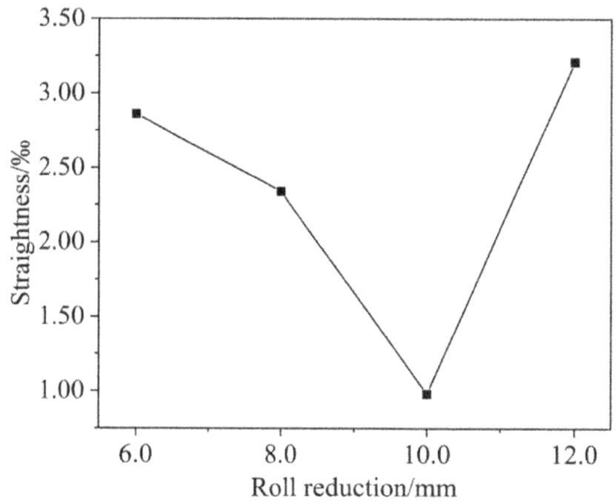

Figure 18. Straightness data of bars after straightening with different roll reductions.

As shown in Figure 18, with other parameters held constant, increasing the roll reduction from 6 mm to 8 mm reduces straightness deviation from 2.86‰ to 2.34‰, indicating a minor improvement in straightening quality. When the roll reduction is further increased to 10 mm, the straightness deviation significantly drops to 0.98‰, demonstrating optimal straightening performance. However, increasing the roll reduction to 12 mm leads to a considerable increase in straightness deviation. Therefore, a reverse bending value of 10 mm enables the bar to undergo the most favorable deformation path, resulting in the best straightening effect.

5.3.3. Effect of Roll Reduction on Equivalent Plastic Strain After Straightening

Figure 19 illustrates the path for section sampling and the effect of roll reduction on the equivalent plastic strain after straightening. As shown in Figure 19a, during the stable straightening process, the strain distribution along any cross-section of the bar can be obtained along the indicated path. The variation in strain from the bar core to its surface is shown in Figure 19b.

According to Figure 19b, a larger roll reduction leads to higher equivalent plastic strains after straightening. When the roll reduction is between 6 mm and 10 mm, the equivalent plastic strain on the surface is about 0.03, while the strain at the core is nearly zero. However, when the reverse bending increases to 12 mm, the surface strain abruptly rises to over 0.06, with the core strain reaching approximately 0.01. This demonstrates that roll reduction significantly influences equivalent plastic strain: the larger the roll reduction, the greater the plastic strain.

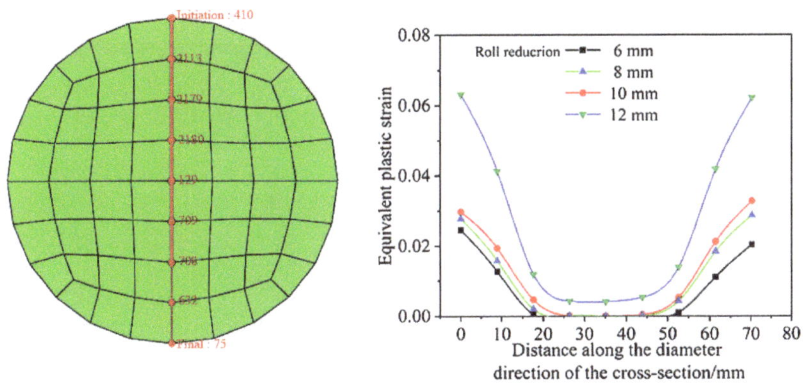

(a) (b)

Figure 19. Selected point paths and equivalent plastic strain evolution in bar section: (**a**) schematic diagram of selected cross-sectional path of the bar; (**b**) effect of roll reduction on post-straightening equivalent plastic strain.

5.4. Effect of Straightening Roll Inclination on Straightening Quality

5.4.1. Effect of Straightening Roll Inclination on Residual Stress After Straightening

Inclination angles of 32°, 34°, 36°, and 38° were selected for the straightening rolls, while other process parameters were maintained at the optimal values obtained from the orthogonal tests. During the straightening process, variations in roll inclination angles change both the contact line length and bending degree between the bar and the rolls, which in turn affects the distribution characteristics of residual stress after straightening. Changes in inclination angle can alter the contact area, loading condition, and deformation pattern, resulting in variations in the magnitude and distribution of residual stresses. The influence of the roll inclination angle on the residual stress of straightened bars is shown in Figure 20. The length of the bar in the figure is one span, specifically 1050 mm.

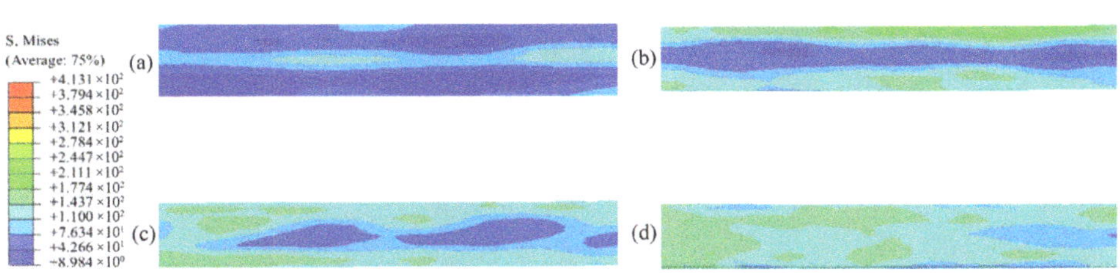

Figure 20. Influence of straightening roll inclination angle on residual stress of bar after straightening: (**a**) 32°; (**b**) 34°; (**c**) 36°; (**d**) 38°.

From Figure 20, it can be observed that when the roll inclination angle is 32°, the residual stress distribution is relatively uniform, and the overall stress level is low. The predominance of blue areas indicates that the residual stress is mainly concentrated in the low-stress range, suggesting good straightening performance. At an inclination angle of 34°, the uniformity of the residual stress distribution decreases slightly, with an increase in green areas, indicating a moderate rise in stress levels. When the inclination angle increases to 36°, the blue areas significantly reduce, and the presence of green and yellow areas becomes more pronounced, suggesting an expansion of high-stress regions. At 38°, a substantial increase in green areas within the bar indicates higher residual stress levels and a corresponding decline in straightening quality.

5.4.2. Influence of Straightening Roll Inclination on Straightness After Straightening

The influence of roll inclination angle on bar straightness is illustrated in Figure 21. As shown, the best straightness is achieved when the roll inclination angle is 32°, which aligns with the conclusions drawn from the orthogonal experiment results. Larger inclination angles result in poorer straightness, likely because greater angles reduce the quality of contact between the straightening rolls and the bar. This suboptimal contact leads to uneven residual stress distribution within the bar after straightening, which negatively impacts straightness and the overall service life of the product.

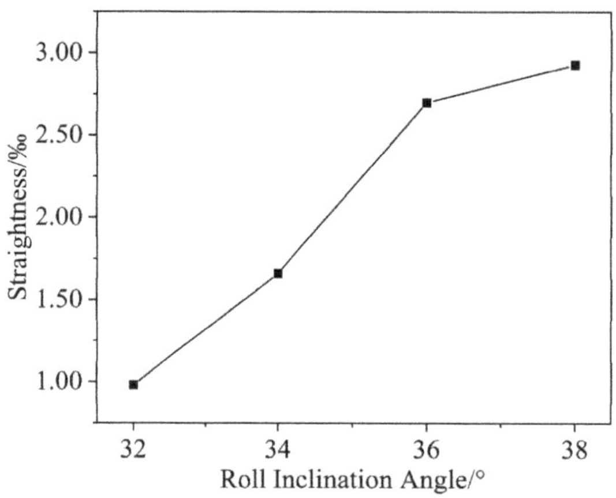

Figure 21. Effect of roll inclination on straightness.

5.5. Effect of Straightening Speed on Straightening Quality

Straightening speed is one of the key process parameters influencing the quality of bar straightening. At lower straightening speeds, plastic deformation and the release of residual stress in the bar are more complete, which is conducive to improved straightening quality. However, excessively low speeds may reduce production efficiency. Conversely, excessively high straightening speeds may lead to insufficient plastic deformation and incomplete stress relief and may even induce vibration or slippage issues. Therefore, investigating the influence of straightening speed on straightening quality is of practical significance.

In this study, to investigate the influence of straightening speed on post-straightening straightness, four straightening speed settings were selected: 20 m/min, 40 m/min, 60 m/min, and 80 m/min. All other process parameters were kept at the optimal values determined from the orthogonal experiment. The influence of straightening speed on post-straightening straightness is illustrated in Figure 22.

As shown in Figure 22, when the straightening speed is 20 m/min, the post-straightening straightness of the bar is 0.33‰. At 40 m/min, the straightness increases slightly to 0.46‰. When the speed reaches 60 m/min, the straightness deteriorates to 1.32‰, and at 80 m/min, it further worsens to 1.89‰. This trend clearly indicates that straightening quality declines as straightening speed increases. The underlying reason may be that, at higher speeds, the contact time between the bar and the rolls is reduced, resulting in insufficient release of internal stresses. These residual stresses negatively impact the straightening effect, thereby reducing the final straightness of the product. Therefore, to balance production efficiency and straightening quality, a medium-speed straightening setting of 40 m/min is recommended.

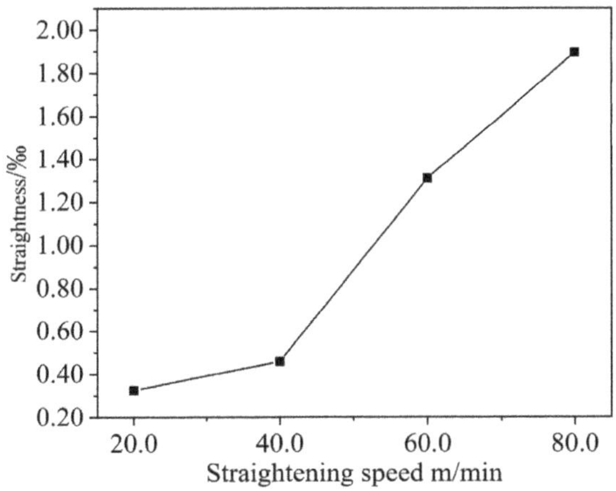

Figure 22. Effect of straightening speed on straightness after straightening.

6. Conclusions

Based on the nonlinear combined hardening model, a finite element model for eleven-roll straightening of 20CrMnTi bars was established. The orthogonal experimental design method was employed to optimize the key process parameters, and the effects of roll gap, roll reduction, straightening speed, and roll inclination angle on straightening quality were investigated. The accuracy of the finite element simulation and the reliability of the optimized process parameters were subsequently verified through a straightening experiment. The main conclusions drawn from this study are as follows:

(1) The finite element simulation results of eleven-roll straightening based on the combined hardening model exhibit good agreement with experimental data. Both the simulated and experimental straightness values were within 1‰ using the optimized process parameters, with a relative error of less than 8%.

(2) Among the four process parameters, their influence on bar straightness, in descending order of significance, is as follows: roll gap > roll reduction > straightening speed > roll inclination angle. Notably, the roll gap exhibits a significantly greater impact than the other factors.

(3) A properly selected roll gap enhances the constraint on the bar during straightening, improving post-straightening straightness. However, an excessively small roll gap can lead to a substantial increase in straightening force. Appropriately adjusting the roll reduction helps release residual stress and improves overall straightening quality.

(4) The roll inclination angle has a considerable influence on both residual stress and straightness. This influence is nonlinear and must be optimized based on actual working conditions. Additionally, a moderate straightening speed of 40 m/min achieves a desirable balance between production efficiency and straightening precision, resulting in the best overall straightening outcome.

Author Contributions: Conceptualization, S.J., S.W. and R.Z.; data curation, S.J., L.B. and Q.M.; formal analysis, L.B., S.W. and R.Z.; funding acquisition, R.Z. and Q.M.; methodology, S.J. and J.Z.; software, L.B. and S.W.; writing—original draft, S.J. and L.B. All authors have read and agreed to the published version of the manuscript.

Funding: This study was funded by the State Key Laboratory of Metal Forming Technology and Heavy Equipment (S2308100.W14), the S&T Program of Hebei (235A4502D, E2025203089), and the S&T Program of Qinhuangdao (202401A013).

Data Availability Statement: The original contributions presented in this study are included in the article. Further inquiries can be directed to the corresponding author.

Conflicts of Interest: Authors Shangwu Jia and Shijie Wang were employed by China National Heavy Machinery Research Institute Co., Ltd. The remaining authors declare that the research was conducted in the absence of any commercial or financial relationships that could be construed as a potential conflict of interest.

References

1. Prager, W. A New Method of Analysing Stresses and Strains in Work Hardening Plastic Solids. *J. Appl. Mech.* **1956**, *23*, 493–496. [CrossRef]
2. Ziegler, H. A Modification of Prager's Hardening Rule. *Q. Appl. Mech.* **1959**, *17*, 55–65. [CrossRef]
3. Armstrong, P.J.; Frederick, C.O. *A Mathematical Representation of the Multiaxial Bauschinger Effect*; GEGB Report; RD/B/N 731; Berkeley Nuclear Laboratories: Berkeley, CA, USA, 1966.
4. Chaboche, J.-L. Constitutive Equations for Cyclic Plasticity and Cyclic Viscoplasticity. *Int. J. Plast.* **1989**, *5*, 247–302. [CrossRef]
5. Chaboche, J.-L. On Some Modifications of Kinematic Hardening to Improve the Description of Ratchetting Effects. *Int. J. Plast.* **1991**, *7*, 661–678. [CrossRef]
6. Han, S.W.; Cho, E.S. Simulation of Cyclic Behavior of Mild Steel with Empirical Model Parameter Equations. *J. Constr. Steel Res.* **2025**, *227*, 109351. [CrossRef]
7. Shi, F.; Wang, D.S.; Chen, L. Cyclic Elastoplastic Constitutive Model for Stainless Steels Compatible with Multiple Strengths. *J. Constr. Steel Res.* **2023**, *205*, 107889. [CrossRef]
8. Yang, M.; Bo, R.Y.; Gou, J.J.; Zhang, Y.; Fan, L.F. A Strain-Space Nonlinear Elasto-Plastic Model Improving Springback Prediction Accuracy and Efficiency. *J. Constr. Steel Res.* **2025**, *226*, 109210. [CrossRef]
9. Okorokov, V.; Gorash, Y.; Mackenzie, D.; van Rijswick, R. New Formulation of Nonlinear Kinematic Hardening Model, Part I: A Dirac Delta Function Approach. *Int. J. Plast.* **2019**, *122*, 89–114. [CrossRef]
10. Okorokov, V.; Gorash, Y.; Mackenzie, D.; van Rijswick, R. New Formulation of Nonlinear Kinematic Hardening Model, Part II: Cyclic Hardening/Softening and Ratcheting. *Int. J. Plast.* **2019**, *122*, 244–267. [CrossRef]
11. Cui, F. *Principles of Straightening and Straightening Machinery*, 2nd ed.; Metallurgical Industry Press: Beijing, China, 2005.
12. Liu, H.; Li, Q. Analysis of Straightening Roll Profiles and Their Close Relationship with Pipe and Bar Straightening. *Steel Pipe* **1995**, *24*, 27–29.
13. Song, H. Study on the Adjustment Angle of Correction Rolls for Pipe Bending Roll Profiles. *Heavy Mach.* **1999**, *299*, 25–28.
14. Zhu, M.; Huang, Y.; Wang, C. Study on Flattening Reduction of Opposed Six-Oblique-Roll Pipe Straightening Machine. *J. Baotou Steel Inst.* **1998**, *19*, 36–38.
15. Zhao, B.; Zhao, H.; Liu, Z.; Li, S. Influence of Roll Profiles of Inclined Roll Straightening Machine on Installation Angle and Contact Line Length. *J. Yanshan Univ.* **1998**, *22*, 74–76.
16. Zheng, G. Study on the Variation Law of Roundness of Steel Pipes Corrected by Inclined Rolls. *Min. Metall. Eng.* **2003**, *23*, 89–92.
17. Zhang, Z.Q. Finite element simulation study on residual cross-sectional Ovalization of thin-walled circular steel tubes in continuous rotary straightening process. *Int. J. Adv. Manuf. Technol.* **2019**, *102*, 2633–2647. [CrossRef]
18. Zhang, Z.Q.; Yan, Y.H.; Yang, H.L. A simplified model of maximum cross-section flattening in continuous rotary straightening process of thin-walled circular steel tubes. *J. Mater. Process. Technol.* **2016**, *238*, 305–314. [CrossRef]
19. Ma, L.-D.; Du, Y.-K.; Meng, Z.-J.; Ma, L.-F.; Liu, Z.-J.; Liu, P.-Y. Effect of process parameters on steel tube roundness in straightening process. *J. Iron Steel Res. Int.* **2020**, *27*, 1270–1283. [CrossRef]
20. Ma, L.; Liu, Z.; Ma, L.; Du, Y. Analysis of eleven cross-roll straightening process of steel tube based on cubic spline function and continuous bending elastic-plastic theory. *Int. J. Adv. Manuf. Technol.* **2021**, *112*, 3235–3245. [CrossRef]
21. Li, Z. Study on the Wear Mechanism of Straightening Rolls in Roll-Type Straightening Machines. Master's Thesis, Taiyuan University of Science and Technology, Taiyuan, China, 2024; pp. 2–39.
22. Yao, Y.; Wu, W.; Liu, R.; Deng, L. Analysis of Factors Affecting Roll Diameter and Roll Distance in Roll-Type Straightening Machines. *Metall. Equip.* **2023**, *45*, 53–55.
23. Hu, Y.; Yuan, J.; Lv, C. Research and Application of an Intelligent Optimization Process Prediction Model for Roll-Type Straightening. *Mod. Manuf. Eng.* **2024**, *46*, 109–117.
24. Gu, C.; Ye, Y.; Fu, T.; Ma, M. Overview of Roll-Type Straightening Technology and Equipment Development. *Heavy Mach.* **2023**, *315*, 12–17.
25. Mwita, W.M.; Akinlabi, E.T. Numerical prediction of tensile yield strengthand micro hardness of Ti6Al4V alloy processed by constrained bending and straightening severe plastic deformation. *Mater. Res. Express* **2019**, *6*, 106560. [CrossRef]

26. Gruber, M.; Kummel, L.; Hirt, G. Control of residual stresses by roller leveling with regard to process stability and one-sided surface removal. *J. Mater. Process. Technol.* **2020**, *280*, 116600. [CrossRef]
27. Petruska, J.; Navrat, T.; Sebek, F. Novel approach to computational simulation of cross roll straightening of bars. *J. Mater. Process. Technol.* **2016**, *233*, 53–67. [CrossRef]
28. Kuboki, T. FEM analysis of tube straightener adopting implicit scheme. In Proceedings of the Metal Forming 2010: Proceedings of the 13th International Conference on Metal Forming, Toyohashi, Japan, 19–22 September 2010; pp. 584–587.
29. Meng, Q.; Zhai, R.; Fu, P.; Zhang, Y.; Zhao, J. Springback Analysis of Rotary Bending Considering Strain Paths. *J. Mater. Process. Technol.* **2023**, *315*, 117930. [CrossRef]
30. Domitner, J.; Schneeberger, P.; Silvayeh, Z.; Schnideritsch, H.; Engel, J.K.; Schider, S.; Klarner, J. Experimental Quantification of the Wear Performance of Rolls Used in Industrial Rotary Straightening of Seamless Steel Tubes. *Wear* **2025**, *578*, 206148. [CrossRef]
31. Niu, T.; Luo, Y.; Chen, F.; Baddour, N.; Li, C.; Peng, B. Investigation of Rotary Straightening Process for the Rollers of Planetary Roller Screw. *J. Braz. Soc. Mech. Sci. Eng.* **2025**, *47*, 116. [CrossRef]

metals

MDPI

Article

Constructal Design and Numerical Simulation Applied to Geometric Evaluation of Stiffened Steel Plates Subjected to Elasto-Plastic Buckling Under Biaxial Compressive Loading

Andrei Ferreira Lançanova [1], Raí Lima Vieira [2], Elizaldo Domingues dos Santos [1,2], Luiz Alberto Oliveira Rocha [1,2], Thiago da Silveira [2], João Paulo Silva Lima [3], Emanuel da Silva Diaz Estrada [1] and Liércio André Isoldi [1,2,*]

1 Graduate Program in Computational Modeling, Federal University of Rio Grande, Rio Grande 96201-900, RS, Brazil; andreiflancanova@furg.br (A.F.L.); elizaldosantos@furg.br (E.D.d.S.); luizrocha@furg.br (L.A.O.R.); emanuelestrada@furg.br (E.d.S.D.E.)

2 Graduate Program in Ocean Engineering, Federal University of Rio Grande, Rio Grande 96201-900, RS, Brazil; rai@furg.br (R.L.V.); thiagods@furg.br (T.d.S.)

3 Faculty of Science and Technology, Federal University of Goiás (UFG), Aparecida de Goiânia 74968-755, GO, Brazil; joaoplima@ufg.br

* Correspondence: liercioisoldi@furg.br

Abstract: Widely employed in diverse engineering applications, stiffened steel plates are often subjected to biaxial compressive loads. Under these conditions, buckling may occur, initially within the elastic range but potentially progressing into the elasto-plastic domain, which can lead to permanent deformations or structural collapse. To increase the ultimate buckling stress of plates, the implementation of longitudinal and transverse stiffeners is effective; however, this complexity makes analytical stress calculations challenging. As a result, numerical methods like the Finite Element Method (FEM) are attractive alternatives. In this study, the Constructal Design method and the Exhaustive Search technique were employed and associated with the FEM to optimize the geometric configuration of stiffened plates. A steel plate without stiffeners was considered, and 30% of its volume was redistributed into stiffeners, creating multiple configuration scenarios. The objective was to investigate how different arrangements and geometries of stiffeners affect the ultimate buckling stress under biaxial compressive loading. Among the configurations evaluated, the optimal design featured four longitudinal and two transverse stiffeners, with a height-to-thickness ratio of 4.80. This configuration significantly improved the performance, achieving an ultimate buckling stress 472% higher than the unstiffened reference plate. In contrast, the worst stiffened configuration led to a 57% reduction in performance, showing that not all stiffening strategies are beneficial. These results demonstrate that geometric optimization of stiffeners can significantly enhance the structural performance of steel plates under biaxial compression, even without increasing material usage. The approach also revealed that intermediate slenderness values lead to better stress distribution and delayed local buckling. Therefore, the methodology adopted in this work provides a practical and effective tool for the design of more efficient stiffened plates.

Keywords: computational modeling; finite element; ultimate buckling stress; stiffened plates

1. Introduction

Plates are two-dimensional structural components whose thickness is significantly smaller than their in-plane length and width dimensions [1,2]. They are commonly used in

https://doi.org/10.3390/met15080879

scenarios subjected to uniaxial, biaxial, and combined loadings [3]. When subjected to compressive loadings, they can suffer an undesirable instability phenomenon called buckling. Buckling phenomena can initially manifest as elastic buckling, where instability occurs in plates while the material remains within its elastic constitutive regime [4]. However, unlike slender columns, plates can resist loads even after elastic buckling has occurred [5]. This behavior can then evolve into elasto-plastic buckling, in which the applied load causes the material to exceed its elastic limit and enter the plastic deformation regime [4].

The buckling resistance of plates is directly proportional to their bending stiffness [6]. Therefore, implementing stiffeners is a common practice, as they increase the plate's stiffness against buckling caused by in-plane compressive and shear loadings [7]. Under uniaxial longitudinal loading, longitudinal stiffeners support part of the applied load, while transverse stiffeners subdivide the plate into smaller sections. Under biaxial loading conditions, longitudinal and transverse stiffeners support the respective loading directions and further divide the plate into smaller panel areas. However, randomly adding stiffeners does not guarantee improved buckling resistance. Therefore, it is necessary to study and identify the optimal number, geometry, and arrangement of longitudinal and transverse stiffeners based on the boundary conditions and loading scenarios [8].

The Constructal Design method, combined with the Exhaustive Search technique, has been used to investigate the influence of the number and geometric configuration of longitudinal and/or transverse stiffeners on the mechanical behavior of stiffened plates. One can highlight studies regarding these structural components subjected to bending due to distributed lateral pressure [9–11], elasto-plastic buckling due to uniaxial compressive load [12,13], or elasto-plastic buckling due to distributed lateral pressure combined with biaxial compressive load [8]. In these analyses, the total steel volume of an unstiffened plate is kept constant, with a portion of this material being transformed into stiffeners. The mechanical behavior of various proposed stiffened plates is then evaluated [8,12,13].

Despite the many plate configurations required to determine the optimized geometry, numerical analysis has proven to be a helpful tool, especially for assessing ultimate buckling resistance compared to analytical methods [12], showing good accuracy and agreement with experimental results [14]. The Finite Element Method (FEM) is commonly used to investigate the buckling of stiffened plates due to its ability to capture buckling modes, as well as its efficiency and simplicity in analyzing and optimizing complex structures [15]. This method is particularly suitable for analyzing plates with stiffeners subjected to compressive loads and operating within the elasto-plastic buckling regime [16]. Ansys Mechanical APDL (MAPDL) software, based on the FEM, has been employed in studies to conduct buckling analysis of plates [8,12,17], using versions 2024R2, 12.1, and 17.1, respectively.

Numerous studies have investigated the buckling behavior of unstiffened plates [18–20] and stiffened plates [21–40] to better understand this instability behavior and identify ways to assess or improve the resistance of these structural components.

Piscopo [19] studied the buckling behavior of unstiffened rectangular plates under uniaxial and biaxial compression using analytical and numerical approaches with simply supported boundary conditions. The author adopted a two-variable refined plate theory from classical thin plate theory to account for bending and shear effects, proposing a new expression for the Euler buckling load and presenting buckling coefficient curves. The analytical results were verified through numerical simulations in ANSYS (version 12.1).

Hanif et al. [41] investigated the ultimate strength of steel stiffened plates under uniaxial compressive loading using nonlinear finite element analysis in ANSYS MAPDL. The authors evaluated the influence of several geometric parameters, including different maximum values of amplitudes and modes of initial imperfections (column-type, local, torsional, and combined), as well as plate and web slenderness. As a result, a simplified formula was proposed to predict the ultimate stress with reasonable accuracy, showing a maximum difference of 2.08% compared to the computational model.

Saad-Eldeen et al. [35] conducted experimental and numerical analyses using ANSYS to evaluate the structural capacity of corroded stiffened steel plates with multiple circular openings under uniaxial compression. The study investigated the effects of opening degree, number, and distribution of openings, initial imperfections, and material corrosion. Results showed that larger imperfection amplitudes and greater opening degrees significantly reduced load capacity, while material properties became less influential as the number of openings increased. Plates with more small openings performed better than those with fewer large ones, especially when openings were placed away from the central region.

Zhang et al. [42] synthesized a decade of experimental, analytical, and numerical research (from 2014 to 2023) in a comprehensive systematic review of stiffened composite plates' elastic and elasto-plastic buckling behavior. The review encompassed over 200 studies, identifying limitations and opportunities for future research. The authors concluded that there is a need to develop more cost-effective experimental methods that better replicate real-world environmental and loading conditions to refine analytical methods to accurately predict the elastic and elasto-plastic behavior of more complex geometries, including three-dimensional effects and to integrate machine learning and artificial intelligence to enhance data interpretation, model validation, and the optimization of stiffened composite plate structures.

Wang et al. [43] presented a new method based on numerical buckling analysis to develop empirical formulas and design charts. This method estimates the maximum lateral pressure that stiffened panels can endure under combined loading, considering various loading conditions, stiffener configurations, and initial imperfections. The authors observed that stiffener location strongly influences ultimate strength and that including local buckling as an initial imperfection improves strength predictions.

Lima et al. [12] developed a computational model to assess the ultimate buckling stress and a Constructal Design model to evaluate the influence of stiffeners and their geometric characteristics on the performance of plates under uniaxial compression. Converting part of the plate volume into stiffeners led to increases in buckling stress of 7.38% and 88.50%, depending on the initial volume considered. Additionally, a variation of 481.24% was observed between the best and worst configurations in terms of ultimate buckling stress, emphasizing the importance of optimizing stiffener geometry. The optimal plate configuration for the second volume scenario featured two longitudinal and two transverse stiffeners.

Baumgardt et al. [44] verified and validated a model in ANSYS Mechanical APDL (2023R1) for predicting critical and ultimate buckling stresses in plates with and without stiffeners, including perforated cases and loading conditions. Maximum deviations were 4.83% and 5.40%, confirming model reliability.

Vieira et al. [8] combined the models by Lima et al. [12] and Baumgardt et al. [45] to analyze stiffened plates with flat stiffeners under elasto-plastic buckling, subjected to biaxial compression and constant lateral pressure P_Z = 0.016 MPa. With 30% of the plate's volume converted into stiffeners, the optimal configuration (five longitudinal and four transverse stiffeners) showed a 284% improvement in ultimate buckling stress. Increasing the height-to-thickness ratio favors local failure, while reducing it synchronizes displacement, decreasing stress concentration. Very low ratios caused premature stiffener buckling and global modes with lower strength.

Although substantial research has been conducted on elasto-plastic buckling and the role of stiffeners in determining the ultimate buckling strength of plates, the effects of plate configuration in relation to stiffeners and the optimization of stiffener geometry under biaxial loading still require further investigation. A more comprehensive understanding of these interactions is crucial for reevaluating the design of structural components subjected to this complex condition, aiming for enhanced structural performance and improved safety. Therefore, guided by the work of Lima et al. [12], the present study aims to apply the Constructal Design method and the exhaustive search technique in numerical analysis, using ANSYS MAPDL (version 2025R2) software, to investigate the phenomenon of elasto-plastic buckling in plates subjected to biaxial compressive loading. The objective is to understand how the plate configuration, the number of stiffeners, and their respective geometries influence ultimate buckling resistance performance indicators. The goal is to identify the optimized configuration of stiffened plates, demonstrating the best performance regarding ultimate buckling resistance under biaxial loading. To achieve this, 30% of the steel volume of an unstiffened plate is converted into flat longitudinal and transverse stiffeners. The number of longitudinal and transverse stiffeners and the ratio between their heights and thicknesses are defined as degrees of freedom. This approach enabled the generation to have various geometric configurations, maintaining the same total volume as the unstiffened reference plate. The ultimate buckling resistances of these configurations are evaluated, allowing for the identification of the highest-performing design for the investigated loading scenario.

Therefore, while most previous studies have addressed uniaxial loading conditions or considered limited stiffener configurations, this work advances the current state of the art by exploring a broader design space defined by variations in stiffener number, geometry, and distribution, while maintaining constant material volume. This study presents a detailed numerical investigation focused on optimizing the geometric configuration of stiffened plates under biaxial compression, aiming to improve buckling performance without increasing material usage. The findings provide new insights into the relationship between stiffener slenderness and structural behavior, leading to the identification of an optimal configuration that enhances the ultimate buckling stress by 472% compared to the unstiffened reference plate.

2. Materials and Methods

2.1. Computational Modeling of Unstiffened and Stiffened Plates

The thin steel unstiffened and stiffened plates are modeled considering the same parameters as Lima et al. [12].

The unstiffened plate has thickness t and total volume V_p illustrated in Figure 1a. The stiffened plates have thickness t_p, stiffeners thickness t_s, stiffeners height h_s, heigh-to-thickness ratio h_s/t_s, number of longitudinal stiffeners N_{ls}, longitudinal stiffeners spacing S_{ls}, number of transverse stiffeners N_{ts}, transverse stiffeners spacing S_{ts}, and total volume of stiffeners V_s depicted in Figure 1b. In this work, the plate and stiffeners present same length a, width b, module of elasticity E, Poisson's ratio ν, and the yield stress σ_y.

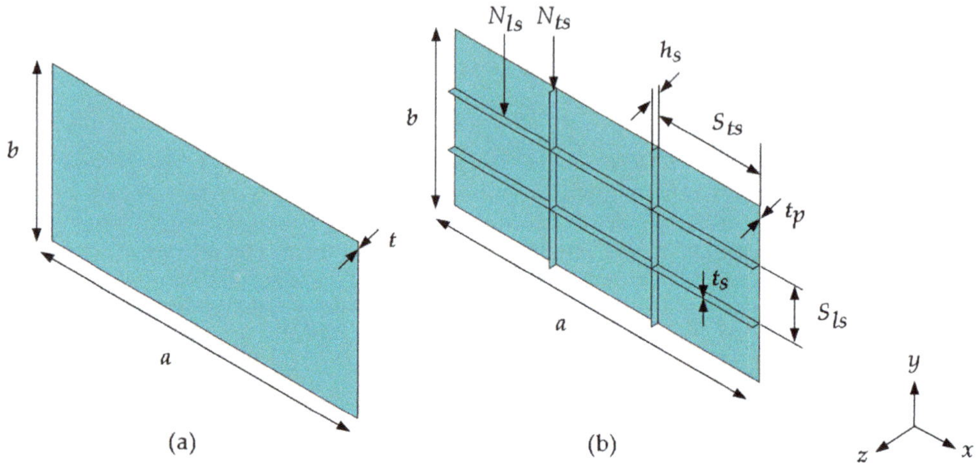

Figure 1. Modeling of: (**a**) unstiffened reference plate and (**b**) stiffened plate.

These plates are numerically simulated using a computational model that initially considers their elastic buckling behavior. Based on the first critical buckling mode, the initial imperfect configuration of each plate is then defined for the subsequent elasto-plastic computational modeling.

2.2. Boundary and Loading Conditions

All simulations' boundary conditions are considered simply supported, restricting the out-of-plane displacement U_z across the four edges of the plate and stiffener boards. Additionally, the horizontal displacement U_x is constrained at the lower-left corner of the plate, while the vertical displacement U_y is constrained at the lower-right corner. The symbols of constraints are illustrated in Figure 2, with the cyan symbols representing the displacement constraints according to the axis directions and the red symbols indicating the applied compressive loading.

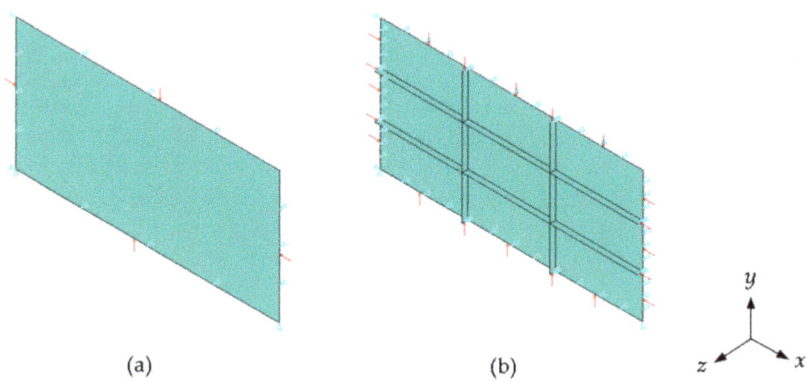

Figure 2. Boundary and loading conditions of: (**a**) unstiffened plate and (**b**) stiffened plates.

The loading condition considered in this study is compressive biaxial loading applied to the borders of the plate and stiffeners, represented by the red arrow in Figure 2. The respective values used in the elastic and elasto-plastic buckling analyses are presented in the following subsections.

2.3. Computational Modeling of Elastic Buckling

The elasto-plastic buckling analysis is based on the eigenvalue problem derived from the total stiffness matrix, combining elastic and geometric stiffness components. Although the fundamental formulations of elastic buckling analysis via FEM are well established, they are presented here to clarify the specific numerical procedures adopted for accurately modeling the elasto-plastic buckling of stiffened plates under biaxial compression, particularly as implemented in ANSYS MAPDL. According to Przemieniecki [45], the displacement equations contain nonlinear terms that must be considered in the calculation of the stiffness matrices for each element $[k]$, represented in the equation:

$$[k] = [k_E] + [k_G], \tag{1}$$

where $[k_E]$ represents the standard elastic stiffness matrix for each element, determined based on the element's initial geometry at the beginning of the load step, and $[k_G]$ represents the geometric stiffness matrix for each element, whose determination depends not only on the geometry but also on the internal forces acting on the element at the start of the loading step. These matrices, $[k_E]$ and $[k_G]$, are computed for each element in the structure:

$$[K_E] = \sum [k_E], \tag{2}$$

$$[K_G] = \sum [k_G], \tag{3}$$

where $[K_E]$ represents the total elastic stiffness matrix and $[K_G]$ represents the total geometric stiffness matrix. The total stiffness matrix $[K]$ is then assembled from them, expressed by:

$$[K] = [K_E] + [K_G], \tag{4}$$

Thus, the global matrix of equations governing the solution of the elastic buckling problem, based on eigenvectors and eigenvalues, is described as:

$$[K] \times \{U\} = \{P\}, \tag{5}$$

where $\{U\}$ is the unknown displacement vector, $[K]$ is the total stiffness, and $\{P\}$ is an external loading vector. The incremental and iterative nature of the analysis necessitates expressing both the total stiffness matrix $[K]$ and the external load vector $\{P\}$ as functions of the load factor λ. To facilitate this, a unit geometric stiffness matrix, denoted by $[K_G^*]$ and a unit external load vector $\{P^*\}$ are defined by setting $\lambda = 1$ on equations:

$$[K_G] = \lambda \times [K_G^*], \tag{6}$$

$$\{F\} = \lambda \times \{P^*\}. \tag{7}$$

Substituting Equation (6) on Equation (4), and considering that the elastic stiffness matrix $[K_E]$ can be regarded as constant for a significant range of displacements, the following expression can be written as:

$$[K] = [K_E] + \lambda \times [K_G^*]. \tag{8}$$

The global matrix equation, Equation (5), can be rewritten as:

$$([K_E] + \lambda \times [K_G^*]) \times \{U\} = \lambda \times \{P\}, \tag{9}$$

Being possible to isolate $\{U\}$ to obtain the displacements:

$$\{U\} = \lambda \times \{P^*\} \times \left([K_E] + \lambda \times [K_G^*]\right)^{-1}. \tag{10}$$

It is noted that as $\left([K_E] + \lambda \times [K_G^*]\right)^{-1}$ is solved, the displacement values tend to infinite under the condition:

$$\det[[K_E] + \lambda \times [K_G]] = 0 \tag{11}$$

Using the Lanczos method, the smallest value of λ, and consequently the respective critical buckling load, is determined by:

$$P_{crit} = \lambda_{crit} \times \{P^*\}, \tag{12}$$

where P_{crit} represents the critical buckling load, the λ_{crit} represents the associated buckling mode, $\{P^*\}$ represents the external load applied. In the elastic buckling analysis of this work, only the first buckling mode is considered. A comprehensive explanation of the Block Lanczos method's operation and implementation can be found in the work of Grimes et al. [46], which serves as the theoretical basis for the eigen solver implemented in MAPDL.

2.4. Computational Modeling of Elasto-Plastic Buckling

In elasto-plastic buckling analyses, both geometric and material nonlinearities are considered. This consideration implies that the total stiffness matrix $[K_G]$ and the global displacements $\{U\}$ no longer exhibit a direct proportional relationship with the load application and resulting stresses, thus characterizing a nonlinear analysis. In the analyses conducted in this work, the selected material is defined with bilinear isotropic hardening; however, for simplification and to obtain more conservative results, a linear elastic-perfectly plastic model is adopted, disregarding the phenomenon of strain hardening. This simplification results in the prediction of lower ultimate buckling resistances, making the analysis more conservative [8].

For elasto-plastic buckling analyses, considering initial imperfections is essential to obtain realistic results regarding its mechanical behavior. The initial imperfections in this study are based on the first elastic buckling mode [4], representing the deformed configuration resulting from the application of the critical buckling load.

The first buckling mode represents the dominant deformation pattern leading to instability in nonlinear buckling studies and exhibits the lowest critical load in an eigenvalue buckling analysis. Although real plate imperfections (originating from manufacturing, transportation, and handling) are often irregular and localized, these deviations can be represented using buckling mode shapes, with the first mode contributing most significantly to the imperfection geometry. Therefore, employing a suitably scaled first buckling mode as the initial imperfection is a practical, conservative approximation widely accepted in buckling analyses [47].

The maximum amplitude of these imperfections is defined according to the recommendations of El-Sawy et al. [4]:

$$w_b = \frac{b}{2000}. \tag{13}$$

The multiplication of this maximum amplitude by the deformed configuration of the first buckling mode defines the imperfect initial geometric configuration for the beginning of the elasto-plastic buckling analysis, as adopted by Fonseca [48].

Once the geometry is updated, as explained by Helbig et al. [49] and Baumgardt et al. [44], a reference load is considered based on the yield stress of the material and applied in small increments, called load sub-steps, to the edges in both directions of the plate, where the reference load is given by:

$$P_y = \sigma_y \times t, \quad (14)$$

where P_y represents the reference load based on the material's yield stress, σ_y represents the yield stress of material and t (or t_p—see Figure 1) the thickness of plate. The application of these sub-steps is governed by the Newton–Raphson iterative method, in which the values of the tangent stiffness matrix $\left[K_{n,i}^T\right]$ and the restoring force vector $\left\{P_{n,i}^{nr}\right\}$ are recalculated for each load sub-step n and iteration i, referring to the configuration of each sub-step of the applied external loading $\{P_n^a\}$:

$$\left[K_{n,i}^T\right]\{\Delta U_i\} = \{P_n^a\} - \left\{P_{n,i}^{nr}\right\}. \quad (15)$$

Also, for each load sub-step n and iteration i, a new value of the displacement vector resulting from each iteration $\{U_{i+1}\}$ is obtained by:

$$\{U_{i+1}\} = \{U_i\} + \{\Delta U_i\}. \quad (16)$$

Repeating the iterative process of updating and obtaining Equations (15) and (16) for each iteration until non-convergence is reached, also called out-of-balance convergence criteria, occurring when:

$$||\{R\}|| < \varepsilon_R R_{ref}, \quad (17)$$

where ε_R represents the convergence tolerance for the criterion, R_{ref} is the reference value of the criterion, and $||\{R\}||$ represents the residual vector as:

$$\{R\} = \{P_n^a\} - \left\{P_{n,i}^{nr}\right\}. \quad (18)$$

Non-convergence indicates that the displacements are so large due to the external loading $\{P_n^a\}$ that the restoring forces $\left\{P_{n,i}^{nr}\right\}$ cannot reach values that respect the criterion of Equation (16), representing that the structure has collapsed. The convergence criteria adopted in this computational model are set to 5% for displacements and 0.5% for both forces and moments values.

2.5. Finite Element

In this study, the finite element SHELL281 is employed to model both the plate and the stiffeners numerically. SHELL281 is an eight-node shell element, with each node featuring six degrees of freedom: three translational (U_x, U_y, U_z) and three rotational (θ_x, θ_y, θ_z). The element is based on the First-Order Shear Deformation Theory (FSDT), also known as the Reissner–Mindlin theory, which accurately represents shear effects in thin to moderately thick structures. SHELL281 is particularly suited for plate and shell applications involving complex geometries, as it accommodates linear and nonlinear analyses. It can model large rotations and large deformations, including changes in thickness. Its advanced features include defining various integration points and support for thickness offsets, drill still factors, and curved shell formulations. These features make it especially effective in capturing geometric nonlinearities and providing reliable results for various structural behaviors [50]. For this computational model, except for the integration points, set as five as recommended by ANSYS, all features of the SHELL281 element are used with the default.

In addition, this finite element supports both quadrilateral and triangular shapes. In general, quadrilateral elements are preferred for simple geometries due to their lower element count and faster convergence. Moreover, triangular elements for SHELL281 are recommended only as fillers in the mesh [50]. For this reason, the quadrilateral shape of the SHELL281 element is adopted in this computational model.

2.6. Constructal Design and Exhaustive Search

The Constructal Design and Exhaustive Search techniques applied to evaluate stiffened plates under biaxial elasto-plastic buckling follow the approach introduced by Lima et al. [12], illustrated in Figure 3.

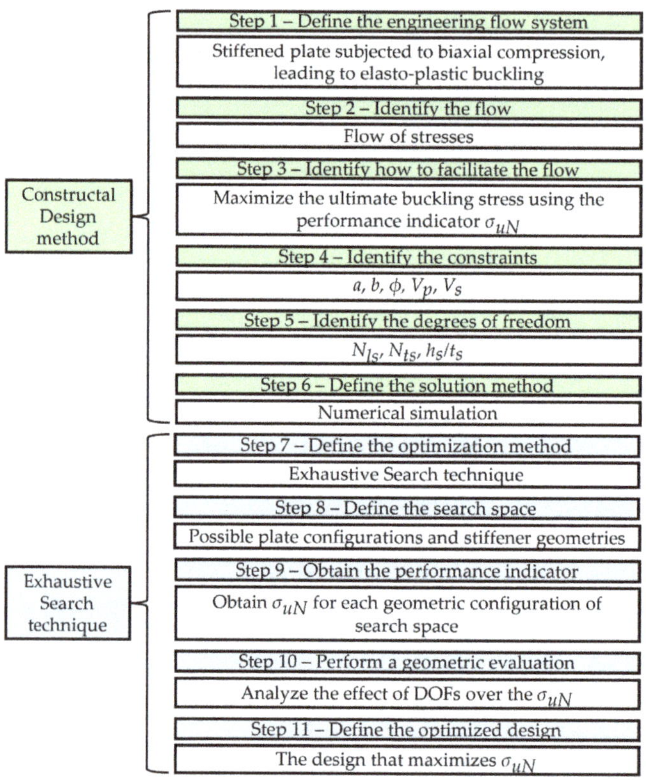

Figure 3. Steps of Constructal Design method and Exhaustive Search technique.

An unstiffened plate is taken as a reference, and a fraction of the volume is redistributed (by reducing its original thickness) to form the stiffeners. This transformation is quantified by the volume fraction ϕ, while the total volume of the plate remains constant:

$$\phi = \frac{V_s}{V_p} = \frac{N_{ls}(ah_st_s) + N_{ts}(b - N_{ls}t_s)h_st_s}{abt}. \tag{19}$$

In this work, an unstiffened plate with defined dimensions (as shown in Figure 1) is taken as the reference configuration. A volume fraction $\phi = 0.3$ was adopted based on findings from previous studies. Lima et al. [12] demonstrated that, for plates with identical in-plane dimensions and varying thickness, redistributing 30% of the original plate volume into stiffeners provided the highest ultimate buckling stress under uniaxial compression, when compared to 10%, 20%, and 40%. Similarly, Vieira et al. [8] employed the same fraction in a study involving combined lateral pressure and biaxial loading. To ensure methodological consistency and enable direct comparison with these previous works, the same redistribution fraction was maintained in the present study. This formulation enables the systematic investigation of multiple geometric configurations by evaluating how variations in the degrees of freedom (DOFs) (N_{ls}, N_{ts}, and ratio h_s/t_s) influence the σ_u.

In this work, an unstiffened plate with dimensions is taken as a reference plate depicted in Figure 1. A volume fraction ϕ = 0.3 was adopted based on findings from previous works. Lima et al. [12] showed that, for plates with identical in-plane dimensions and varying thickness, a 30% redistribution into stiffeners provided the highest ultimate buckling stress when compared to 10%, 20%, and 40% under uniaxial compression. Vieira et al. [8] also used this value in a study involving combined lateral pressure and biaxial loading. To ensure methodological consistency and enable direct comparison with these benchmark studies, the same redistribution fraction was maintained in the present work. This formulation enables the investigation of multiple geometric configurations by analyzing how variations in the degrees of freedom (DOF) (N_{ls}, N_{ts}, and ratio h_s/t_s) influence the σ_u.

The N_{ls} and N_{ts} is varied from 2 to 5, also following the approach adopted by Lima et al. [12], who investigated plates with identical dimensions under uniaxial loading. This range was chosen because it enables, under the volume conservation constraint, the generation of configurations with sufficiently high h_s to trigger local buckling modes, as well as sufficiently low h_s values to allow the development of global buckling behavior. These values yield sixteen plate configurations denoted as P(N_{ls};N_{ts}): P(2;2), P(2;3), P(2;4), P(2;5), P(3;2), P(3;3), P(3;4), P(3;5), P(4;2), P(4;3), P(4;4), P(4;5), P(5;2), P(5;3), P(5;4), and P(5;5). To ensure a symmetric distribution of stiffeners across the plate, the spacing between both longitudinal and transverse stiffeners is defined accordingly based on the selected values of N_{ls} and N_{ts}:

$$S_{ls} = \frac{b}{N_{ls}+1}, \tag{20}$$

$$S_{ts} = \frac{a}{N_{ts}+1}, \tag{21}$$

with S_{ls} as the spacing between longitudinal stiffeners and S_{ts} as the spacing between transverse stiffeners.

The value of t_s is defined as a minimum of 5 mm, incrementally up to a maximum of 40 mm, which, combined with the sixteen different plate configurations, resulted in 128 different stiffened plate designs to have σ_u investigated.

To evaluate and compare the performance of the various stiffened plate configurations and stiffener geometries, σ_u values obtained are non-dimensionalized by normalizing the ultimate buckling stress of the reference plate σ_{uR}, resulting in the normalized ultimate buckling stress σ_{uN}. This normalized parameter serves as a performance indicator and is calculated as:

$$\sigma_{uN} = \frac{\sigma_u}{\sigma_{uR}}. \tag{22}$$

Additionally, the normalized out-of-plane displacements U_{zN} are also calculated, by equation:

$$U_{zN} = \frac{U_z}{U_{zR}}, \tag{23}$$

where U_z represents the maximum value of out-of-plane displacements calculated, and U_{zR} is the maximum value of out-of-plane displacements from the reference plate. In this study, only the σ_{uN} is taken as performance indicator, being U_{zN} calculated only to investigate the relation between stress and displacement.

By varying the DOFs N_{ls}, N_{ts}, and the ratio h_s/t_s, and subsequently calculating the σ_{uN}, the h_s/t_s ratios that maximized σ_{uN} are determined for each plate configuration. These are the once-optimized height-to-thickness ratios $(h_s/t_s)_o$ and the corresponding once-maximized normalized buckling stress $(\sigma_{uN})_m$. From this first optimization step, the highest $(\sigma_{uN})_m$ values and their associated $(h_s/t_s)_o$ and N_{ts} values are identified and redefined, respectively, as the twice-maximized stress $(\sigma_{uN})_{mm}$, the twice-optimized height-to-thickness ratio $(h_s/t_s)_{oo}$, and the once-optimized number of transverse stiffeners $(N_{ts})_o$. Finally, based on these refined values, the plate configuration with the overall highest ultimate buckling stress is established, referred to as the three-times maximized strength $(\sigma_{uN})_{mmm}$, the three-times optimized ratio $(h_s/t_s)_{ooo}$, the twice-optimized number of transverse stiffeners $(N_{ts})_{oo}$, and the once-optimized number of longitudinal stiffeners $(N_{ls})_o$.

The combination of Constructal Design, Exhaustive Search, and Finite Element Method (FEM) is particularly effective for studying plate buckling due to its ability to optimize geometrical configurations and analyze complex mechanical behaviors, as demonstrated in Lima et al. [12] and Vieira et al. [8]. This occurs because it is possible to understand how the variation in degrees of freedom influences the performance indicator.

2.7. Mesh Convergence Test

Mesh convergence tests are a fundamental step in ensuring the reliability of finite element analysis. These tests identify whether the results are independent of mesh size, confirming that the chosen discretization does not compromise solution accuracy. Additionally, they assess whether the achieved level of accuracy is sufficient, ensuring that further mesh refinement would not yield significant improvements relative to the increased computational cost [51].

In verifying the computational model used in this study, the size of the finite elements is determined through mesh convergence tests conducted for each case. However, due to the large number of simulations required by the Constructal Design methodology and the Exhaustive Search technique, a representative mesh convergence test is performed. This test is conducted for both an unstiffened plate and a stiffened plate after calculating all possible values of h_s for each combination of N_{ls}, N_{ts}, and t_s, to identify a representative and more complex plate configuration. The results of this test are then used to standardize the mesh element size across all subsequent simulations.

2.8. Sub-Steps Load Convergence Test

As the computational model is initially applied to only a few simulations for the computational model verification, a high number of 200 sub-steps is considered, with a maximum of 400 and a minimum of 50, depending on the convergence of analysis.

For the case study, once all possible geometries are defined and the finite element mesh shape and size are established, a sub-step load convergence test is also performed to standardize the number of incremental subdivisions used for applying the reference loads. This test is essential due to the many simulations required for the various stiffened plate geometric configurations generated through the Constructal Design method.

2.9. Verification of Computational Model

According to Oñate [52], in the context of structural finite element analysis, building confidence in the numerical results is essential for ensuring that the computational model reliably represents the physical problem under study. This confidence is primarily established through two complementary processes: verification and validation. Verification is concerned with assessing whether the computational model accurately represents the underlying mathematical and structural formulation. It focuses on identifying and minimizing numerical errors by comparing the results of the computational model with established reference solutions. In this work, verification was conducted through comparison with published numerical results from the literature, which, although not analytical, are widely recognized as benchmarks in similar studies. This approach is especially relevant when analytical solutions are not available for complex problems such as biaxial elasto-plastic buckling of stiffened plates. On the other hand, validation involves evaluating how accurately the computational results reflect real-world behavior, typically by comparing numerical predictions with experimental data. In the present study, validation was incorporated through comparisons with selected experimental results available in the literature, thereby reinforcing the reliability of the computational model. Together, verification and validation are fundamental to demonstrating both the correctness of the numerical implementation and the physical representativeness of the model, ensuring that the conclusions drawn from the simulations are robust and trustworthy. Additionally, Morris [53] recommends a one-factor-at-a-time approach to isolate the effect of each parameter. The proposed computational model is therefore verified using reference numerical results and validated through comparison with experimental ultimate loads results for both unstiffened and stiffened plates.

3. Results and Discussion

3.1. Computational Model Verification and Validation

3.1.1. Verification for Elasto-Plastic Buckling and Unstiffened Plates

The first verification for elasto-plastic buckling and unstiffened simply-supported steel plate considered the Lima et al. [12] study, which investigated the uniaxial compressive loading in an unstiffened plate with dimensions a = 2000 mm, b = 1000 mm, and t = 14 mm, with material properties E = 210 GPa, σ_y =355 MPa, and $\nu =$ 0.3, represented in Figure 4.

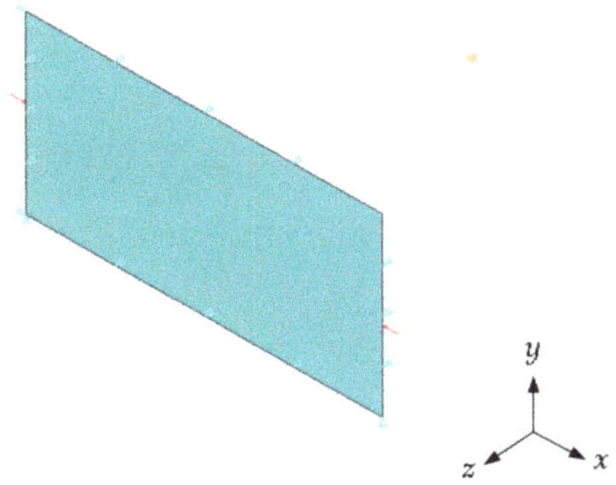

Figure 4. Loading and boundary conditions, represented by red and cyan symbols, respectively, of unstiffened plate considered for the first verification of the elasto-plastic computational model.

The σ_u resultant from this computational model is obtained through the mesh convergence test, as presented in Table 1.

Table 1. Mesh convergence test for the first verification of the elasto-plastic buckling computational model with an unstiffened plate.

Element Length (mm)	Number of Elements	σ_u (MPa)
100	200	186.45
75	378	184.13
50	800	184.13
25	3200	186.45

The mesh convergence test achieved an σ_u = 186.45 MPa, which is 0.62% lower than compared with the σ_u = 187.61 MPa obtained by Lima et al. [12]. This slight difference may be related to the type of finite element used, as the SHELL281 element is adopted in the present study, whereas Lima et al. [12] employed the SHELL93 element.

The second verification of this computational model for elasto-plastic buckling and unstiffened simply-supported steel plate is carried out by the Shanmugam and Narayanan [18] study. This study applied a biaxial compressive loading to an unstiffened plate with dimensions a = 720 mm, b = 240 mm, and t = 4 mm, with material properties E = 205 GPa, σ_y = 245 MPa, and ν = 0.3, represented in Figure 5.

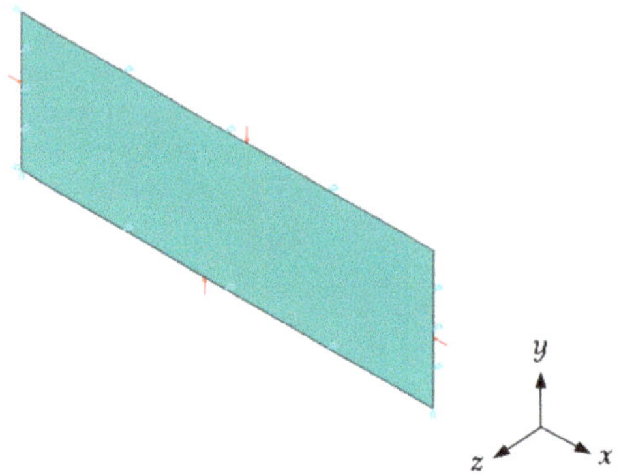

Figure 5. Loading and boundary conditions, represented by red and cyan symbols, respectively, of unstiffened plate considered for the second verification of the elasto-plastic computational model.

The value of σ_u achieved for this verification is obtained through the mesh convergence test, shown in Table 2.

Table 2. Mesh convergence test for the second verification of the elasto-plastic buckling computational model with an unstiffened plate.

Element Length (mm)	Number of Elements	σ_u (MPa)
100	24	55.28
75	40	55.28
50	75	55.28
25	290	55.28
10	1728	55.28

The mesh convergence test achieved an σ_u = 55.28 MPa, which represents a difference of 1.90% lower than compared with the σ_u = 56.35 MPa obtained by Shanmugam and Narayanan [18].

3.1.2. Validation for Elasto-Plastic Buckling and Unstiffened Plates

The validation of this computational model for elasto-plastic buckling and unstiffened plate is realized considering a case from Shanmugam and Narayanan [18], which tested experimentally a simply-supported plate with dimensions $a = b$ = 86 mm, t = 2.032 mm, and material properties E = 205 GPa, σ_y =334.7 MPa, and ν = 0.3, illustrated in Figure 6.

The value of P_u result of this validation is obtained through the mesh convergence test, shown in Table 3.

The mesh convergence test resulted in P_u = 33.05 kN, which represents an error of −7.03% compared with the P_u = 35.55 kN obtained by Shanmugam and Narayanan [18].

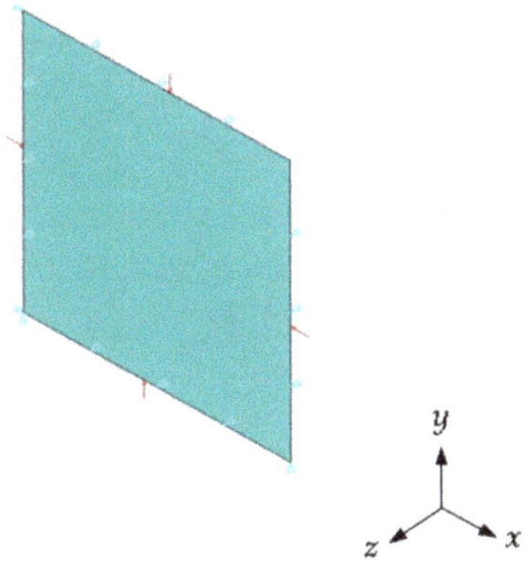

Figure 6. Loading and boundary conditions, represented by red and cyan symbols, respectively, of unstiffened plate considered for the validation of the elasto-plastic computational model.

Table 3. Mesh convergence test for the first verification of the elasto-plastic buckling computational model with an unstiffened plate.

Element Length (mm)	Number of Elements	P_u (kN)
10	81	33.05
7.5	144	33.05
5	324	33.05
2.5	1225	33.05

3.1.3. Verification for Elasto-Plastic Buckling and Stiffened Plates

The first verification of this computational model for elasto-plastic buckling and stiffened plate is also based on Lima et al. [12] study, which applied a uniaxial compressive loading in a simply-supported steel stiffened plate, with the plate presenting a = 2000 mm, b = 1000 mm, t = 18 mm, and $N_{ls} = N_{ts} = 2$. The stiffeners present the same a and b values of plate, h_s = 14 mm, and t_s = 45 mm. The material properties of plate and stiffeners are the same, with E = 210 GPa, σ_y =355 MPa, and $\nu =$ 0.3, represented in Figure 7.

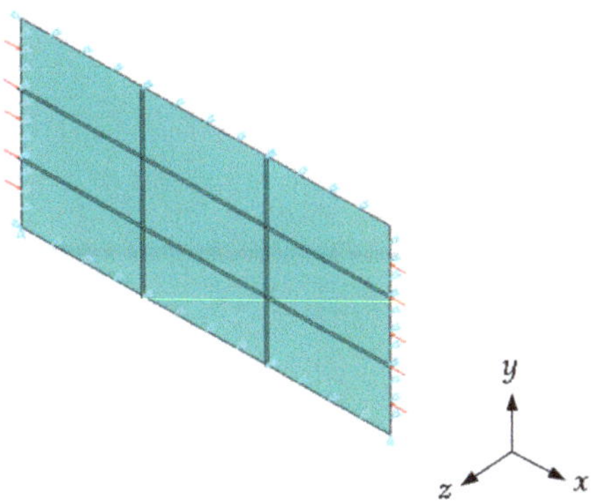

Figure 7. Loading and boundary conditions, represented by red and cyan symbols, respectively, of stiffened plate considered for the first verification of the elasto-plastic computational model.

The value of σ_u resultant is determined based on the mesh convergence results presented in Table 4.

Table 4. Mesh convergence test for the first verification of the elasto-plastic buckling computational model with a stiffened plate.

Element Length (mm)	Number of Elements	σ_u (MPa)
100	318	284.42
75	489	284.10
50	1008	281.77
25	3648	281.22

The mesh convergence test resulted in a σ_u = 281.22 MPa, which is 4.28% lower than the σ_u = 293.78 MPa reported by Lima et al. [12]. As mentioned earlier, this difference may be attributed to the different types of finite elements used.

The second verification of the computational model for elasto-plastic buckling of stiffened plates is based on the study by Paik and Seo [21], which applied biaxial compressive loading to a simply supported steel stiffened plate with dimensions a = 16,300 mm, b = 4300 mm, and thickness t_p = 18 mm. The plate contained N_{ts} = 19 T-shaped stiffeners, extending across the full plate length and width, with h_s = 463 mm, t_s = 8 mm, and flange thickness t_f = 172 mm. The plate and stiffeners present the same material properties, with Young's modulus E = 205.8 GPa, yield strength σ_y = 315 MPa, and Poisson's ratio ν = 0.3. The longitudinal stiffeners are represented indirectly by imposing U_z = 0 boundary conditions along their intersection lines with the plate without explicitly modeling their geometry. The stiffened plate and loading and boundary conditions are illustrated in Figure 8, in which the blue arrows represent the applied compressive loading in x direction, red arrows represent the applied compressive loading in y direction, and cyan symbols indicate the support conditions.

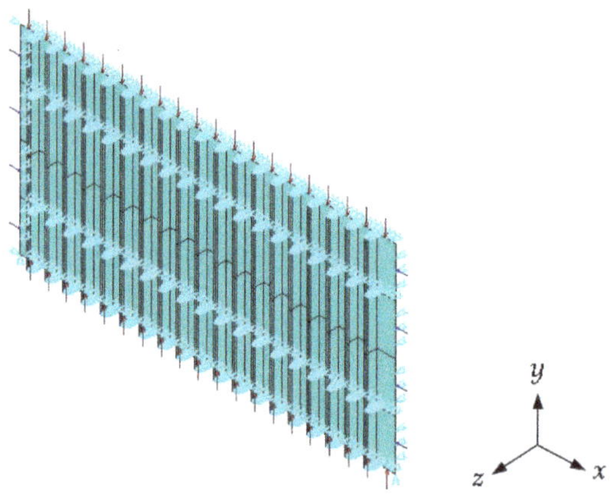

Figure 8. Loading and boundary conditions of stiffened plate considered for the second verification of the elasto-plastic computational model.

The σ_u value is obtained from the mesh convergence analysis, with results summarized in Table 5.

The computational model resulted in a longitudinal ultimate buckling σ_{ux} = 69.30 MPa and transverse ultimate buckling σ_{uy} = 103.95 MPa, which is respectively 0.87% and 0.88% lower than the σ_{ux} = 69.91 MPa and σ_{uy} = 104.87 MPa presented by Paik and Seo [21].

Table 5. Mesh convergence test for the second verification of the elasto-plastic buckling computational model with a stiffened plate.

Element Length (mm)	Number of Elements	σ_{ux} (MPa)	σ_{uy} (MPa)
1000	924	99.54	149.31
750	1164	71.19	106.79
500	1940	69.93	104.90
250	5616	69.30	103.95
100	27,544	69.30	103.95

3.1.4. Validation for Elasto-Plastic Buckling and Stiffened Plates

The validation for elasto-plastic buckling and stiffened plates was carried out by comparing the P_u obtained in the present study with experimental results reported by Kumar et al. [24]. In their investigation, a stiffened steel panel was subjected to uniaxial compressive loading. The geometry of the panel, illustrated in Figure 9, consisted of a plate with dimensions a = 1160 mm, b = 960 mm, and thickness t_p = 5 mm. The material properties of the plate were E = 180 GPa, σ_{yp} = 218 MPa, and Poisson's ratio ν = 0.3. The panel was reinforced with four longitudinal stiffeners, each located 100 mm from the plate edges and spaced 320 mm apart, and four transverse stiffeners placed 60 mm from the panel ends, with a spacing of 280 mm. The stiffeners had thickness t_s = 5 mm and height h_s = 50 mm and were made of material with E = 180 GPa, σ_{ys} = 300 MPa, and ν = 0.3.

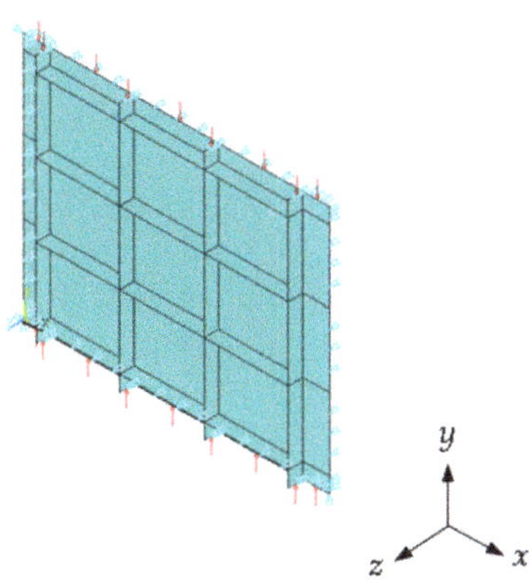

Figure 9. Loading and boundary conditions, represented by red and cyan symbols, respectively, of stiffened plate considered for the validation of the elasto-plastic computational model.

The P_u value is achieved from the mesh convergence test, with results shown in Table 6.

Table 6. Mesh convergence test for the validation of the elasto-plastic buckling computational model with a stiffened plate.

Element Length (mm)	Number of Elements	P_u (kN)
100	246	1169.57
75	382	1131.64
50	894	1118.99
25	2946	1118.99

The present study achieved P_u = 1118.99 kPa, which represents an error of −8.28% relative to the experimental value of P_u = 1220 kN reported by Kumar et al. [21].

3.2. Mesh Convergence Test—Case Study

After calculating all possible values of h_s for each combination of N_{ls}, N_{ts}, and t_s, the mesh convergence test to standardize the finite element size is performed for both the unstiffened reference plate and stiffened plate with configuration P(5;5), with intermediate values of h_s and t_s. This plate configuration represents the case with the highest interaction between the plate and stiffeners due to the most significant number of stiffeners, which is considered the most complex case.

For the simply supported unstiffened reference steel plate with a = 2000 mm, b = 1000 mm, t = 14 mm, E = 210 GPa, ν = 0.3, and σ_y = 355 MPa, the mesh convergence test is shown in Table 7.

Table 7. Mesh convergence test to standardize the finite element size of unstiffened plates of case study.

Element Length (mm)	Number of Elements	σ_u (MPa)
100	200	60.57
75	378	59.68
50	800	59.68
25	3200	59.68

From Table 7, one can observe a value of σ_u= 59.68 MPa, with no variation when comparing element sizes of 75 mm, 50 mm, and 25 mm. As previously demonstrated by Vieira et al. [8], while the element size does not significantly affect the predicted value of σ_u, it can influence the local stress distribution patterns. Therefore, a finite element size of 25 mm was adopted, as it provided both a converged value of σ_u and consistent stress field representation. Given that convergence was already achieved and that further mesh refinement would only escalate computational cost without improving the accuracy of σ_u, no additional refinements were performed. The computational cost remains scalable, and the numerical prediction of σ_u stable, even for highly refined meshes (though at the expense of increased simulation time.)

For the simply-supported stiffened steel plates with a = 2000 mm, b = 1000 mm, t_p = 9.8 mm, N_{ls} = N_{ts} = 5, h_s = 29 mm, t_s = 20 mm, E = 210 GPa, ν = 0.3, and σ_y = 355 MPa, the mesh convergence is shown in Table 8.

Table 8. Mesh convergence test to standardize the finite element size of stiffened plates of case study.

Element Length (mm)	Number of Elements	σ_u (MPa)
100	468	122.70
75	780	122.70
50	1338	122.70
25	4788	122.70

The mesh convergence test presented in Table 8 resulted in a σ_u = 122.70 MPa, without difference due to the element size adopted. Considering the same approach considered for the unstiffened reference plate (see Table 7), all simulations of stiffened plates are performed with an element size of 25 mm.

3.3. *Load-Steps Convergence Test—Case Study*

With all possible geometries defined and the finite element shape and size established, a sub-step convergence test is carried out to standardize the number of incremental subdivisions used for applying the reference loads (see Equation (14)). This load-step convergence test is performed using the same stiffened plate configuration previously adopted in the mesh convergence analysis, as shown in Table 9.

Table 9. Sub-steps convergence test.

Number of Sub-Steps	Maximum Number of Sub-Steps	Minimum Number of Sub-Steps	Processing Time (s)	σ_u (MPa)
50	100	10	91	116.26
100	200	25	94	117.59
200	400	50	153	122.70
300	600	100	195	120.64

From Table 9, it is concluded that dividing the reference load into 200 and 300 sub-steps led to higher values of σ_u. Although the number of sub-steps resulted in differences in the stress distributions [8], this study adopted 200 sub-steps to reduce computational effort. This decision is supported by the convergence test for the plate model considered, which showed a computational cost reduction of approximately 21.54% when using 200 sub-steps instead of 300.

3.4. *Reference Plate*

An unstiffened plate with a = 2000 mm, b = 1000 mm, t = 18 mm, E = 210 GPa, ν = 0.3, and σ_y = 355 MPa is selected as a reference plate and presented σ_{uR} = 59.68 MPa and U_{zR} = 38.05 mm calculated with this computational model. The out-of-plane displacements and von Mises stress distributions are shown in Figure 10.

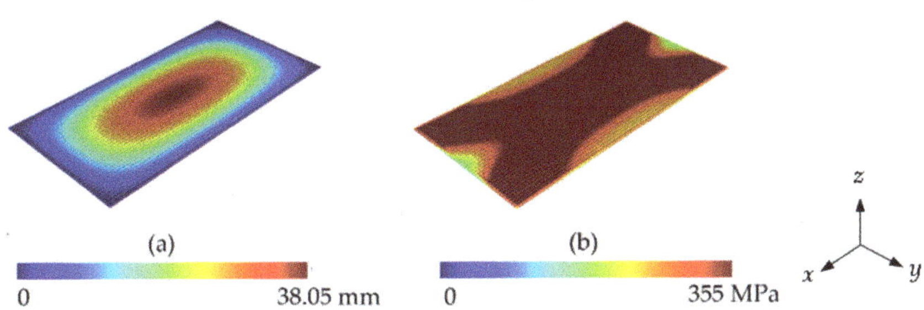

Figure 10. Unstiffened reference plate under biaxial compression: (**a**) out-of-plane displacements distribution and (**b**) von Mises stress distribution.

In Figure 10a, the maximum displacement values are located at the center of the plate, forming a semi-wave pattern indicative of a global buckling failure mode. In Figure 10b, the stress distribution reveals that the material reaches its yield stress across nearly the entire plate. Similar behaviors are reported in unstiffened plates with comparable a and b dimensions, boundary conditions, and biaxial compressive loading, as discussed by Baumgardt et al. [44] and Vieira et al. [8].

3.5. *Influence of* N_{ls}, N_{ts} , *and* t_s *over* h_s

To investigate the influence of N_{ls}, N_{ts}, and t_s over h_s, the plate configurations with less (2) and higher (5) values of N_{ls} are plotted in Figure 11, varying the N_{ts} and t_s.

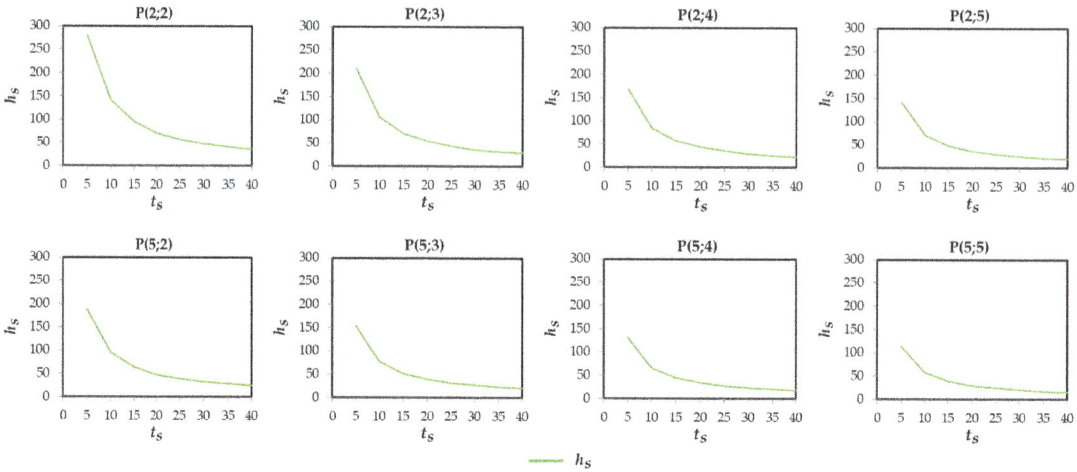

Figure 11. Influence of N_{ls}, N_{ts}, and t_s over h_s on stiffened plates with N_{ls} = 2 and N_{ls} = 5.

In Figure 11, the same behavior can be observed across all graphs: to satisfy the premise of conserving the original material volume of the reference plate (while converting 30% of this volume into stiffeners), together with the N_{ls} and N_{ts} ranging from 2 to 5, and the t_s varying from 5 mm to 40 mm, the resulting h_s becomes a function of these parameters. As N_{ls}, N_{ts} and t_s increase, both the maximum and minimum possible values of h_s decrease, leading to a corresponding reduction in the h_s/t_s ratio. This behavior is consistent across all plate configurations analyzed in this study. Figure 12 further illustrates this trend by visually comparing the geometrical configurations with the lowest (P(2;2)) and highest (P(5;5)) number of stiffeners, as t_s varies.

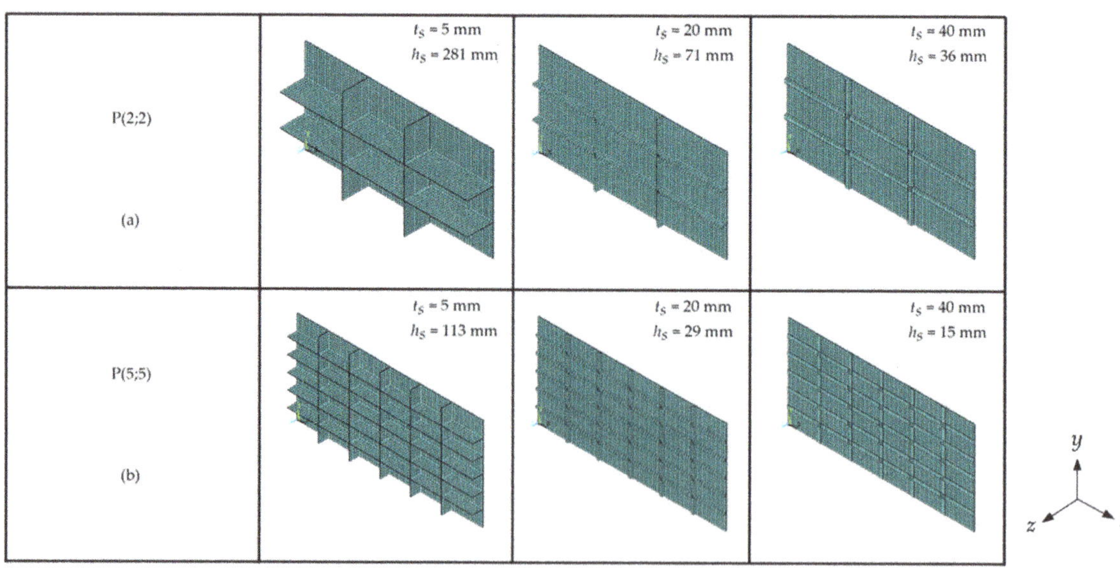

Figure 12. Visual demonstration of the influence of N_{ls}, N_{ts} and t_s over h_s on stiffened plates with N_{ls} = 2 and N_{ls} = 5. (**a**) P(2;2) and (**b**) P(5;5).

Figure 12a shows that the plate configuration P(2;2), which has the lowest number of stiffeners, allows the stiffeners to reach a height of h_s = 281 mm when using the minimum thickness t_s = 5 mm. As t_s increases to its maximum value of 40 mm, the stiffener height decreases to h_s = 36 mm, representing a reduction of approximately 87.2%. In contrast, the configuration with the highest number of stiffeners, P(5;5), reaches a maximum stiffener height of h_s = 113 mm at t_s = 5 mm, which decreases to h_s = 15 mm at t_s= 40 mm, a reduction of about 86.7% (see Figure 12b). These differences in values and the corresponding illustrations in Figure 12 (resulting solely from the transformation of part of the plate volume into stiffener) demonstrate how the application of the Constructal Design can lead to numerous and significantly different geometric configurations, which can be explored to identify the most resistant component without requiring additional material. The complete information on all values of N_{ls}, N_{ts}, h_s, and t_s are available in Supplementary Materials of this article.

3.6. *Influence of h_s/t_s, N_{ls}, and N_{ts} over σ_{uN} and U_{zN}*

For the 128 different stiffened plates defined by the Constructal Design method, the influence of the ratio h_s/t_s, N_{ls}, and N_{ts} is evaluated concerning the σ_{uN} and the U_{zN}; i.e., the effect of the variation in the DOFs on the performance indicators is evaluated. Figure 13 illustrates this influence for plates with N_{ls} = 2 and N_{ls} = 3, while Figure 14 presents the corresponding influence for plates with N_{ls} = 4 and N_{ls} = 5. A large number of curves were plotted to enable the identification of a consistent typical behavior regarding the relationship between the parameters investigated in this subsection.

Regarding the σ_{uN}, in several graphics in Figures 13 and 14, it is observed that, for all stiffened plate geometries analyzed, very low values of the ratio h_s/t_s resulted in low values of σ_{uN}. The same behavior is observed for very high values of this ratio. In all geometric configurations, the best performance in terms of stress occurred at intermediate values of h_s/t_s, with the best results occurring for values of t_s between 15 and 20 mm. As h_s/t_s increased progressively from this optimal value, a decreasing trend in σ_{uN} values are identified. To understand this behavior, plate P(3;2) is selected arbitrarily, and the minimum, optimal, moderate, and maximum values of h_s/t_s are selected to investigate the stress distributions and out-of-plane displacements. Figure 15 presents the behavior of stress distributions and out-of-plane displacements for P(3;2) with the increment of the h_s/t_s value.

Figure 15a illustrates that for the minimum value of the h_s/t_s ratio in the P(3;2) plate configuration, the volume conservation results in stiffeners with low height and large thickness. This geometric combination reduces moments of inertia, thereby providing limited structural reinforcement. As a result, the stiffeners contribute minimally to the overall stiffness of the system, and the structure remains predominantly governed by global buckling. The von Mises stress distribution shows high stress values concentrated in the majority of the plate, but it is also present in the stiffeners.

As the h_s/t_s ratio approaches its optimal value, Figure 15b shows a significantly improved distribution of out-of-plane displacements. The increased stiffener height enhances the overall structural stiffness, which not only reduces the typical concentration of displacements at the center of the plate and along the stiffeners (characteristic of global buckling) but also causes noticeable displacements redistributed symmetrically along the horizontal and vertical axes. This behavior change indicates the onset of local instability, confirming that the stiffened plate begins to exhibit local buckling characteristics. The von Mises stress distribution presents more red regions across the plate and stiffeners, indicating that the stress has been redistributed, occupying larger areas and reducing stress concentration.

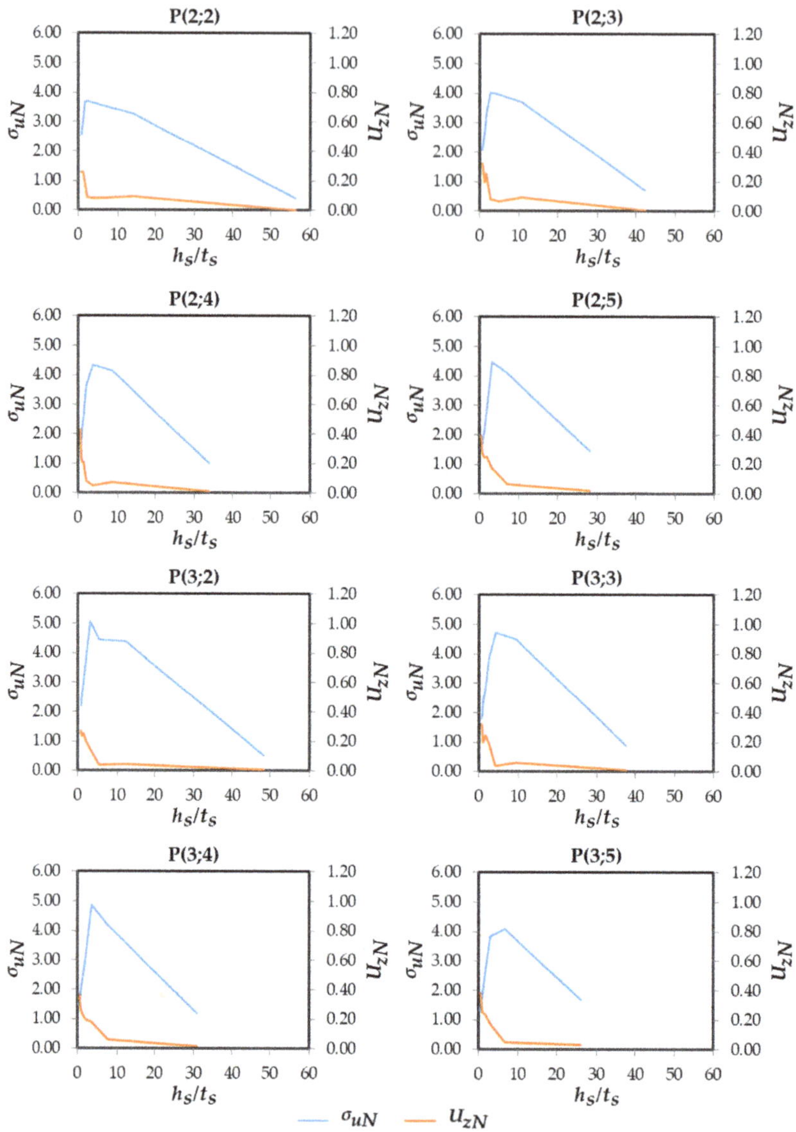

Figure 13. Influence of h_s/t_s, N_{ls}, and N_{ts} over σ_{uN} and U_{zN} for plates with N_{ls} = 2 and N_{ls} = 3.

For a moderate (higher) value of the h_s/t_s ratio, Figure 15c illustrates that the increased h_s leads to a higher moment of inertia among the stiffeners. This behavior enhances their local stiffness, making them more resistant to out-of-plane displacements in the regions where they are located than to the rest of the plate. Consequently, displacements previously distributed between the stiffeners and the plate (as shown in Figure 15b, where blue areas indicate central displacement) become concentrated primarily in the unstiffened regions of the plate.

At the maximum h_s/t_s value for the P(3;2) configuration (Figure 15d), the load applied to the stiffeners resulted in displacements occurring in the opposite direction. This behavior is attributed to the elevated h_s value, which significantly increased the bending moment induced by the applied load. Additionally, the stiffeners' high slenderness promoted their lateral buckling. As a result, the von Mises stress distribution did not exhibit significant stress levels, indicating that the structure failed abruptly under relatively low loading conditions.

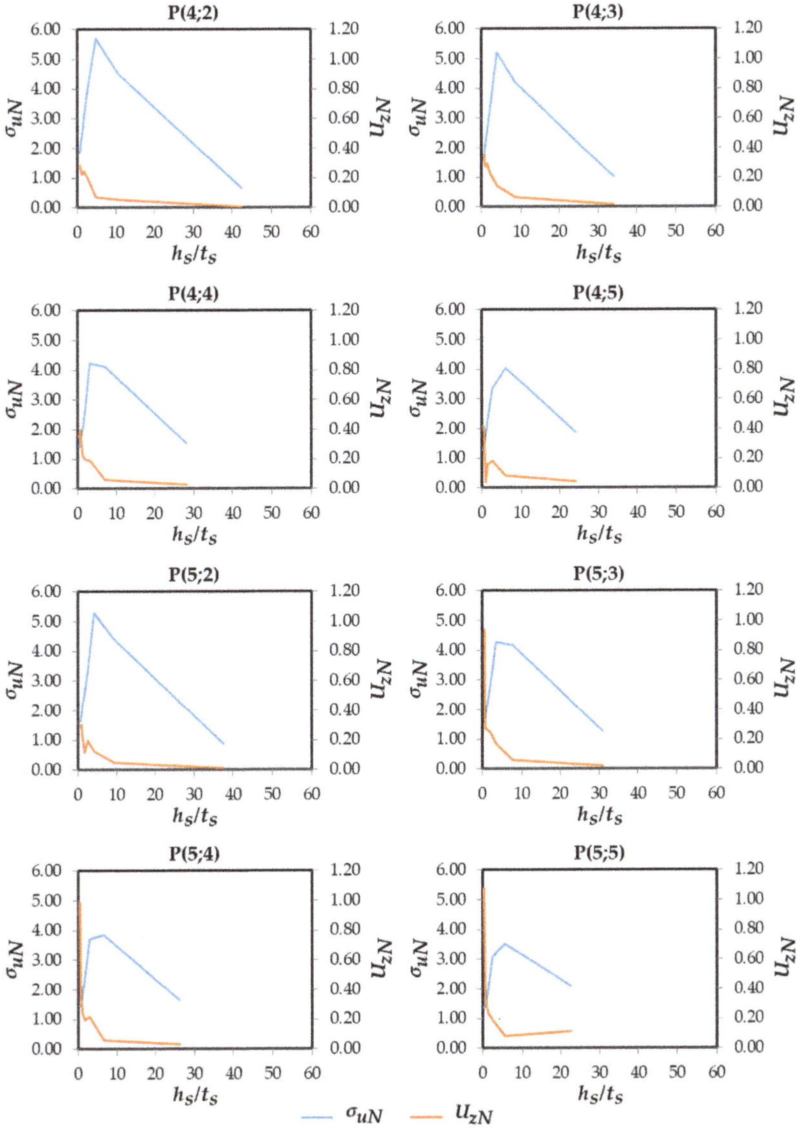

Figure 14. Influence of h_s/t_s, N_{ls}, and N_{ts} over σ_{uN} and U_{zN} for plates with N_{ls} = 4 and N_{ls} = 5.

Regarding U_z, in Figure 15, it can be inferred that their reduction does not necessarily imply an improvement in ultimate buckling stress; rather, it is closely related to the buckling mode that develops. When comparing the different cases, it is evident that the minimum h_s/t_s ratio (Figure 15a) leads to global buckling, characterized by the highest U_z and lowest σ_{uN}. As the h_s/t_s ratio increases to the optimal value (Figure 15b), buckling mode transitions from global to local buckling. This transition is accompanied by a redistribution of displacements, reducing the maximum displacement value and resulting in the highest σ_{uN}.

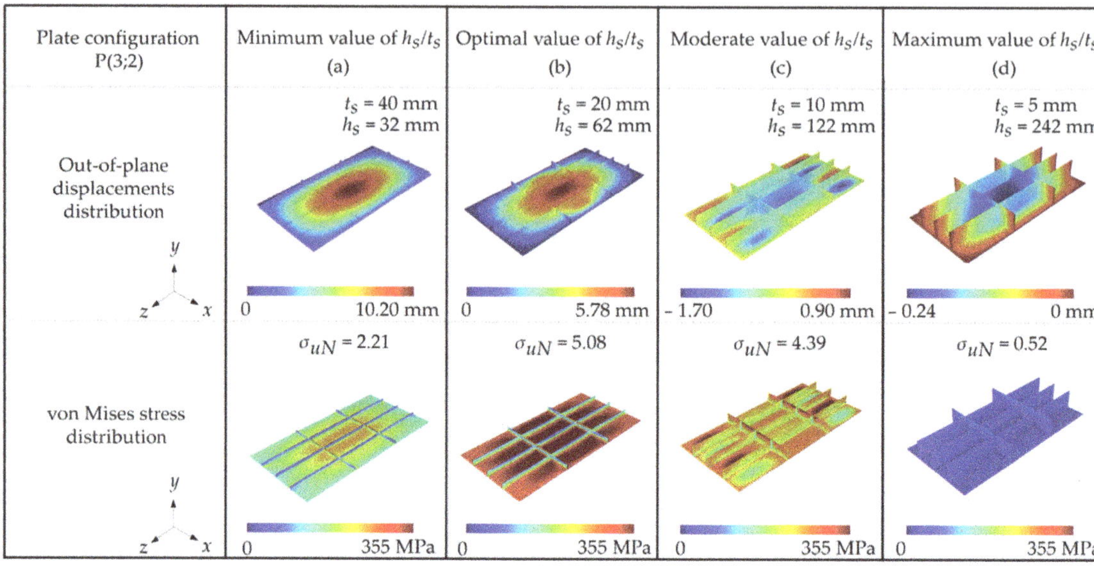

Figure 15. Influence of h_s/t_s over σ_u and U_z of plates: (**a**) P(3;2) and h_s/t_s = 0.80, (**b**) P(3;2) and h_s/t_s = 3.10, (**c**) P(3;2) and h_s/t_s = 12.20, and (**d**) P(3;2) and h_s/t_s = 48.40.

However, when the h_s/t_s ratio is increased beyond the optimal point (Figure 15c), displacements, which are previously concentrated in the center of the plate and along the stiffeners, become more widely distributed across various regions of the plate. This redistribution leads to premature local buckling, resulting in lower ultimate buckling stress than that obtained at the optimal ratio. Therefore, even though the maximum U_z continues to decrease, structural performance in buckling resistance also diminishes.

These findings help explain the trends observed in the σ_{uN} and U_z curves shown in Figures 13 and 14. At lower h_s/t_s values, global buckling dominates, with high displacement levels and low σ_{uN}. As the h_s/t_s ratio increases, an optimal value is reached, marked by redistributed displacements and improved structural performance (lower U_z, higher σ_{uN}). When the h_s/t_s ratio exceeds this optimal point, U_z continues to decrease, but σ_{uN} also declines.

Regarding N_{ls} and N_{ts}, increasing these values reduces the minimum and maximum allowable values of the h_s/t_s ratio. As illustrated in Figure 15a, lower h_s/t_s ratios generally result in global buckling. Nevertheless, across all plate configurations P(N_{ls};N_{ts}) and h_s/t_s values, the minimum h_s/t_s consistently resulted in global buckling for all plate configurations. Additionally, depending on the specific values of N_{ls} and N_{ts}, increasing the h_s/t_s ratio beyond the minimum could either induce a transition to local buckling (at higher h_s/t_s values) or sustain global buckling behavior, as shown in Figure 16, taken at P(4;4) as an investigation example.

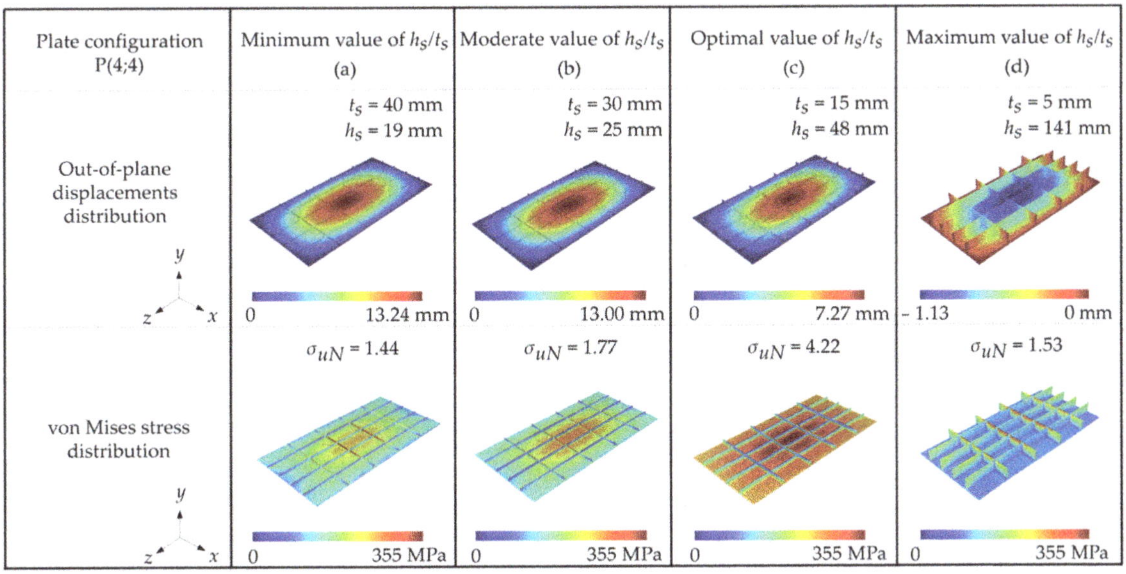

Figure 16. Influence of h_s/t_s over σ_u and U_z of plates: (**a**) P(4;4) and h_s/t_s = 0.48, (**b**) P(4;4) and h_s/t_s = 0.83, (**c**) P(4;4) and h_s/t_s = 3.20, and (**d**) P(4;4) and h_s/t_s = 28.20.

As observed in the plates with lower N_{ls} and N_{ts} values (see Figure 15), the maximum value of σ_{uN} is achieved with an optimized h_s/t_s ratio corresponding to the most efficient stress distribution (Figure 16c). In contrast, Figure 16a shows that, due to the low h_s/t_s ratio, stresses are highly concentrated in the stiffeners. As the h_s/t_s ratio increases, the stiffeners contribute more significantly to the overall stiffness of the plate-stiffeners system. When this ratio reaches its optimal value, a more uniform stress distribution is achieved, with both the plate and the lower regions of the stiffeners sustaining stress levels close to the yield strength. The plates P(4;4), which had the highest h_s/t_s ratio, also exhibited an inverse displacement direction. This behavior is attributed to the influence of the high h_s value, which significantly affects the resulting moment generated by the load acting on the stiffeners. Additionally, the higher values of N_{ls} and N_{ts} contribute to a more effective distribution of this moment over a larger plate area.

In agreement with Bejan and Lorente [53], flow systems naturally exhibit imperfections, which cannot be eliminated but redistributed to promote efficient flow. By utilizing Constructal Design, it becomes possible to develop improved configurations and more effective strategies for generating geometries that enable an optimal distribution of these imperfections. Besides that, structural engineering systems can be interpreted as flow systems that evolve and adapt their shapes to facilitate the flow of stress. While it may seem unconventional to regard stress as a flow, this perspective proves valuable when determining the most effective geometric configuration of structural components under load. Within the framework of material mechanics, imperfections are associated with areas of increased stress concentrations. Thus, improved structural performance is achieved when these peak stresses are distributed more uniformly across the available material. Based on Figures 15 and 16, and the constructal principle of optimal distribution of imperfections [54,55], one can infer that the optimized geometries promote a more uniform distribution throughout the structure. In the context of stress flow, this implies that the most efficient structural geometries allow for a more even distribution of stress, enabling more regions of the stiffened plate to reach the stress limit, enhancing the overall mechanical performance. Notably, this trend—where optimized geometric configurations of steel plates under elasto-plastic buckling exhibit a greater amount of regions reaching the limit stress—is also identified in the studies by Lima et al. [12], Lima et al. [13], and Vieira et al. [8].

3.7. Highest and Lowest Values of h_s/t_s, N_{ls}, and N_{ts} over σ_{uN}

The highest σ_{uN} value observed is 5.72, occurring in the P(4;2) configuration with an h_s/t_s ratio of 4.80. In contrast, the lowest σ_{uN} value, 0.43, is obtained for the P(2;2) configuration with h_s/t_s equal to 56.20. These extremes correspond to a 472% increase and a 57% decrease relative to the reference stress σ_{uR}. The corresponding out-of-plane displacement distribution and von Mises stress distributions for these two configurations are illustrated in Figure 17.

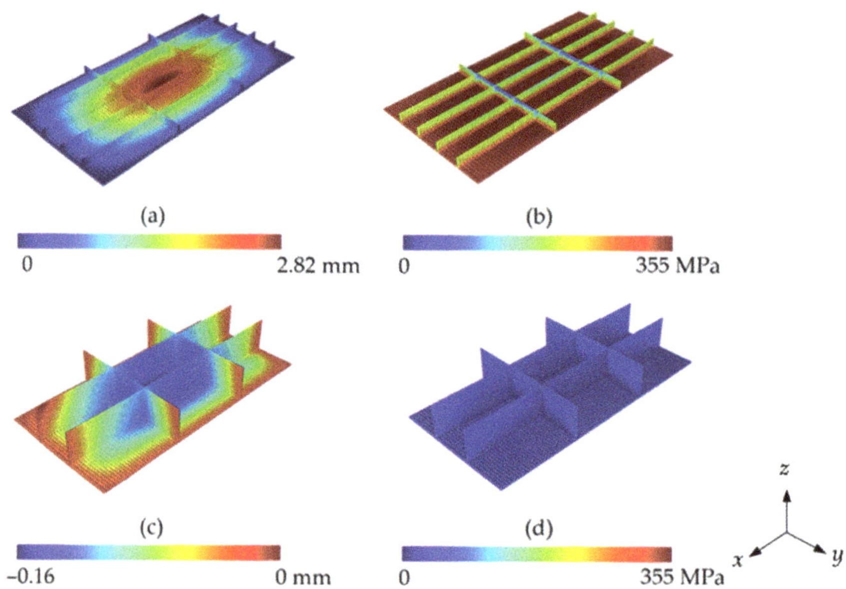

Figure 17. Best and worst plate configurations: (**a**) P(4;2) out-of-plane displacements, (**b**) P(4;2) von Mises stress distribution, (**c**) P(2;2) out-of-plane displacements, and (**d**) P(2;2) von Mises stress distribution.

The out-of-plane displacements (see Figure 17a) are uniformly distributed across the global structure in the optimal plate configuration. The von Mises stress (illustrated in Figure 17b) is also effectively balanced among the structural elements, with values close to the yield stress in the plate and the stiffeners. Conversely, the least effective plate configuration features the highest h_s/t_s ratio (shown in Figure 17c,d), resulting in excessive slenderness. This condition leads to failure due to lateral buckling of the stiffeners under relatively low loads.

3.8. Influence of N_{ls} and N_{ts} over Once Optimized $(h_s/t_s)_o$ and Once Maximized $(\sigma_{uN})_m$

Based on the σ_{uN} values corresponding to each h_s/t_s ratio within the different plate configurations (see Figures 13 and 14), the $(\sigma_{uN})_m$ and its associated $(h_s/t_s)_o$ are determined, as presented in Table 10.

Table 10. $(\sigma_{uN})_m$ and $(h_s/t_s)_o$ for all plate configurations.

Plate Configuration	N_{ls}	N_{ts}	$(h_s/t_s)_o$	$(\sigma_{uN})_m$
P(2;2)	2	2	2.28	3.71
P(2;3)	2	3	2.70	4.04
P(2;4)	2	4	3.80	4.34
P(2;5)	2	5	3.20	4.48
P(3;2)	3	2	3.10	5.08
P(3;3)	3	3	4.27	4.74
P(3;4)	3	4	3.47	4.88
P(3;5)	3	5	6.60	4.11
P(4;2)	4	2	4.80	5.72
P(4;3)	4	3	3.87	5.20
P(4;4)	4	4	3.20	4.22
P(4;5)	4	5	6.10	4.05
P(5;2)	5	2	4.27	5.31
P(5;3)	5	3	3.47	4.29
P(5;4)	5	4	6.60	3.86
P(5;5)	5	5	5.70	3.51

According to Table 10, the maximum value of $(\sigma_{uN})_m$ is 5.72, observed in the P(4;2) configuration with an $(h_s/t_s)_o$ ratio of 4.80. In contrast, the lowest performance is recorded for the P(5;5) configuration, which reached a $(\sigma_{uN})_m$ of 3.51 at an $(h_s/t_s)_o$ ratio of 5.70. These results correspond to improvements of 472% and 251% over σ_{uR}, respectively. The corresponding out-of-plane displacement and von Mises stress distributions for both configurations are illustrated in Figure 18.

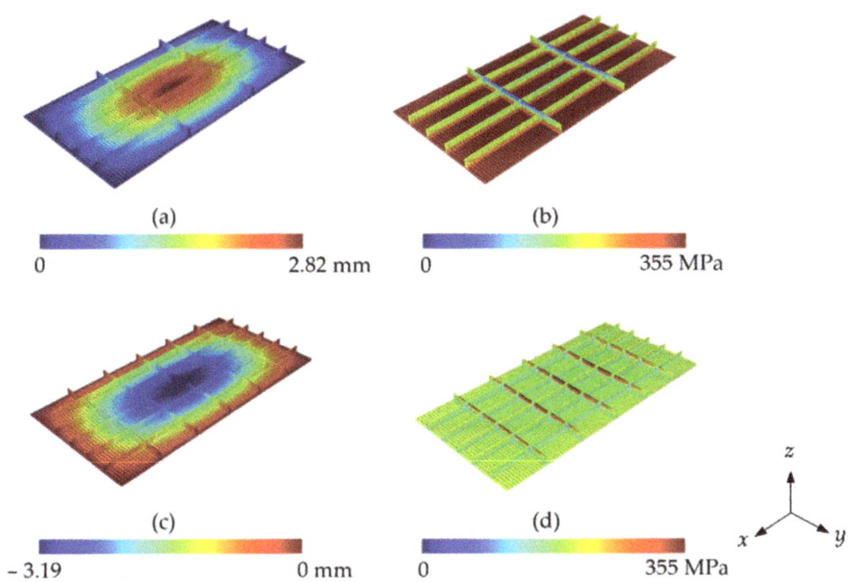

Figure 18. Best and worst plate configurations: **(a)** P(4;2) out-of-plane displacements, **(b)** P(4;2) von Mises stress distribution, **(c)** P(5;5) out-of-plane displacements, and **(d)** P(5;5) von Mises stress distribution.

Comparing the displacement distributions of the best-performing plate configuration in terms of $(\sigma_{uN})_m$ (see Figure 18a) with the worst-performing one (see Figure 18c), the latter exhibits a predominant concentration of out-of-plane displacements at the center of the stiffened plate. This behavior indicates a less efficient structural response than the configuration with the highest $(\sigma_{uN})_m$, where displacements are more evenly distributed. Regarding stress distribution, the better-performing plate (Figure 18b) also shows greater participation of the plate itself in stress, resulting in more uniform stress distribution and, consequently, reducing stress concentrations if compared with the P(5;5) plate (see Figure 18d). The influence of N_{ls} and N_{ts} over $(h_s/t_s)_o$ and $(\sigma_{uN})_m$ from Table 10 is shown in Figure 19.

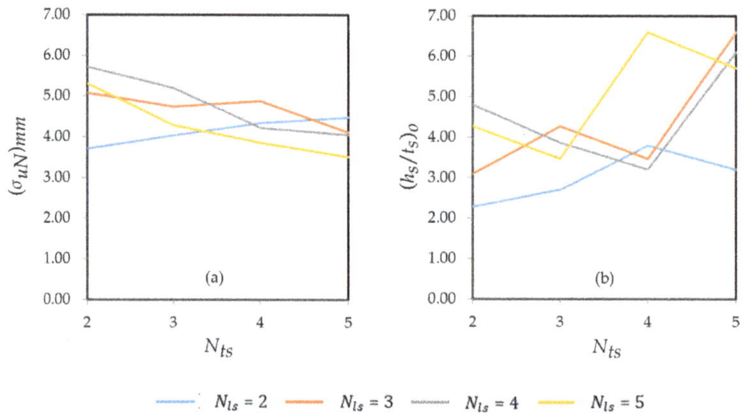

Figure 19. Influence of N_{ls} and N_{ts} on: **(a)** $(\sigma_{uN})_m$ and **(b)** $(h_s/t_s)_o$.

Figure 19a shows that, except for the configuration with $N_{ls} = 2$, there is a general trend of decreasing $(\sigma_{uN})_m$ as N_{ts} increases. This behavior can be attributed to the reduction in the h_s/t_s ratio that results from adding more N_{ls} and N_{ts}, as previously discussed. In the case of plates with $N_{ls} = 2$, however, the increase in N_{ts} appears beneficial. Due to the low N_{ls} value, the resulting h_s/t_s values are relatively high, which is illustrated in Figure 17d, leading to lateral buckling of the stiffeners and ultimately the worst performance in terms of σ_{uN}. In this specific configuration, the available material volume is better utilized by increasing the number of N_{ts}, which helps stabilize the structure and improve stress distribution.

According to Figure 19b, a predicted behavior is noticed, as shown in Figures 15 and 16, that for each plate configuration, the maximized value of σ_{uN} is not necessarily obtained by the highest values of $(h_s/t_s)_o$. When the curves of $(h_s/t_s)_o$ increase with the rise in N_{ts}, it indicates that, despite the reduction in the available h_s due to the increased number of transverse stiffeners, the maximum $(\sigma_{uN})_m$ value had not been previously achieved with the higher $(h_s/t_s)_o$ values.

3.9. Influence of N_{ls}, $(N_{ts})_o$, and $(h_s/t_s)_{oo}$, on $(\sigma_{uN})_{mm}$

Based on the results for N_{ts}, $(h_s/t_s)_o$, and $(\sigma_{uN})_m$, see Table 10 and Figure 19, it is possible to determine the once-optimized number of transverse stiffeners $(N_{ts})_o$, the twice-maximized normalized ultimate buckling stress $(\sigma_{uN})_{mm}$, and the corresponding twice-optimized height-to-thickness ratio $(h_s/t_s)_{oo}$, as summarized in Table 11.

The maximum value of $(\sigma_{uN})_{mm}$ is 5.72, observed in the P(4;2) configuration with $(h_s/t_s)_{oo}$ of 4.80. In contrast, the lowest value, 4.48, is obtained from the P(2;5) configuration with $(h_s/t_s)_{oo}$ equal to 3.20. These values correspond to an increase of 472% and 348% in relation to σ_{uR}, respectively. Figure 20 presents the displacement and von Mises stress distributions for both scenarios.

Table 11. Results of $(N_{ts})_o$, $(h_s/t_s)_{oo}$, and $(\sigma_{uN})_{mm}$ for each N_{ls} plate configuration.

Plate Configuration	N_{ls}	$(N_{ts})_o$	$(h_s/t_s)_{oo}$	$(\sigma_{uN})_{mm}$
P(2;5)	2	5	3.20	4.48
P(3;2)	3	2	3.10	5.08
P(4;2)	4	2	4.80	5.72
P(5;2)	5	2	4.27	5.31

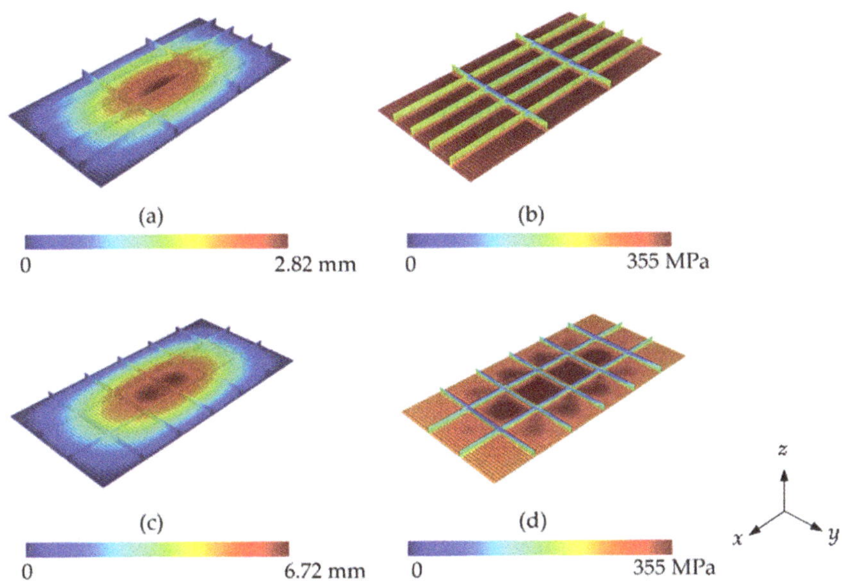

Figure 20. Best and worst plate configurations: **(a)** P(4;2) out-of-plane displacements, **(b)** P(4;2) von Mises stress distribution, **(c)** P(2;5) out-of-plane displacements, and **(d)** P(2;5) von Mises stress distribution.

As expected, and consistent with previous optimizations, the plate that exhibited the highest ultimate buckling stress also showed a better displacement distribution (lower maximum out-of-plane displacement value compared to another plate with the same global buckling mode) in Figure 20a. Supporting this result, the same plate also presented a more efficient stress distribution (Figure 20b); with stress levels close to the yield limit distributed across the entire surface of the plate and along the stiffeners, especially in the contact regions between the plate and the stiffeners. This indicates that both components work together to enhance the structural strength of the system. In contrast, the plate shown in Figure 20c,d, although it exhibits some regions with stress close to the yield limit, shows a concentration of stresses in the center of the plate, while the edges present lower values. This less uniform distribution indicates a lower structural performance compared to the plate shown in Figure 20b, which presented better uniform distribution.

The influence of N_{ls}, $(N_{ts})_o$, and $(h_s/t_s)_{oo}$, over $(\sigma_{uN})_{mm}$ are graphically shown in Figure 21.

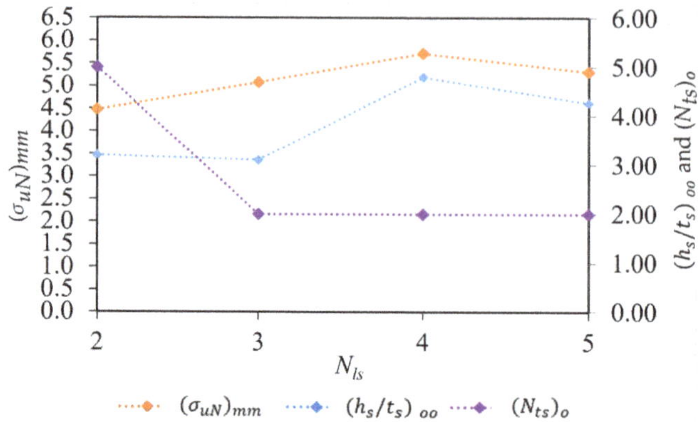

Figure 21. Influence of N_{ls} on $(N_{ts})_o$, $(h_s/t_s)_{oo}$, and $(\sigma_{uN})_{mm}$.

From Figure 21, it can be observed that only plate configuration with N_{ls} = 2 presented the maximum possible value of transverse stiffeners ($(N_{ts})_o$ = 5). The other configurations, with N_{ls} > 2, presented $(\sigma_{uN})_{mm}$ associated with the minimum value of transverse stiffeners ($(N_{ts})_o$ = 2). This behavior is again related to volume conservation, the configuration with N_{ls} = 2 allowed for higher values of $(h_s/t_s)_{oo}$, even with a high value of longitudinal stiffeners. In contrast, in the other configurations, lower values of N_{ts} are obtained so that the values of $(h_s/t_s)_{oo}$ would be sufficient to achieve the corresponding $(\sigma_{uN})_{mm}$.

By comparing the results obtained under the same premises for the application of constructal design and exhaustive search, using plates with identical dimensions and material properties, Lima et al. [12] achieved the optimized configuration for uniaxial loading as plate P(2;2), with $(h_s/t_s)_{ooo}$ = 14.09 and $(\sigma_{uN})_{mmm}$ = 1.89. In this study, considering biaxial loading, the optimized configuration is found to be plate P(4;2), with $(h_s/t_s)_{ooo}$ = 4.80 and $(\sigma_{uN})_{mmm}$ = 5.72. This behavior comparison reveals a substantial increase in ultimate strength: the $(\sigma_{uN})_{mmm}$ under biaxial loading is approximately three times higher than that obtained under uniaxial loading. This indicates that, for the same 30% redistribution of the original plate volume into stiffeners, the configuration optimized for biaxial loading is more effective, resulting in significantly greater structural efficiency in comparison with the respective reference plate. Furthermore, the critical buckling direction is longitudinal since the plate's length is twice its height. This behavior explains why the optimized configuration under biaxial loading featured many longitudinal stiffeners.

4. Conclusions

The verification, validation, and application of a numerical model for elasto-plastic buckling in both stiffened and unstiffened plates under biaxial compression enabled the use of Constructal Design and Exhaustive Search methods to evaluate structural performance in buckling conditions. This approach provided a detailed understanding of how longitudinal and transverse stiffeners (varying in number, height, and thickness) affect the elasto-plastic buckling behavior and the overall structural strength of the plate. It particularly highlighted the distribution of out-of-plane displacements and stress throughout the structure. The verification and validation of the elasto-plastic buckling analysis showed a maximum difference of 1.90% and 4.28% when compared to previous numerical results, and 7.03% and 8.28% when compared to experimental results, for unstiffened and stiffened plates, respectively.

Regarding the influence of the number of transverse and longitudinal stiffeners, the best performances occurred for intermediate values of h_s/t_s with t_s between 15 mm and 20 mm.

This behavior can be associated with a better stress distribution over the plate. Furthermore, concerning the influence of h_s/t_s, it may be inferred that the lower and intermediate values of h_s/t_s resulted in the worst and best performance for σ_{uN}, respectively, while higher values of h_s/t_s led to local buckling of the stiffeners due to the increased slenderness.

With respect to U_z, the results indicate that higher values of U_z are related to global buckling, while intermediate values of U_z are associated with local buckling, which also corresponds to the highest values of σ_{uN}. Moreover, the optimal plate configuration exhibited out-of-plane displacements and von Mises stresses uniformly distributed along both the plate and the stiffeners.

Additionally, the methodology used allowed for the identification of an optimized plate configuration, where the geometry of the stiffeners improves structural performance by redistributing material from the original unstiffened plate to the strengthening elements. The plate configuration that achieved the highest normalized ultimate buckling stress was P(4;2), with $(\sigma_{uN})_{mmm}$= 5.72, $(h_s/t_s)_{ooo}$ = 4.80, $(N_{ts})_{oo}$ = 4, and $(N_{ls})_o$ = 2, representing a 472% increase compared to the reference σ_{uR} of the unstiffened plate. In contrast, the worst-performing stiffened plate configuration was P(2;2), with h_s/t_s = 56.20, N_{ts}= 2, and N_{ls} = 2, which resulted in a 57% reduction in σ_{uN} compared to the unstiffened reference. The performance difference between the best and worst stiffened configurations reached 319%.

As recommendations for future work, it is suggested to investigate the following aspects: the influence of plates with varying aspect ratios (a/b); the impact of different ratios of applied loads in each principal direction; the effect of alternative stiffener geometries and the distribution of stiffener volume; the consideration of larger initial imperfections, in accordance with design standards, and the inclusion of material strain hardening (work hardening) behavior after yielding to better capture the post-yield response of modern steels and to improve the realism and accuracy of elasto-plastic buckling predictions.

Supplementary Materials: The following supporting information can be downloaded at: https://www.mdpi.com/article/10.3390/met15080879/s1, Table S1: Constructal Design; Table S2: Exhaustive Search.

Author Contributions: Conceptualization, A.F.L., R.L.V., J.P.S.L., E.d.S.D.E. and L.A.I.; methodology, A.F.L., R.L.V., E.D.d.S., L.A.O.R., T.d.S., J.P.S.L., E.d.S.D.E. and L.A.I.; software, A.F.L.; verification, A.F.L.; formal analysis, A.F.L., R.L.V., T.d.S., J.P.S.L., E.d.S.D.E. and L.A.I.; investigation, A.F.L., R.L.V., T.d.S., J.P.S.L., E.d.S.D.E. and L.A.I.; resources, E.D.d.S., L.A.O.R., E.d.S.D.E. and L.A.I.; data curation, A.F.L.; writing—original draft preparation, A.F.L., R.L.V. and L.A.I.; writing—review and editing, E.D.d.S., L.A.O.R., T.d.S., J.P.S.L., E.d.S.D.E. and L.A.I.; visualization, E.D.d.S., L.A.O.R., T.d.S., J.P.S.L., E.d.S.D.E. and L.A.I.; supervision, T.d.S., J.P.S.L., E.d.S.D.E. and L.A.I.; project administration, L.A.I.; funding acquisition, E.D.d.S., L.A.O.R. and L.A.I. All authors have read and agreed to the published version of the manuscript.

Funding: This research was funded by Coordination for the Improvement of Higher Education Personnel—Brazil (CAPES), Finance Code 001, for the social demand program, grant number (Process: 88887.501697/2020-00), and Brazilian National Council for Scientific and Technological Development—Brazil (CNPq) for their research grants (Processes: 307791/2019-0, 308396/2021-9, and 309648/2021-1).

Institutional Review Board Statement: Not applicable.

Informed Consent Statement: Not applicable.

Data Availability Statement: The original contributions presented in this study are included in the article/Supplementary Materials. Further inquiries can be directed to the corresponding author.

Acknowledgments: The authors thank the CAPES and CNPQ for their financial support in the form of doctoral and research productivity scholarships.

Conflicts of Interest: The authors declare no conflicts of interest.

References

1. Jones, R.M.R. *Buckling of Bars, Plates and Shells*; Bull Ridge Publishing: Blacksburg, VA, USA, 2006.
2. Szilard, R. *Theories and Applications of Plate Analysis*; John Wiley & Sons: Hoboken, NJ, USA, 2004; Volume 57.
3. Musmar, M.A. Structural Performance of Steel Plates. *Front. Built Environ.* **2022**, *8*, 991061. [CrossRef]
4. El-Sawy, K.M.; Nazmy, Y.A.S.; Martini, M.I. Elasto-Plastic Buckling of Perforated Plates under Uniaxial Compression. *Thin Walled Struct.* **2004**, *42*, 1083–1101. [CrossRef]
5. Trahair, N.S.; Bradford, M.A.; Nethercot, D.A.; Gardner, L. *The Behavior and Design of Steel Structures*, 4th ed.; Taylor & Francis, CRC Press: Abingdon, UK, 2008; ISBN 9780415301565.
6. Ueda, Y.; Yao, T. Ultimate Strength of Compressed Stiffened Plates and Minimum Stiffness Ratio of Their Stiffeners. *Eng. Struct.* **1983**, *2*, 97. [CrossRef]
7. Zhao, W.; Mahdi, M.A. Buckling Load Maximization of Stiffened Plates Using Level Set Topology Optimization and Inverse Isoparametric Mapping Algorithm. In Proceedings of the American Institute of Aeronautics and Astronautics, San Diego, CA, USA, 8 June 2023.
8. Vieira, R.L.; Baumgardt, G.R.; dos Santos, E.D.; Rocha, L.A.O.; da Silveira, T.; Lima, J.P.S.; Isoldi, L.A. Computational Model and Constructal Design Applied to Thin Stiffened Plates Subjected to Elastoplastic Buckling Due to Combined Loading Conditions. *Appl. Sci.* **2025**, *15*, 3354. [CrossRef]
9. Troina, G.; Cunha, M.; Pinto, V.; Rocha, L.; Santos, E.D.; Fragassa, C.; Isoldi, L. Computational Modeling and Constructal Design Theory Applied to the Geometric Optimization of Thin Steel Plates with Stiffeners Subjected to Uniform Transverse Load. *Metals* **2020**, *10*, 220. [CrossRef]
10. de Queiroz, J.P.T.P.; Cunha, M.L.; Pavlovic, A.; Rocha, L.A.O.; dos Santos, E.D.; Troina, G.d.S.; Isoldi, L.A. Geometric Evaluation of Stiffened Steel Plates Subjected to Transverse Loading for Naval and Offshore Applications. *J. Mar. Sci. Eng.* **2019**, *7*, 7. [CrossRef]
11. Kucharski, D.M.P.; Pinto, V.T.; Rocha, L.A.O.; Dos Santos, E.D.; Fragassa, C.; Isoldi, L.A. Geometric Analysis By Constructal Design Of Stiffened Steel Plates Under Bending with Transverse I-Shaped Or T-Shaped Stiffeners. *Facta Univ. Ser. Mech. Eng.* **2022**, *20*, 617–632. [CrossRef]
12. Lima, J.P.S.; Cunha, M.L.; dos Santos, E.D.; Rocha, L.A.O.; Real, M.d.V.; Isoldi, L.A. Constructal Design for the Ultimate Buckling Stress Improvement of Stiffened Plates Submitted to Uniaxial Compressive Load. *Eng. Struct.* **2020**, *203*, 109883. [CrossRef]
13. Lima, J.P.S.; Rocha, L.A.O.; dos Santos, E.D.; Real, M.d.V.; Isoldi, L.A. Constructal Design And Numerical Modeling Applied To Stiffened Steel Plates Submitted To Elasto-Plastic Buckling. *Proc. Rom. Acad. Ser. A—Math. Phys. Tech. Sci. Inf. Sci.* **2018**, *19*, 195–200.
14. Ringsberg, J.W.; Darie, I.; Nahshon, K.; Shilling, G.; Vaz, M.A.; Benson, S.; Brubak, L.; Feng, G.; Fujikubo, M.; Gaiotti, M.; et al. The ISSC 2022 Committee III.1-Ultimate Strength Benchmark Study on the Ultimate Limit State Analysis of a Stiffened Plate Structure Subjected to Uniaxial Compressive Loads. *Mar. Struct.* **2021**, *79*, 103026. [CrossRef]
15. Wang, B.; Tian, K.; Hao, P.; Cai, Y.; Li, Y.; Sun, Y. Hybrid Analysis and Optimization of Hierarchical Stiffened Plates Based on Asymptotic Homogenization Method. *Compos. Struct.* **2015**, *132*, 136–147. [CrossRef]
16. Ghavami, K.; Khedmati, M.R. Numerical and Experimental Investigations on the Compression Behaviour of Stiffened Plates. *J. Constr. Steel Res.* **2006**, *62*, 1087–1100. [CrossRef]
17. Hassan, A.; Kurgan, N. Modeling and Buckling Analysis of Rectangular Plates in ANSYS. *Int. J. Eng. Appl. Sci.* **2019**, *11*, 310–329. [CrossRef]
18. Shanmugam, N.E.; Narayanan, R. Ultimate Strength of Biaxially Loaded Plates. In *Stability and Ductility of Steel Structures*; Elsevier: Amsterdam, The Netherlands, 1998.
19. Piscopo, V. Refined Buckling Analysis of Rectangular Plates Under Uniaxial and Biaxial Compression. *World Acad. Sci. Eng. Technol. Int. J. Mech. Mechatron. Eng.* **2010**, *4*, 1018–1025. [CrossRef]
20. Paik, J.K.; Kim, B.J.; Seo, J.K. Methods for Ultimate Limit State Assessment of Ships and Ship-Shaped Offshore Structures: Part I-Unstiffened Plates. *Ocean. Eng.* **2008**, *35*, 261–270. [CrossRef]
21. Paik, J.K.; Seo, J.K. Nonlinear Finite Element Method Models for Ultimate Strength Analysis of Steel Stiffened-Plate Structures under Combined Biaxial Compression and Lateral Pressure Actions—Part I: Plate Elements. *Thin-Walled Struct.* **2009**, *47*, 1008–1017. [CrossRef]
22. Tanaka, S.; Yanagihara, D.; Yasuoka, A.; Harada, M.; Okazawa, S.; Fujikubo, M.; Yao, T. Evaluation of Ultimate Strength of Stiffened Panels under Longitudinal Thrust. *Mar. Struct.* **2014**, *36*, 21–50. [CrossRef]
23. Anyfantis, K.N.; Pantazopoulou, S.; Papanikolaou, N. Generalized Probabilistic Response Surfaces for the Buckling Strength Assessment of Stiffened Panels. *Thin-Walled Struct.* **2023**, *189*, 110860. [CrossRef]
24. Suneel Kumar, M.; Lavana Kumar, C.; Alagusundaramoorthy, P.; Sundaravadivelu, R. Ultimate Strength of Orthogonal Stiffened Plates Subjected to Axial and Lateral Loads. *KSCE J. Civ. Eng.* **2010**, *14*, 197–206. [CrossRef]
25. Yuan, Y.; Xing, Y. A Semi-Analytical Solution for Critical Buckling Loads of Orthotropic Stiffened Rectangular Thin Plates. *Thin-Walled Struct.* **2024**, *205*, 112449. [CrossRef]

26. Ozdemir, M.; Ergin, A.; Yanagihara, D.; Tanaka, S.; Yao, T. A New Method to Estimate Ultimate Strength of Stiffened Panels under Longitudinal Thrust Based on Analytical Formulas. *Mar. Struct.* **2018**, *59*, 510–535. [CrossRef]
27. Guo, G.; Cui, J.; Wang, D. An Experimental Investigation on the Collapse Modes of Stiffened Plates Subjected to Combined Axial and Lateral Loads. *Ocean. Eng.* **2024**, *299*, 117189. [CrossRef]
28. Ma, H.; Mei, H.; Wang, D. Scale Model Design for the Stiffened Plate Subjected to Combined Longitudinal Compression and Lateral Pressure Considering Collapse Modes. *Ocean. Eng.* **2022**, *243*, 110289. [CrossRef]
29. Xu, M.C.; Song, Z.J.; Zhang, B.W.; Pan, J. Empirical Formula for Predicting Ultimate Strength of Stiffened Panel of Ship Structure under Combined Longitudinal Compression and Lateral Loads. *Ocean. Eng.* **2018**, *162*, 161–175. [CrossRef]
30. Wang, Z.; Yuan, T.; Kong, X.; Wu, W. A Universal Similarity Method and Design Procedure for Buckling Assessment of Stiffened Plates under Compression Load on Real Ships. *Thin-Walled Struct.* **2022**, *181*, 110025. [CrossRef]
31. Ma, H.; Xiong, Q.; Wang, D. Experimental and Numerical Study on the Ultimate Strength of Stiffened Plates Subjected to Combined Biaxial Compression and Lateral Loads. *Ocean. Eng.* **2021**, *228*, 108928. [CrossRef]
32. Fujikubo, M.; Harada, M.; Yao, T.; Khedmati, M.R.; Yanagihara, D. Estimation of Ultimate Strength of Continuous Stiffened Panel under Combined Transverse Thrust and Lateral Pressure Part 2: Continuous Stiffened Panel. *Mar. Struct.* **2005**, *18*, 411–427. [CrossRef]
33. Shi, G.-J.; Xiong, Y.-F.; Cai, S.-J.; Wang, D.-Y. Experiment Study of Dynamic Buckling for Stiffened Panels under Longitudinal Impact. *Ocean. Eng.* **2023**, *284*, 115243. [CrossRef]
34. Anyfantis, K.N. Ultimate Strength of Stiffened Panels Subjected to Non-Uniform Thrust. *Int. J. Nav. Archit. Ocean. Eng.* **2020**, *12*, 325–342. [CrossRef]
35. Saad-Eldeen, S.; Garbatov, Y. Experimental and Numerical Analysis of Structural Capacity of Perforated Stiffened Plates. *J. Mar. Sci. Eng.* **2023**, *11*, 842. [CrossRef]
36. Shanmugam, N.E.; Dongqi, Z.; Choo, Y.S.; Arockiaswamy, M. Experimental Studies on Stiffened Plates under In-Plane Load and Lateral Pressure. *Thin-Walled Struct.* **2014**, *80*, 22–31. [CrossRef]
37. Seo, J.K.; Song, C.H.; Park, J.S.; Paik, J.K. Nonlinear Structural Behaviour and Design Formulae for Calculating the Ultimate Strength of Stiffened Curved Plates under Axial Compression. *Thin-Walled Struct.* **2016**, *107*, 1–17. [CrossRef]
38. Paik, J.K.; Kim, B.J.; Seo, J.K. Methods for Ultimate Limit State Assessment of Ships and Ship-Shaped Offshore Structures: Part II-Stiffened Plates. *Ocean. Eng.* **2008**, *35*, 271–280. [CrossRef]
39. Paik, J.K.; Kim, B.J. Ultimate Strength Formulations for Stiffened Panels under Combined Axial Load, in-Plane Bending and Lateral Pressure: A Benchmark Study. *Thin-Walled Struct.* **2002**, *40*, 45–83. [CrossRef]
40. Zhong, Q.; Wang, D. Ultimate Strength Characteristics and Assessment of Laser-Welded Web-Core Sandwich Plates under Combined Biaxial Compression and Lateral Pressure. *Ocean. Eng.* **2022**, *263*, 112324. [CrossRef]
41. Hanif, M.I.; Adiputra, R.; Prabowo, A.R.; Yamada, Y.; Firdaus, N. Assessment of the Ultimate Strength of Stiffened Panels of Ships Considering Uncertainties in Geometrical Aspects: Finite Element Approach and Simplified Formula. *Ocean. Eng.* **2023**, *286*, 115522. [CrossRef]
42. Zhang, G.; Hu, Y.; Yan, B.; Tong, M.; Wang, F. Buckling and Post-Buckling Analysis of Composite Stiffened Panels: A Ten-Year Review (2014–2023). *Thin-Walled Struct.* **2024**, *205*, 112525. [CrossRef]
43. Wang, Z.; Kong, X.; Wu, W.; Kim, D.K. An Advanced Design Diagram of Stiffened Plate Subjected to Combined In-Plane and Lateral Loads Considering Initial Deflection Effects. *Thin-Walled Struct.* **2024**, *203*, 112144. [CrossRef]
44. Baumgardt, G.R.; Fragassa, C.; Rocha, L.A.O.; dos Santos, E.D.; da Silveira, T.; Isoldi, L.A. Computational Model Verification and Validation of Elastoplastic Buckling Due to Combined Loads of Thin Plates. *Metals* **2023**, *13*, 731. [CrossRef]
45. Przemieniecki, J.S. *Theory of Matrix Structural Analysis*; Dover Publications: New York, NY, USA, 1985; p. 384.
46. Grimesf, R.G.; Lewisf, J.G.; Simon, H.D. A Shifted Block Lanczos Algorithm for Solving Sparse Symmetric Generalized Eigenproblems. *SIAM J. Matrix Anal. Appl.* **1994**, *15*, 228–272. [CrossRef]
47. Ellobody, E.; Feng, R.; Young, B. *Finite Element Analysis and Design of Metal Structures*, 1st ed.; Butterworth-Heinemann: Waltham, MA, USA, 2014.
48. Fonseca, E.M.M. Steel Columns under Compression with Different Sizes of Square Hollow Cross-Sections, Lengths, and End Constraints. *Appl. Sci.* **2024**, *14*, 8668. [CrossRef]
49. Helbig, D.; Da Silva, C.C.C.; Real, M.d.V.; dos Santos, E.D.; Isoldi, L.A.; Rocha, L.A.O. Study about Buckling Phenomenon in Perforated Thin Steel Plates Employing Computational Modeling and Constructal Design Method. *Lat. Am. J. Solids Struct.* **2016**, *13*, 1912–1936. [CrossRef]
50. ANSYS Inc. Mechanical APDL 2024 R2—Element Reference. In *Ansys Mechanical APDL Element Reference*; ANSYS, Inc.: Canonsburg, PA, USA, 2024; pp. 254–265.
51. Bathe, K.J. *Finite Element Procedures*, 2nd ed.; Bathe, K.-J., Ed.; Prentice Hall: Upper Saddle River, NJ, USA, 2014.
52. Oñate, E. *Structural Analysis with the Finite Element Method—Linear Statics*, 2nd ed.; Springer: Dordrecht, The Netherlands, 2009.

53. Morris, M.D. American Society for Quality Factorial Sampling Plans for Preliminary Computational Experiments. *Technometrics* **1991**, *33*, 161–174. [CrossRef]
54. Bejan, A.; Lorente, S. *Design with Constructal Theory*; Wiley & Sons, Inc.: Hoboken, NJ, USA, 2008.
55. Bejan, A. *Shape and Structure: From Engineering to Nature*; Cambridge University Press: Cambridge, UK, 2000.

metals

Article

Numerical and Geometrical Evaluation of Steel Plates with Transverse Hat-Stiffeners Under Bending

Mariana Alvarenga Alves [1,2], Eduarda Machado Rodrigues [2,3], Luiz Alberto Oliveira Rocha [1,2,3], Elizaldo Domingues dos Santos [1,2,3], William Ramires Almeida [2] and Liércio André Isoldi [1,2,3,*]

1 Graduate Program in Computational Modeling (PPGMC), Federal University of Rio Grande—FURG, Rio Grande 96201-900, Brazil; marianaalves1612@hotmail.com (M.A.A.); luizrocha@furg.br (L.A.O.R.); elizaldosantos@furg.br (E.D.d.S.)

2 School of Engineering, Federal University of Rio Grande—FURG, Rio Grande 96201-900, Brazil; eduarda108899@gmail.com (E.M.R.); walmeida@furg.br (W.R.A.)

3 Graduate Program in Ocean Engineering (PPGEO), Federal University of Rio Grande—FURG, Rio Grande 96201-900, Brazil

* Correspondence: liercioisoldi@furg.br; Tel.: +55-53-99109-7356

Abstract: Thin steel plates with stiffeners are widely used in shipbuilding, aeronautics, and civil construction due to their lightness and structural strength. This study presents a numerical model developed using ANSYS Mechanical APDL with SHELL281 finite elements to evaluate the deflection of thin steel plates with trapezoidal-shaped box-beam stiffeners, known as hat-stiffened plates. The structure is analyzed under a uniformly distributed load perpendicular to the plate, with simply supported boundary conditions. The constructal design method combined with the exhaustive search technique is employed to optimize the geometry. A volume fraction of 30% is used, transferring material from the reference plate (without stiffeners) to the stiffeners, defining parameters such as number, height, and thickness—considered degrees of freedom. The stiffener angle is fixed at 120°. The results show that increasing stiffener height and reducing thickness generally improve structural performance by reducing deflections. The best configuration with transverse stiffeners reduced deflection by 97.15% compared to the reference plate, and by 79.27% compared to the best longitudinal configuration from previous studies. Therefore, transverse stiffeners were more effective than longitudinal ones. This study highlights the importance of stiffener orientation and geometry in the structural optimization of thin steel plates.

Keywords: hat-stiffened plates; finite element method; computational modeling; out-of-plane displacements; constructal design

1. Introduction

Steel plates with stiffeners are widely used in naval, automotive, aerospace industries, and in civil engineering structures [1,2]. The stiffeners make the steel plates act simultaneously as both finishing and structural elements that combine good load-bearing capacity and low weight [3]. The shape of the stiffener is critical, as it influences the mechanical behavior of the structural component composed by the plate and stiffeners. Figure 1 shows some types of stiffeners, including the hat-stiffener type illustrated in Figure 1d and investigated in the present work. The flat or I-shaped stiffener (Figure 1a) is well known as the most commonly used in structural engineering; however, the other types (Figure 1b–d) are also adopted in specific applications (Figure 1e,f).

 https://doi.org/10.3390/met15060647

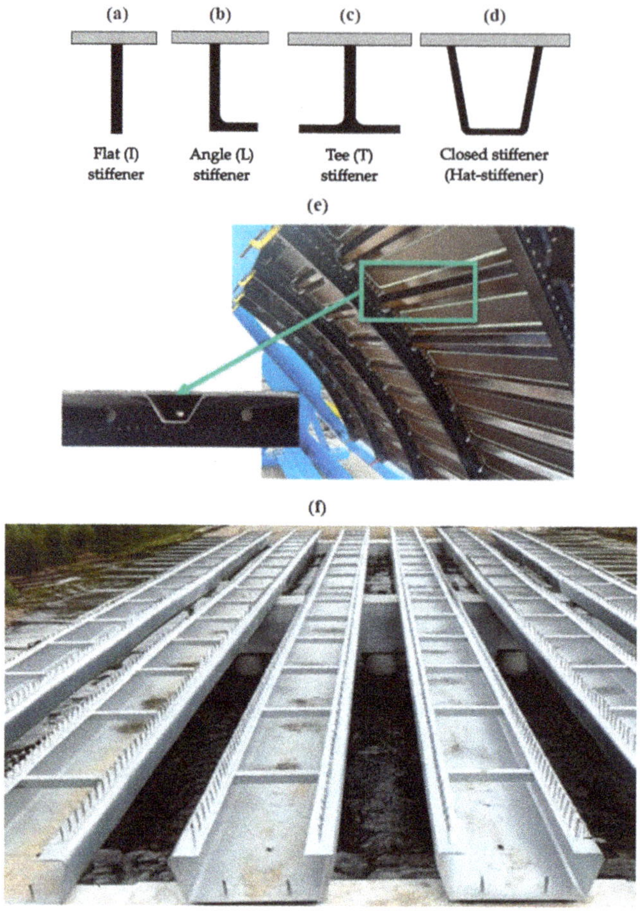

Figure 1. Main types of stiffeners: (**a**) I-shaped; (**b**) L-shaped; (**c**) T-shaped; (**d**) hat-stiffener; (**e**) application of steel hat-stiffeners in aeronautical panels, adapted from [2]; and (**f**) application of steel hat-stiffeners in civil construction (bridge structures), adapted from [4].

Stiffened plates have been investigated by means of computational modeling due to their great potential to develop and study different combinations of plates and stiffeners. The finite element method (FEM) plays a key role in this context, and is widely implemented in commercial software, such as ANSYS and ABAQUS. Several assessments are made during the study and development of plates with stiffeners, including geometric evaluations. For instance, the constructal design method, based on the constructal theory proposed by Adrian Bejan in 1996 [5–9], has proven to be an efficient tool for the geometric analysis of structural engineering problems [10]. The method is based on the constructal law as follows: "For a system with finite dimensions to remain in operation, its geometric configuration must constantly evolve always to allow the best flow of currents that flow within the system" [6–9,11]. This theory affirms that the shapes found in nature are the result of continuous evolution to allow the best flow within them. In the field of structural engineering, a structural system can be analyzed several times, adopting criteria, to find the geometry that provides the best flow of stress within it. Therefore, the application of the constructal design method requires that restrictions, degrees of freedom, and performance indicators be defined so that, in addition to finding the best geometries, it is possible to evaluate the influence of the variation of the degrees of freedom on the performance indicators and better understand the problem [6–9,11,12].

The geometric evaluation with the constructal design of stiffened plates subject to bending has already been carried out through studies that use numerical simulation. Troina et al. [13] studied plates with longitudinal and transverse I-shaped stiffeners having the same height, aiming to minimize the central deflection of these structures. Nogueira et al. [14] also investigated plates with I-shaped stiffeners, but considered different heights for the longitudinal and transverse ones, in order to minimize the maximum and central deflections of the plate.

In turn, according to Tharian and Nandakumar [15], hat-stiffeners (see Figure 1d–e) have greater torsional stiffness and a higher strength/weight ratio when compared to open section stiffeners (see Figure 1a–c). Therefore, concerning hat-stiffened plates that are the focus of the present work, some previous studies can be highlighted: Tharian and Nandakumar [16] performed a FEM numerical analysis comparing open-section stiffeners with hat-stiffeners, and highlighted the advantages of closed box beam stiffeners over open section stiffeners. Pal et al. [17] analyzed the stresses and deflections of plates with trapezoidal box beam stiffeners, keeping constant the plate volume while its geometries and boundary conditions were varied. Virág and Szirbik [18] conducted a study whose objective was to identify potentially dangerous vibration frequencies and eliminate the possibilities of failure in plates with hat-stiffeners, by means of modal analysis. Tharian and Nandakumar [15] performed a structural analysis of bunkers and developed a super element used in the numerical analysis of plates with hat-stiffeners. Filippatos et al. [19] improved the efficiency of components made of composite materials in the aeronautical industry using hat-stiffeners. Aneja et al. [20] investigated the variation of the inclination angle of the sidewalls of hat-stiffeners, indicating that an inclination angle of 120° allows for an increase in mechanical resistance. Recently, Alves et al. [21] applied the constructal design method to perform a geometric evaluation of plates with longitudinal hat-stiffeners, aiming to minimize its maximum and central deflections.

In this context, this work proposes the geometric evaluation and optimization of steel plates with transverse hat-stiffeners, simply supported and under the incidence of a uniformly distributed load. The constructal design method and the exhaustive search technique are employed in association with a FEM numerical model to reduce the maximum and central deflection of plates having transverse hat-stiffeners. For this purpose, a reference plate without stiffeners is considered, and 30% of its volume is redistributed to form hat-stiffeners; i.e., the stiffeners are generated by reducing the reference plate's thickness while maintaining constant its width and length. The angle of the hat-stiffener sidewalls is 120°, as recommended by Aneja et al. [20]. Based on these definitions, it is possible to build hat-stiffened plates with one to nine transverse stiffeners, with heights between 175 mm and 400 mm, and thicknesses from 4.75 mm to 12.7 mm. The FEM computational model is developed in ANSYS Mechanical APDL 2024 R2 software, with the SHELL281 finite element. The obtained results are analyzed and discussed, and then compared with those reported by Alves et al. [21], who adopted a similar approach to study the maximum and central deflections of plates reinforced with longitudinal hat-stiffeners.

In addition, the relevance of the present study also lies in its focus on thin steel plates reinforced with steel hat-stiffeners, a topic that remains relatively underexplored in the current literature. While a considerable number of the published works investigate hat-stiffened plates made of composite materials [22–33], there is a clear gap when it comes to similar studies involving steel, particularly under bending loads. Given the widespread use of steel structures in civil, naval, and offshore engineering, a deeper understanding of the structural behavior of steel hat-stiffened plates is essential. This article contributes to filling this gap by offering detailed numerical analyses and insights that are directly applicable to practical engineering design with conventional construction materials.

2. Materials and Methods

To carry out the evaluation and optimization of the geometric configurations of the simply supported A36 steel plates with transverse hat-stiffeners, the constructal design method was employed in conjunction with the exhaustive search technique. It is important to note that constructal design is a geometric evaluation method and not an optimization method. Therefore, for optimization to take place, the process must be combined with an optimization method, such as the exhaustive search technique. In this way, the constructal design method is responsible for generating the search space (possible geometric configurations) while the exhaustive search technique identifies the geometry that leads to the best system performance. For the constructal design application, it is also necessary to define global and/or local constraints, degrees of freedom (which vary within the defined constraints to generate the geometric configurations), and performance indicators (which can be minimized or maximized to improve the system performance) [12].

In addition, the simply supported boundary conditions were adopted for all numerical simulations. This choice reflects practical situations frequently encountered in structural applications, where stiffened plates are supported along their edges without full rotational restraint. Examples include steel floors, bridge panels, and ship deck structures, where the plate is allowed to rotate at the supports while its vertical displacement is constrained.

In turn, the choice of A36 steel for the present study is justified by its widespread use in civil construction and naval/offshore engineering, where stiffened steel plates are commonly employed to enhance structural performance under various loading conditions. A36 steel offers a balanced combination of mechanical strength, weldability, availability, and cost-effectiveness, making it a practical and widely adopted material for structural components. In civil construction, it is frequently used in floor systems, bridge components, and industrial buildings, where stiffeners improve load-bearing capacity and control deflection. In the naval and offshore sectors, A36 steel stiffened plates are found in ship hulls, decks, bulkheads, and offshore platform modules, where they provide mechanical resistance to bending and buckling. These applications reinforce the relevance of selecting A36 steel as a representative material for investigating the structural behavior of thin plates with hat-stiffeners.

To numerically simulate the mechanical behavior of all the geometries investigated in this work, the finite element method (FEM) was used through the ANSYS Mechanical APDL software (version 2024 R2, ANSYS Inc., Canonsburg, PA, USA). The SHELL281 finite element, illustrated in Figure 2 and suitable for modeling thin to moderately thick plates, was adopted for both the plate and the stiffeners in the present work, following its application in previous studies on plated structures [10,14,21]. SHELL281 is a finite element with 8 nodes and 6 degrees of freedom per node, consisting of 3 rotations (θx, θy, and θz) and 3 translations (Ux, Uy, and Uz) [34]. In the FEM, the unknown displacements are obtained through the matrix manipulation of a system of algebraic equations [1,35,36], represented as follows:

$$[K]\{U\} = \{F\}, \tag{1}$$

where $[K]$ is the global stiffness matrix, $\{U\}$ represents the vector of nodal displacements to be obtained, and $\{F\}$ represents the vector of nodal forces, equivalent to the forces applied to the system. To ensure that the computational model is correctly defined, validations and verifications were carried out, comparing its results with those presented in the references found in the literature.

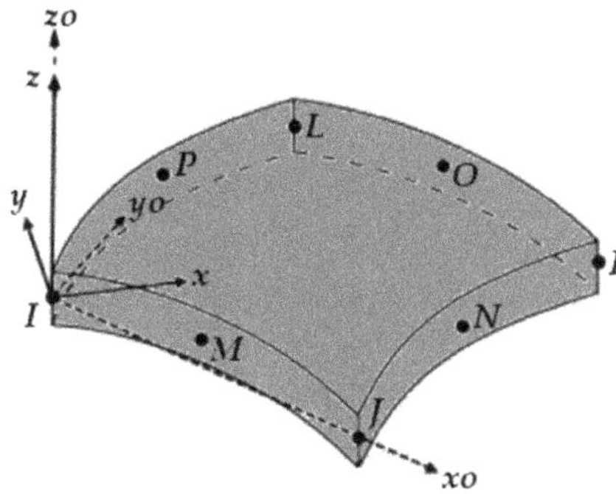

Figure 2. Geometry of the SHELL281 element, adapted from [34].

Regarding the case study, as previously mentioned, this work aims to analyze simply supported rectangular steel plates subjected to uniformly distributed loads, reinforced with trapezoidal hat-stiffeners positioned transversely to the plate's longest dimension. The main objective is to use the constructal design method, combined with the exhaustive search technique, to minimize both the maximum and central displacements of the hat-stiffened plates by varying the height and thickness of the stiffeners. To establish the initial dimensions of the stiffeners, a reference plate (without stiffeners) was considered, with a width of a = 2000 mm, length of b = 1000 mm, and a thickness of t_{rp} = 20 mm. A volumetric fraction corresponding to 30% of the total volume of the plate [13,14,21] was removed and transformed into stiffeners. Since a and b were considered constraints, the reduction was made in the plate's thickness. Thus, the plates with hat-stiffeners had their thickness reduced to t = 14 mm. It is important to mention that the total material volume of the plates with stiffeners remained equal to the reference plate, since there was only a material redistribution, with the removed volume being transformed into hat-stiffeners. The material used was A36 steel, which has an elastic modulus of E = 200 GPa and a Poisson's ratio of ν = 0.3, such as in [13,14,21]. All four edges of the hat-stiffened plates are considered to be simply supported, and a distributed load of 10 kPa is applied [13,14,21]. This load level was chosen to ensure that the structural response remains within the elastic regime. In addition, the sidewalls of the hat-stiffeners have an inclination angle of 120°, as indicated by Aneja et al. [20]. Figure 3 shows a schematic representation of a plate with two transverse hat-stiffeners. The thickness of the hat-stiffeners was based on commercially available plate thicknesses: t_s = 4.75 mm; t_s = 6.35 mm; t_s = 8.00 mm; t_s = 9.53 mm, and t_s = 12.7 mm. The height of the stiffeners, h_s, is related to the number of stiffeners, and the following maximum values were adopted: h_s = 400 mm (one stiffener); h_s = 250 mm (two and three stiffeners), and h_s = 175 mm (four or more stiffeners). The application of the constructal design method allowed for the generation of 224 distinct geometries of plates with transverse hat-stiffeners. Appendix A presents the dimensions of the stiffeners used in each geometric configuration, as well as the numerical results obtained in terms of the maximum and central deflection for each proposed geometric configuration, through the Tables A1–A9.

As can be seen in the example with two stiffeners, as shown in Figure 3, in order to allow multiple plates to be joined together, the distance from the transverse stiffeners to the edge of the plate will always be half the distance between the stiffeners. An exception occurs when only one transverse stiffener is used—in this case, it will be centered along the longest dimension of the plate. Also in Figure 3, b_t represents the base width of the hat-stiffener, and n' represents the distance between two stiffeners.

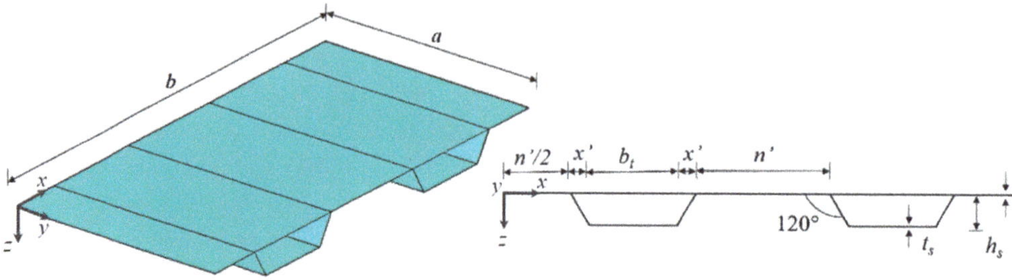

Figure 3. Schematic representation of a plate with two transverse hat-stiffeners.

3. Results and Discussions

3.1. Computational Model Validation and Verification

Although the validation and verification procedures were previously presented by Alves et al. [21], they are reproduced here to clearly show the accuracy of the proposed computational model.

Regarding the model validation, an experimental study developed by Carrijo et al. [37] was numerically simulated. Figure 4a presents the geometry of the plate with I-shaped stiffeners, which has its four corners simply supported. A uniformly distributed load of 0.96 kPa is applied to the stiffened plate. The material of the plate and stiffeners has the following mechanical properties: E = 2.5 GPa and ν = 0.36. For this analysis, a converged regular mesh generated by square SHELL281 finite elements was adopted, each with a side length of 2.436 mm. Figure 4b shows the numerical result for the out-of-plane displacement distribution. The experimental test performed by Carrijo et al. [37] found a central deflection of U_z = 6.2200 mm, whereas the proposed computational model found a central deflection of U_z = 6.5075 mm. Therefore, a relative error of 4.58% between the numerical and experimental results was reached. However, it is worth explaining that the comparison with the experiment presented by Carrijo et al. [37] serves as a representative validation that supports the general reliability of the proposed FEM strategy. Although there are some differences (such as the type of stiffeners, dimensions, material, and boundary conditions), the numerical simulation of this case allows for the assessment of whether the computational model can accurately capture the fundamental physical behavior of the stiffened plates under bending. That said, one can consider the computational model validated through a proof-of-concept strategy, which is commonly adopted when an exact experimental counterpart is not available.

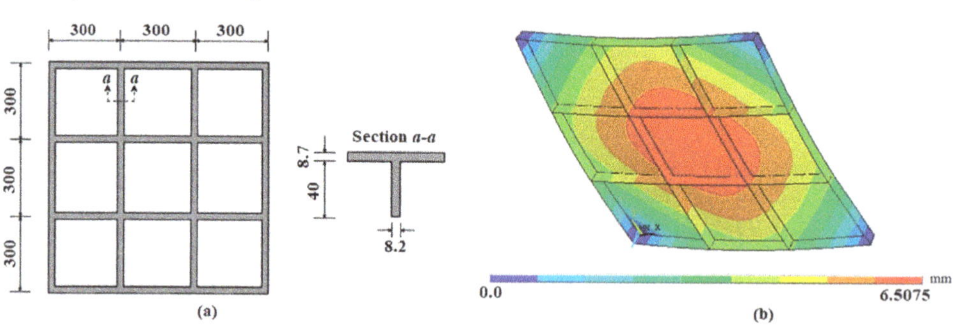

Figure 4. Validation of the computational model: (**a**) dimensions (in mm) of the stiffened plate experimentally tested, adapted from [37]; (**b**) deflection distribution obtained numerically with the proposed computational model (adapted from [21]).

After that, when considering simply supported hat-stiffened steel plates, two computational model verifications were carried out. The first consisted of comparing the results obtained in this study with those of Tharian and Nandakumar [16], who modeled a plate with two stiffeners (Figure 5) using the finite elements SHELL63 and SHELL93. The hat-stiffened plate is subjected to a uniform distributed loading of 10 kPa, and it is made of steel with E = 210 GPa and ν = 0.3.

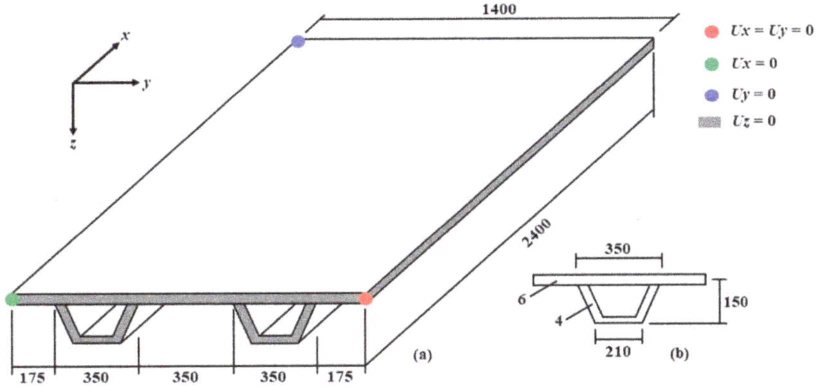

Figure 5. First verification of the computational model, adapted from [16]: (**a**) dimensions (in mm) of the plate with stiffeners, and (**b**) details of the hat-stiffeners.

The results can be seen in Figure 6. Employing a converged mesh of square SHELL281 finite elements with a size of 10 mm, a maximum displacement of 0.7295 mm was found with the proposed numerical model, while Tharian and Nandakumar [16] obtained values of 0.7198 mm (SHELL63) and 0.7214 mm (SHELL93), resulting in relative differences of 1.35% and 1.12%, respectively, thus verifying the proposed numerical model.

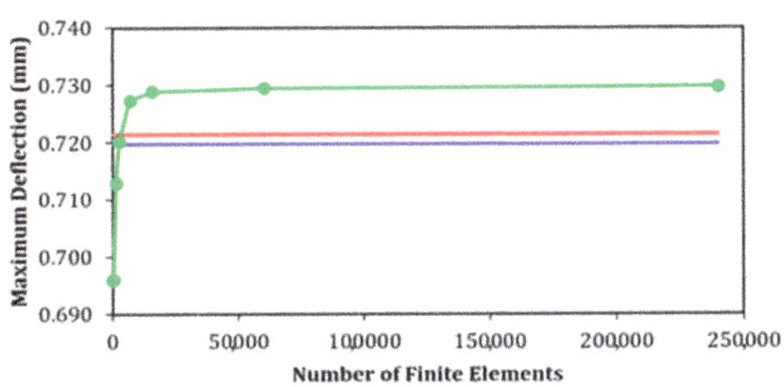

Figure 6. Mesh convergence and results of the first verification: SHELL63 (the blue line, adapted from [16]), SHELL93 (the red line, adapted from [16]) and SHELL 281 (the green line, the present study).

The second verification was carried out considering a simply supported steel plate with a centered hat-stiffener, as shown in Figure 7. A total of 25 hat-stiffener configurations were analyzed, which were simulated using the finite elements SHELL181 for the plate and BEAM3 for the hat-stiffener in the study conducted by Pal et al. [17]. It is worth mentioning that, despite the hat-stiffener having different dimensions (as presented in Table 1), its total volume is kept constant and equal to 320,000 mm^3 in the 25 configurations.

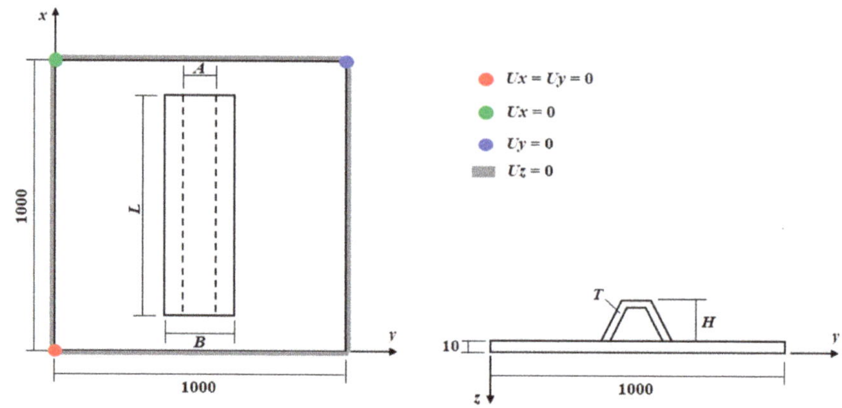

Figure 7. Second verification of the computational model. The plate analyzed with a centered hat-stiffener (in mm), adapted from [17].

Table 1. Dimensions (in mm, see Figure 7) of the hat-stiffener for the second verification [17].

Case	Thickness (*T*)	Shorter Base (*A*)	Longer Base (*B*)	Height (*H*)	Length (*L*)
1	2	35	60	65	955.90
2	3	35	60	65	637.26
3	4	35	60	65	477.95
4	5	35	60	65	382.36
5	6	35	60	65	318.63
6	2	40	60	65	932.78
7	3	40	60	65	621.86
8	4	40	60	65	466.39
9	5	40	60	65	373.11
10	6	40	60	65	310.93
11	2	40	65	70	878.09
12	3	40	65	70	585.39
13	4	40	65	70	439.04
14	5	40	65	70	351.23
15	6	40	65	70	292.70
16	2	40	60	70	881.92
17	3	40	60	70	587.95
18	4	40	60	70	440.96
19	5	40	60	70	352.77
20	6	40	60	70	293.97
21	2	35	65	65	950.02
22	3	35	65	65	633.35
23	4	35	65	65	475.01
24	5	35	65	65	380.01
25	6	35	65	65	316.67

Moreover, both the plate and the hat-stiffener are made of steel with E = 200 GPa and ν = 0.3, being subjected to a uniform distributed load of 1 kPa. A mesh convergence test was carried out, considering Case 1 of Table 1, and defining a mesh generated with square SHELL281 finite elements with a size of 10 mm for the 25 cases.

Figure 8 presents the results obtained with the proposed model in comparison with those of Pal et al. [17]. Among all cases, the average relative difference was 3.3%, and the maximum relative difference was 5%, which verifies the developed computational model.

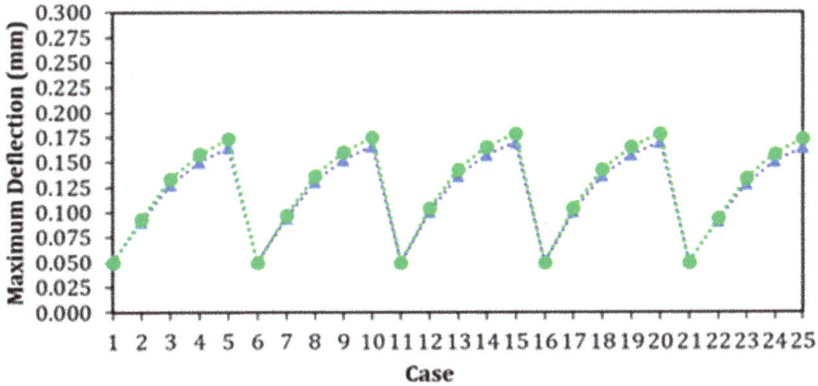

Figure 8. Results of the second verification for the 25 cases: the blue dot line shows the SHELL181 and BEAM3 adapted from [17], and the green dot line shows the SHELL181 and BEAM3 in the present study.

3.2. Case Study

As previously explained, a reference plate without stiffeners was adopted, and all geometric configurations of plates with stiffeners were derived from this plate, maintaining the two conditions: (i) the total material volume of the reference plate and the plates with hat-stiffeners is the same, by transforming 30% of the reference plate's volume into stiffeners; and (ii) the angle of the stiffener's side wall must be 120°, as shown in Figure 3. Based on this approach, it was possible to generate, through the constructal design method, the geometric configurations of plates with transverse stiffeners, varying between one and nine stiffeners, and considering five different thicknesses for the stiffeners.

A mesh convergence test was performed using the hat-stiffened plate with the highest level of complexity, that is, the plate with nine stiffeners. In this test, the SHELL281 element was used, with square shapes forming regular meshes with sizes ranging from 5 to 40 mm. The maximum deflection of the hat-stiffened plate was evaluated for each tested mesh. Observing Figure 9, one can infer that the results stabilized at mesh M5 (10 mm), which was adopted for the spatial discretization of all 224 numerically simulated cases.

As the main purpose of applying the constructal design method is to increase its structural efficiency by understanding how the variation of the geometric configuration leads to superior mechanical performance, the numerical results obtained in terms of the maximum and central out-of-plane displacement were recorded, and can be seen in Figures 10–18 for the plates with one to nine transverse hat-stiffeners, respectively. In addition, the maximum deflection of the reference plate (with no stiffeners) is also plotted in Figures 10–18.

As can be seen, except for a few cases with one stiffener (see Figure 10), all maximum and central deflections were less than those of the reference plate. In other words, for the vast majority of cases, transforming 30% of the reference plate material into hat-stiffeners improved the structural mechanical performance. Furthermore, as illustrated in Figures 10–18, there is a very small difference between the maximum and central deflections, except for specific cases, such as the plate with one stiffener (see Figure 10), with a thickness of 12.70 mm and heights greater than 200 mm, and the plate with two stiffeners, with thicknesses of 6.35 mm and 8.00 mm (see Figure 11). In general, it can also be observed that, as the hat-stiffener height increases, the hat-stiffened plate displacements decrease.

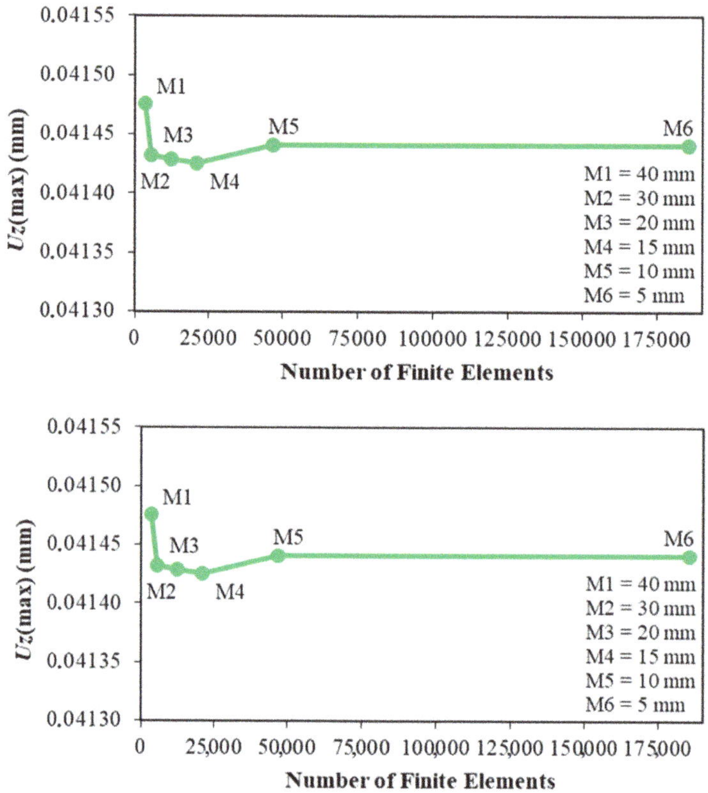

Figure 9. Convergence test for the present study.

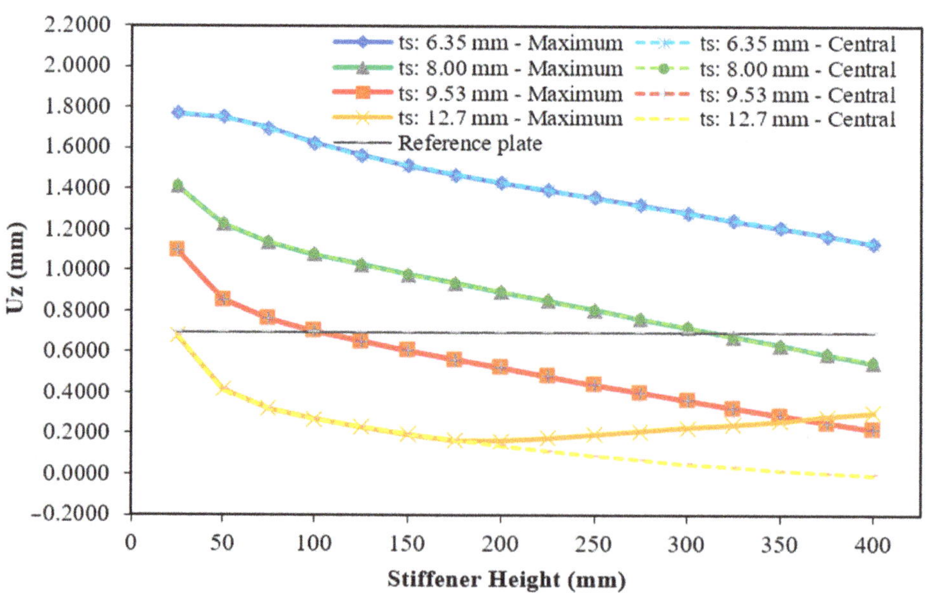

Figure 10. Maximum and central deflection for the plate with one hat-stiffener.

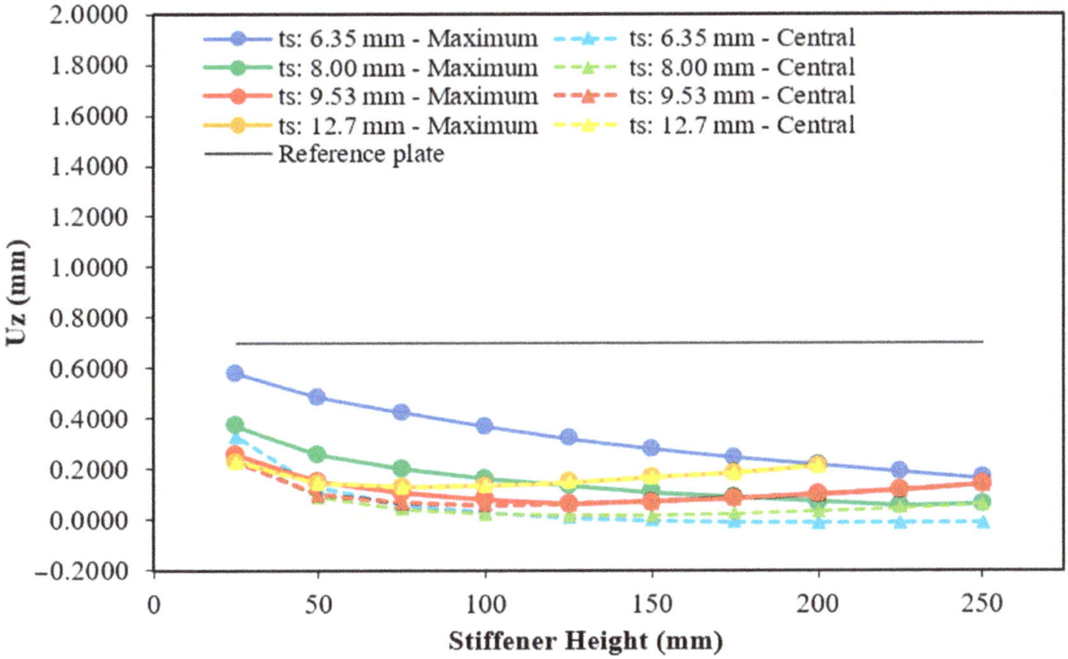

Figure 11. Maximum and central deflection for the plate with two hat-stiffeners.

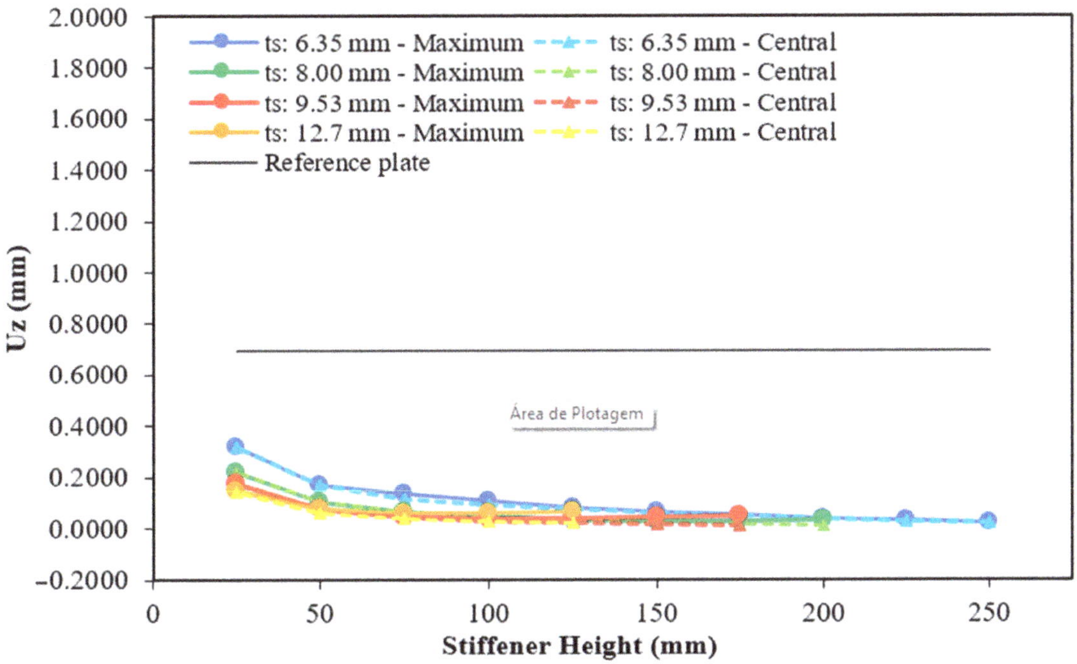

Figure 12. Maximum and central deflection for the plate with three hat-stiffeners.

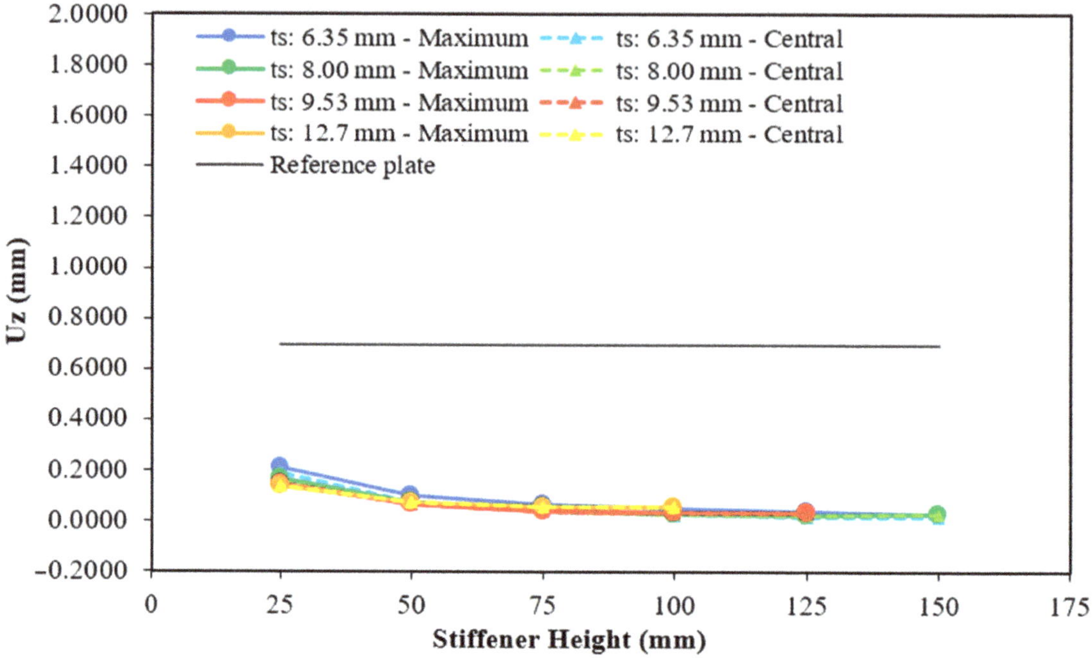

Figure 13. Maximum and central deflection for the plate with four hat-stiffeners.

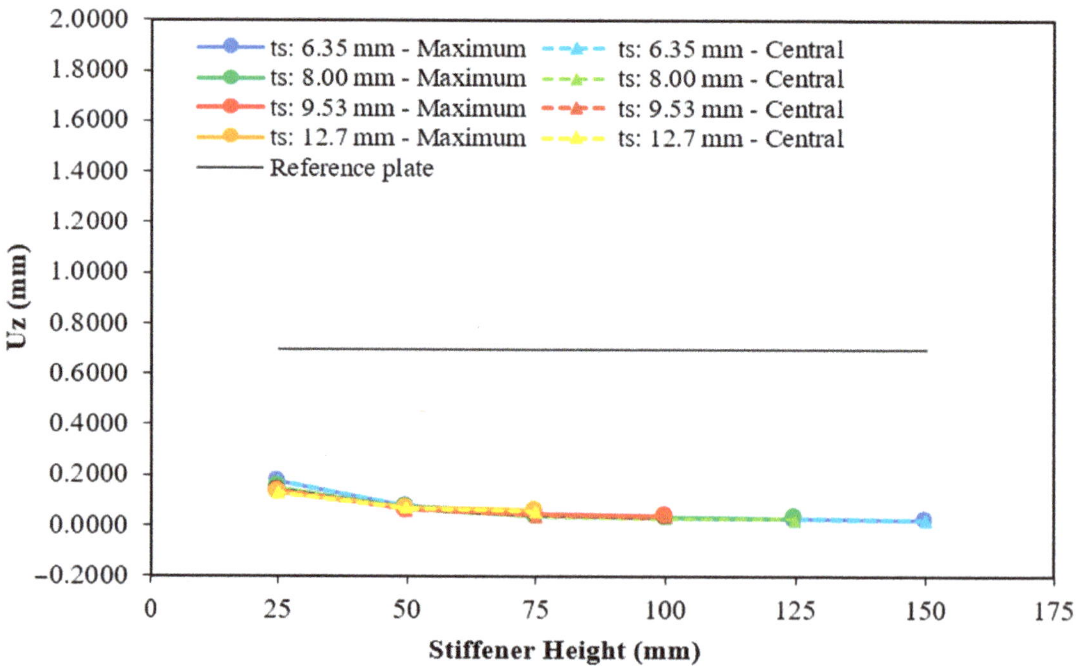

Figure 14. Maximum and central deflection for the plate with five hat-stiffeners.

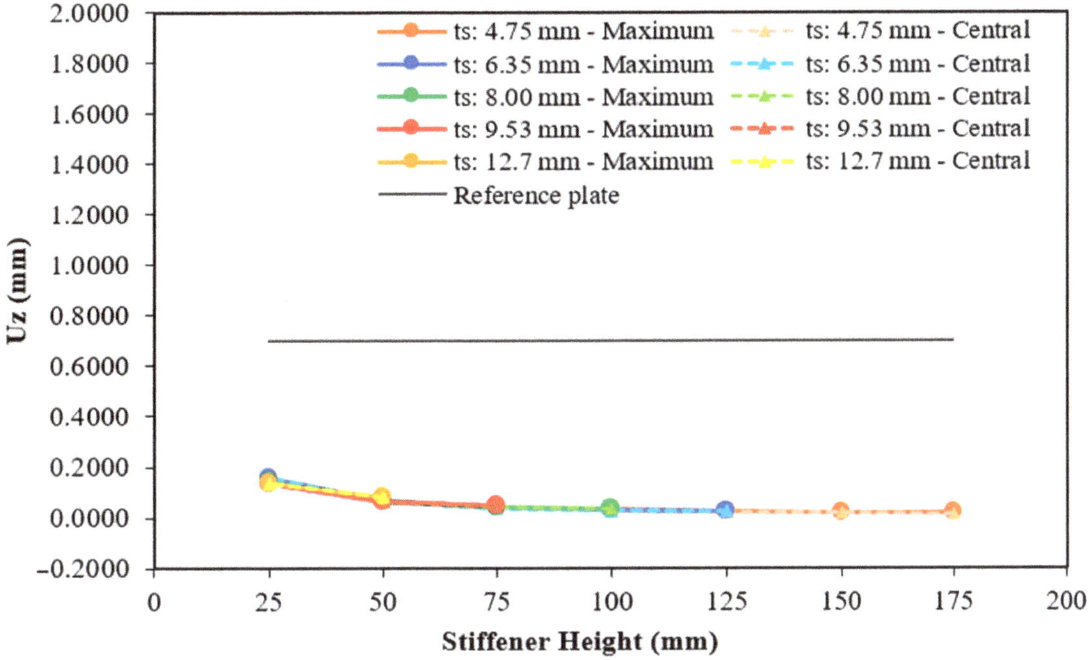

Figure 15. Maximum and central deflection for the plate with six hat-stiffeners.

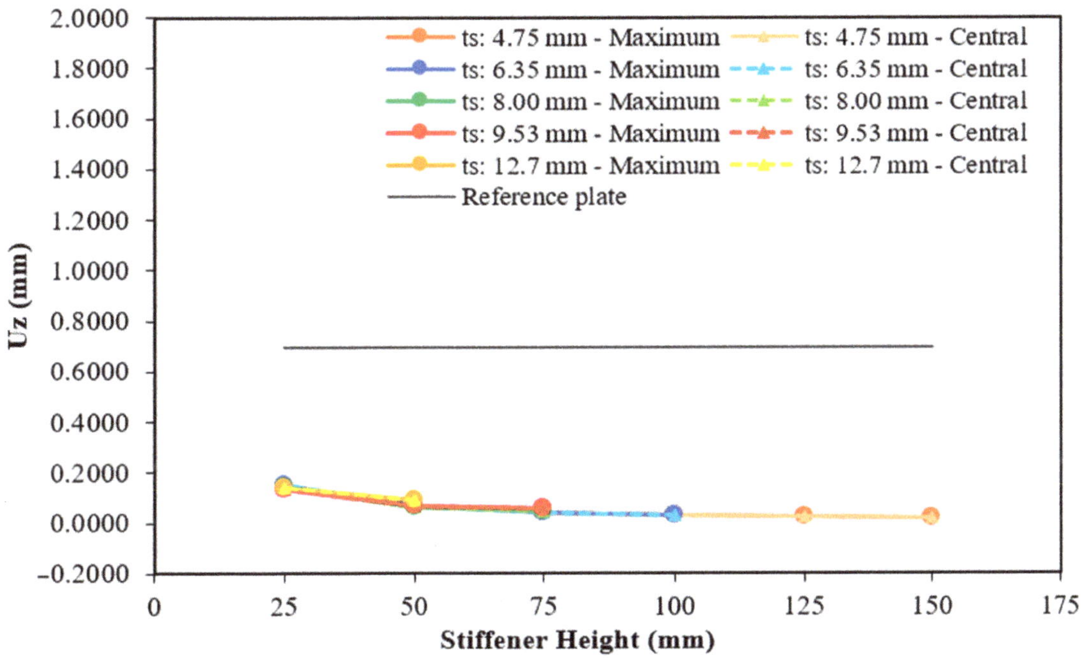

Figure 16. Maximum and central deflection for the plate with seven hat-stiffeners.

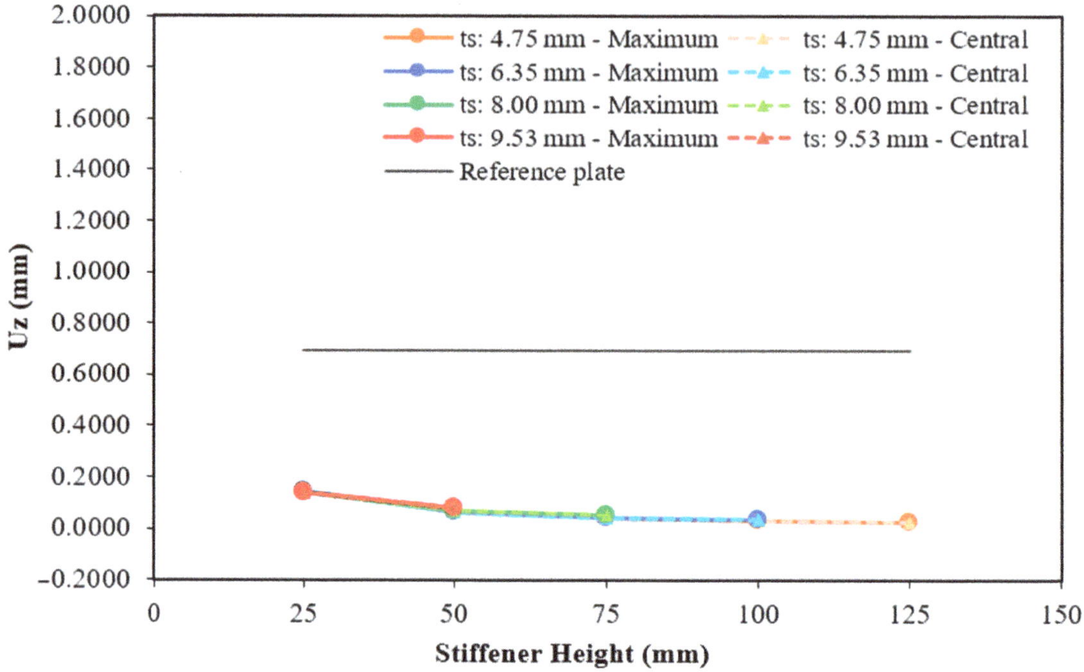

Figure 17. Maximum and central deflection for the plate with eight hat-stiffeners.

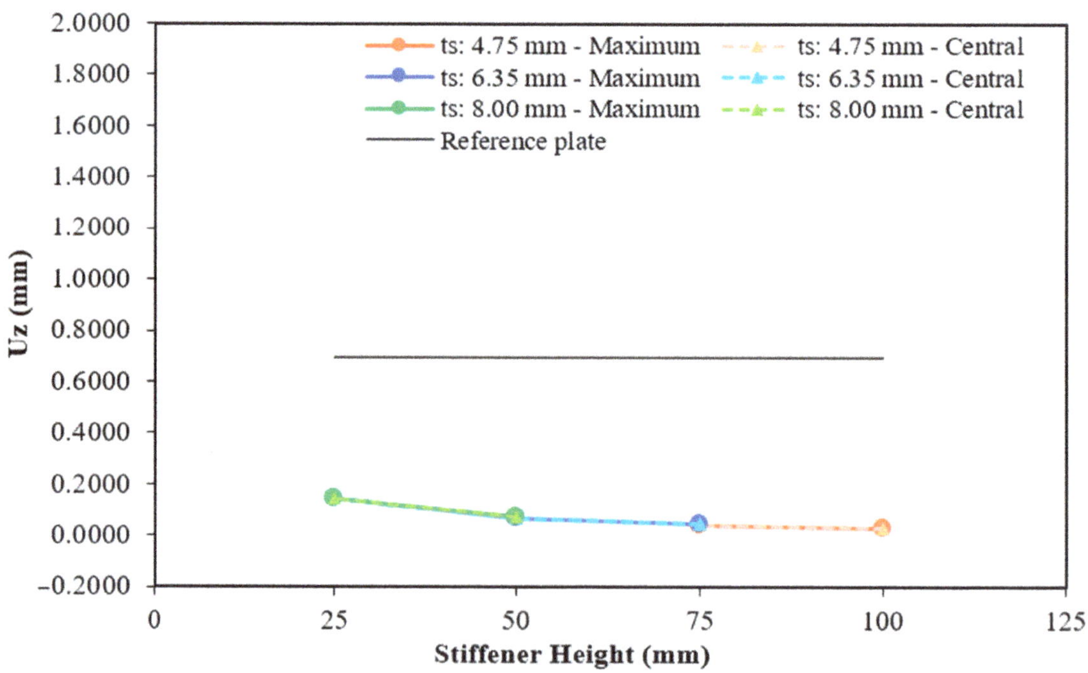

Figure 18. Maximum and central deflection for the plate with nine hat-stiffeners.

Regarding the case with one stiffener (see Figure 10), 66 geometries were evaluated considering four commercial thicknesses. In general, one can observe that the largest deflections occur with the smallest stiffener thickness, while the smallest deflections occur with the largest thickness. The best result is achieved when the stiffener has a height of 200 mm and a thickness of 12.70 mm, showing an improvement of 76.39% in the maximum deflection and 80.04% in the central deflection compared to the reference plate. Unlike other configurations, for the 12.70 mm thickness, only the central deflection of the plate follows the pattern in which the greater stiffener heights result in smaller deflections—even generating a negative central deflection at the maximum height (400 mm). Meanwhile, the results for the maximum deflection initially decrease up to the intermediate height considered, and then increase as the hat-stiffener height increases. This behavior occurs due to two factors: (i) the transverse stiffener is located in the central region of the plate, leaving large areas of the plate "unstiffened"; and (ii) at greater heights, the hat-stiffener takes on a geometric shape that increases the stiffness of this region, causing the largest displacements to occur in the "unstiffened" regions of the plate, as can be seen in Figure 19.

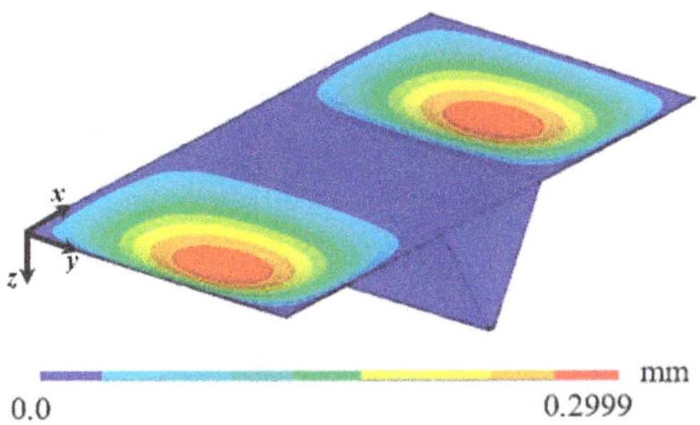

Figure 19. Displacement distribution of the plate having one transverse hat-stiffener, with h_s = 400 mm and t_s = 12.70 mm.

In turn, when two hat-stiffeners are considered (see Figure 11) it is possible to identify that the maximum and central deflections coincide only for the cases having thickness of 12.70 mm and heights greater than 100 mm for the 9.53 mm thickness. Unlike the other cases presented, in which the deflections decrease as the height increases, in these thicknesses, the deflections decrease up to an intermediate height (75 mm for the 12.70 mm thickness) and then increase, because, as in the plate with one stiffener, the geometry of the stiffeners and their location influence the distribution of displacements along the structure, as can be seen in Figure 20. For the other thicknesses (6.35 mm and 8.00 mm), although the maximum and central deflections do not coincide, their values decrease with the increasing height, with the central deflection always being smaller than the maximum. When adopting the 6.35 mm thickness, the central deflection above a height of 150 mm assumed negative values, because the central region of the plate has greater stiffness due to the geometry of the transverse hat-stiffener. The maximum height adopted for the stiffeners in this case was 250 mm, making it possible to carry out 38 geometric analyses. The smallest maximum deflection occurs at a height of 225 mm when using a stiffener with a thickness of 8.00 mm. Thus, the maximum and central deflections were 0.0545 mm and 0.0466 mm, respectively. These results show a reduction of 92.19% and 93.32% in relation to the maximum and central deflections of the reference plate. On the other hand, the worst result occurs at a height of 25 mm and a thickness of 6.35 mm, with values of 0.5790 mm and 0.3262 mm for the maximum and central deflection, with a reduction of 17.00% and 53.24%, respectively.

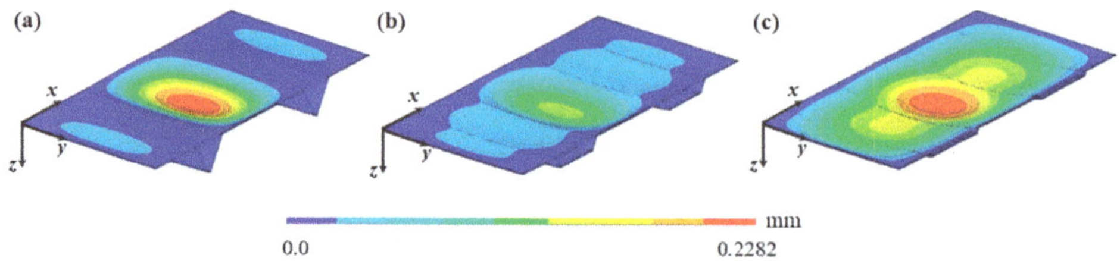

Figure 20. Displacement distribution of the plate having two transverse hat-stiffeners for a t_s = 12.70 mm: (**a**) h_s = 200 mm; (**b**) h_s = 75 mm; and (**c**) h_s = 25 mm.

For the plates with three transverse hat-stiffeners, Figure 12 presents the results of the 30 geometric configurations investigated, indicating a reduction in the maximum and central deflections as the height of the stiffeners increases. For the thicknesses of 6.35 mm and 8.00 mm, small differences between the maximum and central deflections were observed. However, for the thickness of 9.53 mm, the difference between the maximum and central deflection values starts to increase at heights above 75 mm. When adopting the thickness of 12.70 mm, there is also a difference between the maximum and central deflection, with the central deflection being smaller than the maximum. These differences between the maximum and central deflections are associated with the presence of a stiffener at the center of the plate, leading to a phenomenon similar to the plates with one or two stiffeners, where changes in the geometry cause displacements to concentrate in regions with lower structural stiffness. Unlike the previous geometric configurations, where the lowest deflection occurs either in the largest thickness or in an intermediate thickness, for the plates with three hat-stiffeners, the lowest deflection was achieved in the smallest thickness of 6.35 mm and at a height of 250 mm—the largest among those analyzed—with values of 0.0252 mm for the maximum deflection and 0.0227 mm for the central deflection. This result shows a reduction of 96.38% and 96.74% in relation to the maximum and central deflections of the reference plate. On the other hand, the worst result also occurs in the 6.35 mm thickness, but at the smallest height of 25 mm, 2.2 times smaller than the result of the reference plate, with the maximum and central deflection being 0.3169 mm.

From Figure 13 the results for the plate with four transverse hat-stiffeners can be viewed. There is no variation between the maximum and central deflections for stiffener thicknesses greater than 8 mm. The 6.35 mm thickness showed both the highest and lowest deflection values, showing variations of up to 49%. Still, for the 6.35 mm thickness, greater displacements were observed in the outermost stiffeners compared to the central stiffeners, as depicted in Figure 21, which are probable causes of the significant variations recorded for this hat-stiffeners thickness. The maximum height for this stiffeners arrangement was 150 mm, resulting in 21 geometric configurations analyzed. The lowest maximum deflection occurs when stiffeners with a thickness of 8.00 mm and a height of 125 mm are used, resulting in a maximum and central deflection of 0.0253 mm—a reduction of 96.38%. The worst result corresponds to 0.2115 mm and 0.1882 mm for the maximum and central deflection, respectively, with stiffeners of 25 mm in height and 6.35 mm in thickness. However, even in this case, there is still an improvement of 69.68% and 73.03% over the maximum and central deflections of the reference plate.

When using five transverse hat-stiffeners in the plate (see Figure 14), the stiffeners' height restrictions become more severe as its thickness increases. Thus, 18 geometric analyses were carried out, with the maximum height being 150 mm for a thickness of 6.35 mm and 75 mm of the maximum height for a thickness of 12.70 mm. The smallest and largest maximum deflection results occur when the stiffeners have a thickness of 6.35 mm.

The best result happens at the greatest height of 150 mm, with the maximum and central deflections of 0.0211 mm, about 33 times smaller than the deflections of the reference plate. On the other hand, the worst result, which occurs at the smallest height (25 mm), presents the maximum and central deflections of 0.1771 mm, a relative difference of 74.61% compared to the reference plate.

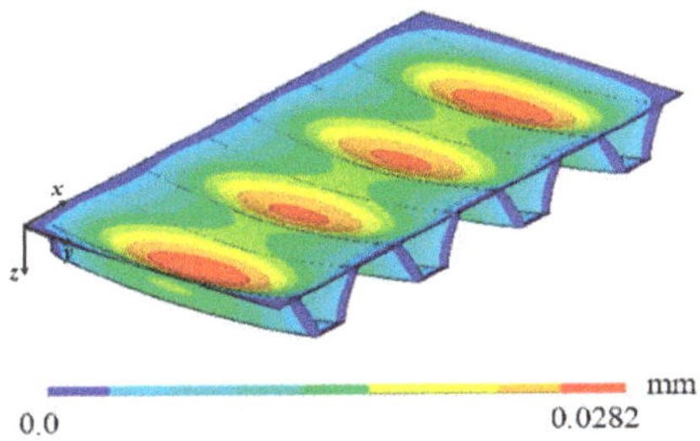

Figure 21. Displacement distribution in the plate with four transverse stiffeners with t_s = 6.35 mm and h_s = 150 mm.

Using six hat-stiffeners, it was also possible to numerically investigate 18 geometric configurations of stiffened plates (see Figure 15), varying the stiffener thickness between 4.75 mm and 12.70 mm. The geometry that achieved the lowest deflection result used transverse stiffeners with a thickness of 4.75 mm and a height of 175 mm (a combination of the smallest thickness and the greatest height), resulting in a maximum deflection of 0.0199 mm and a central deflection of 0.0166 mm. These values represent reductions of 97.15% and 97.62%, respectively, compared to the deflections of the reference plate. The highest deflection result occurs with stiffeners of 25 mm in height and 6.35 mm in thickness, with values of 0.1594 mm for the maximum deflection and 0.1562 mm for the central deflection. These values are approximately 4.4 times smaller than those of the reference plate.

For the plates with seven transverse hat-stiffeners (see Figure 16), it was possible to perform 16 geometric analyses, from which the lowest deflection result was obtained with a height of 150 mm and a thickness of 4.75 mm. Both the maximum and central deflections were 0.0220 mm, representing a 96.84% improvement over the reference plate. As in the previous case, the worst result occurs in the plate with stiffeners of 25 mm in height and 6.35 mm in thickness, with the maximum and central deflections of 0.1525 mm, corresponding to a reduction of 78.14%.

By adding eight transverse hat-stiffeners to the plate (see Figure 17), the number of analyses was reduced to 12 due to the problem's constraints. There was little variation between the maximum and central deflection and, in general, the best results were found with the smallest stiffener thicknesses. The smallest deflection occurred for the plate with hat-stiffeners having 125 mm in height and 4.75 mm in thickness. The maximum and central deflections achieved reached a reduction of approximately 96% in the plate's displacements, with values of 0.0257 mm and 0.0255 mm, respectively. On the other hand, the highest deflection was 0.1478 mm for the maximum deflection and 0.1473 mm for the central deflection, approximately 78.80% lower than the displacements of the reference plate.

Finally, from Figure 18, only seven geometric configurations were possible for the plates with nine transverse hat-stiffeners. The lowest deflection result was 0.0315 mm for both the maximum and central deflections, achieved by adopting a stiffener height of 75 mm and a thickness of 4.75 mm, representing a 95.34% reduction compared to the reference plate. The highest values for the maximum and central deflections were 0.1466 mm, obtained with a height of 25 mm and a thickness of 6.35 mm, corresponding to a 4.76-fold reduction in plate deflections compared to the reference plate.

Based on the results presented in Figures 10–18, Table 2 compiles the best and worst cases according to the number of transverse hat-stiffeners in the plate, as well as the relative difference (RD) between the maximum and central deflections of the hat-stiffened plates and the reference plate.

Table 2. Best and worst results of the maximum and central deflections according to the number of hat-stiffeners in the transverse direction of the plate.

Number of Hat-Stiffeners	h_s (mm)	t_s (mm)	U_z^{max} (mm)	$U_z^{central}$ (mm)	RD (%) U_z^{max}	RD (%) $U_z^{central}$
1	200	12.7	0.1647	0.1392	−76.39	−80.04
	25	6.35	1.7712	1.7712	153.90	153.90
2	225	8.00	0.0545	0.0466	−92.19	−93.32
	25	6.35	0.5790	0.3262	−17.00	−53.24
3	250	6.35	0.0252	0.0227	−96.38	−96.74
	25	6.35	0.3169	0.3169	−54.56	−54.56
4	125	8.00	0.0253	0.0253	−96.38	−96.38
	25	6.35	0.2115	0.1882	−69.68	−73.03
5	150	6.35	0.0211	0.0211	−96.97	−96.97
	25	6.35	0.1771	0.1771	−74.61	−74.61
6	175	4.75	0.0199	0.0166	−97.15	−97.62
	25	6.35	0.1594	0.1562	−77.15	−77.61
7	150	4.75	0.0220	0.0220	−96.84	−96.84
	25	6.35	0.1525	0.1525	−78.14	−78.14
8	125	4.75	0.0257	0.0245	−96.31	−96.49
	25	6.35	0.1478	0.1473	−78.82	−78.88
9	100	4.75	0.0315	0.0315	−95.48	−95.48
	25	6.35	0.1466	0.1466	−78.98	−78.98

From Table 2, one can infer that the configurations with 3 and from 5 to 9 transverse hat-stiffeners, the lowest displacements occur in the configurations with greater heights and smaller thickness. On the other hand, with a single transverse stiffener, the maximum displacement occurred at an intermediate height with the greatest thickness. Table 2 reinforces the observation that displacements decrease with the increase in the height of the transverse hat-stiffeners.

Figure 22 shows the displacement distribution of the best case for each of the nine proposed groups of transverse hat-stiffened plate geometries. It is worth noting that the same color scale was used for all geometric configurations, allowing a visual identification of how the variation in geometry influences the magnitude of out-of-plane displacements.

The observation of Figure 22 indicates that reducing the number of transverse stiffeners leads to a concentration of the displacement field in specific regions, accentuating the maximum displacements. On the other hand, increasing the number of transverse stiffeners leads to a more uniform displacement distribution, with a tendency to concentrate along the longitudinal central axis (perpendicular to the transverse stiffeners). This behavior is in agreement with the constructal principle of the optimal distribution of imperfections [9,10], allowing to identify the case having six hat-stiffeners (Figure 22f) as the optimized geometric configuration that conducted to the superior structural performance, corroborating the data presented in Table 2.

It was also observed among the obtained results and illustrated in Figure 22 that, mainly in the cases of plates with one (Figure 22a) and three (Figure 22c) transverse hat-stiffeners, the maximum deflection is different from the central deflection of the stiffened plate. The existence of a transverse hat-stiffener aligned with the transverse central axis of the plate increased the stiffness in this region and directed the displacement field toward the 'non-stiffened' regions, located laterally to the stiffener in the case of the plate with one hat-stiffener, and between stiffeners, in the case of the plate with three hat-stiffeners. The size of the 'non-stiffened' regions in these two cases may also have influenced this behavior.

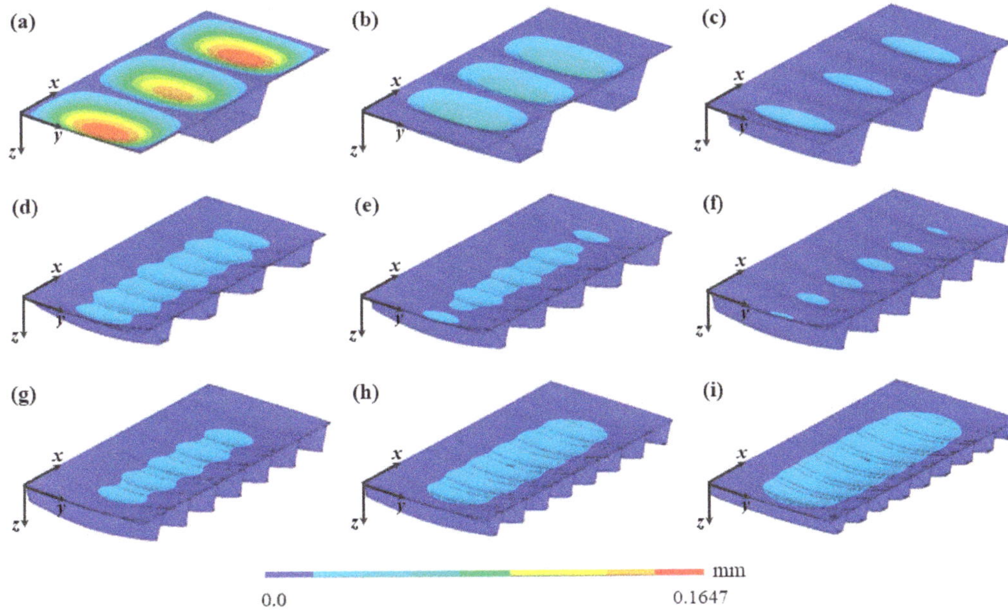

Figure 22. Deflection distribution of the best geometric configurations among the studied plates, with: (**a**) one hat-stiffener; (**b**) two hat-stiffeners; (**c**) three hat-stiffeners; (**d**) four hat-stiffeners; (**e**) five hat-stiffeners; (**f**) six hat-stiffeners; (**g**) seven hat-stiffeners; (**h**) eight hat-stiffeners; and (**i**) nine hat-stiffeners.

3.3. Comparison Between Plates Reinforced with Transverse or Longitudinal Hat-Stiffeners

As previously mentioned, Alves et al. [21] studied a structural component with the same characteristics considered in this work, but with hat-stiffeners oriented longitudinally on the plate. Both works adopted the same approach, i.e., the constructal design method combined with the exhaustive search technique, and the constraint that a maximum of 30% of the reference plate volume could be transformed into longitudinal or transverse hat-stiffeners. In addition, the dimensions of the reference plate, boundary conditions, and applied loading are the same in both works, thus allowing a fair comparison between the hat-stiffened plates with transverse or longitudinal stiffeners.

Considering the constraints and degrees of freedom, five groups of geometries were generated, with plates containing from one to five longitudinal hat-stiffeners in Alves et al. [21]. The hat-stiffeners height ranged from 25 mm to 300 mm. The plate thickness and the lateral wall angle of the stiffeners are the same as those adopted in the present work (120°). In total, 100 different geometric configurations were generated, numerically simulated, and analyzed by Alves et al. [21]. Table 3 presents the best and worst results in terms of the central and maximum deflection for each number of longitudinal hat-stiffeners.

When comparing the results related to transverse hat-stiffeners (presented in Table 2) with those related to longitudinal stiffeners (presented in Table 3) for analogous plates under the same boundary and loading conditions, it is observed that the transverse hat-stiffeners demonstrated greater structural efficiency. This statement is supported by the fact that the results obtained using the hat-stiffeners in the transverse direction of the plates showed a noticeable reduction in both the maximum and central displacements when compared to those achieved in the configuration with the hat-stiffened plates in the longitudinal direction.

Table 3. Best and worst results of the maximum and central deflections according to the number of hat-stiffeners in the longitudinal direction of the plate.

Number of Hat-Stiffeners	h_s (mm)	t_s (mm)	U_z^{max} (mm)	$U_z^{central}$ (mm)	RD (%) U_z^{max}	RD (%) $U_z^{central}$
1	250	9.53	0.0958	0.0958	−86.26	−86.26
	250	4.75	1.7735	1.7735	154.23	154.23
2	150	6.35	0.1381	0.1266	−80.20	−81.84
	25	6.35	0.5371	0.5371	−23.01	−23.01
3	150	4.75	0.1244	0.1244	−82.17	−82.17
	25	6.35	0.4497	0.4497	−35.53	−35.53
4	125	4.75	0.1650	0.1650	−76.34	−76.34
	25	9.53	0.6344	0.6345	−9.06	−9.04
5	100	4.75	0.2259	0.2259	−67.61	−67.61
	25	8.00	0.6014	0.6014	−13.79	−13.79

In Figure 23, the out-of-plane displacement distributions of the cases that achieved the best performance with the longitudinal hat-stiffeners (Figure 23a) and the transverse hat-stiffeners (Figure 23b) are depicted. It is observed that the use of a single longitudinal hat-stiffener in the plate, with a height of h_s = 250 mm and a thickness of t_s = 9.53 mm, resulted in a reduction of 86.26% in both the maximum and central deflections when compared to the values obtained for the reference plate. On the other hand, when employing six hat-stiffeners in the transverse direction of the plate, with a height of h_s = 175 mm and a thickness of t_s = 4.75 mm, there was a reduction of 97.62% in the central deflection and 97.15% in the maximum deflection, when compared to the reference plate. The direct comparison between the best case with the longitudinal hat-stiffeners and the best case with the transverse hat-stiffeners shows that the maximum deflections obtained using the transverse stiffeners are 79.27% smaller. The greater efficiency of the transverse stiffeners in reducing deflections can be explained by the fact that their walls are parallel to the shortest span. According to Araújo [38] and Nogueira et al. [14], the bending moment demand is higher in the direction of the shortest span. Therefore, using a geometric configuration that increases the stiffness in the direction of the shortest span leads to a reduction in deflections.

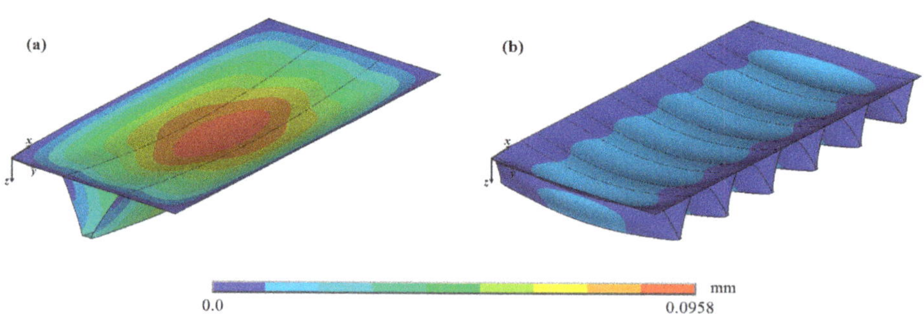

Figure 23. Best cases obtained using hat-stiffeners: (**a**) longitudinal direction and (**b**) transverse direction.

4. Conclusions

This study investigated the structural efficiency, in terms of deflection, of a steel plate with hat-stiffeners installed in the transverse direction of the plate. The constructal design method was employed together with the exhaustive search technique to convert 30% of the volume of an unstiffened reference plate into transverse stiffeners. Considering the imposed constraints and degrees of freedom, a total of 224 geometries were generated. The numerical simulation of these geometries was carried out using a computational model developed in the FEM, which was verified and validated.

As one of the main purposes of using stiffeners is to reduce plate deflection, the primary objective of this work was to minimize the displacements occurring in the hat-stiffened plates. The results obtained showed that the vast majority of the tested configurations reduced the displacements when compared to the reference plate. The best result was achieved by using six transverse hat-stiffeners with a height of 175 mm and a thickness of 4.75 mm, leading to a reduction of approximately 97% in both the maximum and central deflections of the plate compared to the unstiffened reference plate. This demonstrates that the strategic development of hat-stiffeners can significantly improve the efficiency of steel plates in terms of deflection reduction.

Comparing the present study with that conducted by Alves et al. [21], which applied the same approach but with longitudinal hat-stiffeners, it is evident that the best-performing plate with one longitudinal hat-stiffener (see Figure 23a) showed inferior performance compared to the best plate with six transverse hat-stiffeners (see Figure 23b). Although the plates with longitudinal stiffeners demonstrated a significant ability to reduce out-of-plane displacements—by approximately 86% relative to the reference plate—this value was about 11% lower than the reduction achieved using transverse stiffeners.

In general, considering the results of Alves et al. [21] and those obtained in the present study, it is observed that, while maintaining a constant material volume, the addition of stiffeners does not necessarily lead to a reduction in the displacements of the plate. This behavior was observed both with the use of longitudinal hat-stiffeners [21] and with transverse hat-stiffeners (present study). It was also noted that the height of the hat-stiffeners has a significant influence on the deflection obtained. As expected, increasing the stiffener height usually results in a reduction of the deflection.

Finally, it is worth noting that constructal theory states that a system can undergo continuous evolution over time in order to improve its internal flow patterns. In the case of the constructal design method, this evolution can be understood as the variation of degrees of freedom to improve the performance indicators, always maintaining the total volume constant [9,21]. In the present study, the material redistributes itself due to the variation of these degrees of freedom, generating new geometries that adapt to achieve a better performance, while respecting the imposed constraints and the search space. Therefore, it can be considered that the constructal principle of the optimal distribution of imperfections [7,9] has been achieved, generating the geometry that best adapts to the investigated situation within the proposed constraints. In the case of structural systems, the internal flow referred to by constructal theory can be understood as a stress flow [7], which changes as the geometry assumes different shapes. According to constructal theory and as stated by da Silveira et al. [10], the geometry that best meets the situation is the one that best distributes imperfections, facilitating the stress flow and resulting in lower displacements.

Future research may continue this study by considering different aspect ratios for the plate dimensions, different boundary conditions, and other volumetric ratios between the reference plate and the volume converted into the stiffeners. Additionally, including von Mises stresses as a performance indicator could provide a deeper understanding of the structural behavior.

Author Contributions: Conceptualization, M.A.A., W.R.A. and L.A.I.; methodology, M.A.A. and L.A.I.; software, M.A.A. and E.M.R.; validation, M.A.A. and E.M.R.; formal analysis, L.A.O.R., E.D.d.S., W.R.A. and L.A.I.; investigation, M.A.A., E.M.R. and L.A.I.; resources, L.A.O.R., E.D.d.S. and L.A.I.; data curation, M.A.A. and W.R.A.; writing—original draft preparation, W.R.A. and L.A.I.; writing—review and editing, M.A.A., L.A.O.R., E.D.d.S., W.R.A. and L.A.I.; visualization, L.A.O.R.,

E.D.d.S., W.R.A. and L.A.I.; supervision, W.R.A. and L.A.I.; project administration, L.A.I.; funding acquisition, L.A.O.R., E.D.d.S. and L.A.I. All authors have read and agreed to the published version of the manuscript.

Funding: This research was funded by Coordination for the Improvement of Higher Education Personnel—CAPES, funding code 001 and National Council for Scientific and Technological Development—CNPq, grant numbers: 307791/2019-0, 308396/2021-9, and 309648/2021-1.

Data Availability Statement: The original contributions presented in this study are included in the article. Further inquiries can be directed to the corresponding author.

Acknowledgments: The authors acknowledge the financial support for conducting this research provided by CAPES (funding code 001) and CNPq (processes: 307791/2019-0, 308396/2021-9, and 309648/2021-1).

Conflicts of Interest: The authors declare no conflicts of interest and the funders had no role in the design of this study; in the collection, analyses, or interpretation of data; in the writing of the manuscript; or in the decision to publish the results.

Appendix A

Here, all the geometric configurations numerically simulated, generated through the application of the constructal design method, and evaluated in this study are presented. Tables A1–A9 show the hat-stiffener height, h_s, and the respective thicknesses, t_s, adopted for each case. Subsequently, the maximum deflection, $U_z{}^{max}$, and the central deflection, $U_z{}^{central}$, are presented. Finally, the percentage difference between these two deflections is shown.

Table A1. Plate with one transverse hat-stiffener.

h_s (mm)	t_s (mm)	U_z^{max} (mm)	$U_z^{central}$ (mm)	RD (%) $U_z^{central} - U_z^{max}$
400	6.35	1.1309	1.1310	0.005
375	6.35	1.1700	1.1700	−0.003
350	6.35	1.2083	1.2084	0.007
325	6.35	1.2462	1.2461	−0.004
300	6.35	1.2833	1.2834	0.006
275	6.35	1.3202	1.3202	−0.003
250	6.35	1.3569	1.3569	0.003
225	6.35	1.3938	1.3939	0.007
200	6.35	1.4316	1.4316	−0.003
175	6.35	1.4713	1.4713	0.003
150	6.35	1.5146	1.5146	−0.002
125	6.35	1.5644	1.5645	0.004
100	6.35	1.6248	1.6248	0.002
75	6.35	1.6953	1.6954	0.005
50	6.35	1.7542	1.7542	0.002
25	6.35	1.7712	1.7712	0.002
400	8.00	0.5481	0.5481	0.000
375	8.00	0.5906	0.5907	0.014
350	8.00	0.6337	0.6337	0.000
325	8.00	0.6767	0.6768	0.012
300	8.00	0.7201	0.7201	0.000
275	8.00	0.7634	0.7635	0.010
250	8.00	0.8067	0.8067	0.000
225	8.00	0.8500	0.8501	0.009
200	8.00	0.8933	0.8934	0.009
175	8.00	0.9370	0.9370	0.000

Table A1. *Cont.*

h_s (mm)	t_s (mm)	U_z^{max} (mm)	$U_z^{central}$ (mm)	RD (%) $U_z^{central} - U_z^{max}$
150	8.00	0.9812	0.9813	0.008
125	8.00	1.0274	1.0274	−0.001
100	8.00	1.0776	1.0777	0.006
75	8.00	1.1383	1.1383	0.000
50	8.00	1.2264	1.2265	0.007
25	8.00	1.4100	1.4100	0.001
400	9.53	0.2203	0.2203	0.000
375	9.53	0.2537	0.2538	0.024
350	9.53	0.2887	0.2887	0.000
325	9.53	0.3248	0.3249	0.018
300	9.53	0.3623	0.3623	0.000
275	9.53	0.4007	0.4008	0.017
250	9.53	0.4401	0.4401	0.000
225	9.53	0.4803	0.4803	0.000
200	9.53	0.5212	0.5213	0.015
175	9.53	0.5630	0.5630	0.000
150	9.53	0.6059	0.6060	0.012
125	9.53	0.6508	0.6508	0.000
100	9.53	0.6998	0.6999	0.011
75	9.53	0.7599	0.7599	0.000
50	9.53	0.8545	0.8546	0.008
25	9.53	1.0965	1.0965	−0.002
400	12.7	0.2999	−0.0049	−101.644
375	12.7	0.2810	0.0057	−97.989
350	12.7	0.2625	0.0185	−92.967
325	12.7	0.2445	0.0334	−86.337
300	12.7	0.2269	0.0505	−77.756
275	12.7	0.2100	0.0696	−66.856
250	12.7	0.1939	0.0908	−53.192
225	12.7	0.1787	0.1140	−36.233
200	12.7	0.1647	0.1392	−15.461
175	12.7	0.1666	0.1666	0.030
150	12.7	0.1966	0.1966	0.000
125	12.7	0.2299	0.2300	0.026
100	12.7	0.2692	0.2693	0.022
75	12.7	0.3218	0.3218	0.000
50	12.7	0.4138	0.4139	0.014
25	12.7	0.6799	0.6799	0.000

Table A2. Plate with two transverse hat-stiffeners.

h_s (mm)	t_s (mm)	U_z^{max} (mm)	$U_z^{central}$ (mm)	RD (%) $U_z^{central} - U_z^{max}$
250	6.35	0.1646	−0.0107	−106.521
225	6.35	0.1894	−0.0125	−106.616
200	6.35	0.2163	−0.0119	−105.515
175	6.35	0.2458	−0.0088	−103.560
150	6.35	0.2793	−0.0025	−100.899
125	6.35	0.3188	0.0079	−97.515
100	6.35	0.3670	0.0255	−93.060
75	6.35	0.4245	0.0578	−86.382
50	6.35	0.4853	0.1277	−73.678
25	6.35	0.5790	0.3262	−43.656

Table A2. *Cont.*

h_s (mm)	t_s (mm)	U_z^{max} (mm)	$U_z^{central}$ (mm)	RD (%) $U_z^{central} - U_z^{max}$
250	8.00	0.0612	0.0612	0.000
225	8.00	0.0545	0.0466	−14.532
200	8.00	0.0702	0.0345	−50.940
175	8.00	0.0882	0.0252	−71.435
150	8.00	0.1086	0.0193	−82.190
125	8.00	0.1323	0.0180	−86.411
100	8.00	0.1611	0.0234	−85.485
75	8.00	0.1989	0.0415	−79.146
50	8.00	0.2556	0.0911	−64.347
25	8.00	0.3690	0.2500	−32.246
250	9.53	0.1404	0.1404	0.000
225	9.53	0.1192	0.1192	0.000
200	9.53	0.1003	0.1003	0.040
175	9.53	0.0839	0.0839	0.000
150	9.53	0.0705	0.0705	0.043
125	9.53	0.0612	0.0612	0.000
100	9.53	0.0793	0.0581	−26.796
75	9.53	0.1066	0.0662	−37.923
50	9.53	0.1515	0.1009	−33.415
25	9.53	0.2566	0.2269	−11.580
200	12.7	0.2107	0.2107	0.000
175	12.7	0.1864	0.1864	0.027
150	12.7	0.1645	0.1646	0.030
125	12.7	0.1462	0.1462	0.000
100	12.7	0.1326	0.1327	0.038
75	12.7	0.1280	0.1280	0.000
50	12.7	0.1436	0.1437	0.028
25	12.7	0.2282	0.2282	0.000

Table A3. Plate with three transverse hat-stiffeners.

h_s (mm)	t_s (mm)	U_z^{max} (mm)	$U_z^{central}$ (mm)	RD (%) $U_z^{central} - U_z^{max}$
250	6.35	0.0252	0.0227	−9.905
225	6.35	0.0326	0.0303	−6.882
200	6.35	0.0416	0.0394	−5.405
175	6.35	0.0528	0.0499	−5.527
150	6.35	0.0668	0.0620	−7.203
125	6.35	0.0847	0.0759	−10.436
100	6.35	0.1080	0.0928	−14.077
75	6.35	0.1369	0.1176	−14.100
50	6.35	0.1710	0.1692	−1.093
25	6.35	0.3169	0.3170	0.009
200	8.00	0.0336	0.0130	−61.399
175	8.00	0.0277	0.0177	−35.960
150	8.00	0.0268	0.0246	−8.427
125	8.00	0.0362	0.0339	−6.272
100	8.00	0.0494	0.0469	−5.022
75	8.00	0.0689	0.0668	−3.063
50	8.00	0.1055	0.1055	0.019
25	8.00	0.2184	0.2184	0.000
175	9.53	0.0497	0.0128	−74.139
150	9.53	0.0422	0.0156	−62.989

Table A3. *Cont.*

h_s (mm)	t_s (mm)	U_z^{max} (mm)	$U_z^{central}$ (mm)	RD (%) $U_z^{central} - U_z^{max}$
125	9.53	0.0379	0.0212	−44.093
100	9.53	0.0380	0.0305	−19.700
75	9.53	0.0463	0.0463	0.000
50	9.53	0.0788	0.0788	0.013
25	9.53	0.1750	0.1750	−0.006
125	12.7	0.0678	0.0226	−66.603
100	12.7	0.0616	0.0266	−56.913
75	12.7	0.0630	0.0374	−40.638
50	12.7	0.0799	0.0629	−21.252
25	12.7	0.1497	0.1410	−5.851

Table A4. Plate with four transverse hat-stiffeners.

h_s (mm)	t_s (mm)	U_z^{max} (mm)	$U_z^{central}$ (mm)	RD (%) $U_z^{central} - U_z^{max}$
150	6.35	0.0283	0.0162	−42.640
125	6.35	0.0369	0.0190	−48.563
100	6.35	0.0488	0.0254	−47.961
75	6.35	0.0648	0.0391	−39.698
50	6.35	0.0992	0.0729	−26.592
25	6.35	0.2115	0.1882	−11.049
150	8.00	0.0263	0.0263	0.000
125	8.00	0.0253	0.0253	0.040
100	8.00	0.0306	0.0283	−7.800
75	8.00	0.0445	0.0381	−14.398
50	8.00	0.0743	0.0650	−12.604
25	8.00	0.1642	0.1578	−3.886
125	9.53	0.0350	0.0350	0.057
100	9.53	0.0349	0.0349	0.000
75	9.53	0.0420	0.0420	0.000
50	9.53	0.0651	0.0649	−0.384
25	9.53	0.1464	0.1464	0.000
100	12.7	0.0539	0.0539	−0.019
75	12.7	0.0539	0.0539	0.000
50	12.7	0.0707	0.0707	0.014
25	12.7	0.1383	0.1383	0.000

Table A5. Plate with five transverse hat-stiffeners.

h_s (mm)	t_s (mm)	U_z^{max} (mm)	$U_z^{central}$ (mm)	RD (%) $U_z^{central} - U_z^{max}$
150	6.35	0.0211	0.0212	0.047
125	6.35	0.0251	0.0251	−0.040
100	6.35	0.0324	0.0325	0.031
75	6.35	0.0462	0.0462	−0.022
50	6.35	0.0768	0.0768	0.013
25	6.35	0.1771	0.1771	0.006
125	8.00	0.0295	0.0263	−10.885
100	8.00	0.0306	0.0299	−2.290
75	8.00	0.0404	0.0404	−0.025
50	8.00	0.0663	0.0663	0.000
25	8.00	0.1499	0.1499	−0.007

Table A5. *Cont.*

h_s (mm)	t_s (mm)	U_z^{max} (mm)	$U_z^{central}$ (mm)	RD (%) $U_z^{central} - U_z^{max}$
100	9.53	0.0386	0.0341	−11.580
75	9.53	0.0433	0.0411	−4.948
50	9.53	0.0638	0.0637	−0.266
25	9.53	0.1390	0.1390	−0.007
75	12.7	0.0598	0.0537	−10.224
50	12.7	0.0713	0.0674	−5.445
25	12.7	0.1334	0.1312	−1.634

Table A6. Plate with six transverse hat-stiffeners.

h_s (mm)	t_s (mm)	U_z^{max} (mm)	$U_z^{central}$ (mm)	RD (%) $U_z^{central} - U_z^{max}$
175	4.75	0.0199	0.0166	−16.566
150	4.75	0.0224	0.0178	−20.651
125	4.75	0.0269	0.0212	−21.176
100	4.75	0.0346	0.0277	−19.763
125	6.35	0.0256	0.0250	−2.265
100	6.35	0.0303	0.0283	−6.796
75	6.35	0.0417	0.0383	−8.017
50	6.35	0.0690	0.0648	−6.118
25	6.35	0.1594	0.1562	−1.989
100	8.00	0.0360	0.0360	0.000
75	8.00	0.0417	0.0417	0.000
50	8.00	0.0645	0.0637	−1.318
25	8.00	0.1422	0.1422	−0.007
75	9.53	0.0487	0.0487	−0.021
50	9.53	0.0664	0.0664	0.000
25	9.53	0.1376	0.1376	0.000
50	12.7	0.0785	0.0785	−0.013
25	12.7	0.1361	0.1361	0.000

Table A7. Plate with seven transverse hat-stiffeners.

h_s (mm)	t_s (mm)	U_z^{max} (mm)	$U_z^{central}$ (mm)	RD (%) $U_z^{central} - U_z^{max}$
150	4.75	0.0220	0.0220	0.000
125	4.75	0.0248	0.0248	0.000
100	4.75	0.0309	0.0309	0.032
75	4.75	0.0432	0.0432	−0.023
100	6.35	0.0324	0.0324	0.000
75	6.35	0.0414	0.0414	0.000
50	6.35	0.0665	0.0665	−0.015
25	6.35	0.1525	0.1525	−0.007
75	8.00	0.0464	0.0462	−0.539
50	8.00	0.0661	0.0661	−0.015
25	8.00	0.1408	0.1408	0.000
75	9.53	0.0589	0.0576	−2.224
50	9.53	0.0706	0.0701	−0.581
25	9.53	0.1376	0.1375	−0.065
50	12.7	0.0910	0.0895	−1.714
25	12.7	0.1395	0.1386	−0.667

Table A8. Plate with eight transverse hat-stiffeners.

h_s (mm)	t_s (mm)	U_z^{max} (mm)	$U_z^{central}$ (mm)	RD (%) $U_z^{central} - U_z^{max}$
125	4.75	0.0257	0.0245	−4.779
100	4.75	0.0303	0.0286	−5.638
75	4.75	0.0415	0.0395	−4.816
100	6.35	0.0377	0.0377	−0.053
75	6.35	0.0433	0.0427	−1.410
50	6.35	0.0661	0.0651	−1.468
25	6.35	0.1478	0.1473	−0.318
75	8.00	0.0543	0.0543	0.000
50	8.00	0.0692	0.0692	−0.014
25	8.00	0.1409	0.1409	−0.007
50	9.53	0.0774	0.0774	0.000
25	9.53	0.1406	0.1406	−0.007

Table A9. Plate with nine transverse hat-stiffeners.

h_s (mm)	t_s (mm)	U_z^{max} (mm)	$U_z^{central}$ (mm)	RD (%) $U_z^{central} - U_z^{max}$
100	4.75	0.0315	0.0315	0.000
75	4.75	0.0415	0.0414	−0.024
75	6.35	0.0472	0.0472	0.000
50	6.35	0.0675	0.0675	0.000
25	6.35	0.1466	0.1466	−0.007
50	8.00	0.0708	0.0708	0.000
25	8.00	0.1422	0.1422	−0.007

References

1. Szilard, R. *Theories and Applications of Plate Analysis: Classical, Numerical and Engineering Methods*; Wiley: Hoboken, NJ, USA, 2004. [CrossRef]
2. Li, B.; Gong, Y.; Gao, Y.; Hou, M.; Li, L. Failure Analysis of Hat-Stringer-Stiffened Aircraft Composite Panels under Four-Point Bending Loading. *Materials* **2022**, *15*, 2430. [CrossRef] [PubMed]
3. Ventsel, E.; Krauthammer, T. *Thin Plates and Shells: Theory: Analysis, and Applications*; CRC Press: Boca Raton, FL, USA, 2001.
4. Michigan DOT Selects Steel for 19-Bridge Bundling Project. Available online: https://www.shortspansteelbridges.org/mdot-bridge-bundling-project/ (accessed on 26 May 2025).
5. Bejan, A. Constructal-Theory Network of Conducting Paths for Cooling a Heat Generating Volume. *Int. J. Heat Mass Transf.* **1997**, *40*, 799–816. [CrossRef]
6. Bejan, A. *Shape and Structure, from Engineering to Nature*; Cambridge University Press: New York, NY, USA, 2000.
7. Bejan, A.; Lorente, S. *Design with Constructal Theory*; John Wiley & Sons: Hoboken, NJ, USA, 2008.
8. Bejan, A.; Zane, J.P. *Design in Nature: How the Constructal Law Governs Evolution in Biology, Physics, Technology, and Social Organization*; Anchor Books: New York, NY, USA, 2013.
9. Bejan, A. *The Physics of Life: The Evolution of Everything*; St. Martin's Press: New York, NY, USA, 2024.
10. da Silveira, T.; Pinto, V.; Neufeld, J.P.; Pavlovic, A.; Rocha, L.; dos Santos, E.; Isoldi, L.A. Applicability Evidence of Constructal Design in Structural Engineering: Case Study of Biaxial Elasto-Plastic Buckling of Square Steel Plates with Elliptical Cutout. *J. Appl. Comput. Mech.* **2021**, *7*, 922–934. [CrossRef]
11. Reis, A.H. Constructal Theory: From Engineering to Physics, and How Flow Systems Develop Shape and Structure. *Appl. Mech. Rev.* **2006**, *59*, 269–282. [CrossRef]
12. Dos Santos, E.D.; Isoldi, L.A.; Gomes, M.N.; Rocha, L.A.O. The Constructal Design Applied to Renewable Energy Systems. In *Sustainable Energy Technologies*; Rincón-Mejía, E., Heras, A., Eds.; CRC Press–Taylor and Francis: Boca Raton, FL, USA, 2017; pp. 63–87.
13. Troina, G.; Cunha, M.; Pinto, V.; Rocha, L.; dos Santos, E.; Fragassa, C.; Isoldi, L. Computational Modeling and Constructal Design Theory Applied to the Geometric Optimization of Thin Steel Plates with Stiffeners Subjected to Uniform Transverse Load. *Metals* **2020**, *10*, 220. [CrossRef]

14. Nogueira, C.M.; Pinto, V.T.; Rocha, L.A.O.; dos Santos, E.D.; Isoldi, L.A. Numerical Simulation and Constructal Design Applied to Plates with Different Heights of Traverse and Longitudinal Stiffeners. *Eng. Solid Mech.* **2021**, *9*, 221–238. [CrossRef]
15. Tharian, M.; Nandakumar, C.G. Superelement for Structural Analysis of Steel Bunkers. *SSRN J.* **2023**. [CrossRef]
16. Tharian, M.; Nandakumar, C.G. Hat stiffened plates for ship building. *Int. J. Agric. Econ. Rural. Dev.* **2014**, *4*, 43–52.
17. Pal, A.K.; Harry, N.N.; Upadhyay, R.; Kushwaha, Y.K. Static Analysis of hat stiffened plate: A parametric study. *Int. J. Res. Eng. Sci. Manag (IJRESM)* **2018**, *1*, 128–131.
18. Virág, Z.; Szirbik, S. Modal Analysis of Optimized Trapezoidal Stiffened Plates under Lateral Pressure and Uniaxial Compression. *Appl. Mech.* **2021**, *2*, 681–693. [CrossRef]
19. Filippatos, A.; Markatos, D.; Tzortzinis, G.; Abhyankar, K.; Malefaki, S.; Gude, M.; Pantelakis, S. Sustainability-Driven Design of Aircraft Composite Components. *Aerospace* **2024**, *11*, 86. [CrossRef]
20. Aneja, R.; Choudharry, A.; Jain, K.K.; Dave, R.K. Design and Optimization of Hat Stiffened Plate using Finite Element Method. *Int. Res. J. Eng. Technol.* **2018**, *5*, 578–584.
21. Alves, M.A.; Rodrigues, E.M.; Pinto, V.T.; Rocha, L.A.O.; dos Santos, E.D.; Isoldi, L.A. Numerical Simulation, Constructal Design, and Systematic Search Applied to the Geometrical Evaluation of Hat-Stiffened Plates under Bending. *Res. Eng. Struct. Mater.* **2025**. [CrossRef]
22. Kim, G.-H.; Choi, J.-H.; Kweon, J.-H. Manufacture and performance evaluation of the composite hat-stiffened panel. *Compos. Struct.* **2010**, *92*, 2276–2284. [CrossRef]
23. Jin, B.C.; Li, X.; Mier, R.; Pun, A.; Joshi, S.; Nutt, S. Parametric modeling, higher order FEA and experimental investigation of hat-stiffened composite panels. *Compos. Struct.* **2015**, *128*, 207–220. [CrossRef]
24. Yetman, J.E.; Sobey, A.J.; Blake, J.I.R.; Shenoi, R.A. Investigation into skin stiffener debonding of top-hat stiffened composite structures. *Compos. Struct.* **2015**, *132*, 1168–1181. [CrossRef]
25. El Samrout, A.; Braydi, O.; Younes, R.; Trouchu, F.; Lafon, P. A New Hybrid Method to Solve the Multi-objective Optimization Problem for a Composite Hat-Stiffened Panel. In *Bioinspired Heuristics for Optimization. Studies in Computational Intelligence*; Talbi, E.G., Nakib, A., Eds.; Springer: Cham, Switzerland, 2019; Volume 774. [CrossRef]
26. Murthy, V.R.; Annamalai, K.; Elango, M. Numerical analysis of hat stiffened composite panels for pre and post buckling conditions. *IOP Conf. Ser. Mater. Sci. Eng.* **2021**, *1128*, 012021. [CrossRef]
27. Shi, M.; Chen, P. Simulation of manufacture of the hat-stiffened composite plate based on multidisciplinary coupling. *Acta Mater. Compos. Sin.* **2021**, *38*, 4150–4160. [CrossRef]
28. Wang, T.; Bai, R.; Wei, C.; Huang, X.; Bai, H. Interface damage analysis of composite hat-stiffened panels. *J. Phys. Conf. Ser.* **2021**, *1948*, 012139. [CrossRef]
29. Wang, Z.; Liu, K.; Yu, T.; Zong, S.; Wang, X. Structural deformation mechanism of the hat-stiffened plate used in marine structures under impact load. *Ocean. Eng.* **2022**, *266*, 112736. [CrossRef]
30. Hochster, H.; Ranatunga, V.; Shemesh, N.N.; Haj-Ali, R. Surrogate PHFGMC micromechanical models for multiscale analysis: AI-enhanced low-velocity impact analysis of hat-stiffened composite panels. *J. Compos. Mater.* **2024**, *59*, 305–320. [CrossRef]
31. Shi, G.-J.; Ji, Y.-H.; Xu, J.-B.; Wang, D.-Y.; Xu, Z.-T. Experimental study of structural failure and ultimate strength of GFRP girder with hat stiffeners and foams under bending load. *Mar. Struct.* **2024**, *96*, 103607. [CrossRef]
32. Liu, B.; Zhang, L.; Liu, A.; Guedes Soares, C. Integrated design method of marine C/GFRP hat-stiffened panels towards ultimate strength optimization. *Ocean. Eng.* **2025**, *317*, 120052. [CrossRef]
33. Yang, X.; Li, G.; Sun, C.; Niu, S.; Yang, Y.; Liu, X.; Shao, C. The influence of high toughness resin region on the pull-off failure process of hat-stiffened composite structures. *Eng. Fail. Anal.* **2025**, *169*, 109214. [CrossRef]
34. ANSYS. *Release 2021 R2 Engineering What's Ahead–Element Reference*; ANSYS: Canonsburg, PA, USA, 2021.
35. Zienkiewicz, O.C. *The Finite Element Method*; McGraw-Hill: London, UK, 1986.
36. Moaveni, S. *Finite Element Analysis: Theory and Application with ANSYS*, 3rd ed.; Pearson Prentice Hall: Hoboken, NJ, USA, 2008.
37. Carrijo, E.C.; Paiva, J.B.; Giogo, J.S. A numerical and experimental study of stiffened plates in bending. *Trans. Model. Simul.* **1999**, *21*, 12–18.
38. Araújo, J.M. *Curso de Concreto Armado*, 4th ed.; Dunas: Rio Grande, RS, Brazil, 2014; Volume 2. (In Portuguese)

metals

MDPI

Article

The Effects of Pass Number and Die Channel Angle of Equal Channel Angular Pressing on Innovative Magnesium Composite Material

Xin Zhang [1,†], Jian Han [2,*,†], Jing Tian [1], Lisong Zhu [2], Peng Zhang [3], Yue Wang [3,*] and Zhengyi Jiang [2]

[1] School of Automobile Engineering, Changshu Institute of Technology, Suzhou 215500, China; zhangxin@cslg.edu.cn (X.Z.); 072422134@cslg.edu.cn (J.T.)
[2] School of Mechanical, Materials, Mechatronic and Biomedical Engineering, University of Wollongong, Wollongong, NSW 2522, Australia; lz131@uowmail.edu.au (L.Z.); jiang@uow.edu.au (Z.J.)
[3] School of Materials Science and Engineering, Tianjin University of Technology, Tianjin 300384, China; zhangpeng@emails.bjut.edu.cn
* Correspondence: jianh@uow.edu.au (J.H.); wangyue212039398@163.com (Y.W.)
† These authors contributed equally to this work.

Abstract: The effects of the designed equal channel angular pressing (ECAP) procedures on microstructures, mechanical properties and corrosion resistances of newly developed nano-MgO/Mg–Zn–Ca composite materials have been investigated in this study. The die channel angles selected by the ECAP processes are 90°and 120°, and the corresponding composite materials are kept for 15 min in the ECAP mold at 300 °C before 1, 4, and 8 passes through route B_C. It can be understood that the sizes of grains and second phases were significantly reduced because of continuous dynamic recrystallization (C-DRX) and mechanical shearing, and the ECAP process with the die angle of 90° shows more evidence of grain refinement owing to the higher shear stress. The obtained mechanical properties stipulated that both the yield and ultimate strength were improved after ECAP, which is related to the interaction of grain and texture evolution, while the elongation increases drastically from 14% (as-extruded state) to 34% (ECAP-ed state). Meanwhile, the improvement of corrosion resistance by microstructural evolution is more significant than adverse effects originating from the internal defects of the material itself as well as the defects originating from the number of passes. Ultimately, the conclusions were made based on the results regarding performance improvement by the optimized parameters designed and utilized in ECAP for this novel Mg composite material.

Keywords: MgO nanoparticles; ECAP; microstructure; mechanical properties; corrosion resistance

1. Introduction

In recent years, magnesium and its alloys have shown great potential in bone implantation as biodegradable metal biomaterials [1,2]. The main advantages of magnesium-based implants are the biodegradable and absorbable properties of magnesium, by which the degradation products of a magnesium alloy can be excreted or used in metabolic processes; magnesium is one of the most abundant cations in human cells and extracellular fluids, which is crucial for the formation of bones and teeth. Magnesium-based alloys have good biocompatibility, such as Mg–Zn–Ca matrix composites, with low development costs. The formation of stable intermetallic compounds between Zn, Ca, and Mg gives them high hardness and good creep resistance. However, the Mg–Zn–Ca alloy is difficult to manufacture as an implant that is easy to produce and hard at room temperature; it has processing problems and a fast corrosion rate. Therefore, it is proposed to add nano-MgO particles to the Mg–Zn–Ca alloy to improve its mechanical properties and corrosion resistance effectively [3,4]. The addition of MgO nanoparticles can effectively block the crack extension of the corrosion product layer and make the corrosion product layer denser [5]. Goh et al. [6] reported that adding MgO nanoparticles was an important factor in inhibiting the growth of grains, and the mechanical shearing process in the ECAP process made the MgO particles evenly distributed, then achieved the refinement of the grains. In the subsequent deformation process, the stable intermetallic compound $Ca_2Mg_6Zn_3$ in Mg–Zn–Ca alloys limits grain size.

The hexagonal close-packed (hcp) structure of magnesium alloys results in very few slip systems at ordinary temperatures, resulting in processing performance being poor [7–10]. The severe plastic deformation (SPD) process imposes a large plastic strain on lightweight materials, improving the micro-plasticity of the materials and refining the microstructure. ECAP, one of the SPD methods, is a common method for refining grain and microstructure homogenization of hexagonal close-packed crystal structures like magnesium alloys [10,11]. During the ECAP deformation process of a magnesium alloy, the deformation energy storage begins to accumulate, but the high-energy state is unstable. High-temperature conditions can induce recrystallization behavior, and the deformation energy accumulated during the deformation process can be the driving force for recrystallization, thereby releasing the deformation energy through the recrystallization process to achieve a stable energy state [12,13]. Jin et al. [14] and Figueiredo et al. [15] proposed a grain refinement mechanism based on dynamic recrystallization and indicated that the new grains were formed by the initial grain boundaries during the deformation process. In addition to grain refinement, the size of MgO and other second phases decreases and are more evenly distributed in the matrix with the increase in the number of ECAP passes. During the deformation process, the recrystallized grains have a preferred orientation, and the non-basal slip system of the crystal is activated, which is beneficial to the improvement of its plasticity, deforming at a higher temperature. ECAP improves mechanical properties and the corrosion resistance of the specimens. The process of ECAP also leads to texture changes, and the texture softening can well support the experimental result of the formation of a geometric softer zone during compression deformation of the alloy [16,17].

Under the ECAP parameters of processing temperature (250 °C) and die channel angle (90°), L. B. Tong et al. [18] used routes of A, Bc and C to perform four passes of extrusion on a Mg–Zn–Ca alloy, and found that route of Bc is the most effective in grain refinement and formation of high-angle grain boundaries, which has great reference significance for optimizing the microstructure and mechanical properties of a Mg–Zn–Ca alloy. Zhang et al. [19] heated a specimen at 300 °C for 15 min in the mold, extruded the specimen into one, four and eight passes through the route B_C, and found that the ECAP process has a significant effect on the microstructure homogenization of the composites, which is more obvious in the initial deformation stage. The work of Zhang et al. complemented the study of the microstructure and mechanical properties of Mg–Zn–Ca alloys under different numbers of passes in the route of Bc. Zhang et al. [20] conducted electrochemical tests and simulated body fluid immersion experiments on MgO/Mg–Zn–Ca composites; however, the authors discussed the effects of only two processing strategies on the corrosion resistance of this new composite material, which is not comprehensive for the study of the corrosion resistance of new composite materials. Although the previous work was rather valuable, it failed to systematically summarize the influence of different die channel angles and number of passes on the properties of MgO/Mg–Zn–Ca composites. In this work, the effects of two different mold angles (90° and 120°) and three passes (1,4, and 8) on the microstructure, mechanical properties and corrosion resistance of innovative magnesium alloys were systematically studied to perfect exploration on improving the properties of MgO/Mg–Zn–Ca composites.

2. Experimental Procedure

2.1. Melting and Fabrication of Composite Materials

The 0.6 wt.% MgO/Mg-3Zn-0.2Ca composite was prepared using high-purity magnesium (99.99%) ingots, Zn (99.99 wt.%) granules, a Mg–Ca master alloy (containing 25 wt.% Ca), and spherical MgO nanoparticles with an average diameter of 50–100 nm. Under the protection of an SF_6/N_2 gas mixture, pure magnesium ingots were melted at 720 °C, followed by the addition of calculated amounts of pure Zn and a Mg–Ca alloy into the molten magnesium, which was maintained at this temperature for 30 min. The MgO nanoparticles were then introduced at the bottom of a steel crucible preheated to 690 °C and subsequently incorporated into the molten magnesium. To ensure uniform dispersion of the MgO nanoparticles, a high-shear dynamic and static mixer was employed to disperse the nanoparticles within the Mg–3Zn–0.2Ca alloy melt. After successfully incorporating the MgO nanoparticles into the matrix melt, the composite melt underwent intensive shear mixing using a high-shear rotor–stator mixer at 4000 r/min for 5 min. The melt was then allowed to cool to 690 °C before being cast into a low-temperature steel mold at 680 °C. After solidification and cooling, the composite ingot was demolded. Following casting, all ingots underwent mechanical machining to remove surface oxidation scales.

2.2. Hot Extrusion

After the composite material was prepared, the ingots were first hot-extruded into square bars with a cross-section of 15 mm × 15 mm using a YJQ-300 extruder (Wuxi Linlian Machinery Manufacturing Co., Ltd., Jiangsu, China) (Figure 1c). Once the furnace temperature of the YJQ-300 extruder reached and stabilized at 300 °C, the extrusion was carried out at a steady speed of 2–3 mm/s. After extrusion, the square bars were cooled to room temperature and then cut into 15 mm × 15 mm × 100 mm sections to fit the ECAP die channel and facilitate the subsequent ECAP process.

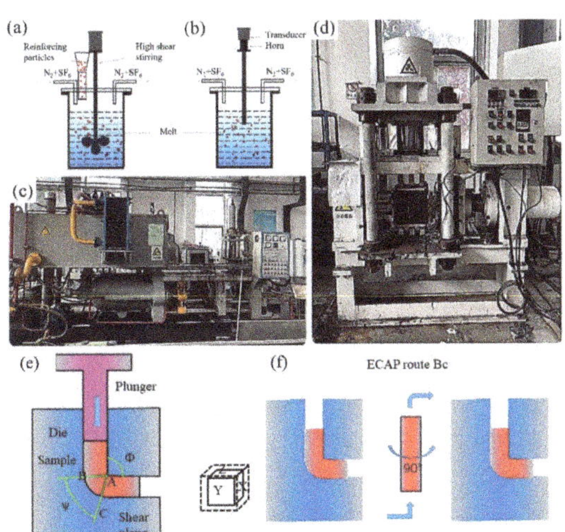

Figure 1. Experimental equipment: (**a**) High-shear stirring, (**b**) Ultrasonic treatment, (**c**) YJQ-300 hot extruding machine, (**d**) ECAP machine, (**e**) ECAP machining principle and (**f**) ECAP route Bc.

2.3. ECAP Deformation of the Composite Material

A graphite-based alcohol lubricant was evenly applied to the surface of the pre-prepared sample and the die channel. The ECAP machine was heated to the specified temperature (300 °C), which was maintained for 30 min. The sample was placed into the die channel, and after both the sample and the die channel were maintained at that temperature for another 30 min, the ECAP processing was carried out according to the specified parameters. The extrusion path followed the Bc path, meaning that the sample was rotated 90° in the same direction before each subsequent pass.

2.4. ECAP Procedure

The die channel angles of the ECAP extruder were 90° and 120°. The selected route was B_C (Figure 1f) as the passing channel for extruding the 1st, 4th and 8th passes after being kept in the ECAP mold at 300 °C for 15 min. The B_C route was rotated 90° counterclockwise after each pass. Ignoring the friction between the sample and the channel, the accumulated equivalent strain values (ε_r) of each of these processes were calculated by Equation (1), proposed by Iwahashi et al. [21].

$$\varepsilon_r = \frac{N}{\sqrt{3}}[2cot\left(\frac{\varphi}{2}+\frac{\psi}{2}\right)+\varphi cosec\left(\frac{\varphi}{2}+\frac{\psi}{2}\right)] \quad (1)$$

where N represents the number of passes, φ the die channel angle, and ψ the corner angle. Through this formula, it can be found that when the angle is 90°, the total deformation strain is more significant than when it is 120°.

2.5. Microstructure Characterization

After ECAP, the cross-section microstructure of specimens in the extrusion direction (ED) was investigated. The specimens were mechanically polished to 5000# using SiC abrasive papers, and the etchant was composed of 2.75 g picric acid, 45 mL ethanol, 2.5 mL acetic acid, and 5 mL distilled water. A scanning electron microscope (SEM, Quanta FEG 250, FEI Co., Ltd., Oregon, OR, USA), and its energy-dispersive spectrometer (EDS) were relied on for microstructural observations. An X-ray diffractometer (Rigaku Ultima IV, Rigaku Corporation Co., Ltd., Tokyo, Japan) was used to scan in the range of 20°–80° at a speed of $8°\cdot min^{-1}$, adopting a Cu target, a 9KW rotating anode target, and a working current of 40 kv, 150 mA. Electron back-scattered diffraction (EBSD) was used to detect textures in materials for further analyzing the extruded and ECAP-ed samples. Mechanical grinding and polishing methods were processed on the obtained specimens for the EBSD testing, and further ion polishing was performed using an ion etching machine (Leica RES101, Leica Microsystems Co., Ltd., Wetzlar, Germany). Owing to the difference in grain size, the original extruded and ECAP-ed specimens were measured with different magnifications for EBSD, and the Channel 5 software was relied on for data analysis.

2.6. Mechanical Test

Compression samples with dimensions of Φ4 mm × 8 mm were cut from the central region of the composite material using wire electrical discharge machining (Taizhou Hengtian Mechanical Manufacture Co., Ltd., Taizhou, Jiangsu, China) along the extrusion direction (ED). The mechanical test was conducted according to the GB/T 7314–2005 standard [22]. The two ends and the outer surface of the samples were polished to remove the oxide layer before testing. The samples were then positioned precisely on the compression platform of an OOL10 universal testing machine. No lubricant was applied between the sample and the compression tools. The test was terminated when the sample exhibited evident damage.

Compression tests were conducted at a strain rate of 0.5×10^{-3} s^{-1} at room temperature, and the corresponding data were recorded to generate compression stress–strain curves.

2.7. Electrochemical Measurements

The size of the specimens for electrochemical testing was 5 mm × 5 mm × 3 mm. To make the specimens reach the equilibrium potential, the specimens were placed in a constant-temperature simulated body fluid (SBF) at 37 °C for 30 min, then subjected to a traditional three-electrode system consisting of a platinum electrode, a saturated calomel electrode (SCE) and the specimen. The exposed surface of the specimen was 0.25 mm^2, ground using silicon papers up to 3000#. Tests of potentiodynamic polarization were conducted at 37 °C on an electrochemical workstation (Zennium, Kronach, Germany) by exerting a potential from the self-corrosion of −500 mV to +500 mV at a scan rate of 1 mV/s.

3. Results and Discussion

3.1. Microstructure Analysis

The SEM of the as-extruded and ECAP-ed 0.6 wt.% MgO/Mg–3Zn–0.2Ca composite is shown in Figure 2, and the specific grain size is shown in Table 1. The average grain size and standard deviation were obtained through EBSD analysis. Figure 2a shows that the grain-size distribution of the as-extruded specimen is not homogenized, presenting the distribution of large grains around small grains. In the ECAP-ed specimens, the distribution of the microstructure was more uniform, and the grains evolved into equiaxial crystals. The significant changes in microstructure can be explained by the following aspects. The processing temperature is kept at 300 °C to reach the recrystallization temperature of Mg alloy during the ECAP process and the deformed grains recover and recrystallize, resulting in grain refinement. Nevertheless, the specimens are also subjected to strain along with the recrystallization process, such that the mechanical shearing effect breaks coarse grains into refined ones. Mechanical actions, such as shear stress concentration during extrusion, induce lattice twisting at grain boundaries, leading to the formation of high-angle grain boundaries and grain refinement. Dislocation accumulation and cross-slip contribute to a banded structure. As stress increases, sub-grain boundaries form and migrate, further promoting the development of high-angle grain boundaries and finer grains. Magnesium alloys have a low stacking fault energy (SFE), making it difficult for dislocations on slip planes to rearrange through climb and cross-slip. As a result, during hot deformation, the dynamic recovery process in magnesium alloys is relatively slow, causing local dislocation density to increase with strain, which consequently promotes the initiation of dynamic recrystallization [23,24].

Table 1. The average grain size of as-extruded and ECAP-ed specimens (um).

Sample	90°-1-Pass	90°-4-Pass	90°-8-Pass	120°-1-Pass	120°-4-Pass	120°-8-Pass
Average grain size	13.66	5.86	5.31	19.7	6.86	6.54
Standard deviation	2.73	1.01	1.15	2.91	1.37	1.25

There are a large number of coarse grains in the extruded specimen, while the coarse grains are basically eliminated in the ECAP specimens. The specimens in the same pass of ECAP using different die channel angles exhibited different grain sizes. The specimens after ECAP when $\varphi_1 = 90°$ exhibited finer grains than the specimens after ECAP when $\varphi_2 = 120°$, indicating that a larger amount of deformation occurred in the ECAP specimens at 90°; the higher strain led to more deformation energy being stored during ECAP, which promotes the process of recrystallization. Agwa et al. [25], using finite element (FE) simulation analysis, reported that enormous equivalent plastic strains occurred in the right-angle channel rather than in the obtuse-angle channel, which was consistent with the current experimental results. The grain size cannot invariably be decreased with an increased number of passes; when the number of passes reaches four, the grain size is in a stable state, and the dynamic recrystallization process achieves a balance. A larger strain in the ECAP-ed specimens results in a higher nucleation rate and finer grains. During the processing, a highly localized lattice misorientation around the particles can be caused in the deformation zone of the nano-Mgo particles, which can be used as an effective nucleation site for the newly recrystallized grains, achieving particle-stimulated nucleation (PSN) and MgO particles; a heterogeneous nucleating agent has a fixed effect on dislocations and grain boundaries during dynamic recrystallization, so adding MgO nanoparticles is beneficial to the grain refinement.

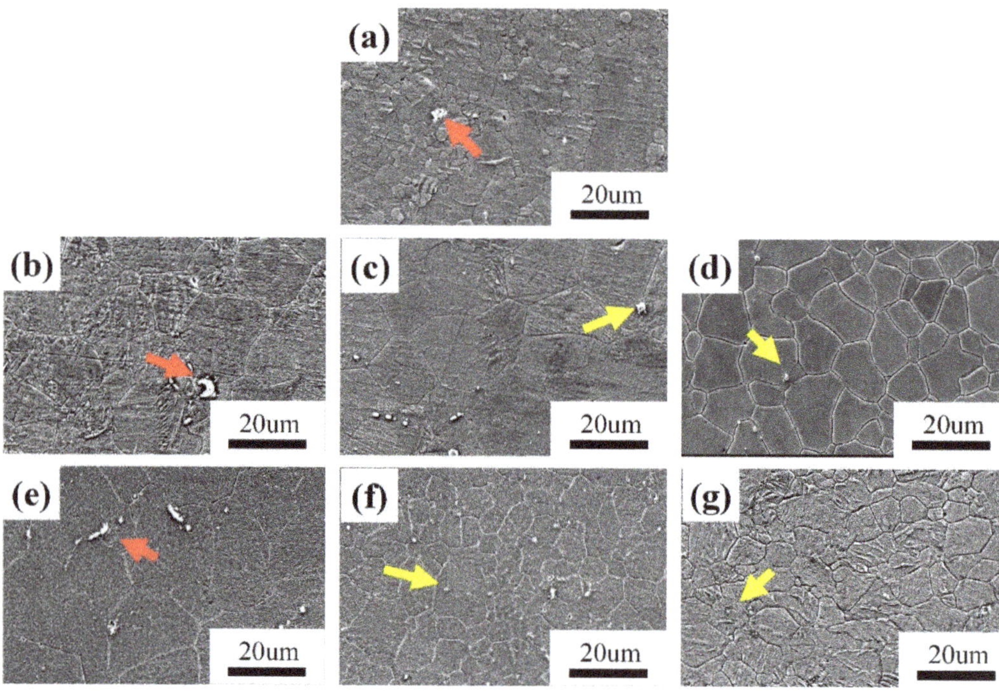

Figure 2. SEM of 0.6wt.% MgO/Mg–3Zn–0.2Ca composite material. (**a**) As-extruded, (**b**) 1-pass ECAP at 120°, (**c**) 4-pass ECAP at 120°, (**d**) 8-pass ECAP at 120°, (**e**) 1-pass ECAP at 90°, (**f**) 4-pass ECAP at 90° and (**g**) 8-pass ECAP at 90°.

The flocculent second phase (as indicated by the red arrow) appears in the grain boundary, and the spherical second phase (as indicated by the yellow arrow) appears inside the grains, as shown in Figure 2. Table 2 shows the EDS result of the four-pass ECAP-ed specimen marked in Figure 3c. Through energy spectrum analysis and the XRD phase analysis results, it can be seen that the atomic ratio Mg:Ca:Zn is close to 6:2:3; therefore, it can be considered that the second phase at the grain boundary (A and B) are $Ca_2Mg_6Zn_3$ molecules. Similarly, the flocculent second phases (C and D) are marked as MgZn compounds. The white particles at position E are identified as MgO, and it can be seen that the atomic percentage of Mg and O elements in Table 2 is not 1, because the size of the MgO particles is so small that the Mg matrix will be scanned in point scanning, resulting in a higher content of the Mg element.

Table 2. EDS result of the 4-pass ECAP-ed specimen marked in Figure 3.

Location	Element (wt.%)				Component
	Mg	Zn	Ca	O	
A	46.6	40.3	13.1		MgZnCa
B	64.1	27.0	8.9		MgZnCa
C	94.0	6.0			MgZn
D	98.7	1.3			MgZn
E	93.0			7.0	nano-MgO

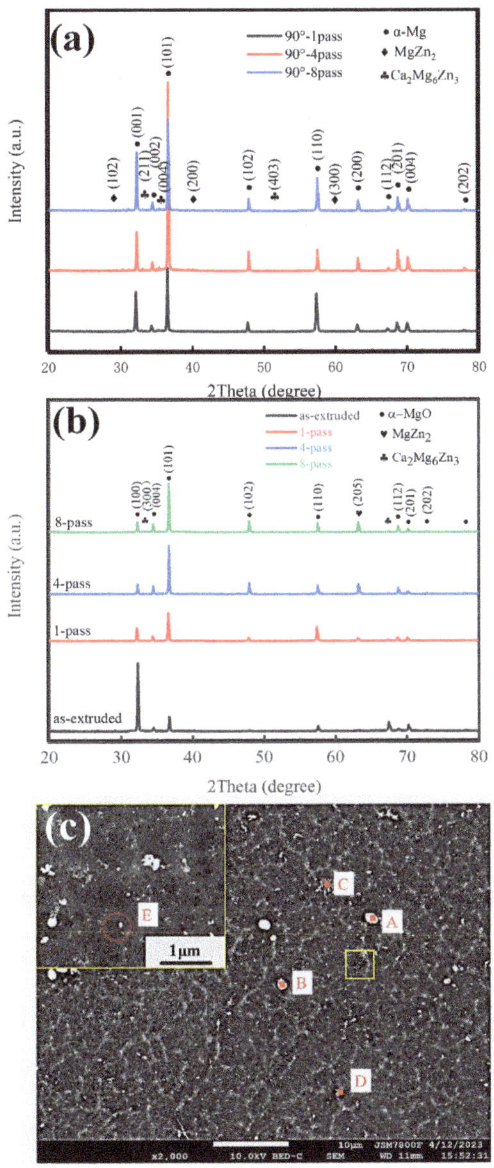

Figure 3. XRD (**a**,**b**) of as-extruded composite 1-, 4-, 8-pass ECAP at 120° and 1-, 4-, 8-pass ECAP at 90°, and (**c**) SEM of 4-pass ECAP at 120°.

The banded and spherical second phases are larger and haphazardly distributed in the as-extruded specimen, which is related to the precipitation behavior during the casting process. After one-pass ECAP-ing, the distribution had a significant improvement; the refining effect of ECAP on the second phase was noticeable, and the refining effect was continuously improving, accompanying the increase in number of passes. The dimensions of the second phase, like the grain size, came into balance after four passes; therefore, it could be inferred that the sample after four-pass ECAP treatments could obtain better performance, and the increase in number of ECAP passes had little effect on its improvement. MgO particles exhibited pinning effects on dislocations and grain boundary movement during dynamic recrystallization, which also confirmed that MgO nanoparticles were an effective heterogeneous nucleating agent.

The as-extruded and ECAP-ed specimen XRD patterns are presented in Figure 3a,b. The as-extruded and ECAP-ed specimens show the same phase peaks: α-Mg matrix, $MgZn_2$, and $Ca_2Mg_6Zn_3$, indicating that the ECAP process can change the distribution of second phases but does not initiate a phase transition during ECAP [26]. MgO is not detected in the XRD results due to the low content, i.e., only 0.6 wt.%, which is below the measurable range of the instrument. The orientation of the second phase is also changed, such that the (004) orientation peak intensity of $Ca_2Mg_6Zn_3$ increases, but the (643) orientation peak intensity decreases as the number of ECAP passes increases, as shown in Figure 3a. The intensity of (100) and (201) cylindrical orientation peaks of α-Mg decreases, while the intensity of (101), (102), and (103) peaks of basal and conical orientation increases, which will have a certain impact on the mechanical properties of the material, since greater basal slip and pyramidal slip can effectively improve the plasticity of the material. At $\varphi_1 = 90°$, the (001) and (101) peak intensities of α-Mg in the composites are significantly improved, and new orientations of $MgZn_2$ and $Ca_2Mg_6Zn_3$ phases appear. This is because changing the channel angle generates higher strain, which facilitates the dynamic precipitation of the second phase.

Figure 4 shows the fraction content of grain type of the specimens. The as-extruded specimen exhibits a typical deformed structure; the fraction of recrystallized grain is just 7.4%, and most of the grains are substructure and deformed grains; the scale of substructure and deformed grains is close to 1:1, while in the ECAP-ed specimen, after eight passes at 120°, the recrystallized grains increase to 60.3%, and the fraction of deformed grains is 5.0%, which indicates an improvement in recrystallization. However, the grains have completed recrystallization in the ECAP-ed specimen after eight passes at 90°, almost no deformed grains are left, and the recrystallized grain is up to 71.5%. The main difference in eight-pass ECAP-ed specimens at different angles lies in the proportion of recrystallized grains and subgrains. In addition, the proportion of recrystallized grains in samples subjected to ECAP at 90° is higher because the ECAP-ed specimen at 90° obtains greater heterogeneity of the distribution of the stored energy in neighboring crystallites, which acts as a driving force for recrystallization during the recrystallization process, promoting its recrystallization behavior.

Figure 5 presents the pole figures of the as-extruded and eight-pass ECAP-ed 0.6 wt.% MgO composite. The fabric texture {0001} <1010> in the as-extruded specimen indicates that the {0001} basal plane and <10–10> direction of most grains are parallel to the extrusion direction (ED), as shown in Figure 5a. The strong basal plane orientation of the coarse grains explains that the pole density of the extruded state (12.49) multiple of random distribution (MRD) is higher than that of the ECAP-ed specimens, indicating that the basal texture decreases after ECAP. The prismatic surface slip is the major deformation mechanism due to the equivalent axisymmetric compressive stress of extrusion and the axial tensile stress, while the {0001} basis plane is parallel to the c-axis direction, and {10–12} tensile twinning occurs when the plane is compressed or stretched along the c-axis direction. The research shows the {0001} basal texture is decomposed into {10–10} and {2-1–10} textures with the increase in the extent of compressive deformation, resulting in texture softening, which can decrease the yield strength [27]. Figure 5c presents the pole diagram of the composite after eight-pass ECAP. After the specimen is processed by eight-pass ECAP at 90°, it is subjected to strong shear force from passing through the included angle, and the basal plane slip system is activated to form a {11–20} <0001> texture; that is, the (0001) basal plane has a vertical oblique texture in the theoretical shear plane. The strong point in the pole figure is rotated about 70° counterclockwise around the ED direction, deviating from the orientation position of the basal plane and significantly weakening the basal plane texture. It is known that the rigid rotation of the lattice is 45° during the ECAP deformation at φ_1 = 90°; however, the rotation of the lattice after eight passes is significantly larger than this angle, indicating the rotation of the lattice is not limited to the rotation of the crystal. In the early stage of deformation, strong shear deformation occurred during the ECAP process, and the coarse grains were broken to form cell blocks which rotated to match the strain between adjacent cell blocks to form a new texture. The grains had been refined, and the texture evolution in the grains was mainly formed by the rotation of the whole grains in the later stage of deformation, thereby gradually forming the ECAP shear texture.

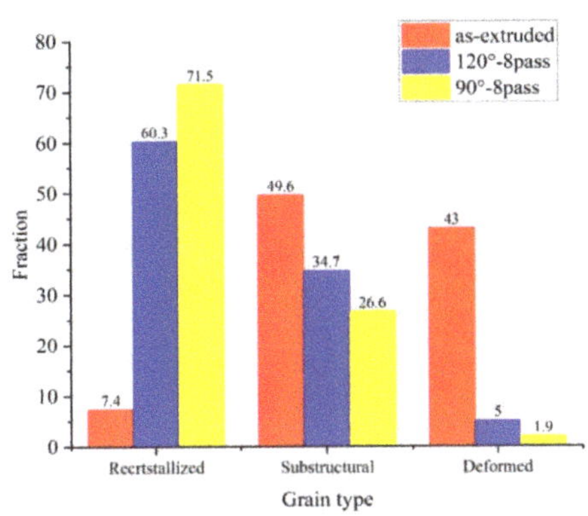

Figure 4. Grain type of different ECAP-ed specimens.

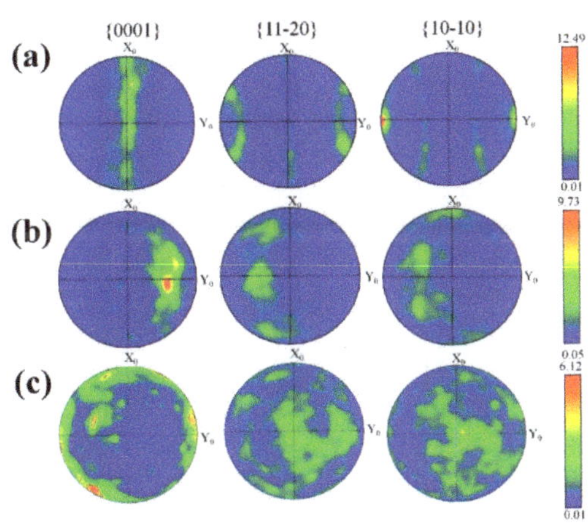

Figure 5. Pole figures of composite. (**a**) As-extruded, (**b**) 8-pass ECAP at 120°, and (**c**) 8-pass ECAP at 90°.

Figure 6 presents the Kernel average misorientation (KAM) and local misorientation of the as-extruded and ECAP-ed specimens. The KAM method is used for Geometrically Necessary Dislocation (GND) of composite materials under different processes, using Equation (2) to calculate the GND density in different regions; the relation between KAM and GND is shown in Equation (2) [28].

$$\rho^{GND} = \frac{2KAM_{ave}}{ub} = KAM_{ave} \tag{2}$$

where ρ^{GND} presents the GND density, KAM_{ave} presents the weighted average 4 of the local misorientation, μ presents the unit length of 75 nm, b presents the Burgers vector and $B = 2.6 \times 1015\ m^{-2}$. The KAM_{ave} in as-extruded ECAP-ed specimens of eight passes at 120°and 90° are 0.071, 0.097, and 0.034, respectively, and the GND in as-extruded eight-pass ECAP-ed specimens at 120° and 90° is $2.522 \times 10^{14}\ m^{-2}$, $1.846 \times 10^{14}\ m^{-2}$, and $8.840 \times 10^{13}\ m^{-2}$ [20].

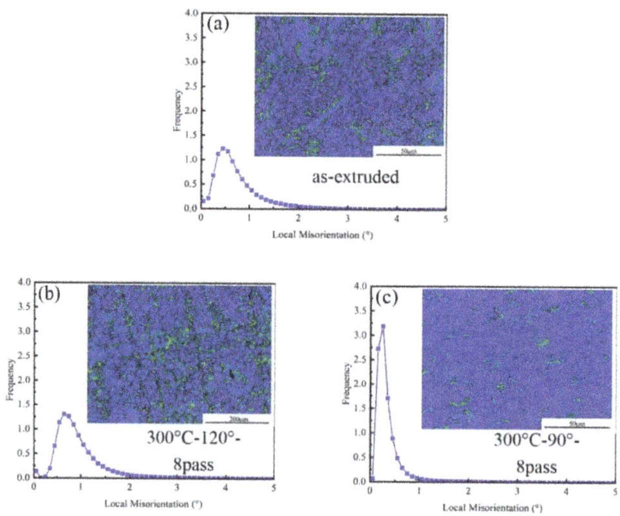

Figure 6. Kernel average misorientation and local misorientation of specimens. (**a**) As-extruded, (**b**) 8-pass ECAP at 120°, and (**c**) 8-pass ECAP at 90°.

In Figure 6, green represents the local misorientation, which is caused by lattice distortion resulting from large deformations. In Figure 6a, the grain structure shows a higher content of green lines, which is due to the large strain experienced by the alloy during the hot extrusion process, leading to dislocation accumulation. The GND density of the eight-pass ECAP specimen at 120° in Figure 6b is high, indicating that after ECAP processing, the matrix generates a large number of dislocations. Under unidirectional compressive stress, dislocations form dislocation pile-ups during their movement, leading to higher stress concentrations around the matrix and precipitate particles. The activation of new dislocations increases the stress on the second-phase particles, ultimately causing microcracks due to the fracture of the second-phase particles and matrix. In Figure 6c, the grain structure is predominantly covered in blue, with less green, indicating that reducing the die angle results in a decrease in the GND density of the composite material. This is because, during ECAP deformation, recrystallization occurs within the 0.6 wt.% MgO/Mg–3Zn–0.2Ca composite material. The recrystallization process leads to a reduction in dislocation density, which can absorb a large number of dislocations and hinder strain hardening during deformation. This is the main reason for the observed strain softening and improved formability. As the die angle decreases, the recrystallized grain size reduces, and most of the dislocations generated during alloy deformation accumulate at the grain boundaries. Due to the presence of non-equilibrium grain boundaries, dislocations accumulated at the grain boundaries are more easily absorbed, triggering dynamic recovery. As a result, the GND density decreases, providing the magnesium alloy with higher stress and strain-hardening rates.

3.2. Mechanical Property

Since the Mg–Zn–Ca alloy under study is primarily intended for biomedical composites, it is likely to experience mainly compressive effects in the human body. Therefore, compression testing can reflect its mechanical behavior in the application environment. The compressive stress–strain curve of the as-extruded and ECAP-ed composite is shown in Figure 7, and the specific values are shown in Table 3. The ability to resist plastic deformation of ECAP-ed specimens was weaker than the as-extruded specimen; the one-pass ECAP-ed specimens at 90° and 120° had the lower ultimate compressive strength (UCS), while gradually rising with the increases in number of passes; the eight-pass ECAP-ed specimens achieved the approximate UCS with the as-extruded specimen. Recrystallization was an important factor in the decrease in UCS in the initial ECAP process. The specimen was subjected to significant deformation during the extrusion process, which caused the work-hardening effect; the formation of textures was the best proof, and the max pole density was 11.29 MRD in the as-extruded specimen. Higher temperatures promoted their recrystallization process, which reduced the orientation trend of the grains, leading to the evolution of their texture and reducing the work hardening when the ECAP process was conducted. It is worth noting that, although the ECAP-ed specimens obtain a similar UCS with the as-extruded specimen, this does not mean that both have the same performance, which mainly depends on their internal structural differences. In the as-extruded specimen, coarse grains are generally considered the source of stress concentration during working, which can cause cracks to initiate at these locations, finally leading to failure. In the ECAP-ed specimens, the stress concentration effect may not be obvious, so when the work hardening is lower than for the as-extruded specimen, the UCS still reaches a similar level because of the refinement and uniform distribution of grains; the performance is considered to be superior to the as-extruded specimen, so the ECAP process is expected to improve its performance without affecting its overall strength. The UCS of the one-pass and four-pass ECAP-ed specimens are at the same level, while the UCS increases after the eight-pass ECAP. Therefore, it can be inferred that dynamic recrystallization is in a balanced state when the number of passes is below four. However, as the number of passes increase, the recrystallization effect is suppressed because the grains are already very small, while the effect of work hardening is enhanced when the deformation rate remains unchanged. In polycrystals with small grain sizes, the non-uniform deformation of adjacent crystallites is not constrained, resulting in variations in stored energy. This variation maintains the driving force for recrystallization, which plays a key role in influencing the work-hardening effect.

There is an interesting phenomenon in Figure 7, which is that the yield strength of the alloy processed by high number of ECAP passes has no obvious change, although the grain size is refined. This phenomenon can be explained by the following aspects. After ECAP processing, there are still large grains in the material structure, which is not the complete grain refinement in the strict sense, and the phenomenon of uneven grain size appears. The preferred orientation of texture affects the mechanical properties of magnesium alloys [29]. Studies have shown that the elongation of the extruded magnesium alloy is greatly improved after equal channel angular extrusion, but the strength has not changed significantly, which is consistent with the findings of [17]. The compressive yield strength (CYS) has different performances at 90° and 120° after eight-pass ECAP; in the ECAP-ed specimens at 90°, the CYS increases with the increase in number of passes because of the effect of grain refinement, verified by the Hall–Petch effect. But it has the opposite trend in the ECAP-ed specimen at 120°; overall, it is in a relatively balanced state with a small downward trend, which is related to the texture softening effect; in the ECAP-ed specimen at 120°, the specimen is prone to form a basal fiber texture during the deformation processes, the {0001} basal plane is parallel to the c-axis direction, and {10–12} tensile twinning can occur when compressing or stretching along the c-axis direction. The {0001} basal texture is decomposed into {1010} and {2-1–10} textures with the increase in the degree of compressive deformation, resulting in texture softening, then a reduction in the CYS.

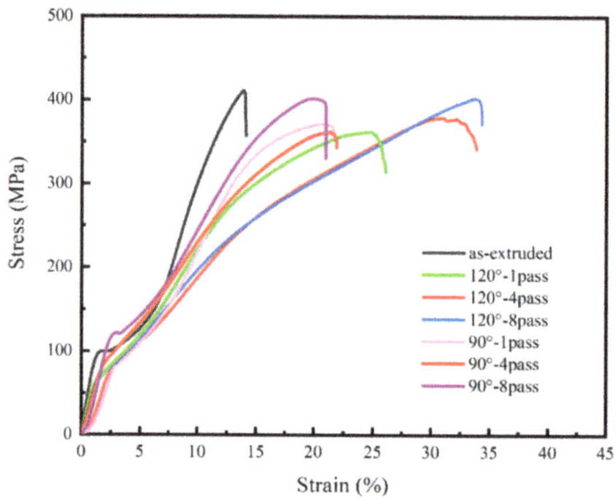

Figure 7. Compressive stress–strain curve of as-extruded composite and 1-, 4-, 8-pass ECAP at 90° and 120°.

Table 3. Compressive properties of the specimens.

Specimen	CYS (MPa)	UCS (MPa)	CSF (%)
As-extruded	107.39	409.08	14.08
90°-1-pass	81.56	370.96	21.61
90°-4-pass	98.94	360.54	22.78
90°-8-pass	113.97	401.76	20.45
120°-1-pass	106.85	362.35	26.31
120°-4-pass	104.74	379.06	34.05
120°-8-pass	97.38	405.77	34.18

In the ECAP-ed specimens at 90° and 120°, the compressive strain of fracture (CSF) shows a great improvement, reaching 1.5 times and 2.4 times that of the as-extruded specimen, respectively. The improvement of CSF can be attributed to the homogenization of microstructure, grains, and second phases; in the as-extruded specimen, there exist many coarse grains which will act as areas of stress concentration. Meanwhile, the larger-sized phases can also be harmful to its performance; cracks can initiate in areas of stress concentration and spread along coarse grains, leading to a decrease in plasticity. The ECAP processing can refine the grains and phases and decrease the areas which can cause stress concentration. Meanwhile, the inhibiting effect of grain boundaries on crack propagation should not be underestimated. Cracks normally spread along the coarse grains and large phases; the ECAP-ed specimen has more grain boundaries and finer second phases, so the plasticity can be greatly improved by suppressing the propagation of cracks. The texture softening during ECAP can improve the anisotropy of the specimens and CSF. The value of CSF of the eight-pass ECAP-ed specimens at 120° is the highest; the specimens have the proximate grain size with it at 90° but exhibit better plasticity.

As compressive deformation increases, the {0001} basal texture decomposes into {10–10} and {2-1–10} textures, leading to texture softening and reduced yield strength. The weakening effect of the extrusion-induced texture surpasses the strengthening effect of grain refinement, while grain refinement activates more slip systems, enhancing plastic deformation. During early ECAP processing, UCS decreases due to dislocations and defects introduced in the composite. As ECAP continues, dislocation accumulation reaches a critical level, hindering movement and making deformation more difficult. With more ECAP passes, the second-phase size decreases, reducing crack initiation and improving strength. A smaller channel angle decreases plasticity due to increased strain and work hardening. The high yield strength results from grain refinement, second-phase and texture strengthening. According to the Hall–Petch relationship, smaller grain size increases yield strength, while the Orowan mechanism suggests second-phase dispersion contributes to strength. In magnesium alloys, basal slip dominates at room temperature [30]. A strong basal texture inhibits basal slip activation, raising yield strength. Additionally, MgO and other second-phase particles at grain boundaries exert a pinning effect, effectively hindering dislocation motion and grain boundary sliding, thereby enhancing the composite's strength.

Figure 8 presents the Schmid factors of as-extruded and eight-pass ECAP-ed specimens. Different colors in the figure represent different deformation capabilities of the grains, and the difficulty of opening the slip in different colors in the figure represent different deformation capability of the grains. In the as-extruded specimen, the distribution of the Schmid factor has a large deviation, indicating a large difference in grain orientation, which explains the reason for the low plasticity of the as-extruded specimen. The texture softening effect and the recrystallization process make the distribution of the Schmid factor of the ECAP specimens finer, and that of the eight-pass ECAP-ed specimen at 120° has a smooth trend; the higher area is greater than 0.3, which is preferred to a soft orientation which undergoes greater deformation and stores more energy [18].

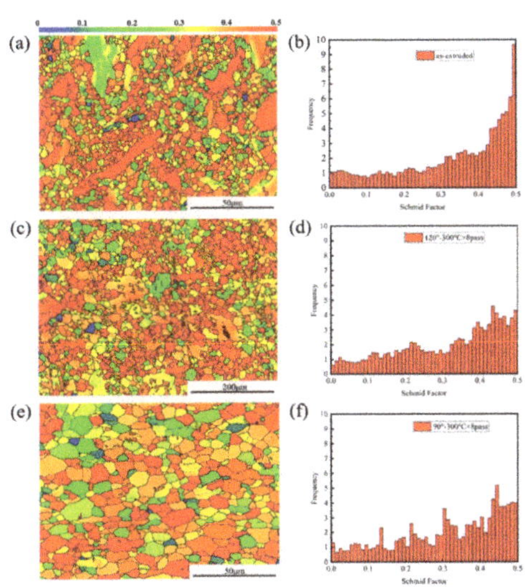

Figure 8. Schmid factor of different specimens. (**a**,**b**) As-extruded, (**c**,**d**) 8-pass ECAP at 120° and (**e**,**f**) 8-pass ECAP at 90°.

3.3. Corrosion Resistance

The dynamic potential polarization curves of composites, corrosion potential (E_{corr}), and corrosion current density (I_{corr}) are shown in Figures 9 and 10, respectively; b_c is the cathode Tafel slope, and b_a is the anode Tafel slope in Figure 10. The corrosion resistance of the prepared innovative magnesium alloy was reflected by dynamic potential polarization curves and impedance spectroscopy to explore the effect of microstructure on corrosion resistance. Table 4 shows the result of corrosion potential (E_{corr}), corrosion current (I_{corr}), cathode Tafel slope (b_c), and anode Tafel slope (b_a); the Tafel slope represents the blocking of the electrode process. Impedance spectroscopy, as shown in Figure 11, reflects the effectiveness of the passivation film formed on the surface. The radius of the capacitive loop is affiliated with the surface film resistance (R1); the small capacitive reactance loop represents the charge transfer resistance (R2), while CPE1 and CPE2 are the constant phase elements of the charge transfer on the surface film, as shown in Figure 11c.

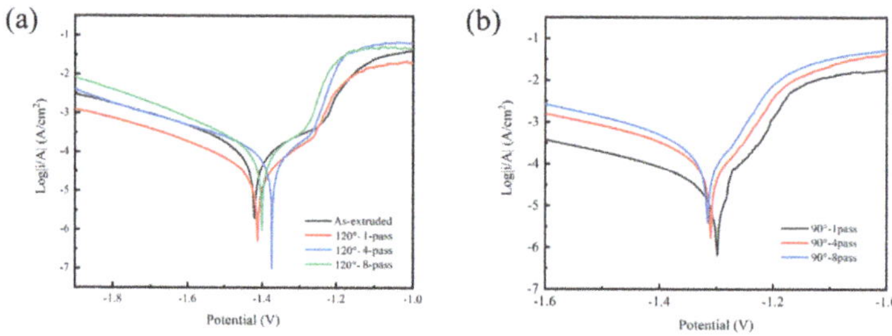

Figure 9. Dynamic potential polarization curves of composites. (**a**) As-extruded and 1-, 4-, 8-pass ECAP at 120°, and (**b**) 1-, 4-, 8-pass ECAP at 90°.

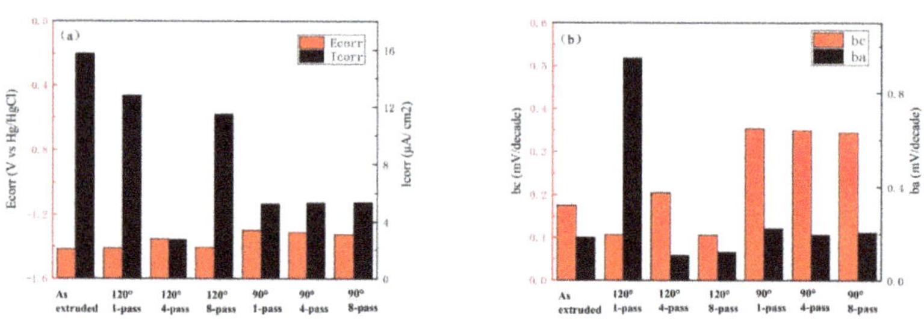

Figure 10. Electrochemical parameters for different specimens in SBF solution. (**a**) Corrosion potential and corrosion current density of extruded and ECAP-ed specimens, and (**b**) cathode Tafel slope and anode Tafel slope of extruded and ECAP-ed specimens.

Table 4. Electrochemical parameters for different specimens in SBF solution.

Specimen	E_{corr} (V vs. Hg/HgCl)	I_{corr} ($\mu A/cm^2$)	b_c (mV/decade)	b_a (mV/decade)
As-extruded	−1.416	15.739	0.173	0.180
120°-1-pass	−1.412	12.784	0.107	0.950
120°-4-pass	−1.355	2.723	0.205	0.106
120°-8-pass	−1.406	11.495	0.106	0.120
90°-1-pass	−1.298	5.248	0.353	0.223
90°-4-pass	−1.310	5.322	0.349	0.195
90°-8-pass	−1.322	5.361	0.339	0.205

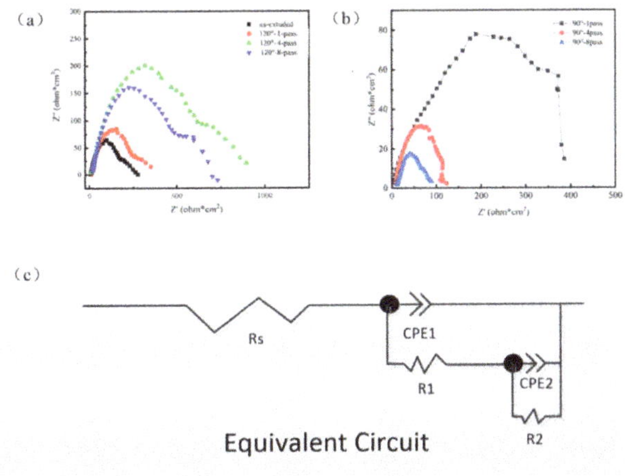

Figure 11. Impedance spectroscopy of composites. (**a**) As-extruded and 1,4,8-pass ECAP at 120°; and (**b**) 1,4,8-pass ECAP at 90°; (**c**) Equivalent circuit model of specimens under corrosion in SBF Solution.

The corrosion potential of the as-extruded specimens is the lowest, but the corrosion current density is the highest, indicating that the as-extruded specimens have the largest corrosion rate. The factors that affect corrosion performance are related to the size of the second phase, which is usually considered the main reason for causing potential differences and accelerating the corrosion process. Larger second phases will exacerbate the pitting process, and the distribution state of the second phase will also affect the corrosion performance; the specimens which have an interrupted distribution of the second phase have better corrosion resistance. The electrochemical corrosion between the second phase and the substrate will be separated independently; because the presence of grain boundaries prevents the diffusion of corrosion and allows it to exist in a small area without affecting its overall corrosion performance, the continuous distribution of the second phase leads to intensified intergranular corrosion, and the corrosion effect will intensify. Moreover, the strengthening effect of grain boundaries will suppress corrosion performance, as the size of corrosive ions decreases. The more grain boundaries there are, the stronger the ability to inhibit the propagation of these corrosive ions; therefore, as the number of grain boundaries increases, the corrosion resistance improves. The ECAP-ed specimens of 90° display the lower I_{corr} and higher E_{corr}, and the ECAP-ed sample of 90°-1-pass has the best corrosion resistance. With a greater strain created by adjusting the mold angle, the I_{corr} reduced significantly, attributing to a decline in the dimension of the second phase and a multiplication grain boundary density during ECAP. From the dynamic potential polarization curves, the corrosion resistance of ECAP-ed specimens was improved by increasing strain to refine grain size; when specimens are of the same grain size, it is necessary to analyze the inner structures.

Figure 11 presents the impedance spectroscopy of these specimens. The capacitive behavior is large, owing to the charge transfer process of $Mg \rightarrow Mg^{2+}$ at the double layer formed by the surface film, while the capacitance loop is small because of the relaxation of the corrosion product film formed on the alloy surface; the resistance of this oxide film is low due to its porous and partially protective properties [31]. The composite materials have capacitive arcs in the high-frequency region and the low-frequency region, indicating that local corrosion occurs in the electrochemical corrosion process. The AC impedance spectrum shows that the capacitor arc processed by ECAP tends to continue to spread, indicating that the constant temperature capacitor arc tends to continue to spread, indicating that the constant temperature ECAP processing has not broken and does not destroy the uniform and slow corrosion of the substrate. Interface bonding between MgO and the matrix has a significant impact on corrosion initiation, while grain homogenization slows down the potential difference between large and small grains, which can explain the phenomenon of improving corrosion resistance and reducing the corrosion rate. Larger-size agglomerates in the extruded state and good interfacial bonding will not cause damage to the matrix at the initiation of corrosion. Dynamic recovery and recrystallization processes homogenize the structure and reduce the susceptibility of corrosion before ECAP, and the cathode current density of the composites after ECAP is the lowest, indicating that the ECAP process improves the cathode reaction resistance. Generally speaking, the bulk deposits act as a cathode during the corrosion process, causing more severe corrosion.

The MgO particles in the ECAP samples are finer and more uniform due to the mechanical shearing, which creates the uniform structure of the second phase without lumps, which improves the corrosion resistance, making the corrosion surface protective film denser and complete, accelerates the passivation speed of the magnesium alloy, reduces the secondary corrosion, and thus reduces the corrosion rate. During the corrosion process of the 0.6 wt.% MgO/Mg–3Zn–0.2Ca composite, the grain boundaries can serve as the cathodic protection matrix and generate $Mg(OH)_2$, which can form a protective film that improves the corrosion resistance. But the Cl^- existing in humans can damage the $Mg(OH)_2$ protective film, causing localized pitting corrosion, and grain refinement will bring more flaws. The as-extruded specimen has many refined grains, whose microstructure is the most inhomogeneous, and the volume fraction of the second phase is the largest; therefore, the corrosion resistance of the as-extruded specimen is the worst [32].

4. Conclusions

The microstructure, mechanical properties, and corrosion resistance of a 0.6wt.% MgO/Mg3Zn0.2Ca composite treated with ECAP (1-, 4-, 8-pass) with die channel angles of 90° and 120° were studied and compared with that of the extruded state. The main results are as follows:

1. The microstructure homogenization of the composite material is affected by the ECAP process significantly; the function of mechanical shear and recovery recrystallization during ECAP can not only refine the grains but also homogenize the second phases. Due to the higher total deformation strain of the ECAP-ed specimen at the die channel angle of 90°, the grain size and second phases are more uniform than those at 120°, and the proportion of recrystallized grains is higher, which causes the dislocation density to be lower than that at 120°. After the ECAP, the {10–10} cylindrical texture strength of the ECAP-ed specimen decreases, yet the {0001} basal texture and {11–20} pyramidal texture are enhanced.

2. The results show that the {0001} basal texture is decomposed into {10–10} and {2-1–10} textures with the increase in compression deformation degree, resulting in texture softening, thus reducing the yield strength. Grain refinement can activate more slip systems, thereby improving the plastic deformation ability of the material. In addition, the size of the second phase decreases, which reduces the possibility of cracking at the second phase and increases the strength with the increase in number of passes.

3. The electrochemical measurement results show that the corrosion resistance of the ECAP-ed sample is stronger due to grain refinement and homogenization; however, the corrosion resistance decreases due to the defects caused by ECAP with the increase in number of passes. The experimental results indicate that the ECAP-ed sample of 90°-1-pass has the best corrosion resistance.

Author Contributions: Conceptualization, X.Z., J.H., J.T. and L.Z.; methodology, L.Z.; software, J.T.; validation, P.Z., Y.W., and Z.J.; formal analysis, Y.W. and Z.J.; Investigation, P.Z. and Z.J.; resources, X.Z. and J.T.; data curation, J.H. and L.Z.; writing—original draft preparation, X.Z. and J.T.; writing—

review and editing, J.H. and L.Z.; visualization, Y.W. and Z.J.; supervision, Y.W. and Z.J.; project administration, J.H. and L.Z.; funding acquisition, J.H., J.T. and Z.J. All authors have read and agreed to the published version of the manuscript.

Funding: This work was supported by the Special Fund for Frontier Technology Research/Advanced Materials of Suzhou. Fund No.: SYG202353.

Data Availability Statement: The original contributions presented in this study are included in the article. Further inquiries can be directed to the corresponding authors.

Conflicts of Interest: The authors declare no conflict of interest.

References

1. Li, D.; Zhang, D.; Yuan, Q.; Liu, L.; Li, H.; Xiong, L.; Guo, X.; Yan, Y.; Yu, K.; Dai, Y.; et al. In Vitro and in Vivo Assessment of the Effect of Biodegradable Magnesium Alloys on Osteogenesis. *Acta Biomater.* **2022**, *141*, 454–465. [CrossRef] [PubMed]
2. Aksenov, D.; Nazarov, A.; Shishkunova, M.; Asfandiyarov, R.; Raab, A.; Sementeeva, Y. Bulk Ultrasonic Treatment of Magnesium and Mg-Zn-Zr Alloy Subjected to ECAP. *J. Alloys Compd.* **2025**, *1014*, 178632. [CrossRef]
3. He, M.; Chen, L.; Yin, M.; Xu, S.; Liang, Z. Review on Magnesium and Magnesium-Based Alloys as Biomaterials for Bone Immobilization. *J. Mater. Res. Technol.* **2023**, *23*, 4396–4419.
4. Wang, X.J.; Nie, K.B.; Sa, X.J.; Hu, X.S.; Wu, K.; Zheng, M.Y. Microstructure and Mechanical Properties of SiCp/MgZnCa Composites Fabricated by Stir Casting. *Mater. Sci. Eng. A* **2012**, *534*, 60–67. [CrossRef]
5. Tang, C.; Lyu, S.; Zhao, Z.; Chen, M. Effects of MgO Nano Particles on the Mechanical Properties and Corrosion Behavior of Mg–Zn–Ca Alloy. *Mater. Chem. Phys.* **2023**, *297*, 127380. [CrossRef]
6. Goh, C.S.; Gupta, M.; Wei, J.; Lee, L.C. Characterization of High Performance Mg/MgO Nanocomposites. *J. Compos. Mater.* **2007**, *41*, 2325–2335. [CrossRef]
7. Han, W.Z.; Zhang, Z.F.; Wu, S.D.; Li, S.X. Investigation on the Geometrical Aspect of Deformation during Equal-Channel Angular Pressing by in-Situ Physical Modeling Experiments. *Mater. Sci. Eng. A* **2008**, *476*, 224–229. [CrossRef]
8. Luis-Pérez, C.J.; Luri-Irigoyen, R.; Gastón-Ochoa, D. Finite Element Modelling of an Al-Mn Alloy by Equal Channel Angular Extrusion (ECAE). *J. Mater. Process. Technol.* **2004**, *153–154*, 846–852. [CrossRef]
9. Horky, J.; Bryła, K.; Krystian, M.; Mozdzen, G.; Mingler, B.; Sajti, L. Improving Mechanical Properties of Lean Mg–Zn–Ca Alloy for Absorbable Implants via Double Equal Channel Angular Pressing (D-ECAP). *Mater. Sci. Eng. A* **2021**, *826*, 142002. [CrossRef]
10. Li, J.; He, T.; Du, X.Y.; Vereschaka, A.; Zhang, J.J. Regulating Hardness Homogeneity and Corrosion Resistance of Al-Zn-Mg-Cu Alloy via ECAP Combined with Inter-Pass Aging. *Mater. Charact.* **2024**, *218*, 114489. [CrossRef]
11. Gazizov, M.R.; Mironov, S.Y.; Holmestad, R.; Gazizova, M.Y.; Kaibyshev, R.O. Effect of ECAP and Aging on Microstructure of an Al-Cu-Mg-Si Alloy. *Mater. Charact.* **2024**, *218*, 114500. [CrossRef]
12. Huang, H.; Liu, H.; Wang, C.; Sun, J.; Bai, J.; Xue, F.; Jiang, J.; Ma, A. Potential of Multi-Pass ECAP on Improving the Mechanical Properties of a High-Calcium-Content Mg-Al-Ca-Mn Alloy. *J. Magnes. Alloys* **2019**, *7*, 617–627. [CrossRef]
13. Cabibbo, M.; Santecchia, E.; Mengucci, P.; Bellezze, T.; Viceré, A. The Role of Cryogenic Dipping Prior to ECAP in the Microstructure, Secondary-Phase Precipitation, Mechanical Properties and Corrosion Resistance of AA6012 (Al-Mg-Si-Pb). *Mater. Sci. Eng. A* **2018**, *716*, 107–119. [CrossRef]
14. Jin, Z.; Yu, D.; Wu, X.; Yin, K.; Yan, K. Drag Effects of Solute and Second Phase Distributions on the Grain Growth Kinetics of Pre-Extruded Mg-6Zn Alloy. *J. Mater. Sci. Technol.* **2016**, *32*, 1260–1266. [CrossRef]
15. Figueiredo, R.B.; Langdon, T.G. Analysis of the Creep Behavior of Fine-Grained AZ31 Magnesium Alloy. *Mater. Sci. Eng. A* **2020**, *787*, 139489. [CrossRef]
16. Yang, Z.; Ma, A.; Xu, B.; Jiang, J.; Sun, J. Corrosion Behavior of AZ91 Mg Alloy with a Heterogeneous Structure Produced by ECAP. *Corros. Sci.* **2021**, *187*, 109517. [CrossRef]
17. Figueiredo, R.B.; Beyerlein, I.J.; Zhilyaev, A.P.; Langdon, T.G. Evolution of Texture in a Magnesium Alloy Processed by ECAP through Dies with Different Angles. *Mater. Sci. Eng. A* **2010**, *527*, 1709–1718. [CrossRef]
18. Tong, L.B.; Zheng, M.Y.; Hu, X.S.; Wu, K.; Xu, S.W.; Kamado, S.; Kojima, Y. Influence of ECAP Routes on Microstructure and Mechanical Properties of Mg-Zn-Ca Alloy. *Mater. Sci. Eng. A* **2010**, *527*, 4250–4256. [CrossRef]
19. Zhang, S.; Liu, Z.; Xin, Y.; Cai, Y.; Han, J. Effect of Equal Channel Angular Pressing on Microstructure and Mechanical Performance of Innovative Nano MgO-Added Mg-Zn-Ca Composite as a Biomaterial. *Mater. Lett.* **2021**, *304*, 130604. [CrossRef]
20. Zhang, S.; Zhu, L.; Song, J.; Liu, Z.; Chen, M.; Han, J.; Jiang, Z. Effect of ECAP on Corrosion Behavior of Innovative Nano MgO/Mg-Zn-Ca Composite as a Biomedical Material in Simulated Body Environment. *Mater. Today Commun.* **2023**, *35*, 106345. [CrossRef]

21. Iwahashi, Y.; Horita, Z.; Nemoto, M.; Langdon, T.G. An Investigation of Microstructural Evolution during Equal-Channel Angular Pressing. *Acta Mater.* **1997**, *45*, 4733–4741. [CrossRef]
22. *GB/T 7314–2005*; Metallic materials-Compresion testing at ambient temperature. National Standardization Administration: Beijing, China, 2005.
23. Khani, S.; Aboutalebi, M.R.; Salehi, M.T.; Samim, H.R.; Palkowski, H. Microstructural Development during Equal Channel Angular Pressing of As-Cast AZ91 Alloy. *Mater. Sci. Eng. A* **2016**, *678*, 44–56. [CrossRef]
24. Zhang, L.; Li, Y. Dynamic Recrystallization Mechanism, Texture Evolution Development and Mechanical Characteristics of a Mg–8.7Gd–4.18Y–0.42Zr Magnesium Alloy by ECAP. *Prog. Nat. Sci. Mater. Int.* **2024**, *34*, 376–388. [CrossRef]
25. Agwa, M.A.; Ali, M.N.; Al-Shorbagy, A.E. Optimum Processing Parameters for Equal Channel Angular Pressing. *Mech. Mater.* **2016**, *100*, 1–11. [CrossRef]
26. Wu, F.; Jiang, F.; Ye, P.; Su, Y.; Long, M. A Bimodal Grain Structured Al-Mg-Sc-Zr Alloy with Excellent Strength and Ductility by the Combination of Hot Rolling and Thermal-ECAP. *Mater. Today Commun.* **2025**, *43*, 111632. [CrossRef]
27. Sun, Z.; Li, Y.; Ma, M.; Li, X.; Shi, G.; Yuan, J.; Chen, D.; Zhang, K. Study on the Effect of the ECAP Deformation on the Organization and Properties of the Extruded Mg-Sn-Al Alloys. *Mater. Lett.* **2024**, *357*, 135775. [CrossRef]
28. Calcagnotto, M.; Ponge, D.; Demir, E.; Raabe, D. Orientation Gradients and Geometrically Necessary Dislocations in Ultrafine Grained Dual-Phase Steels Studied by 2D and 3D EBSD. *Mater. Sci. Eng. A* **2010**, *527*, 2738–2746. [CrossRef]
29. Paudel, Y.R.; Indeck, J.; Hazeli, K.; Priddy, M.W.; Inal, K.; Rhee, H.; Barrett, C.D.; Whittington, W.R.; Limmer, K.R.; El Kadiri, H. Characterization and Modeling of {101¯2} Twin Banding in Magnesium. *Acta Mater.* **2020**, *183*, 438–451. [CrossRef]
30. Wang, Y.; Choo, H. Influence of Texture on Hall-Petch Relationships in an Mg Alloy. *Acta Mater.* **2014**, *81*, 83–97. [CrossRef]
31. Liu, Q.; Ma, Q.X.; Chen, G.Q.; Cao, X.; Zhang, S.; Pan, J.L.; Zhang, G.; Shi, Q.Y. Enhanced Corrosion Resistance of AZ91 Magnesium Alloy through Refinement and Homogenization of Surface Microstructure by Friction Stir Processing. *Corros. Sci.* **2018**, *138*, 284–296. [CrossRef]
32. Cubides, Y.; Ivan Karayan, A.; Vaughan, M.W.; Karaman, I.; Castaneda, H. Enhanced Mechanical Properties and Corrosion Resistance of a Fine-Grained Mg-9Al-1Zn Alloy: The Role of Bimodal Grain Structure and β-Mg17Al12 Precipitates. *Materialia* **2020**, *13*, 100840. [CrossRef]

metals

Article

Mechanical Properties of 7075-T6 Aluminum Alloy in Electrically Assisted Forming

Shasha Dou , Zhuang Liu, Zhijun Li, Haojie Shi , Kang Zhou and Jiansheng Xia *

College of Mechanical Engineering, Yancheng Institute of Technology, Yancheng 224051, China; lisadou@ycit.edu.cn (S.D.); lzjxzjx@163.com (Z.L.); 19962412659@163.com (Z.L.); 17851736608@163.com (H.S.); weirdozhouk@163.com (K.Z.)
* Correspondence: xiajs@ycit.edu.cn; Tel.: +86-15861988970

Abstract: The coupling effects of electrical pulse, temperature, strain rate, and strain on the flow behavior and plasticity of 7075-T6 aluminum alloy were investigated and characterized. The isothermal tensile test and electrically assisted isothermal tensile test were performed at the same temperature, and the typical models were further embedded in ABAQUS for numerical simulation to illustrate the electroplastic effect. The results showed that electrical pulses reduced deformation resistance but greatly increased elongation. Compared with the traditional Johnson–Cook model, the proposed modified electroplasticity constitutive equations have a certain improvement in calibration accuracy for a highly nonlinear and thermoelectric coupling dynamic behavior. Moreover, combined with the electrically assisted three-point bending experiment, it was found that the springback angle decreases with the increase in current density. This is very close to the experimental result, further verifying the effectiveness of the thermoelectric coupling constitutive equation.

Keywords: 7075-T6 aluminum alloy; material characterization; electroplastic effects; Johnson–Cook constitutive equation; uniaxial tensile

1. Introduction

The 7075-T6 aluminum alloy has excellent properties such as a high strength-to-density ratio, high fracture toughness, and resistance to stress corrosion cracking. However, its poor formability at room temperature restricts its application scope. How to effectively improve its formability has become a hot topic in the research field. Electrically assisted stamping forming is a new technology with great application prospects. Compared with traditional hot forming, its non-thermal effect can effectively improve the formability of metal materials and reduce residual stress. At present, during the electrically assisted plastic deformation process, the influence of pulsed current on the mechanical properties of the 7075-T6 aluminum alloy and its mechanism of action are still unclear. During the electrically assisted plastic deformation process, in addition to the thermal effect under the action of current, there is also a non-thermal effect. However, due to the different mechanisms of action for different materials, a unified theory has not been formed yet. Therefore, determining the rheological mechanical properties of materials under the action of pulsed current and establishing accurate constitutive equations are particularly important for improving the simulation accuracy of software. The mechanical properties [1–3] of the 7075-T6 aluminum alloy were obtained through electrically assisted uniaxial tensile experimental analysis and numerical simulation, including thermal and non-thermal effects of the material [4,5]. To further utilize the mathematical model method to represent the relationship between flow stress and strain of materials under plasticity effects, a

 https://doi.org/10.3390/met15020117

traditional constitutive equation was used to link current density with thermal activation behavior [6,7]. Additionally, the thermoelectrically coupled constitutive equation of the material needs to be established. The equation can be effectively imported into the finite element software for simulation analysis to improve the simulation accuracy.

Since the 1960s, the theory of electroplastic deformation [6,8–12] has been studied, but there are few reports on its industrial applications. Electrically assisted production creates complex shapes for forming aluminum alloy components, especially in lightweight automotive design. Applying an electric current reduces the material's yield strength when machining aluminum and copper alloys, facilitating processes like stamping and tensile. Roh et al. [13] modified the power-law Hollomon hardening model by fitting the electroplastic experimental data. They developed a comprehensive phenomenological model that includes Joule heating and electroplastic effects to quantify their contribution to mechanical behavior. However, the model did not capture the stress drop [14,15]. Wang et al. [16] separated the Joule heating effect from the microscopic thermal effect caused by electrical pulses to construct a composite model. DINH K-A [17] found that the current increased elongation in electrically assisted two-stage forming experiments on Al-Mg and Al-Si-Mg alloys and the quantitative effect of the current on the synthesized microstructures [18] depended on the type of aluminum alloy. Adam Jordan [19] demonstrated through electrically assisted bending tests that applying electric current to the Al6111 aluminum alloy reduced its deformation resistance [11,20] and inhibited springback [12,21]. The DIC measurement system found a more homogeneous strain distribution over the thickness, particularly for the coarse grain structure, related to the electrophysical effect.

The objective of this study is to investigate the effect of electrical pulse on the dynamic mechanical responses of the 7075 aluminum alloy and its analytical modeling approached for numerical simulation. The conventional Johnson–Cook constitutive equation was appropriately modified based on the stress–strain curves obtained from unidirectional tensile experiments on the 7075-T6 aluminum alloy. By combining high-temperature and thermoplastic parameters, a new thermoelectrically coupled constitutive equation, EA-Johnson–Cook, suitable for this material, was developed. After obtaining the relevant parameters, the new equation's ability to predict rheological stresses is analyzed. Finally, based on Huber-von Mises theory of plasticity, the modified constitutive equation is implemented in the ABAQUS software through the UMAT (UMAT stands for "User-defined Material Subroutine" and refers to a user-defined material modeling subroutine in ABAQUS software. Using UMAT, the user can implement customized constitutive equations to simulate the behavior of materials in finite element analysis (FEA).) subroutine to evaluate the effectiveness of the constitutive equation algorithm. This paper discusses the effects of strain rate and current density on the mechanical properties of the 7075 aluminum alloy. The EA-Johnson–Cook constitutive equation proposed in this paper is superior in accuracy to the traditional Johnson–Cook constitutive equation and is more suitable for thermoelectric coupling applications. It quantifies the impact of each parameter through constitutive equations, providing a reference for the application of electrically assisted machining.

2. Experimental Equipment and Materials

2.1. Experimental Materials

The thickness of the test material, a 7075-T6 aluminum alloy sheet supplied by Chalco Ruimin Company, was 1 mm (The city of origin of the device is Fujian Province and the country is China.). Its chemical composition is shown in Table 1, and its mechanical properties are represented in Table 2. The sheet was processed into the required shape for the tensile test by punching, and the dimensions of the specimen are illustrated in Figure 1, considering the gauge and high-temperature tensile test design. The units in the figure were in millimeters.

Table 1. Chemical composition of 7075-T6 aluminum alloy (mass fraction, %).

Element	Cu	Mg	Fe	Ti	Zn	Si	Cr	Al
Quality score	1.63	3.161	0.1309	0.2113	6.10	0.03	0.22	Balanced

Table 2. The main mechanical properties of 7075-T6 aluminum alloy.

Tensile Strength (MPa)	Yield Strength (MPa)	Elongation (%)	Elastic Modulus (GPa)
547.5	490.7	13.4	70

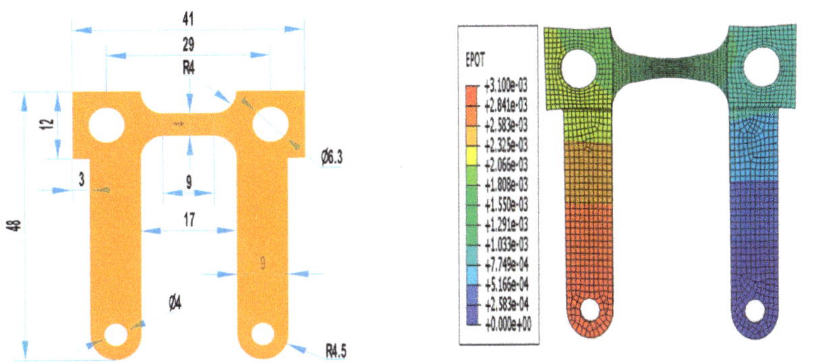

(**a**) (**b**)

Figure 1. (**a**) Dimensions of electrically assisted tensile specimens; (**b**) voltage distribution of 7075-T6 aluminum alloy sample.

2.2. Experimental Equipment

(1) Pulse power supply and thermal imager

As shown in Figure 2a, the SMD-100 dual-pulse electroplating power supply was utilized, capable of operating in unidirectional or bidirectional modes. The waveform was rectangular, with a current range of 0 to 200 A and a duty cycle range of 1 to 99%. By adjusting the current magnitude and duty cycle, this power supply could generate the required pulse current for the experiment. Due to the relatively high current intensity used in the experiment, it was essential to wear insulating gloves to prevent safety hazards. Additionally, as shown in Figure 2b, a FLIR E5 WiFi model thermal imager was employed, and it features a spectral range of 7.5 to 13 μm and a measurable temperature range of −20 to 900 °C. When current passes through the material, it introduces heat into the material. Simultaneously, heat exchanged with the surrounding air and heat radiation contributed to heat loss.

(2) Electrically assisted tensile platform

A current-assisted uniaxial tensile testing machine for sheet metal was designed to integrate current parameters, temperature detection, and temperature control. A pinning device was included for insulation to prevent current damage to the machine. Figure 3a illustrates the quasi-static uniaxial tensile test apparatus supported by pulsed current. The conductor was wrapped around the energized interface of the specimen, which was coated with the PTFE adhesive and sprayed with black boron nitride paint. The fixture structure is shown in Figure 3b.

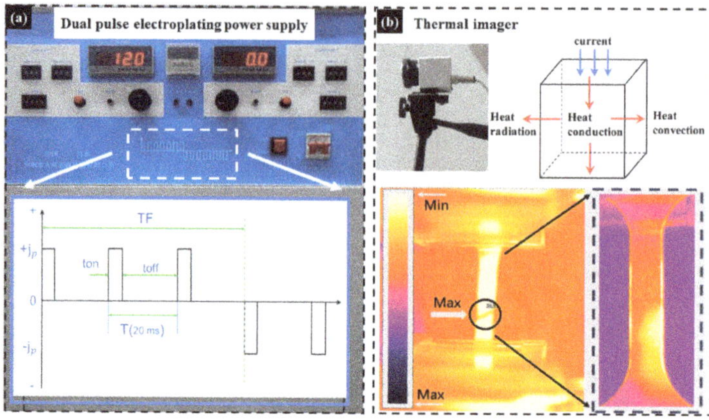

Figure 2. Experimental equipment diagram: (**a**) pulse power supply and waveform schematic and (**b**) thermal imaging camera and heat transfer schematic.

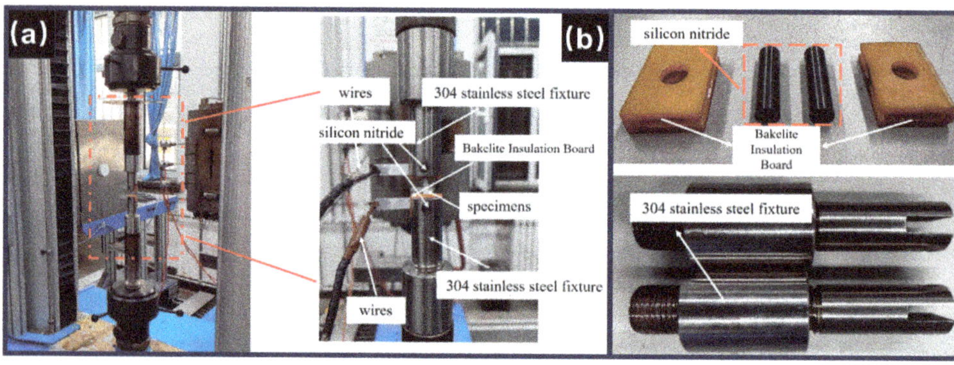

Figure 3. Electrically assisted tensile platform: (**a**) electrically assisted tensile test platform and (**b**) fixture design.

As shown in Figure 3, the pin material was silicon nitride. It was known for its excellent flexural and shear strength, capable of withstanding thermal shocks. Bakelite served as insulation, while the upper and lower fixtures were made from high-temperature 304 stainless steel. The tensile testing of 7075-T6 aluminum alloy commenced, with the pulsed power supply requiring heating or cooling at the beginning and end of each test to ensure the current was effective.

2.3. Experimental Principle

An electrically assisted uniaxial tensile test involves introducing a pulse current into the traditional tensile process. Experimental platforms include a fixture insulation design in which a plastic or wood insulator is inserted between the original universal tensile testing machine fixture. This design prevents electrical conductivity, thereby ensuring normal equipment operation. The test principle is illustrated in Figure 4.

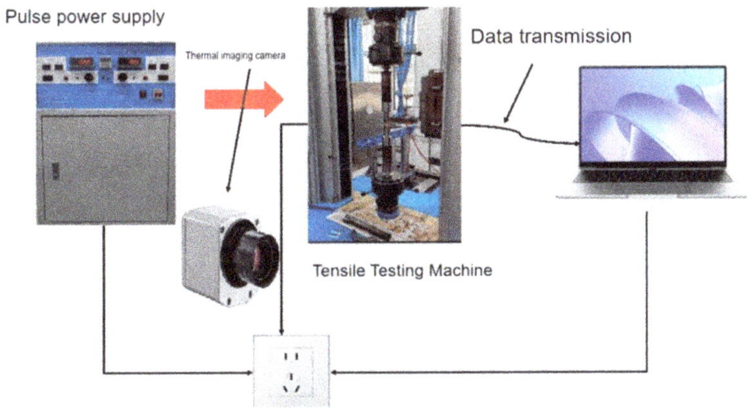

Figure 4. Experimental process schematic.

The current-assisted tensile testing device mainly comprised four components: the tensile testing platform, pulse power supply, control system, and data acquisition platform. The tensile testing platform included a tensile fixture, specimen, and bench. The power supply consisted of the pulse power supply unit, insulated fixture, and electrode connector, ensuring a closed loop during testing to adjust current and voltage parameters. The control system was primarily composed of a tensile testing machine controller that regulates the speed. The data acquisition platform comprises a computer, force sensor, electronic extensometer, and USB interface. The data acquisition platform mainly consisted of a laptop, a force sensor, an electronic extensometer, and a USB interface. Utilizing the M223C testing measurement and control system, the tensile force and displacement were measured in real-time during the tensile test. The software generated the force–displacement and stress–strain curves, enabling automated data acquisition.

2.4. Experimental Arrangement

During sheet metal forming simulations, inaccurate material stress–strain parameters can lead to low accuracy. In current-assisted metal tensile testing, stress and strain varied inconsistently, requiring precise measurement. Four variables—current density, pulse frequency, shear rate, and accurate strain–strain curves—were established through electrically assisted tensile tests. This process helped create a new material constitutive equation, improving the accuracy of simulations and examining the impact of pulse current on the mechanical properties of aluminum alloy sheets. During tensile testing, this section focused on studying the effects of varying current densities and strain rates on the mechanical properties of the 7075-T6 aluminum alloy. The test parameters are shown in Table 3, where the four sets of temperatures (150 °C, 210 °C, 270 °C, and 330 °C) represent the reference temperatures measured at four sets of current densities (8 A/mm^2, 14 A/mm^2, 20 A/mm^2, and 26 A/mm^2).

Table 3. Experimental schedule.

Current Density (A/mm^2)	Pulse Frequency (HZ)	Title Strain Rate (s^{-1})	Temperature (°C)
8	200	0.01	150
14	200	0.1	210
20	200	1	270
26	200	10	330

2.5. Experimental Results

When the pulse frequency is 200 Hz, the stress is obtained at four different strain rates and four different current densities (8 A/mm^2, 14 A/mm^2, 20 A/mm^2, and 26 A/mm^2) during the tensile process. The strain curve is shown in Figure 5. The analysis of the high-temperature tensile stress–strain curve revealed a decrease in flow stress as the temperature rose to 150 °C. Plasticity remained stable due to the accelerated heat-activated slip mechanism at high temperatures, which quickly eliminated dislocations and reduced tensile strength. There are no obvious signs of temperature softening at 210 °C. The most notable stress reduction occurred between 270 °C and 330 °C, with a sharp decrease in tensile strength at 330 °C. At the same time, the increase in elasticity is related to the thermally activated slip mechanism in the crystals, because the generated thermal energy promotes the rapid movement of dislocations and reduces the concentration of stress in the lattice, thus increasing the plasticity of the material.

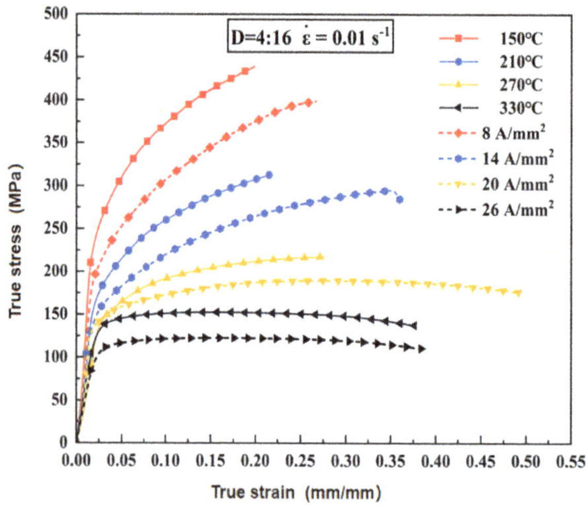

Figure 5. True stress–strain curves of isothermal temperature tensile and electrically assisted tensile strength.

The significant decrease in tensile strength and the increase in ductility at 330 °C are attributed to the thermally activated slip mechanism within the crystals. The primary driving mechanism is thermal energy, which promotes the rapid movement of dislocations and reduces stress concentration within the lattice. This process lowered the yield strength to approximately 150 MPa, enhancing the plasticity. The electrically assisted tensile curve shows that stress decreases and increases material toughness at the same temperature. In addition to the Joule heating effect, the electroplastic impact is also evident, enhancing the plasticity of the material.

In contrast, the Joule heating effect is more significant. When the temperature reaches a certain threshold, the material softens, and the phenomenon of sequestration and entanglement [22,23] is substantial. Introducing electric current to the drift electrons can reduce resistance, enhance mobility, and facilitate slip, potentially lowering the strength of the metal sheet.

As shown in Figure 6, the ultimate tensile stress (UTS) under both high-temperature tensile (TAT) and electrically assisted tensile (EAT) conditions exhibits a stepwise decreasing trend. The ultimate tensile strengths under the influence of electric current decrease to 301.84 MPa, 231.85 MPa, 189.42 MPa, and 144.03 MPa, respectively. Additionally, there is a gradual increase in the post-break elongation of the specimens at high temperatures ($\varepsilon_{fracture}$), highlighting the differences observed under the influence of current. Under different current densities of 39.94%, 44.49%, 49.12%, and 37.33%, the ultimate tensile stress decreased by 76.4 MPa as the current density increased from 20 to 26 A/mm^2. Additionally, the post-break elongation decreased by 10.79%. This is due to the decrease in the fracture area of the steel plate, the increase in the relative current density, and the concentration of heat at the midpoint of the specimen, resulting in an uneven heat distribution.

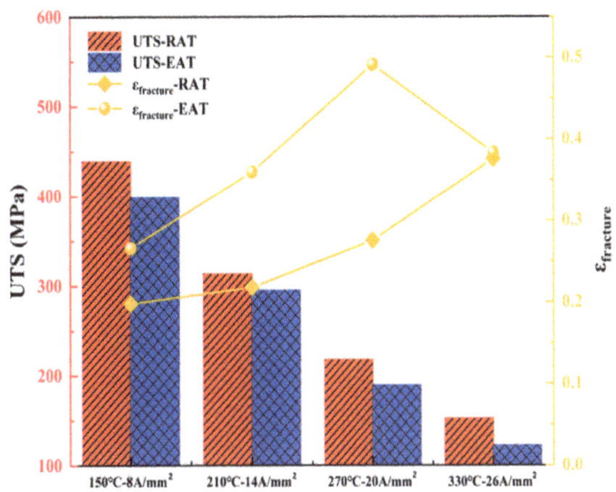

Figure 6. Comparison of ultimate tensile lightness and elongation at break data under high-temperature tensile (TAT) and electrically assisted tensile (EAT) conditions.

2.6. Electroplastic Effect Coefficient Solution

(1) Electroplastic effect decoupling

The difference in flow stress between room temperature and electrically assisted heating is $\Delta\sigma_1$, where σ_R represents the room-temperature tensile rheological stress and σ_E represents the rheological stress obtained through electrically assisted heating. The relationship is expressed in Equation (1):

$$\Delta\sigma_1 = \sigma_R - \sigma_E \tag{1}$$

The difference in flow stress between furnace heating and electrically assisted heating at the same temperature is $\Delta\sigma_2$, where σ_T represents the ultimate tensile strength obtained through furnace heating. The relationship related to the thermoplastic effect is shown in Equation (2):

$$\Delta\sigma_2 = \sigma_R - \sigma_T \tag{2}$$

As presented in Table 4, based on the high-temperature tensile experimental data under electrically assisted heating and at the same temperature, the fracture strain value of the material increases in the high-temperature state. Therefore, the difference in stress cannot be achieved solely through the corresponding strain. Instead, the difference can be observed through variations in peak stress values under different conditions, reflecting changes in plasticity. The maximum stress, or ultimate tensile strength, determines the proportion of purely electrically induced plastic deformation, denoted as ψ in Equation (3):

$$\psi = \frac{\Delta\sigma_1 - \Delta\sigma_2}{\Delta\sigma_1} \times 100\% \tag{3}$$

Table 4. Decoupling of effects at different temperatures under 1 s^{-1}.

Percentage of Electrophysical Effects (A/mm^2)	8 (A/mm^2)	14 (A/mm^2)	20 (A/mm^2)	26 (A/mm^2)
Thermoplastic (%)	48.882	50.029	66.986	75.726
Electrically plasticized	50.254	52.859	69.817	80.481
Purely electro plastic	5.025	5.353	4.056	5.908

(2) Electroplastic effect coefficient solution and law

The ratio of the work performed by the current during plastic deformation to the total power consumed by the pulsed power supply characterized the electrophysical effect coefficient [24,25]. This portion of the electrical power provided sufficient energy for dislocations, enabling them to overcome lattice obstacles and continue their movement. It is assumed that the total power consumed during the plastic deformation stage of the 7075 aluminum alloy remained constant when the sheet temperature was constant, regardless of the current intensity. The total energy consumed during electrically assisted uniaxial tensile was as follows:

$$P_{Total} = P_M + P_E \tag{4}$$

P_{Total} in Equation (4) is the total power during tensile, P_M in Equation (6) is the mechanical power of the tensile testing machine, and P_E in Equation (7) is the electrical power consumed during tensile, where the experimental procedure is all 10 V voltage:

$$P_{Total} = A\sigma_T * \dot{\varepsilon} * l_0 \tag{5}$$

$$P_M = A\sigma_E * \dot{\varepsilon} * l_0 \tag{6}$$

$$P_E = \eta\xi VI = 10AJ_e \tag{7}$$

where A is the instantaneous cross-sectional area of the material, η is the power conversion efficiency, $\dot{\varepsilon}$ is the strain rate, and l_0 is the length of the scalar segment from the above equation:

$$A\sigma_T * \dot{\varepsilon} * l_0 = \eta\xi VI + A\sigma_E * \dot{\varepsilon} * l_0 \tag{8}$$

Referring to Equation (8), assuming a power conversion efficiency of 100% (η = 1) and a scalar segment length of 20 mm, the coefficient of the electrophysical effect could be derived from Equation (9):

$$\xi = \frac{(\Delta\sigma_1 - \Delta\sigma_2)\dot{\varepsilon}}{2J_e} \tag{9}$$

Equation (9) revealed that the variable ξ is correlated with the current density J_e, specimen size, and strain rate ε. For instance, considering a strain rate of 1 s^{-1}, Figure 7 illustrates the trend of the coefficient ξ with the flow stress difference for various current densities. Generally, the electroplastic effect coefficient ξ is not a fixed value [26,27]; it is influenced by factors such as specimen size, current density J_e, and strain rate $\dot{\varepsilon}$.

As shown in Figure 7, the coefficient of the electroplastic effect ξ increases with the current density J_e. The maximum values are summarized in Table 5, which show differences in the contribution of current density to plasticity change and indicate the threshold for enhanced plasticity at a given current density. Therefore, pure electrophilic plasticity can be harnessed to lower the forming temperature and offset the decrease in plasticity resulting from temperature reduction.

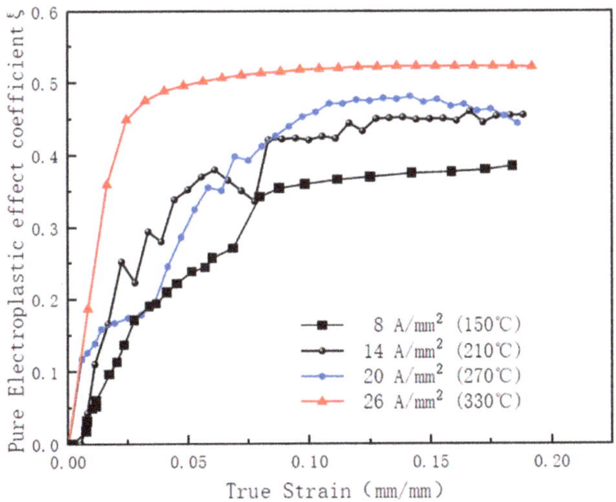

Figure 7. Electroplating effect coefficients at different current densities.

Table 5. Maximum values of purely electroplastic effect coefficient A at different current densities.

Current Density J_e	Purely Electroplastic Effect Coefficient ξ
8 A/mm^2	0.385
14 A/mm^2	0.461
20 A/mm^2	0.482
26 A/mm^2	0.523

3. 7075-T6 Electroplasticity Constitutive Equations

3.1. Johnson–Cook Constitutive Equation

Johnson–Cook develops an image-only constitutive model that considers the strain hardening, strain rate, and thermal softening [28,29] described above. It creates expressions for ε_p, $\dot{\varepsilon}$, and T that are independent. Equation (10) is as follows:

$$\sigma(\varepsilon_p, \dot{\varepsilon}, T) = (A + B{\varepsilon_p}^n)[1 + Cln(\dot{\varepsilon}^*)][1 - T^{*m}] \quad (10)$$

where σ is the rheological stress, ε_p is the equivalent plastic strain, $\dot{\varepsilon}^*$ is the dimensionless strain rate, C is the strain rate sensitivity factor, T^* is the temperature effect coefficient, $T^* = (T - T_r)/(T_m - T_r)$, where T_r is the reference temperature, T_m is the melting point temperature, and m is the temperature effect coefficient.

3.2. Electrothermal Conversion

Magargee's experiments [12] observed that, when the metal temperature was cooled to room temperature, there was minimal change in the flow stress of electrically assisted metal deformation, and it suggested that most electric heat was transferred as thermal energy. Therefore, in the investigation of electrically assisted forming, it was crucial first to analyze the conversion of electrical energy into thermomechanical energy and examine the direct conversion of electrical and thermal energy.

(1) Conversion of electrical energy and thermal energy

In electrically assisted forming, the heating of the metal material is closely related to the energizing time and current density. Assuming that the whole heat transfer process is adiabatic [30], then the Joule heating (Q_H) of the heat conduction entering the material is stored in the system in proportion to the heat capacity of the material (Q_R). The applied Joule thermal energy is the same as the thermal energy stored by the capacitor, and the energy conversion Equation (11) is as follows:

$$Q_H = Q_R \tag{11}$$

where Q_H is Joule thermal energy;

Q_R is thermal energy stored in the material system.

According to the Joule heat [19,31] equation $Q_H = I^2 R \Delta t$, where $I = J_e A$, from the equation defining resistance (J_e is the current density, ρ_E is the resistivity of the material, and Δt is the time of energization). According to the thermal energy formula $Q_R = mC_P\Delta T$ (m is the mass of the material, C_P is the specific heat capacity, and ΔT is the temperature difference), where $m = \rho_D AL$ (ρ_D is the mass density, A is the cross-sectional area of the center of the specimen at the time of current flow, and L is the length of the material), as shown in Table 6:

Table 6. Material parameters of the 7075-T6 aluminum alloy at room temperature.

ρ_d(t/mm^3)	C_p(J/t·°C)	ρ_E(Ω·mm)	T_m(°C)
12.81×10^{-9}	9.454×10^5	5.19×10^{-5}	477

Substituting the above equation into the energy conversion Equation (11), Equation (12) is as follows:

$$\frac{(J_e A)^2 \rho_E L}{A}\Delta t = \rho_D ALC_P\Delta T \tag{12}$$

The deformation is derived and is as follows:

$$\frac{\Delta T}{\Delta t} = \frac{\rho_E}{\rho_D C_P}{J_e}^2 \tag{13}$$

During the experiment, the temperature at the center of the sheet can be measured using a thermal imager after increasing the current. Figure 8 shows the relationship between the energizing time and temperature under various currents. As the current density increases, the temperature rises. At 0–8 s, temperature rises faster, and at 8–40 s, temperature rises slower until the sheet breaks.

(2) Thermoelectric conversion functions

According to the data on the tensile strength of the 7075-T6 aluminum alloy at high temperatures, the material parameter "thermoelectric conversion parameter" is defined. $T_v(J_e)$ is the ratio of high-temperature tensile strength to tensile strength at room temperature, and Equation (14) can be converted into the following:

$$T_v(J_e) = \frac{T - T_R}{T_m - T_R} = \frac{\Delta T}{T_m - T_R} = \frac{\rho_E \Delta t}{\rho_D C_P (T_m - T_R)}{J_e}^2 = K{J_e}^2 \tag{14}$$

where K is the time-dependent softening time function.

The relationship is established between the thermal-softening parameters generated by current Joule heating and the effective current density, which ends when the temperature rises to the material's melting point. The thermoelectric conversion parameters increased with the increase in current density. The growth rate is slower at the beginning, and the temperature of the aluminum alloy increases faster after the current density reaches 8 A/mm^2; when the current density further increases to 15~25 A/mm^2, the temperature rises to the melting point. It is shown that the thermal-softening parameter value increases with a longer energizing time at the same current density, leading to a more pronounced thermal-softening effect induced by Joule heating.

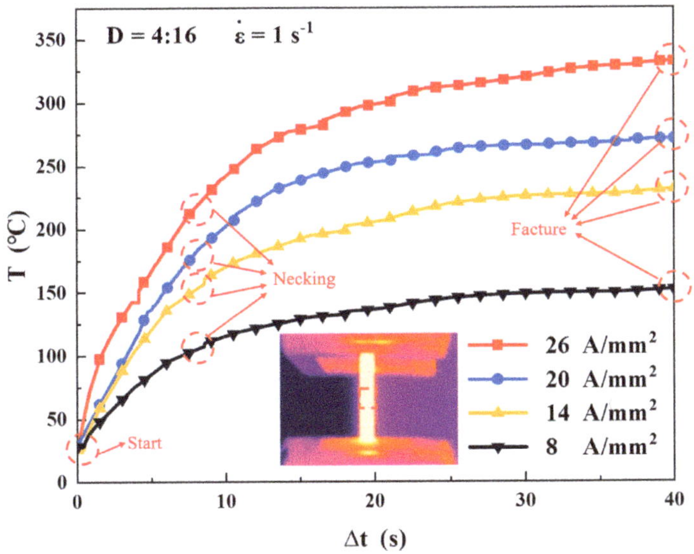

Figure 8. Temperature rise curves at different current densities.

For aluminum alloys with low melting points (<1000 °C), thermoplastic deformation is usually characterized by a wide range of stresses and temperatures. Sheikh-Ahmad utilizes this approach to showcase the efficacy of electrically assisted tensile tests for high-temperature uniaxial tests at varying strain rates [9]. He employs an s-shaped exponential form to express the empirical correlation between the thermal-softening parameters and temperature. This correlation is known as the thermoelectric softening function, as shown in Equation (15):

$$f(T) = \frac{\lambda_1}{\lambda_1 + \exp[\lambda_2 T_V(J_e)]} \tag{15}$$

Substitution of the electrothermal conversion parameters concerning the current density leads to Equation (16):

$$f(T) = \frac{\lambda_1}{\lambda_1 + \exp\left[\frac{\lambda_2 {J_e}^2 \rho_E \Delta t}{(T_m - T_R)\rho_D C_P}\right]} \tag{16}$$

The sum of the equation is the parameters of λ_1, λ_2. The least squares fitting method and experimental data can determine the conversion function.

The fitting curves for the 7075-T6 aluminum alloy at different times are shown in Figure 9. At lower current densities, the current does not significantly affect the material's behavior. However, small changes in the current density can dramatically alter the material's properties at higher densities, reaching a critical value known as the "current density threshold". For the 7075-T6 aluminum alloy, the change in tensile strength is observed to be very small at the effective current density below 5 A/mm^2, but the tensile strength is significantly reduced between 5~25 A/mm^2.

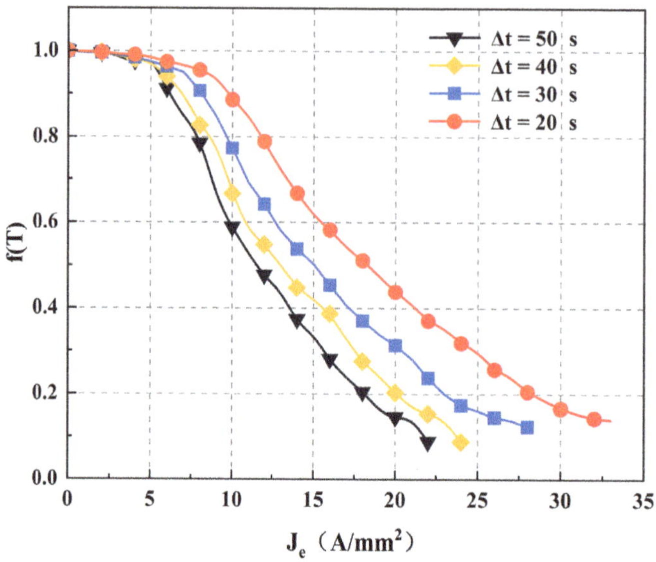

Figure 9. Relationship curves under different power-on times $Je-(T)$.

(3) Current density threshold

By computing the rate of thermal-softening change concerning the effective current density and formulating the function, a useful approach was presented to quantify the position and limit of the current density threshold. This method helped to determine the relative impact of the effective current density on the thermal-softening rate, known as the "current density sensitivity". It clarified how thermal softening varies with respect to the current density. The current density needed for the optimal thermal softening of the material could be determined through analysis. When an electric current induced thermal softening in a low-melting-point metal, the required current density for maximum effectiveness could be estimated within the appropriate "current density sensitivity range". Consequently, the thermal-softening Equation (17) can be established.

$$\left|\frac{\partial f(J_e)}{\partial J_e}\right| = \left|\frac{2cd\rho_E J_e exp\left(\frac{d\rho_E {J_e}^2}{\rho_D c_{p(T_m-T_R)}}\right)}{\left(c+exp\left(\frac{d\rho_E {J_e}^2}{\rho_D c_{p(T_m-T_R)}}\right)\right)^2 \rho_D c_{p(T_m-T_R)}}\right| \tag{17}$$

Figure 10 illustrates that the current density helps to identify the required current density for effective thermal softening. As the energizing time increases within a specific range, the peak value and the adequate current density sensitivity increase. Evaluating the current density sensitivity of a particular material allows us to optimize and select the most appropriate current density for inducing softening. This process also enables us to assess the effect of electrically assisted deformation on a given workpiece material. When the power-on time is 40 s, the sensitive narrow-band range aligns with the density gradient used in the test.

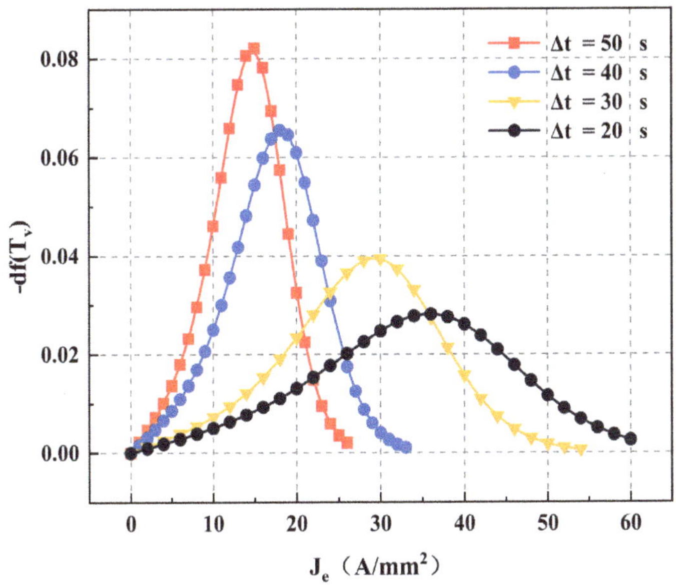

Figure 10. Different power-on-times relationship curves of $J_e - df(T_v)$.

3.3. Electroplasticity Constitutive Equations

Utilizing the Johnson–Cook model and electroplasticity analysis, the electrically assisted plastic deformation of the 7075-T6 aluminum alloy was characterized, which led to the establishment of the electroplasticity constitutive model, EA-Johnson–Cook. Initially, the model's strength and strain-hardening coefficients were derived from room-temperature tensile tests. Subsequently, the thermal-softening term governing the stress behavior at elevated temperatures was determined. Finally, the electroplasticity constitutive model for aluminum alloy materials was analyzed and validated through integration with the finite element software [32].

(1) EA-Johnson–Cook constitutive equations

Based on the Johnson–Cook model at high temperatures, an electrical and thermal energy conversion term, the electrothermal conversion function $f(T)$, is added to characterize the electrically assisted tensile behavior. The electroplasticity constitutive equation EA-Johnson–Cook of the material can be expressed as follows:

$$\sigma(\varepsilon_\rho, \dot{\varepsilon}, T) = F(\varepsilon_p)G(\dot{\varepsilon})f(T) = (A + B\varepsilon_p{}^n)\left[1 + Cln\left(\frac{\dot{\varepsilon}}{\dot{\varepsilon}_0}\right)\right]f(T) \tag{18}$$

where $F(\varepsilon_p)$ is the strain-hardening function;

$G(\dot{\varepsilon})$ is the strain rate function;

$f(T)$ is the electrothermal conversion function.

(2) Determination of strain-hardening function

When $\varepsilon^* = 1$ and $T^* = 0$, and when the stress changes with strain, the strain-hardening function of the material is as follows:

$$F(\varepsilon_p) = A + B\varepsilon_p{}^n \tag{19}$$

A, B, and n represent the initial yield stress, the material strain-hardening modulus, and the hardening index at the reference strain rate and temperature. The above equation shows that it has a linear relationship. When the temperature is 25 °C, and the strain rate is 0.001 s^{-1}, the material's unidirectional tensile true plastic stress–strain curve is shown in Figure 11. At that time, $\varepsilon_P = 0$, and A = 547.512 MPa.

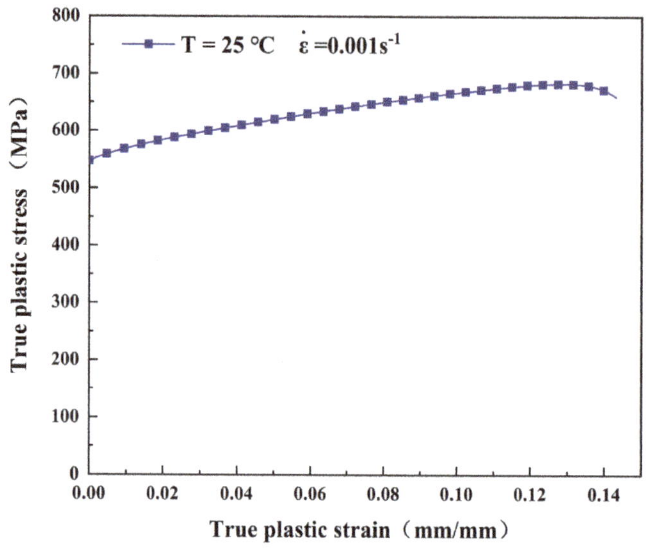

Figure 11. Room-temperature stress–strain curve and fitting with 0.001 s^{-1}.

To calculate the value of n, the least squares fitting method is used, and the natural logarithm is taken on both sides of the equal sign. Then, Equation (20) can be rewritten as follows:

$$ln(\sigma - A) = lnB + nln\varepsilon_P \tag{20}$$

The relationship between the $ln\varepsilon_P$ and $ln(\sigma - A)$ is linear, the slope of the straight line in the graph is the hardening index, and n is calculated at 0.751.

To calculate the value of B, Equation (21) can be rewritten as follows:

$$\sigma - A = B\varepsilon_P{}^n \tag{21}$$

As shown in Figure 12, the relationship curve is plotted. The relationship between $(\sigma - A)$ and $\varepsilon_P{}^n$ is approximately linear, and B is the slope of the curve, and B = 671.202 is obtained by linear fitting.

(3) Determination of strain rate parameters

$G(\dot{\varepsilon})$ is the strain rate function, where $G(\dot{\varepsilon}) = 1 + Cln(\dot{\varepsilon}/\dot{\varepsilon}_0)$, $\dot{\varepsilon}$ is the strain rate, $\dot{\varepsilon}_0$ is the reference strain rate, Equation (22) is as follows, and the real stress–strain data (strains of 0.1 to 0.3 at intervals of 0.05) at four different strain rates at a reference temperature of 25 °C are selected as shown in Figure 13, substituting the true stress–strain data into Equation.

$$\frac{\sigma}{547.512 + 671.202\varepsilon_p^{0.751}} = 1 + Cln\left(\frac{\dot{\varepsilon}}{\varepsilon_0}\right) \tag{22}$$

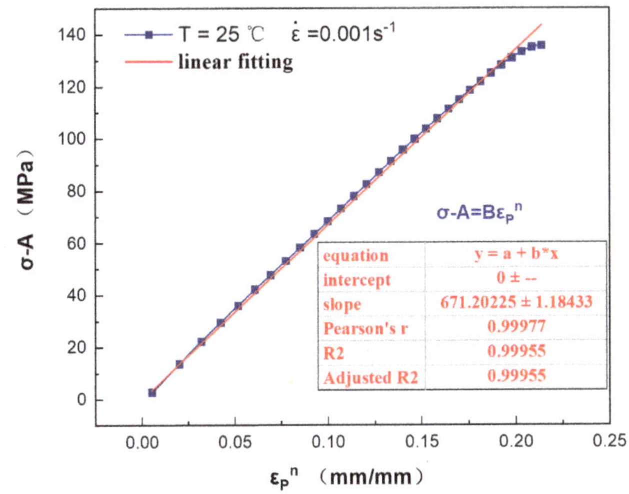

Figure 12. Relationship between $(\sigma - A)$ and $B\varepsilon_p{}^n$.

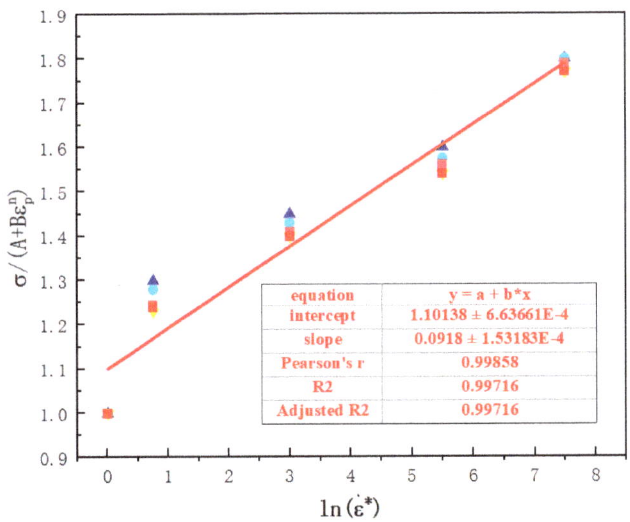

Figure 13. $\sigma/(A + B\varepsilon_p{}^n) - ln\left(\dot{\varepsilon}^*\right)$ fitting curve.

The relationship curve of $\sigma/(A + B\varepsilon_p{}^n) - ln(\dot{\varepsilon}/\dot{\varepsilon}_0)$ is shown in Figure 13, and the value of parameter c is calculated as 0.116 by linear fitting.

(4) Solution of thermal-softening parameter m

Compared to the room-temperature tensile strength, the flow stress of the 7075-T6 aluminum alloy under electric current is much lower, attributed to the thermal-softening effect. $f(T)$ can also be interpreted as the ratio of the strength of high-temperature tensile or electrically assisted tensile to room-temperature tensile as shown in Equation (23):

$$f(T) = \frac{\sigma_E}{\sigma_R} = \frac{\sigma(\varepsilon_\rho, \dot{\varepsilon}, T)}{(547.512 + 671.202\varepsilon_p{}^n)\left[1 + 0.116ln\left(\frac{\dot{\varepsilon}}{\dot{\varepsilon}_0}\right)\right]} \tag{23}$$

Recalling the JC model, we can directly fit the straight line in Figure 14 to obtain Equation (24) to obtain the slope values and the model parameter m.

$$ln\left(1-\frac{\sigma_E}{\sigma_R}\right)=mln\left(\frac{T-T_r}{T_m-T_r}\right) \tag{24}$$

where σ_E is the electrically assisted tensile strength and σ_R is the room-temperature tensile strength.

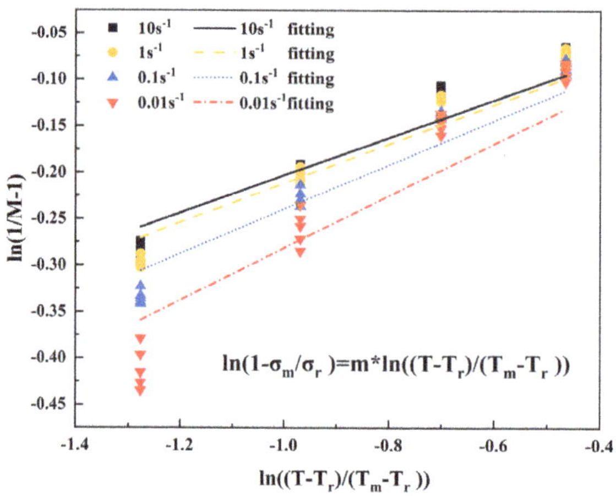

Figure 14. $ln\left(1-\frac{\sigma_m}{\sigma_r}\right)ln\left(\frac{T-T_r}{T_m-T_r}\right)$ fitting curves.

As seen from Table 7, the parameter m increases with increasing strain rate, as higher strain rates lead to more significant plastic deformation. R^2 is maximum at 0.1 s^{-1}, indicating the best model fit at this rate.

Table 7. The analysis of the m-value of the coefficient and the fitting result.

Strain Rate	m	R	R^2	R^2 After Adjustment
10 s^{-1}	0.203	0.98999	0.98009	0.97904
1 s^{-1}	0.212	0.99327	0.98402	0.98318
0.1 s^{-1}	0.239	0.99327	0.98658	0.98588
0.01 s^{-1}	0.281	0.98541	0.97104	0.96952

(5) The electrothermal conversion function

Compared to room-temperature tensile strength, the flow stress of the 7075-T6 aluminum alloy under electric current is significantly lower, attributed to the thermal-softening effect. T_V is a material property parameter, with a value of 0.00289 that is dependent on temperature. $f(T)$ represents the thermal energy function. It is defined as the ratio of the strength of high-temperature tensile or electrically assisted tensile to that of room-temperature tensile, as shown in Equation (25):

$$f(T)=\frac{\sigma(\varepsilon_p,\dot{\varepsilon},T)}{\sigma(\varepsilon_p,\dot{\varepsilon})}=\frac{\lambda_1}{\lambda_1+\exp[\lambda_2 T_V(J_e)]} \tag{25}$$

Let the left side be M to simplify Equation (25), and it leads to Equation (26):

$$l_m\left(\frac{1}{M}-1\right) = \lambda_1 K(T) J_e^2 - ln\lambda_1 \tag{26}$$

Table 8 shows the parameter values for λ_1 and λ_2 at different strain rates.

Table 8. $ln(1/M-1) - J_e$ fitting parameter.

Strain Rate	λ_1	λ_2
10 s^{-1}	0.24925	1.69977
1 s^{-1}	0.25495	1.38498
0.1 s^{-1}	0.37355	1.34597
0.01 s^{-1}	0.82821	1.33816

Taking the rate as 1 s^{-1} as an example, the EA-Johnson–Cook model connecting the current density parameters is presented as Equation (27):

$$\sigma(\varepsilon_\rho, \dot{\varepsilon}, J_e) = (547 + 814.6{\varepsilon_p}^{0.915})\left[1 + 0.1043ln\left(\frac{\dot{\varepsilon}}{\dot{\varepsilon_0}}\right)\right]\frac{0.25495}{0.25495 + \exp[0.004{J_e}^2]} \tag{27}$$

4. Numerical Simulation of Uniaxial Tensile

4.1. Analysis of Current and Temperature Field During Pulsed Current Loading Process

Then, we simulate the current-assisted tensile process, setting a power-on time of 40 s, and four groups current densities (8 A/mm^2, 14 A/mm^2, 20 A/mm^2, and 26 A/mm^2) for comparison. This analysis aims to examine the distribution patterns of the temperature field, current field, and strain field during the energized tensile process. The simulation results are shown in Figure 15, which illustrates the current distribution and uniform distribution of current density across the marked distance section of the specimen.

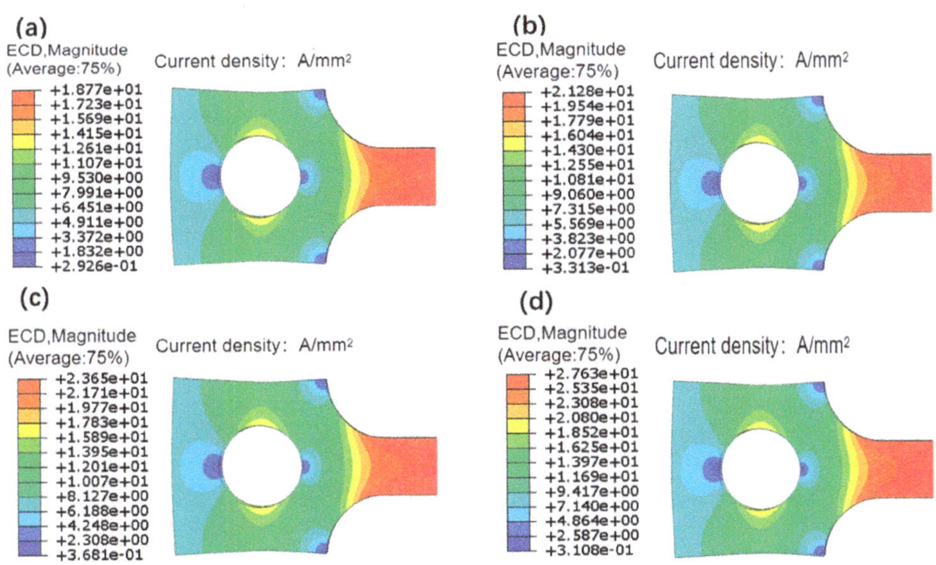

Figure 15. Current density distribution of tensile specimens under pulsed currents: (**a**) 8 A/mm^2, (**b**) 14 A/mm^2, (**c**) 20 A/mm^2, and (**d**) 26 A/mm^2.

Figure 16 illustrates the temperature change along the length with different current densities. The temperature increases with the current density. Notably, the temperature distribution gradually converges to the middle section, forming a curve similar to a quadratic function with a smooth transition at the peak temperature. Moreover, with higher current densities, the temperature elevation area expands. At a current density of 26 A/mm^2, the temperature rise area extends about 1 mm further on both sides compared to 8 A/mm^2.

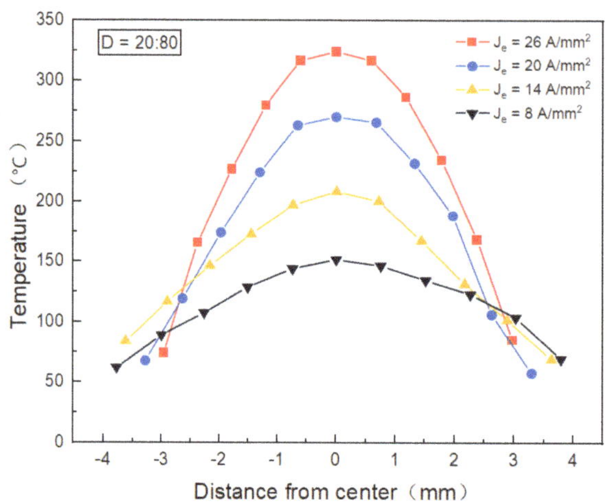

Figure 16. Temperature distribution in the center axis of specimens with different current densities.

4.2. Stress and Strain Field Analysis During Pulsed Current Loading Process

It involves coupling electric, thermal, and force fields, requiring the observation of the stress–strain field distribution. A path is established in the direction of the length with current densities of 8 A/mm^2, 14 A/mm^2, 20 A/mm^2, and 26 A/mm^2, respectively. Figure 17a,b show the stress and strain change curves along the length of the plate. The rapid increase in the current density due to rising temperature gradually reduces stress and strain. The stress–strain and temperature fields exhibit nearly trapezoidal distributions, with higher values at the middle and lower at the sides. This pattern results from the current-assisted tensile process affecting the elastic modulus and Poisson's ratio due to temperature changes, which leads to a similarity between the stress–strain and temperature distributions.

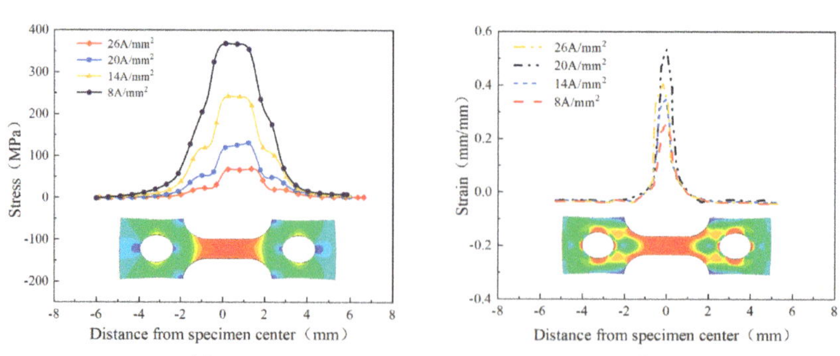

Figure 17. Distribution of stress–strain field at different current densities in the center of the sample: (**a**) stress field distribution and (**b**) strain field distribution.

4.3. Comparison of Experimental and Predicted Values

Through implicit analysis to customize the material principal structure [33,34], the primary task of UMAT is based on finite element calculations.

The modified Johnson–Cook model combined with the ABAQUS software predicted the flow stress behavior of electrically assisted tensile specimens at different rates. After conducting uniaxial tensile tests at different rates, Figure 18 compares experimental and predicted values. The results show that the model's predictions are highly consistent with the experimentally observed flow stress trends, which indicates that the error of EA Johnson–Cook model is tiny. Three standard statistical parameters were introduced [35] to quantify the accuracy and reliability of the response model, that is, correlation coefficient (R), mean absolute error (AARE), and root mean square error (RMSE), with their expressions given in Equations (28)–(30).

$$R = \frac{\sum_{i=1}^{i=N}\left(\sigma_E^i - \overline{\sigma}_E\right)\left(\sigma_P^i - \overline{\sigma}_P\right)}{\sqrt{\sum_{i=1}^{i=N}\left(\sigma_E^i - \overline{\sigma}_E\right)^2 \sum_{i=1}^{i=N}\left(\sigma_P^i - \overline{\sigma}_P\right)^2}} \tag{28}$$

$$AARE = \frac{1}{N}\sum_{i=1}^{i=N}\left|\frac{\sigma_E^i - \sigma_P^i}{\sigma_E^i}\right| \times 100 \tag{29}$$

$$RMSE = \sqrt{\frac{1}{N}\sum_{i=1}^{i=N}\left(\sigma_E^i - \sigma_P^i\right)^2} \tag{30}$$

where N is the number of (strain) data points, σ_E^i is the yield stress, σ_P^i is the model predicted yield stress, $\overline{\sigma}_E$ is the average of the experimental yield stress, and $\overline{\sigma}_p$ is the average of the predicted yield stress. The correlation coefficient (R) indicates the linearity of the relationship between the experimental and predicted data. By definition, larger R, smaller $AARE$, and $RMSE$ values indicate better predictive performance.

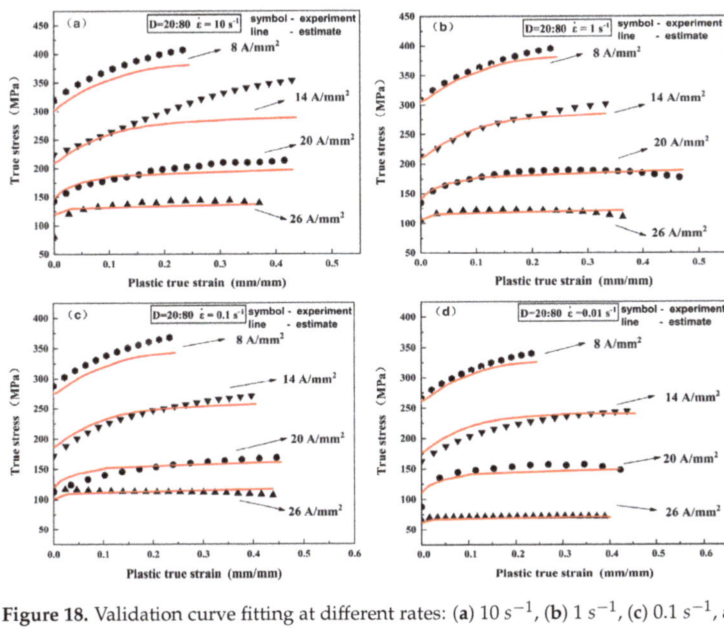

Figure 18. Validation curve fitting at different rates: (**a**) 10 s^{-1}, (**b**) 1 s^{-1}, (**c**) 0.1 s^{-1}, and (**d**) 0.01 s^{-1}.

Figure 19 shows the overall standard statistical results and the correlation between the experimental values and the predicted values of the intrinsic model. Data points near the straight line indicates less deviation between the predicted and experimental values, including the statistical parameters *R*, *AARE*, and *RMSE*. The correlation coefficient of the model is 0.99608, indicating that the correlation between the experimental data and the data predicted by the model is in good agreement. In addition, the *AARE* and *RMSE* of the model are 2.2633% and 5.678633 MPa, respectively. These results are attributed to the EA Johnson–Cook model using fractional versus exponential thermal-softening terms to describe thermally activated plastic deformation.

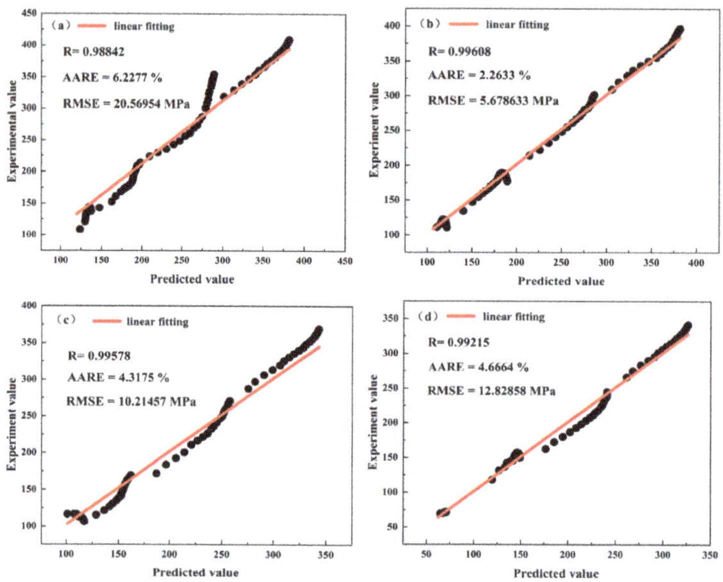

Figure 19. Overall standardized statistical results and correlation between experimental stresses and predicted stresses at different strain rates: (**a**) 10 s^{-1}, (**b**) 1 s^{-1}, (**c**) 0.1 s^{-1}, and (**d**) 0.01 s^{-1}.

4.4. Electrically Assisted Three-Point Bending Platform Construction

The experimental verification of formability of the 7075 aluminum alloy under electrified conditions with a three-point bending test. Figure 20 shows the three-point bending experimental setup. Insulation is applied to the punch and die to ensure measurement accuracy. The downward pressure speed of the punch is set at 10 mm/min for consistency.

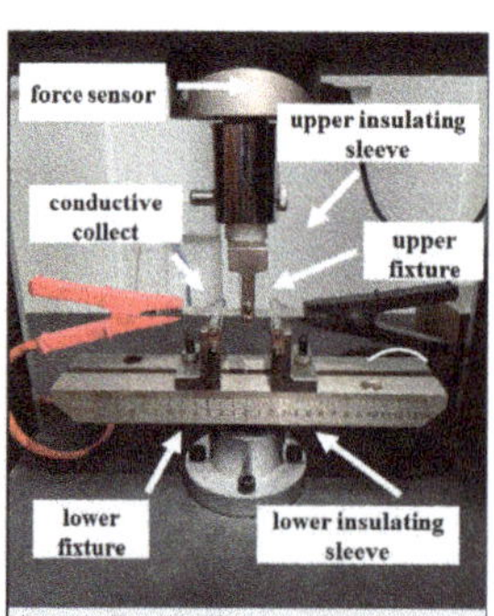

Figure 20. Three-point bending test platform stress–strain curves with different current densities.

4.5. Effect of Different Current Densities on Stress-Strain and Angle of Rebound

As shown in Figure 21, the stress–strain curve at various current densities decreases the bending stress as the current density increases, demonstrating the current's capacity to enhance material plasticity. The figure shows a significant decrease in the stress yield section, with flexural strength at the yield point dropping by 21–24% at its maximum.

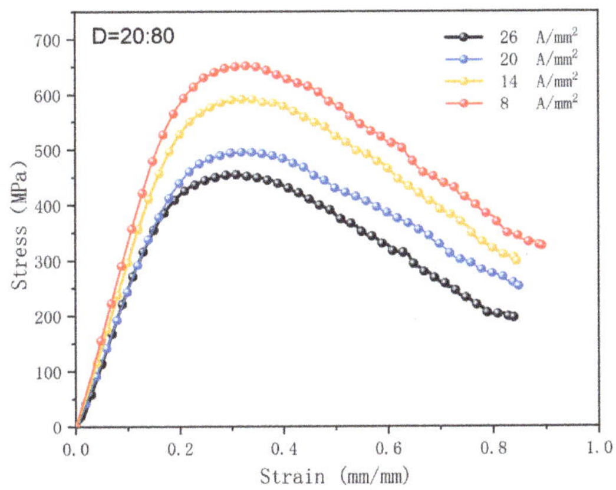

Figure 21. Stress–strain at different current densities.

Figure 22 shows the springback angle of the 7075 aluminum alloy sheet after forming with various electrical pulse parameters. With a specific duty cycle, the springback angle notably decreased as the pulse current density rose, which suggested that applying pulse current could effectively enhance the resilience of the plates post-forming. Adjusting the pulse current density appropriately minimizes plate bending springback, improving the forming effect. The springback angle was smaller at a 20% duty cycle, resulting in better suppression. Notably, at D = 20% and a current density of 20 A/mm^2, the springback angle measures 4°, nearly eliminating the rebound effect.

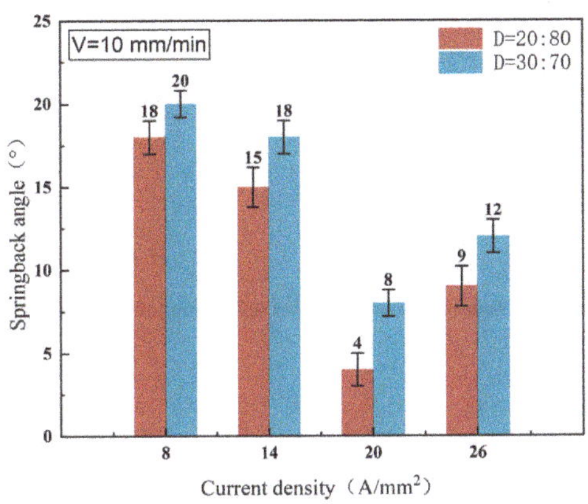

Figure 22. Rebound for different current parameters.

4.6. Effect of Different Current Densities on Temperature

In Figure 23, the specimen temperature measurement locations are segmented into three positions. When the response values peak, the temperature rises the fastest and highest at reference point 1, corresponding to the bending rounded corner. This region is more prone to softening than the surrounding areas, facilitating bending deformation. The temperature increase accelerates residual stress release, promotes stress relaxation, and reduces bending resilience. Reference point 2 lies midway between reference point 1 and reference point 3 along the span. Consequently, the temperature at reference point 2 is higher than at reference point 3 due to increased friction with the rounded corners of the die. The overall temperature is notably lower compared to that in the tensile test. This discrepancy can be attributed to the superior thermal efficiency of the 7075 aluminum alloy, which features a significantly larger contact area between the plate and the surrounding air.

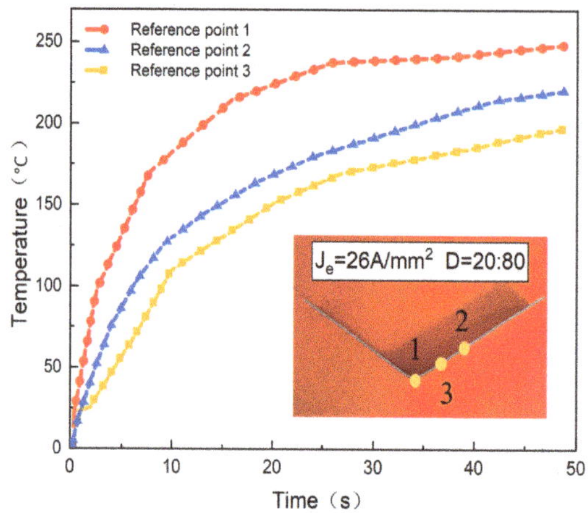

Figure 23. Temperature variation with time at three positions.

Figure 24 illustrates the temperature variations over time under different current densities. The temperature rise rate varied with current densities, with higher current densities causing faster temperature increases in the specimen. Elevated current densities allow the plate to absorb more energy, rapidly increasing thermal activation energy. This trend aligned with findings from the tensile test. By adjusting the current density, operators can determine optimal heating and molding temperatures, improving efficiency and reducing costs.

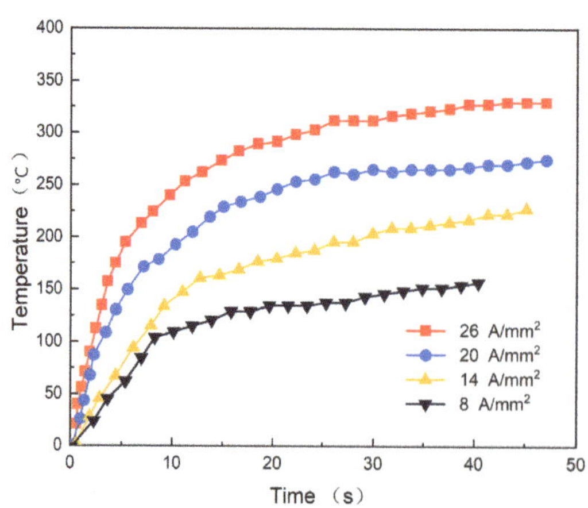

Figure 24. Temperature variation at different times in the length direction.

4.7. Numerical Simulation of Three-Point Bending

(1) Modeling and Material Properties

The finite element model of the three-point bending test is shown in Figure 25a, which mainly consists of three parts: the convex die, the concave die, and a plate made of the 7075 aluminum alloy. The die material is P20 die steel.

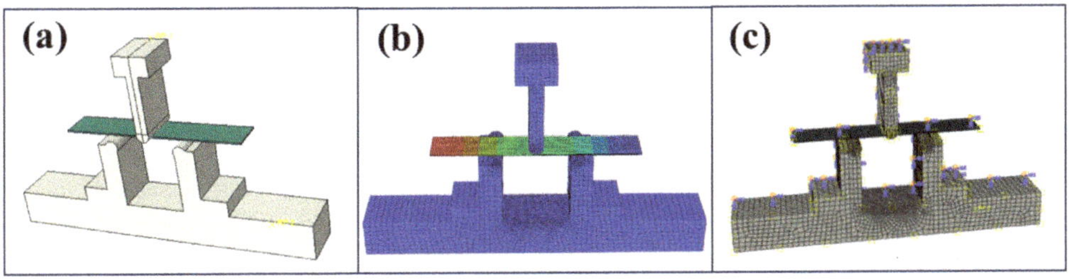

Figure 25. Three-point bending finite element model: (**a**) modeling and assembly, (**b**) electric potential field, and (**c**) meshing and constraints.

(2) Mesh division and rigid body constraints

The grid cell size of the plate is 0.4 mm, while the grid cell size of the mold is set to 0.75 mm. Both use thermoelectric structure coupling cells Q3D8R. First, the absolute zero of the software environment is defined, followed by the setting of the room-temperature environment using the predefined field. For contact, the friction coefficient between the 7075 plate and P20 mold steel is interpolated and inputted using the friction model [36] from the same group. Rigid body constraints can be established by setting the reference point during the three-point bending simulation.

(3) Boundary conditions and analysis step

Regarding boundary conditions, the thermoelectric structural coupling element necessitates the application of current. A surface current is established at the left end. Given the stringent accuracy demands on parameters in thermoelectric structural coupling, to ensure convergence, the current loading method is selected as the current density. The electric potential field is depicted in Figure 25b, with the potential direction aligned along the two sides of the plate, thereby ensuring the flow of current. The three-point bending process, akin to the tensile process, involves multiple physical fields. Under the coupled influence of the electric field, temperature field, and force field, the analysis step is chosen to be thermoelectrical–structural, which also requires the application of current, leading to the coupling of the electric field, force field, and temperature field. Consequently, the thermoelectric structural analysis step is employed. As illustrated in Figure 25c, this approach enhances the computational efficiency of the model. Furthermore, to ensure that the material undergoes rigid body displacement during the three-point bending simulation process, it is imperative to set fixed constraints for the left and right dies to guarantee the precision of the simulation results. For the control of the upper die, the objective of bending is achieved by employing displacement. In the analysis step, a vertical displacement is specified, and the output of the displacement load is controlled through a smooth step.

4.8. Bending Stress Field Analysis

Figure 26 illustrates the distribution of bending stresses at different current densities (8 A/mm^2, 14 A/mm^2, 20 A/mm^2, 26 A/mm^2). Following yielding, there was a significant decrease in the bending stress. The ultimate bending strength can be analyzed by adjusting the analysis step to coincide with the moment of maximum stress. As shown in the cloud diagram, the stress distribution gradually becomes more concentrated. The stress distribution region exhibits a stepwise uniform pattern, highlighting the bending rounded corners as areas of maximum force. The bending stress greatly exceeds the tensile stress and decreases as the current density of the energized surface increases. This occurs because the bending stress significantly decreases after yielding due to the onset of plastic deformation in the material. Additionally, the increase in the current density further reduces stress concentration by inducing thermal effects and changes in the microstructure.

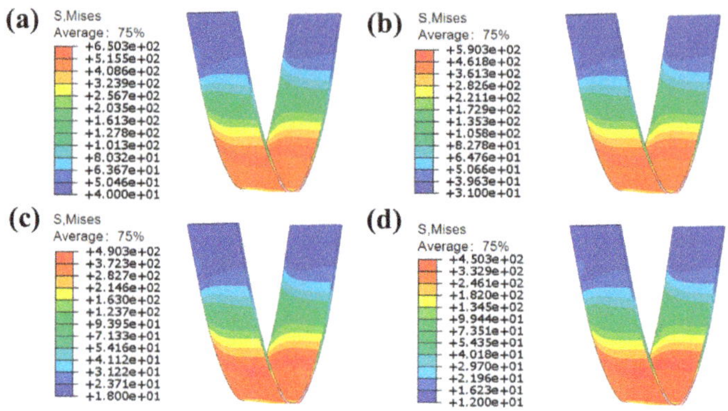

Figure 26. Stress field clouds at different current densities: (**a**) 8 A/mm^2, (**b**) 14 A/mm^2, (**c**) 20 A/mm^2, and (**d**) 26 A/mm^2.

5. Conclusions

(1) Based on the electrically assisted tensile test platform, the variation law of yield strength of the 7075-T6 aluminum alloy was obtained. The yield strength decreases with the increase in the current density.
(2) Through the decoupling of thermal and non-thermal effects, it was found that compared with traditional electric furnace heating, electrically assisted heating reduces yield strength and increases elongation. The higher the current density, the greater the electroplastic effect coefficient, and pure electroplasticity can be used to reduce the forming temperature.
(3) A thermal electroplasticity constitutive equations was constructed, and through subroutine and error analysis, it was found that the correlation between strain rate 1 s^{-1} was as high as 0.99, with a minimum average relative error of 2.26% and a root mean square error of 5.68 MPa.
(4) The verification of the electrically assisted three-point bending example shows that, as the current density increases, the springback angle decreases, the rebound suppression effect is better, the bending stress decreases with the increase in the current density, and the yield cross-section of stress significantly decreases.

Author Contributions: Conceptualization, S.D.; methodology, J.X.; software, Z.L. (Zhuang Liu), H.S., K.Z. and Z.L. (Zhijun Li); validation, Z.L. (Zhuang Liu), H.S., K.Z. and Z.L. (Zhijun Li); investigation, S.D.; resources, S.D.; data curation, J.X.; writing—original draft preparation, Z.L. (Zhuang Liu); writing—review and editing, S.D. and J.X.; visualization, Z.L. (Zhuang Liu), H.S., K.Z. and Z.L. (Zhijun Li); supervision, J.X.; project administration, S.D.; funding acquisition, S.D. All authors have read and agreed to the published version of the manuscript.

Funding: This research received no external funding.

Data Availability Statement: Data are contained within the article.

Acknowledgments: We would like to express our sincere gratitude to Chunyu Zhu for their valuable contributions to the formal analysis of this research. Their expertise and insights have greatly enhanced the quality of this study. We are truly grateful for their support and guidance throughout the process.

Conflicts of Interest: The authors declare no conflicts of interest.

References

1. Dalong, L.; Yanting, L.; Enlin, Y.; Yi, H.; Feng, L. Theoretical and experimental study of the drawing force under a current pulse. *Int. J. Adv. Manuf. Technol.* **2018**, *97*, 1047–1051. [CrossRef]
2. Li, C.; Xu, Z.; Peng, L.; Lai, X. An electric-pulse-assisted stamping process towards springback suppression and precision fabrication of micro channels. *Int. J. Mech. Sci.* **2022**, *218*, 107081. [CrossRef]
3. Stolyarov, V.; Misochenko, A. A Pulsed Current Application to the Deformation Processing of Materials. *Materials* **2023**, *16*, 6270. [CrossRef] [PubMed]
4. Liu, J.; Jia, D.; Fu, Y.; Kong, X.; Lv, Z.; Zeng, E.; Gao, Q. Electroplasticity effects: From mechanism to application. *Int. J. Adv. Manuf. Technol.* **2023**, *131*, 3267–3286. [CrossRef]
5. Lv, Z.; Zhou, Y.; Zhan, L.; Zang, Z.; Zhou, B.; Qin, S. Electrically assisted deep drawing on high-strength steel sheet. *Int. J. Adv. Manuf. Technol.* **2020**, *112*, 763–767. [CrossRef]
6. Mai, J.; Peng, L.; Lin, Z.; Lai, X. Experimental study of electrical resistivity and flow stress of stainless steel 316L in electroplastic deformation. *Mater. Sci. Eng. A* **2011**, *528*, 3539–3544. [CrossRef]
7. Tskhondiya, G.A.; Beklemishev, N.N. Simulating the effect of a high density electric current pulse on the stress field during plastic deformation. *Int. J. Mater. Form.* **2011**, *5*, 157–162. [CrossRef]
8. Okazaki, K.; Kagawa, M.; Conrad, H. A study of the electroplastic effect in metals. *Scr. Metall.* **1978**, *12*, 1063–1068. [CrossRef]
9. Molotskii, M.; Fleurov, V. Magnetic effects in electroplasticity of metals. *Phys. Rev. B* **1995**, *52*, 15829. [CrossRef]
10. Goldman, P.D.; Motowidlo, L.R.; Galligan, J.M. The absence of an electroplastic effect in lead at 4.2 K. *Scr. Metall.* **1981**, *15*, 353–356. [CrossRef]
11. Fan, R.; Magargee, J.; Hu, P.; Cao, J. Influence of grain size and grain boundaries on the thermal and mechanical behavior of 70/30 brass under electrically-assisted deformation. *Mater. Sci. Eng. A* **2013**, *574*, 218–225. [CrossRef]
12. Magargee, J.; Morestin, F.; Cao, J. Characterization of Flow Stress for Commercially Pure Titanium Subjected to Electrically Assisted Deformation. *J. Eng. Mater. Technol.* **2013**, *135*, 041003. [CrossRef]
13. Roh, J.H.; Seo, J.J.; Hong, S.T.; Kim, M.J.; Han, H.N.; Roth, J.T. The mechanical behavior of 5052-H32 aluminum alloys under a pulsed electric current. *Int. J. Plast.* **2014**, *58*, 84–99. [CrossRef]
14. Hu, L.; Jiang, S.; Zhou, T.; Tu, J.; Shi, L.; Chen, Q.; Yang, M. Multiscale Modeling of Polycrystalline NiTi Shape Memory Alloy under Various Plastic Deformation Conditions by Coupling Microstructure Evolution and Macroscopic Mechanical Response. *Materials* **2017**, *10*, 1172. [CrossRef]
15. Ao, D.; Chu, X.; Yang, Y.; Lin, S.; Gao, J. Effect of electropulsing on springback during V-bending of Ti-6Al-4V titanium alloy sheet. *Int. J. Adv. Manuf. Technol.* **2018**, *96*, 3197–3207. [CrossRef]
16. Wang, X.; Xu, C.; Li, Y.; Wang, B. Respective roles of the thermal and electromigration effect in AZ31 Mg alloy during low-frequency electropulsing tension. *J. Alloys Compd.* **2020**, *846*, 156074. [CrossRef]
17. Dinh, K.A.; Hong, S.T.; Choi, S.J.; Kim, M.J.; Han, H.N. The Effect of Pre-strain and Subsequent Electrically Assisted Annealing on the Mechanical Behaviors of Two Different Aluminum Alloys. *Int. J. Precis. Eng. Manuf.* **2020**, *21*, 2345–2358. [CrossRef]
18. Fu, J.; Ma, D.; Fan, L.; Yu, Z.; Yin, H.; Ma, C. Tribological Properties of Solid Lubricant WS(2) in Dimples on the Cylinder of Diesel Engine at High Temperature. *Materials* **2022**, *15*, 8161. [CrossRef] [PubMed]
19. Jordan, A.; Kinsey, B.L. Investigation of thermal and mechanical effects during electrically-assisted microbending. *J. Mater. Process. Technol.* **2015**, *221*, 1–12. [CrossRef]
20. Wagner, K.C.; Byrd, G.D. Evaluating the effectiveness of clinical medical librarian programs: A systematic review of the literature. *J. Med. Libr. Assoc.* **2012**, *92* (Suppl. S4), J.
21. Shi, C.; Mao, W.; Chen, X.G. Evolution of activation energy during hot deformation of AA7150 aluminum alloy. *Mater. Sci. Eng. A* **2013**, *571*, 83–91. [CrossRef]
22. Islam, Z.; Wang, B.; Haque, A. Current density effects on the microstructure of zirconium thin films. *Scr. Mater.* **2018**, *144*, 18–21. [CrossRef]
23. Li, X.; Yang, W.; Xu, D.; Ju, K.; Chen, J. A new ductile fracture criterion considering both shear and tension mechanisms on void coalescence. *Int. J. Damage Mech.* **2020**, *30*, 374–398. [CrossRef]
24. Xu, S.; Xiao, X.; Zhang, H.; Cui, Z. Electroplastic Effects on the Mechanical Responses and Deformation Mechanisms of AZ31 Mg Foils. *Materials* **2022**, *15*, 1339. [CrossRef]

25. Song, P.; Li, X.; Ding, W.; Chen, J. Electroplastic Tensile Behavior of 5A90 Al–Li Alloys. *Acta Metall. Sin. (Engl. Lett.)* **2014**, *27*, 642–648. [CrossRef]
26. Indhiarto, I.; Shimizu, T.; Yang, M. Effect of Peak Current Density on Tensile Properties of AZ31B Magnesium Alloy. *Materials* **2021**, *14*, 1457. [CrossRef]
27. Dobras, D.; Bruschi, S.; Simonetto, E.; Rutkowska-Gorczyca, M.; Ghiotti, A. The Effect of Direct Electric Current on the Plastic Behavior of AA7075-T6 Aluminum Alloy in Different States of Hardening. *Materials* **2020**, *14*, 73. [CrossRef] [PubMed]
28. Shang, H.; Wang, S.; Zhou, L.; Lou, Y. Neural network-based ductile fracture model for 5182-O aluminum alloy considering electroplastic effect in electrically-assisted processing. *Eng. Fract. Mech.* **2023**, *290*, 109476. [CrossRef]
29. Zhou, Y.; Zhu, R.; Zuo, X.; Xie, W. Tribo-electrical behaviors of CNTs-MoS2/Cu composites under sliding electrical contact with brass. *Tribol. Int.* **2023**, *180*, 108207. [CrossRef]
30. Zhao, Y.C.; Wan, M.; Meng, B.; Xu, J.; Shan, D.B. Pulsed current assisted forming of ultrathin superalloy sheet: Experimentation and modeling. *Mater. Sci. Eng. A* **2019**, *767*, 138412. [CrossRef]
31. Ruszkiewicz, B.J.; Grimm, T.; Ragai, I.; Mears, L.; Roth, J.T. A Review of Electrically-Assisted Manufacturing With Emphasis on Modeling and Understanding of the Electroplastic Effect. *J. Manuf. Sci. Eng.* **2017**, *139*, 110801. [CrossRef]
32. Zhou, M.; Lin, Y.C.; Deng, J.; Jiang, Y.Q. Hot tensile deformation behaviors and constitutive model of an Al–Zn–Mg–Cu alloy. *Mater. Des.* **2014**, *59*, 141–150. [CrossRef]
33. Sheng, Y.; Hua, Y.; Wang, X.; Zhao, X.; Chen, L.; Zhou, H.; Wang, J.; Berndt, C.C.; Li, W. Application of High-Density Electropulsing to Improve the Performance of Metallic Materials: Mechanisms, Microstructure and Properties. *Materials* **2018**, *11*, 185. [CrossRef] [PubMed]
34. Xu, Z.; Guo, P.; Peng, L.; Lai, X. Electroplasticity mechanism study based on dislocation behavior of Al6061 in tensile process. *J. Alloys Compd.* **2022**, *910*, 164890.
35. Lu, J.; Song, Y.; Zhou, P.; Lin, J. Rheological behavior and dynamic softening mechanism of AA7075-T6 sheet under isothermal tensile deformation. *J. Mater. Res. Technol.* **2020**, *9*, 9784–9797. [CrossRef]
36. Xia, J.; Dou, S. Theory and finite element simulation analysis of plate U-bending forming. *Mech. Des. Manuf.* **2022**, 238–241.

metals

MDPI

Article

Effect of Electric Pulse Treatment on the Interfacial Properties of Copper/304 Stainless Steel Composite Thin Strips Fabricated by Roll Bonding

Zefeng Wang [1], Xiaomiao Niu [1,2,3], Ming Wang [1], Yu Yang [1], Dongping He [1,2,3] and Wangzhe Du [1,2,3,*]

1 College of Mechanical Engineering, Taiyuan University of Technology, Taiyuan 030024, China; 2023510125@link.tyut.edu.cn (Z.W.); niuxiaomiao@tyut.edu.cn (X.N.); 17735576485@163.com (M.W.); 2024520176@link.tyut.edu.cn (Y.Y.); hedongping@tyut.edu.cn (D.H.)

2 National Key Laboratory of Metal Forming Technology and Heavy Equipment, Taiyuan 030024, China

3 Engineering Research Center of Advanced Metal Composites Forming Technology and Equipment, Ministry of Education, Taiyuan 030024, China

* Correspondence: duwangzhe@tyut.edu.cn

Abstract: Annealing is a commonly used post-processing method for composite thin strips but suffers from drawbacks such as long processing time, high energy consumption, and susceptibility to oxidation. Replacing annealing with electric pulse treatment (EPT) can address these issues. In this study, a specially designed fixture was used to investigate the effects of pulsed current on the bonding strength of T2 copper (Cu)/304 stainless steel (SS) composite thin strips. The initial strip, with a 50% reduction rate, was prepared using a two-high mill, resulting in a Cu/SS composite strip with a thickness of 0.245 mm. Pulsed current treatment was applied with peak temperatures ranging from 350 °C to 600 °C. The results showed that EPT significantly improved the bonding strength. A pulsed current of 55 A resulted in the highest average peel strength of 10.66 ± 0.93 N/mm, with a maximum Fe content on the Cu side of 7.39 ± 0.84%, while a pulsed current of 65 A resulted in the highest Cu content on the SS side, reaching 57.54 ± 2.06%. This study demonstrates that EPT effectively controls the deformation behavior and interface state of composite strips, producing Cu/SS composite thin strips with high bonding strength.

Keywords: roll bonding; Cu/SS composite thin strips; electric pulse treatment; heat treatment; bonding mechanism

1. Introduction

Metal composite thin strips usually integrate the unique properties of each constituent to achieve superior performance over single-metal materials [1–5]. Copper/stainless steel (Cu/SS) ultrathin composite strips, known for their extremely thin dimensions, high specific surface area, excellent electrical and thermal conductivity, superior mechanical strength, and outstanding corrosion resistance, are promising in advanced applications such as sensor diaphragms and flexible display substrates [6–9].

However, the significant differences in the physical and chemical properties of Cu and SS hinder interdiffusion, resulting in weak interfacial bonding [10]. The interface cracking of the composite ultrathin strips limits further processing and applications. Fabrication methods such as spray deposition [11], magnetron sputtering [12], and diffusion bonding [13] each present inherent limitations, including process complexity, high costs, and low efficiency. Roll bonding is a scalable and reliable method for fabricating ultrathin composite strips but often relies on prolonged annealing to improve interfacial bonding [14,15]. However, the high costs, extended processing times, and harmful emissions of annealing present challenges to sustainable production [16]. For example, Yanyang Qi et al. [17] prepared ultrathin stainless steel/copper composite materials by heating and cooling them with the furnace and holding them at the target temperature for 5 min. Chen Wang et al. [18] Cu/Al annealed composite thin strips in a tube furnace for 1 h to achieve a higher bonding strength.

Current-assisted processing, particularly pulsed current, has emerged as a promising alternative due to its high instantaneous energy density, enabling improved deformation behaviors [19], microstructural refinement, and interfacial bonding [20]. Tingting Zhang et al. [21] successfully prepared AZ31B Mg/5052 Al alloy composite plates with a thickness of 3.8 mm by pulsed current-assisted rolling welding. Xiongwei Guo et al. [22] applied a pulse current to the TA1/304 composite plate during the rolling process, which effectively improved the bonding strength of the composite plate. In the current research of Niu X. et al. [10], there are problems such as long time and high energy consumption, but electrical treatment can greatly shorten the treatment time of Cu/SS composite thin strips, reduce energy consumption, and greatly improve their bonding strength. However, in the current research, the influence mechanism of current processing parameters on the interface bonding state of composite thin bands is not clear. Therefore, it is necessary to study the effect of current on the bonding strength and microstructure of T2 Cu/304 SS composite thin strip.

This study investigates the impact of short-time pulsed current on the bonding performance and interfacial microstructure of T2 Cu/304 SS composite ultrathin strips. Results reveal that pulsed current significantly enhances interfacial bonding strength, offering insights into the mechanisms of bonding improvement. These findings provide a theoretical foundation for developing efficient, sustainable post-treatment methods and expanding the applications of composite materials in advanced industries.

2. Experimental

2.1. Fabrication of the Composite Thin Strips

The raw materials selected for this study include T2 pure Cu sheets measuring 100 mm × 30 mm × 0.3 mm and 304 SS sheets measuring 100 mm × 30 mm × 0.2 mm. The raw materials were subjected to annealing before roll bonding. The T2 pure copper strip underwent stress relief annealing at a low temperature of 260 °C for 1 h, while the 304 stainless steel strip underwent homogenized solution annealing at 1050 °C for 4 h. The chemical composition of the original 304 stainless steel strip and T2 pure copper used was detected by spectroscopic analysis, as shown in Table 1. Cu/SS composite thin strips were prepared using a combination of cold rolling and EPT. The cold rolling was performed on a two-high rolling mill equipped with custom tungsten steel rollers, with a roller diameter of Φ150 mm and a roller speed of 37.7 rad/s and the rolling force was 90 kN.

Table 1. Chemical compositions of the strips (wt%).

Materials	Cr	Ni	C	O	Mn	Si	P	S	Fe	Cu
SS304	18.16	7.97	0.06	—	1.20	0.58	0.43	0.02	Bal.	—
T2 Copper	—	≤0.004	—	≤0.005	—	—	—	≤0.005	—	Bal.

The preparation and post-treatment processes of the Cu/SS composite thin strips are depicted in Figure 1. Prior to assembly, the oxide layer and contaminants on the bonding surfaces were removed using a steel wire brush. The SS strip (upper layer) and Cu strip (lower layer) were then stacked and fed into a ZJ150 two-high rolling mill (XFRMM Ltd., Shenyang, China). To achieve a 50% reduction rate in the Cu/SS composite thin strip, the rolling force was set to 90 kN. The rolled Cu/SS composite strip was subsequently cut into 8 mm-wide strips using wire electrical discharge machining. These strips served as specimens for electric pulse treatment (EPT), while two additional groups underwent corresponding heat treatments (HTs) as control groups. During the EPT process, thermocouples connected to a temperature recorder with the model TCP-500XL (MEASURE FINE Ltd., Hangzhou, China) were placed in contact with the SS strip to monitor the temperature of the Cu/SS composite thin strips. Finally, peeling tests were performed to evaluate the bonding strength under varying parameters.

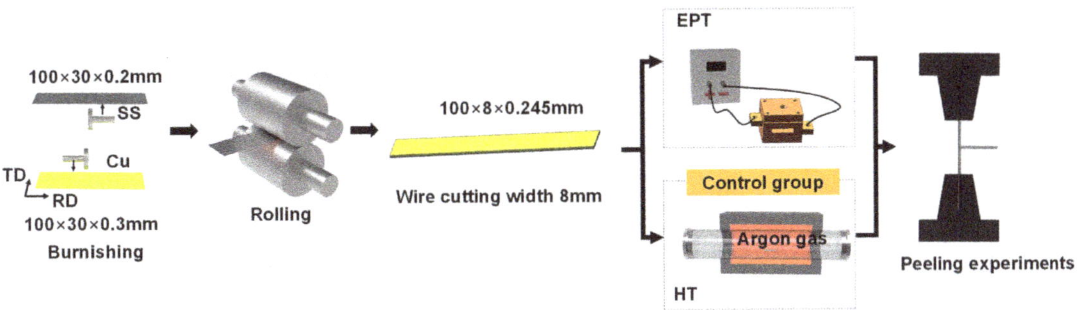

Figure 1. Roll bonding and its post-processing processes.

2.2. EPT and HT Experiments

The Cu/SS composite thin strips after rolling and EPT are shown in Figure 2. To ensure an initial bonding strength after a single-pass rolling process, a high reduction rate was required to achieve preliminary bonding. The reduction rate was set at 50%, resulting in a post-rolling thickness of the composite thin strips ranging from 0.245 mm to 0.25 mm. The thickness of Cu is about 0.14 mm, and the thickness of SS is about 0.11 mm, and their reduction rates are 53.3% and 45%, respectively. Due to the mismatch in deformation behavior between pure Cu and SS, significant warping occurred in the composite thin strips after cold rolling. However, the application of EPT eliminated internal stresses, resulting in a flattened composite thin strip.

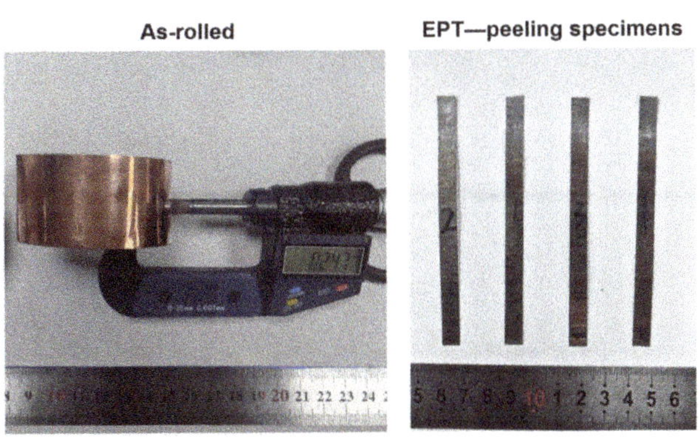

Figure 2. As-rolled specimens and EPT specimens.

Based on our preliminary experiments, a fixture capable of providing stable current conduction for composite thin strips was designed. As shown in Figure 3, the fixture adopts a sequentially moving configuration with positive and negative electrodes, where the distance between the two electrodes is 12 mm. By moving the electrodes, the composite thin strip is continuously subjected to pulsed current. The positive electrode contacts the SS side, while the negative electrode contacts the Cu side. When the pulse power supply is activated, the higher electrical conductivity of copper compared to SS causes the current to flow from the positive electrode through the steel strip and then immediately to the copper side. Since the Cu and SS strips are preliminarily bonded by the first pass of cold rolling, a small portion of the current also flows through the bonding interface and the SS strip.

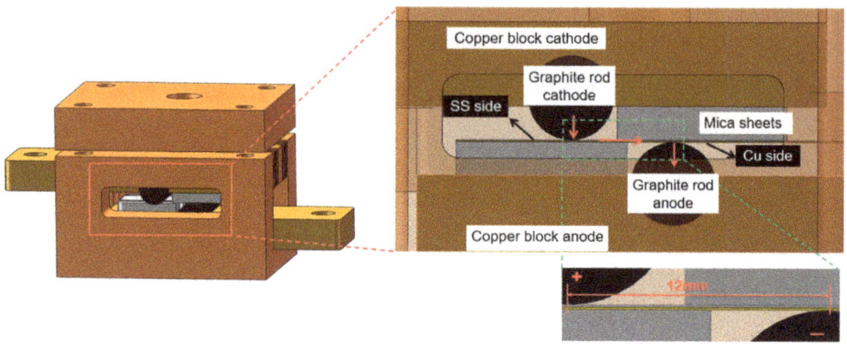

Figure 3. The schematic diagram of the EPT fixture and electrode arrangement.

The composite thin strips were placed into the fixture and connected to a low-frequency pulse power supply. Uniform sequential current conduction was applied, with each conduction cycle lasting 5 s. The pulse current frequency was set to 500 Hz with a duty cycle of 20%. The bonding strength of copper/stainless steel composite thin strips was investigated under different current densities. In this study, HT-450 and HT-600 refer to annealing at 450 °C and 600 °C, respectively, while EPT-350, EPT-400, EPT-450, EPT-500, EPT-550, and EPT-600 represent the electrical parameters corresponding to the composite thin strips under different peak temperatures induced by varying EPT currents. The detailed HT and EPT parameters are summarized in Table 2.

Table 2. Parameters of HT and EPT.

No.	Reduction Rate	Peak Temperature (°C)	Effective Current (A)	Processing Time (s)
As-rolled	50%	—	—	—
HT-450		450	—	100
HT-600		600		
EPT-350		350	45	5
EPT-400		400	50	
EPT-450		450	55	
EPT-500		500	59	
EPT-550		550	62	
EPT-600		600	65	

The temperature–time curves for different HT and EPT parameters are shown in Figure 4. The maximum temperature achieved after 5 s of pulse current for each EPT parameter was recorded (Figure 4b). The highest bonding strength was observed when the maximum temperature reached 450 °C, while at 600 °C, the composite exhibited reasonable metallurgical bonding. Annealing at 450 °C and 600 °C (HT-450 and HT-600) served as control groups for comparison.

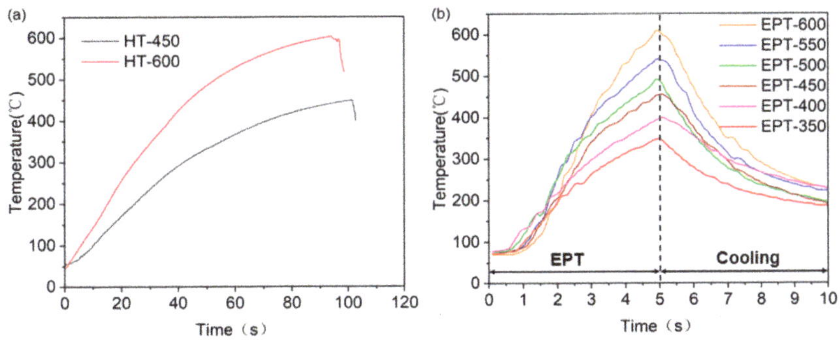

Figure 4. Temperature curves of HT and EPT: (**a**) HT temperature curve and (**b**) EPT temperature curve.

2.3. Mechanical Test and Microscopic Characterization

The peeling test, conducted using an INSTRON 5969 universal testing machine (ITW Inc., Norwood, MA, USA), evaluated the interfacial bonding strength of composite thin strips. Static tensile forces were simultaneously applied to the Cu and SS sides at the opening of the strips, with a peeling rate of 25 mm/min, enabling progressive separation along the longitudinal interface. The peeling strength was determined from the stable region of the peeling curve over the last 20 mm of a total 70 mm peeling length. Five samples were tested under each parameter to obtain the average peel strength. Sample dimensions and testing procedures followed the GB/T 2792-2014 standard [23].

Microscopic characterization was performed using an electron microscope with the model JSM-IT 500 (JEOL Ltd., Tokyo, Japan). Scanning Electron Microscopy (SEM) was used to examine the bonding interface morphology in as-rolled, HT, and EPT states. Energy Dispersive Spectroscopy (EDS) was used to characterize elemental distributions at the interfaces. The microstructural analysis focused on unpeeled regions of the peeled specimens. Sample preparation included water-bath polishing with quartz sandpaper, mechanical polishing with a diamond suspension, and extracting 1 cm sections from both Cu and SS sides of the peeled region to study the bonding interface features. The Vickers microhardness of SS and Cu side surfaces was measured using an HVT-1000 microscopic Vickers hardness tester (SCTMC Ltd., Shanghai, China) in the unpeeled area. Three samples were taken under each parameter, and three points were taken for each sample to be averaged. The residence time was 10 s with a load of 500 g.

3. Experimental Results

3.1. Bonding Properties of the Specimen

The rolled composite thin strips exhibit a porous bonding interface and low bonding strength, with an average peel strength of 0.44 ± 0.10 N/mm. As shown in Figure 5, both EPT and HT significantly influence bonding strength. Increasing the HT temperature enhances the metallurgical bonding effect. Specifically, HT-450 results in a peel strength of only 0.96 ± 0.39 N/mm, while HT-600 increases the peel strength to 4.00 ± 0.49 N/mm.

EPT of 5 s can rapidly enhance the bonding strength of the composite thin strips. The peel strength exhibits a two-phase trend, initially increasing and then decreasing. In the first phase, with current parameters between 45 A and 55 A, the bonding strength increases sharply as the pulsed current rises. Notably, under the EPT-450 condition, the average peel strength at the bonding interface reaches its highest value of 10.66 ± 0.93 N/mm. In the second phase, with current parameters between 55 A and 65 A, the bonding strength decreases as the pulse current increases. This is due to the damage to the copper substrate, which lowers the deformation resistance of copper. As a result, the composite strip primarily exhibits fracture of the Cu substrate during the peel test. Under the EPT-600 condition, the average peel strength of the composite thin strip reaches its lowest value of 5.29 ± 0.40 N/mm.

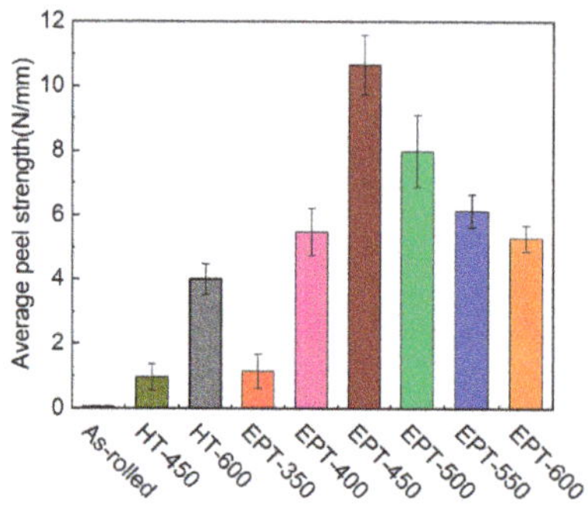

Figure 5. Average peel strength of the as-rolled, HT, and EPT specimens.

A comparison of HT-450 with EPT-450 and HT-600 with EPT-600 reveals that, while both processes reach the highest temperature before post-treatment, EPT has a significantly greater effect on the bonding interface than annealing. When the peak temperature is 450 °C, the peel strength of EPT-450 is 11.1 times that of HT-450, while the peel strength of EPT-600 is 1.3 times that of HT-600. The increase in peel strength at 600 °C when applying EPT compared to HT at the same temperature is insignificant, which is attributed to the instantaneous high temperature generated by the large pulsed current, leading to the formation of a strong metallurgical bond at the interface [24]. Peel failure occurs on the Cu substrate, which makes the bond strength lower. In contrast, HT at 600 °C accelerates element diffusion [17], promoting metallurgical bonding in localized regions, at which time the bonding strength of the bonding interface is weaker than that of the copper substrate, and peel failure occurs at the Cu/SS interface.

3.2. Interfacial Structures of the As-Rolled and HT Specimens

Figure 6 shows the SEM images and corresponding EDS line scan spectra of the Cu/SS composite thin strip in both as-rolled and HT states. Figure 6a,c,e, represent the composite interface states in the as-rolled and annealed conditions and the yellow line represents the line scan path, while Figure 6b,d,f show the diffusion thickness of Cu atoms towards the SS side. No plateau was observed in the EDS line scan spectra at the bonding interface of the samples, indicating that no intermetallic compounds (IMCs) were formed at the Cu/SS bonding interface [14]. As shown in Figure 6a,c,e, defects can be observed at the composite interface in both the as-rolled and HT conditions. From Figure 6a, it is evident that there are significant long gaps and pores at the composite interface (marked by red dashed boxes), indicating poor bonding in the as-rolled Cu/SS composite thin strip. From Figure 6b, it can be seen that the thickness of the diffusion layer is only 1.022 μm. From Figure 6c, it can be seen that an incomplete hardened layer exists at the composite interface, which was caused by the breakage of the SS hardened layer under the rolling force, damaging the Cu substrate surface. The rolling process caused fresh Cu to bond with the SS substrate, resulting in a mechanical bond at the interface. However, pores remain at the interface, suggesting that annealing at 450 °C did not significantly improve the bonding strength, and the diffusion layer thickness slightly increased to 1.046 μm (Figure 6d). As shown in Figure 6e, at 600 °C annealing, most of the pores are eliminated, and the bonding state improves. As shown in Figure 6f, the thickness of the diffusion layer increased to 1.272 μm.

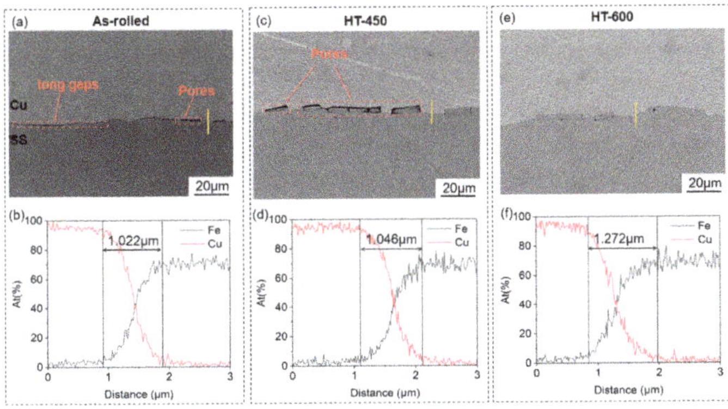

Figure 6. SEM images and EDS line scans (the yellow lines in the figure) of the Cu/SS interface between as-rolled and HT states: (**a**,**b**) as-rolled; (**c**,**d**) HT-450 and (**e**,**f**) HT-600.

By observing the morphology of the peeled Cu/SS composite thin strips in both the as-rolled and HT states, EDS elemental analysis was performed on the Cu elements remaining on the SS surface after peeling. As shown in Figure 7a, the EDS scan reveals that the Cu remaining on the SS side in the as-rolled composite thin strip is insignificant, with a content of only 1.46%. As shown in Figure 7b,c, with the increase in annealing temperature, the diffusion area at the composite interface enlarges. After HT at 450 °C and 600 °C, the Cu content retained on the SS side slightly increases, reaching 5.09% and 10.30%, respectively. This Cu is mainly distributed in the cracks of the fractured hardened layer. A partial enlargement of Figure 7c (marked by red boxes), a small metallurgical bonding region can be observed, accompanied by the appearance of tiny ductile dimples, indicating that plastic fracture of the Cu substrate occurs in this area, and the bonding strength has been improved to some extent.

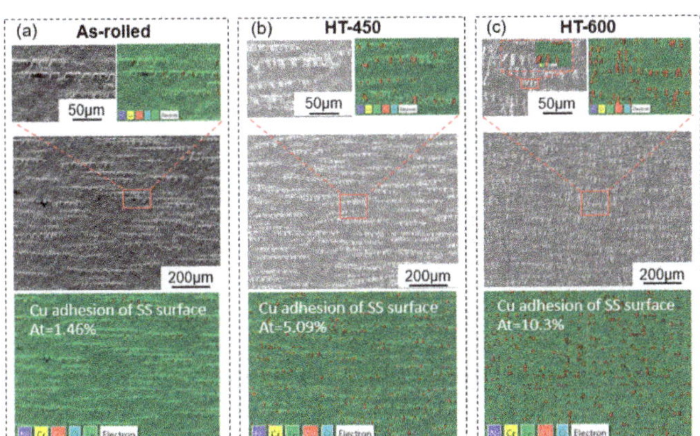

Figure 7. SEM images of the SS side and the corresponding EDS maps after peeling of as-rolled and HT states: (**a**) as-rolled; (**b**) HT-450 and (**c**) HT-600.

3.3. Interface Structure Analysis for EPT

Figure 8a,c,e,g,i,l represent the composite interface states after EPT, while Figure 8b,d,f,h,j,k show the thickness of Cu atom diffusion towards the SS side. As shown in Figure 8a,c, although pores are still observed at the composite interface under the conditions of EPT-350 and EPT-400, there are also many areas with strong bonding, indicating that the interface bonding state has improved compared to the as-rolled condition. As shown in Figure 8e,g,i,l, the interface bonding is tight, with no obvious cracks, voids, or delamination defects, and the bonding interface forms a jagged structure, which tends to become smoother with increasing effective current. This improvement is likely due to the local high temperatures generated by the pulsed current, which causes partial melting at the interface. The diffusion of Cu and Fe atoms, combined with the slight clamping force from the electrical contacts, facilitates the reorganization of the hardened layer and effectively fills the defects and voids at the interface, significantly relieving the residual stress in the hardened layer, thereby making the layer smoother.

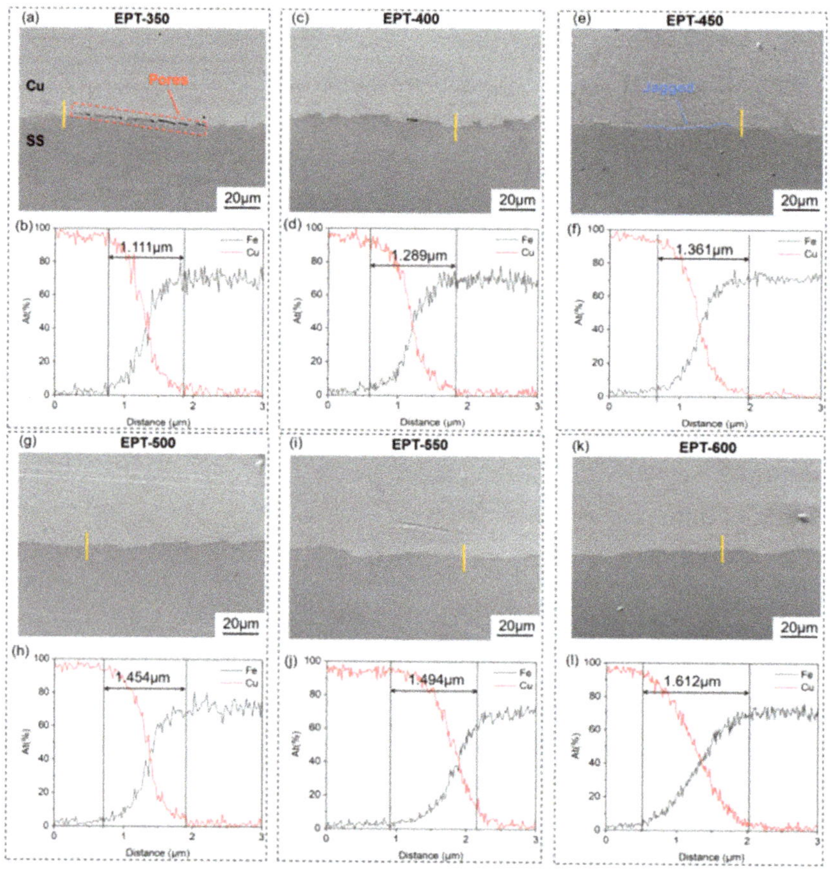

Figure 8. SEM image and EDS line scan (the yellow lines in the figure) of the Cu/SS interface after EPT: (**a**,**b**) EPT-350; (**c**,**d**) EPT-400; (**e**,**f**) EPT-450; (**g**,**h**) EPT-500; (**i**,**j**) EPT-550 and (**k**,**l**) EPT-600.

The EDS line scan results in Figure 8b,d,f,h,i,k show that the concentration of Cu rapidly decreases from the Cu side to the SS side, while the concentration of Fe increases sharply. No plateau was observed at the bonding interface of all samples, indicating that the pulsed current does not lead to the formation of IMCs. Therefore, IMCs do not affect the bonding quality and performance of the Cu/SS composite thin strip. Additionally, the thickness of the diffusion layer increases with the increase in effective current. Under the condition of EPT-450, the diffusion layer thickness is 1.361 μm, and under EPT-600, the diffusion layer thickness reaches its maximum value of 1.612 μm.

By observing the morphology of the peeled Cu/SS composite thin strip after pulsed current treatment, EDS elemental analysis was conducted on the Cu elements remaining on the SS surface after peeling. As shown in Figure 9a–f, with the increase in effective current, the Cu content remaining on the SS side of the composite thin strip gradually increases. As seen in Figure 9a–c, with the increase in current, the Cu content progressively rises, and the Cu remaining on the SS side is distributed in dot-like metallurgical bonding regions. Under the EPT-450 condition, larger Cu flakes appear on the SS side, with a Cu content of 35.23%, and the bonding strength reaches its maximum. This suggests a positive correlation between Cu content and bonding strength.

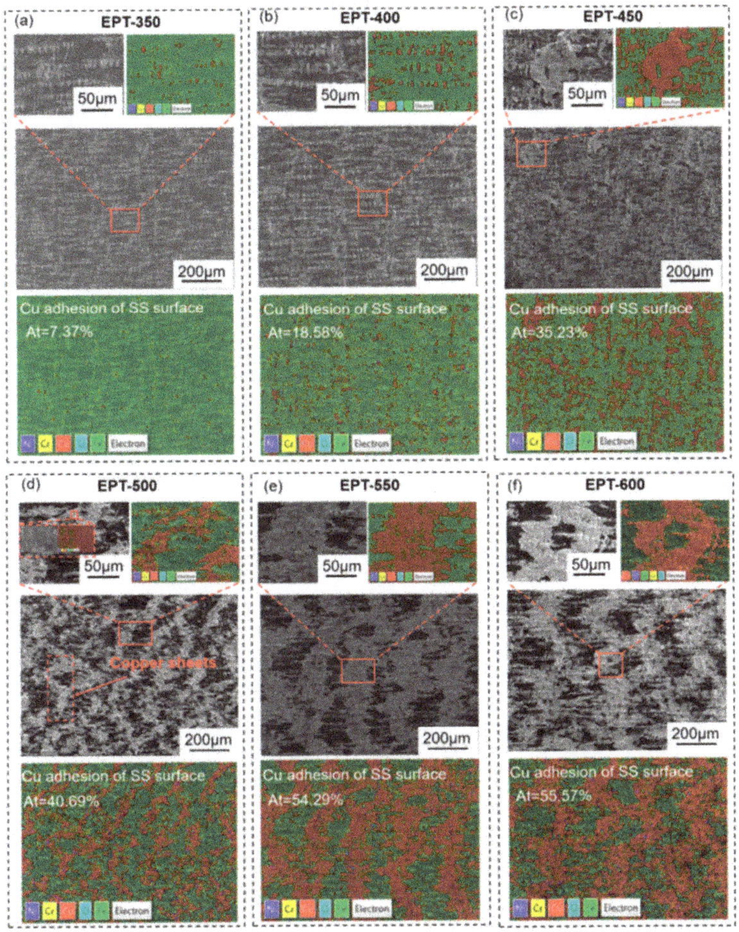

Figure 9. SEM images of the SS side and corresponding EDS surface scan spectra after EPT and peeling: (**a**) EPT-350; (**b**) EPT-400; (**c**) EPT-450; (**d**) EPT-500; (**e**) EPT-550 and (**f**) EPT-600.

From Figure 9d–f, it can be observed that starting from EPT-500, the exposed fresh SS metal surface is almost entirely covered by strip-like Cu sheets and scattered dot-like metallurgical bonding regions. In this stage, although the Cu content is high, the peel strength decreases with the increasing Cu content. This is because the Cu/SS composite thin strip forms large, localized, strong metallurgical bonding regions. The strength of the bonding interface of the Cu/SS composite thin strip is greater than the strength of the fractured Cu substrate at the interface. During peeling, microcracks generated at the bonding interface propagate along the Cu grain boundaries, and when the bonding interface strength becomes weaker than that of the Cu substrate, peeling occurs along the interface. Since large areas of the Cu substrate are peeled off, and plastic fracture occurs in the Cu substrate at this point, larger ductile dimples are formed (Figure 9d). The highest Cu content is observed under the EPT-600 condition, reaching 55.57%. At this point, the entire Cu/SS composite thin strip is almost entirely in a metallurgical bonding state, and after peeling, a uniform copper layer adheres to the SS side.

As shown in Figure 10a,c–g, EDS elemental analysis was performed on the Fe content of the Cu surface of the composite thin strip after different post-treatments and peeling. From Figure 10a, it can be seen that the Cu surface in the as-rolled state contains 0.63% Fe, which is due to the rolling pressure and friction during the composite process, causing the Cu and SS metals to be in close contact and flow together, thus promoting the diffusion of Fe elements into the Cu side and Cu elements into the SS side.

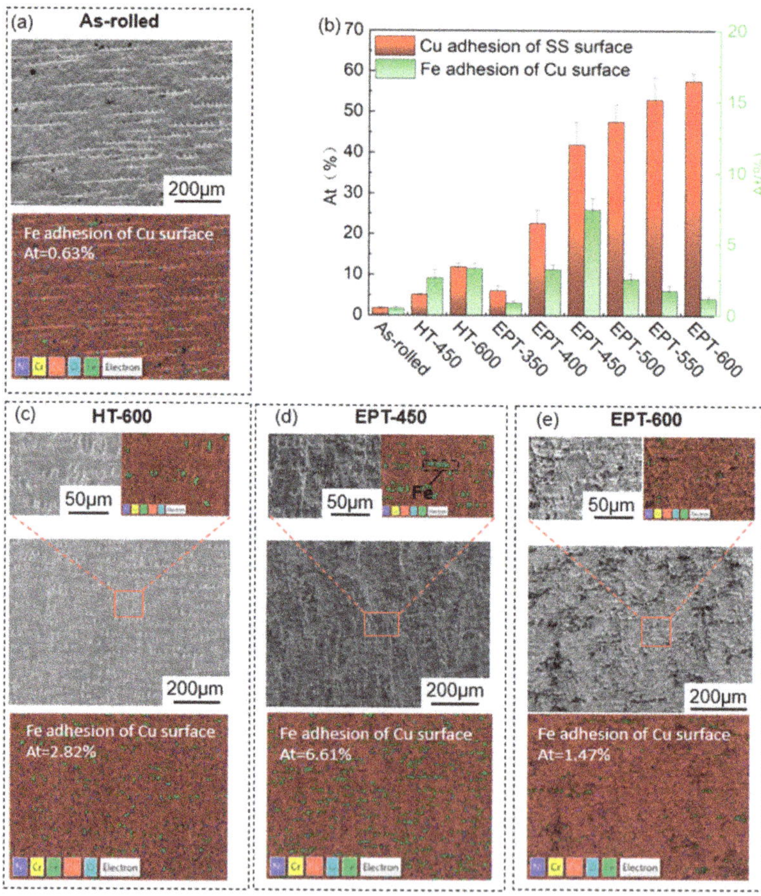

Figure 10. SEM images of Cu side, EDS scan, Cu content on SS side, and SS content on Cu side after peeling under different conditions: (**a**) as-rolled; (**b**) Cu and Fe content; (**c**) HT-600; (**d**) EPT-450 and (**e**) EPT-600.

Figure 10b shows that with the increase in annealing temperature, the Fe content on the Cu surface and the Cu content on the SS surface both increases. At 600 °C, the Fe content on the Cu surface reaches 2.82%, while the Cu content on the SS side is 10.3%. As the pulsed current increases, the Cu content on the SS side surface increases. The Fe content on the Cu surface, however, shows a positive correlation with the pulsed current up to

EPT-450. This is because, at this stage, peeling occurs primarily at the bonding interface. Under the EPT-450 condition, peeling happens from the entire bonding interface of the composite thin strip with maximum bonding strength, resulting in the highest Fe content on the Cu surface, which is 6.61%. At this point, the bonding strength of the composite thin strip is at its highest (10.66 ± 0.93 N/mm).

However, after EPT-500, the Fe content on the Cu surface becomes negatively correlated with the pulsed current. This is because, at this stage, peeling mainly occurs on the Cu substrate. Under the EPT-600 condition, since the SS side is entirely covered by a layer of Cu sheet, the Fe content on the Cu surface is only 1.47%.

4. Discussion

4.1. Effects of HT and EPT on Cu/SS Composite Interface Morphology

As shown in Figure 11, during the cold-rolling composite process, an effective mechanical bond is formed to some extent, while some unbonded areas (pores) also remain. This bonding is mainly physical and typically does not form metallurgical bonding at room temperature [10]. Research has shown that as the annealing temperature increases, atomic diffusion at the interface becomes stronger [25–27]. During annealing, atoms near the pre-bonding points are activated, and elements from both the Cu and SS substrates diffuse at the interface, creating new bonding points. This results in the closure of pores and the formation of dot-like metallurgical bonding regions, thus improving the bonding strength of the composite strip. Gondcharton P [28] and others studied the void phenomena in copper–copper bonding layers at temperatures between 300 and 400 °C and found that at certain temperatures, vacancy accumulation promotes atomic diffusion.

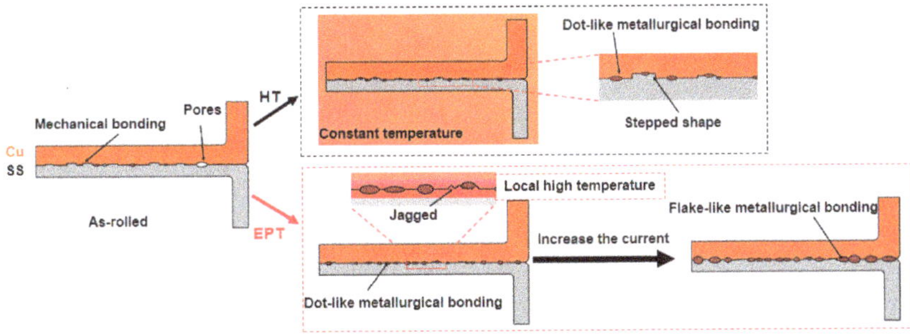

Figure 11. Interfacial bonding status of the composite thin strips processed after EPT and HT.

When the annealing temperature reaches 450 °C, the Cu and Fe atoms receive relatively low energy, leading to some degree of diffusion, but at a slow rate, resulting in fewer metallurgical bonding regions and a low bonding strength. At 600 °C, the higher temperature provides more energy for atomic diffusion, significantly accelerating the diffusion of Fe and Cu atoms, which increases the Cu content on the SS side to 10.3%, and significantly increases the number of metallurgical bonding regions.

In the as-rolled state of the Cu/SS composite thin strip, the bonding interface contains many defects (long gaps and pores), and the resistivity at these defects is high. The high-energy drift electrons carried by the pulsed current interact extensively with the Fe/Cu atoms in the area, rapidly converting energy into heat and generating local high temperatures [29–31]. The pulsed current also induces periodic thermal expansion and contraction of the composite strip, which disrupts the brittle hardened layer at the bonding interface, causing it to melt. The electrical contacts must maintain good contact with the composite strip, thus applying a slight clamping pressure to the interface, making the bonding surface flatter [21,32].

When a pulsed current of 45 A to 55 A is applied, the energy generated gradually increases with increasing current, promoting a gradual increase in the diffusion rate of Cu atoms. After peeling, many dot-like metallurgical bonding regions form on the SS side. When the effective current exceeds 55 A, the diffusion rate of Cu atoms further increases, resulting in the Cu on the SS side of the peeled composite strip exhibiting a flake-like structure.

4.2. Mechanism of Action of EPT on Interfaces

The magnitude of the pulsed current affects the heating rate, thereby influencing the atomic diffusion rate [33,34]. The pulsed current flows from the SS side to the Cu side along the rolling direction, and dislocations move in the direction of the electron wind in the bonding interface region [35]. This results in the rearrangement of surrounding atoms, which, to some extent, causes the hardened layer at the bonding interface to become more even. Overheated dislocations and grain boundaries promote thermally activated diffusion, accelerating the diffusion rate of Cu and Fe atoms [33]. Between EPT-350 and EPT-450, the bonding mode of the Cu/SS composite thin strip is primarily mechanical bonding, with randomly dispersed small metallurgical bonding regions. During the peeling process, the metallurgical bonding is not strong, and most of the applied force acts at the bonding interface, leading to fractures at the interface. In this stage, the peel strength increases with the growth of metallurgical bonding regions. At the same time, the pulsed current disrupts part of the hardened layer, forming an irregular "jagged" structure, which increases the contact area at the bonding interface, making the mechanical bonding more robust and enhancing the overall bonding strength.

From EPT-450 to EPT-600, the bonding mode of the Cu/SS composite thin strip is mainly characterized by flake-like, strong metallurgical bonding, with mechanical bonding and dot-like metallurgical bonding as secondary. The further increase in pulsed current leads to higher temperatures at the bonding interface. The localized regions of Cu melt, making the bonding interface flatter and directly adhere to the SS surface, forming flake-like metallurgical bonding. In areas with relatively lower temperatures, mechanical bonding and dot-like metallurgical bonding dominate.

During peeling, when the composite strip peels from the regions with flake-like strong metallurgical bonding, the bonding strength of the Cu/SS interface exceeds the strength of the Cu substrate at the interface [36]. Since the strength of SS is much greater than that of Cu, the pulsed current can reduce the deformation resistance of Cu and improve its plastic deformation ability. This causes plastic deformation, crack propagation, and fracture within the Cu substrate, leading to peeling from the Cu side of the bonding interface. Under SEM, uniform, stripe-like copper layers adhered to the SS side are observed, and they exhibit characteristics of plastic fracture with ductile dimples [37].

When force is applied to regions with less strong metallurgical bonding, the bonding strength of the Cu/SS interface becomes weaker than the strength of the Cu substrate at the interface, causing peeling to initiate again from the bonding interface. Therefore, in this stage, peeling is the result of both partial peeling of the Cu substrate and partial peeling of the bonding interface.

4.3. Hardness Test

Figure 12 shows a comparison of the Vickers hardness between the SS side and Cu side surfaces as raw materials, in the as-rolled state, and after post-treatment (HT and EPT). After rolling, the micro-Vickers hardness on the SS side increased to 460.04 HV, with an increase of

113.5%, which was consistent with the results of Hedayati, A. et al. [38]. The micro-Vickers hardness on the Cu side increased to 135.40 HV, and the increase reached 18.1%.

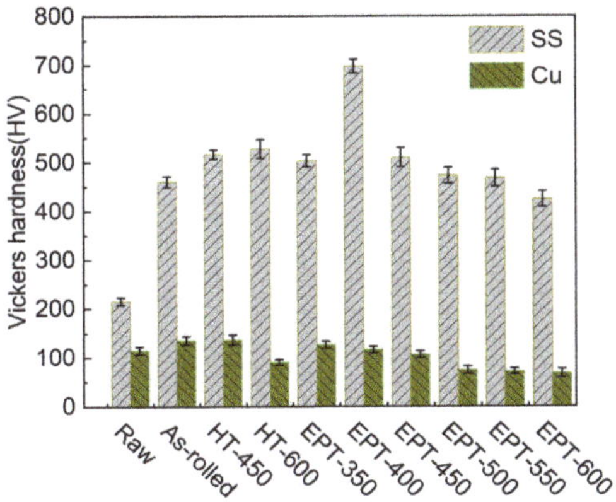

Figure 12. Effects of HT and EPT on the Vickers hardness of the surface of the composite thin strip.

After HT-600 treatment, the micro-Vickers hardness on the SS side increased to 527.64 HV, which was 14.7% higher than that of the as-rolled state due to the large and uneven grain size of the SS in the as-rolled state, and the redistribution of residual stresses and the appearance of fine recrystallized grains due to short-term annealing at 600 °C [10].

After EPT-400 treatment, the micro-Vickers hardness on the SS side reaches a maximum of 697.87 HV, which is 1.5 times that of the as-rolled state. This is due to the fact that the pulse current causes smaller recrystallized grains on the surface of the SS than in the as-rolled state, increasing its dislocation density and promoting surface hardening [39,40]. As the pulse current continues to increase, the recrystallization is more complete, and its surface hardness gradually decreases. Both HT and EPT caused the recrystallization of Cu, resulting in a decrease in its micro-Vickers hardness [41].

In summary, EPT can significantly improve the bonding strength of Cu/SS composite thin strips and retain the hardness of the raw material after rolling to a certain extent (as shown in Figure 12). Compared with the Cu/SS composite thin strip with a bonding strength of about 8 N/mm and 3 N/mm, respectively, prepared by intermediate annealing and two-pass rolling at 400 °C and 600 °C [10], the bonding strength was significantly improved to 10.66 N/mm after EPT-450 treatment. However, in the future, it is still necessary to study the evolution of the interface state corresponding to different rolling processes and electrical treatment parameters. It is necessary to study the problems faced by industrial applications, etc.

5. Conclusions

This study investigates the preparation of Cu/SS composite thin strips with high bonding strength by sequentially applying uniform pulsed currents. The pulsed current applied to the surface can promote the mutual diffusion of elements at the bonding interface, significantly enhancing the bonding strength of the composite thin strips. The research findings are as follows:

EPT demonstrates superior efficiency and effectiveness over traditional heat treatment, achieving significantly higher peel strength and copper content in less time. After annealing at 450 °C for 100 s, the peel strength is 0.96 ± 0.39 N/mm, with the copper content on the SS side being 5.06 ± 0.20%. After annealing at 600 °C, the peel strength increases to 4.00 ± 0.40 N/mm, with the copper content on the SS side reaching 11.83 ± 1.00%. After annealing, the Fe content on the Cu side is relatively low. In contrast, after applying pulsed current for 5 s, the peel strength reaches 10.66 ± 0.93 N/mm, with the copper content on the SS side being 41.86 ± 5.67%, and the Fe content on the Cu side is 7.39 ± 0.84%, which significantly outperforms the heat treatment effect. A pulsed current of 55 A is identified as the optimal parameter.

Effect of pulsed current on bonding strength: The bonding strength under EPT shows two distinct phases. In the low-current stage (45–55 A), high instantaneous heat flux density and non-thermal effects significantly accelerate the diffusion of Cu and Fe, increasing the number of dot-like metallurgical bonding regions and strengthening mechanical bonding, thus greatly improving bonding strength. In the high-current stage (55–65 A), excessive peak current causes the bonding strength at the interface to exceed that of the copper substrate, resulting in a decrease in bonding strength.

Comparison between HT and EPT: HT promotes interfacial bonding through prolonged diffusion at lower temperatures, leading to a gradual improvement in bonding strength. In contrast, EPT through instantaneous high heat flux density and non-thermal effects, rapidly accelerates the diffusion of Cu and Fe, repairing interface defects and increasing metallurgical bonding regions. However, excessively high currents cause the metallurgical bonding regions to form a flake-like structure, leading to a decrease in bonding strength.

Author Contributions: Conceptualization, Z.W. and X.N.; methodology, Z.W., Y.Y. and M.W.; data curation, Z.W. and M.W.; writing—original draft preparation, Z.W. and X.N.; Visualization Z.W. and Y.Y.; writing—review and editing, X.N., W.D. and D.H.; supervision and project administration, X.N. and W.D.; funding acquisition, D.H. and W.D. All authors have read and agreed to the published version of the manuscript.

Funding: The work is financially supported by National Natural Science Foundation of China (No. 52105391, No. U22A20188, No. 52305404); National Key Laboratory of Metal Forming Technology and Heavy Equipment Open Fund (S2308100.W21, S2308100.W17, B2408100.W13).

Data Availability Statement: The original contributions presented in the study are included in the article. Further inquiries can be directed to the corresponding author.

Conflicts of Interest: The authors declare no conflicts of interest.

References

1. Yu, C.; He, Z.; Lv, Q.; Yu, J.; Xiao, H. Preparation of Ti/Al Composite Plates by Differential Temperature Rolling with Induction Heating. *Int. J. Adv. Manuf. Technol.* **2021**, *117*, 383–394. [CrossRef]
2. Huang, G.; Shen, Y. The Effects of Processing Environments on the Microstructure and Mechanical Properties of the Ti/5083Al Composites Produced by Friction Stir Processing. *J. Manuf. Process.* **2017**, *30*, 361–373. [CrossRef]
3. Yang, M.; Chen, D.; Zhou, H.; Xu, J.; Ma, H.; Shen, Z.; Zhang, B.; Tian, J. Experimental and Numerical Investigation of Microstructure and Evolution of TiNi Alloy/Q235 Steel Interfaces Prepared by Explosive Welding. *J. Mater. Res. Technol.* **2021**, *15*, 5803–5813. [CrossRef]
4. Yan, M.; Wang, M.-Y.; Cui, Z.-Y.; Xu, J.-B.; Huang, H.-G. The Effect of a Coating Sprayed Using Supersonic Flame Coating Technology on the Mechanical Properties and Interface Structure of a Thick Steel/Aluminum Composite Plate during Hot Rolling. *Metals* **2024**, *14*, 450. [CrossRef]
5. Zhao, S.; Hu, Y.; Li, S.; Wang, T. Mechanical Properties and Bonding Mechanism of the Mg/Al Clad Sheet Manufactured by the Corrugated Roll. *Metals* **2023**, *13*, 503. [CrossRef]
6. Zhang, Z.; Zhang, H.; Liu, X.; Wang, T.; Huang, Q.; Liao, X. Effect of Roll Surface Topography on Microstructure and Mechanical Properties of 304 Stainless Steel Ultra-Thin Strip. *J. Manuf. Process.* **2023**, *108*, 764–778. [CrossRef]
7. Cestari, A.; De Araújo, M.; De Oliveira, D.C. Corrosion Behavior of Metallic Surfaces in Biodiesel Evaluated by Atomic Force Microscopy, Vickers Micro Hardness, and Copper Strip Test. *Eng. Fail. Anal.* **2021**, *124*, 105329. [CrossRef]
8. Cui, C.; Gu, K.; Weng, Z.; Zhang, M.; Wang, J. Martensitic Transformation in Rolled 301 Stainless Steel Induced by Cryogenic Treatment. *Mater. Today Commun.* **2024**, *38*, 108531. [CrossRef]

9. Liu, X.; Liao, W.; Yang, Y. Thermal Characteristics and Uniformity of Microstructures during Temperature Controlled Mold Continuous Casting Profiled Copper Alloy Strip. *Int. Commun. Heat Mass Transf.* **2020**, *110*, 104414. [CrossRef]
10. Niu, X.; Ding, Q.; Zhang, H.; Liu, X.; Wang, T. Research on Fabricating Cu/Stainless Steel Composite Thin Strips by Two-Pass Cold Roll-Bonding with Intermediate Annealing. *Int. J. Adv. Manuf. Technol.* **2024**, *130*, 3323–3339. [CrossRef]
11. Zhang, T.; Zhai, H.; Li, W.; Hong, H.; Li, Y. XRD and EBSD Evaluation on Deposition Behavior and Microstructure Characteristic of HVOF Sprayed 304SS Coating on Aluminum Substrate. *Surf. Coat. Technol.* **2025**, *496*, 131614. [CrossRef]
12. Lablali, Y.; Oubaki, R.; Ghailane, A.; Alami, J.; Makha, M. Correlation between Sputtering Method, Microstructure and Properties of TiOx Thin Films Deposited by Reactive Direct-Current and High-Power Impulse Magnetron Sputtering. *Thin Solid Film.* **2024**, *808*, 140573. [CrossRef]
13. Wang, C.; Zhou, T.; Xu, X.; Wu, T.; Zhang, M.; Wu, J.; Zhan, L.; Wang, G. Evolution of Microstructure and Mechanical Properties in TiBw/Ti65 Composites during Vacuum Solid-Phase Diffusion Bonding. *Mater. Today Commun.* **2024**, *41*, 110961. [CrossRef]
14. Ren, M.; Xie, H.; Lin, F.; Jia, F.; Huo, M.; Wu, H.; Yang, M.; Jiang, Z. Effect of Heat Treatment on the Microstructure and Mechanical Properties of Copper/SS304L Composite Sheets. *Vacuum* **2022**, *204*, 111370. [CrossRef]
15. Chen, D.; Zhang, H.; Li, H.; Zhu, R.; Zhu, Y.; Jiang, Z. Study on Microstructure and Properties of Ultra-Thin Cu/Al Composite Sheets Using the Cold-Rolled Composite Method at the Microscale. *Metals* **2023**, *13*, 780. [CrossRef]
16. Krechkovska, H.; Tsybailo, I.; Dzioba, I.; Student, O.; Pała, R. Restoration of Properties of Heat-Resistant Steel After Long-Term Operation in Steam Pipeline Bends of TPP by Heat Treatment. *Metals* **2024**, *15*, 21. [CrossRef]
17. Qi, Y.; Ma, X.; Ma, L.; Zhou, C.; Jiang, Z.; Zhao, J. A Study on the Microstructural Evolution, Interfacial Diffusion and Mechanical Properties of Ultra-Thin Stainless Steel–Copper Composites Fabricated by Roll Bonding. *Met. Mater. Int.* **2024**, *30*, 2925–2941. [CrossRef]
18. Wang, C.; Ma, L.; Ma, X.; Wang, T.; Jiang, Z.; Hasan, M.; Zhao, J. Effect of Annealing Temperature on Microstructure and Tensile Properties of Copper/Aluminum Composite Thin Strip. *Trans. Nonferrous Met. Soc. China* **2023**, *33*, 701–713. [CrossRef]
19. Zhao, Z.; Hou, H.; Zhang, N.; Zhang, Y.; Wang, Y.; Wang, G. Effect of High-Energy Electro-Pulses on the Compression Deformation Behavior of Ti-6Al-4V Alloy. *Met. Mater. Int.* **2016**, *22*, 585–593. [CrossRef]
20. Wang, H.; Song, G.; Tang, G. Effect of Electropulsing on Surface Mechanical Properties and Microstructure of AISI 304 Stainless Steel during Ultrasonic Surface Rolling Process. *Mater. Sci. Eng. A* **2016**, *662*, 456–467. [CrossRef]
21. Zhang, T.; Wang, Y.; Xu, Z.; Zhu, K.; Bian, G.; Wang, T.; Fu, X. A New Method for Fabricating Mg/Al Alloy Composites by Pulse Current-Assisted Rolled Welding. *Mater. Lett.* **2023**, *330*, 133247. [CrossRef]
22. Guo, X.; Ren, Z.; Zhang, P.; Zhang, C.; Jiang, S.; Zhang, Q.; Wang, T.; Huang, Q. Effect of Pulse Current on Interface Microstructure and Bonding Properties of TA1/304 Double-Layer Clad Plates. *Chin. J. Mech. Eng.* **2024**, *37*, 116. [CrossRef]
23. *E8/E8M-24*; Standard Test Methods for Tension Testing of Metallic Materials. ASTM International: West Conshohocken, PA, USA, 2024.
24. Liu, Z.; Liu, P.; Zhou, L.; Wang, L. Effects of Pulsed Current on the Microstructure and Properties of Laser Cladded TC17 Titanium Alloy. *Materials* **2023**, *17*, 91. [CrossRef] [PubMed]
25. Cooper, D.R.; Allwood, J.M. Influence of Diffusion Mechanisms in Aluminium Solid-State Welding Processes. *Procedia Eng.* **2014**, *81*, 2147–2152. [CrossRef]
26. Sabetghadam, H.; Hanzaki, A.Z.; Araee, A.; Hadian, A. Microstructural Evaluation of 410 SS/Cu Diffusion-Bonded Joint. *J. Mater. Sci. Technol.* **2010**, *26*, 163–169. [CrossRef]
27. Chen, Z.; Wang, D.; Cao, X.; Yang, W.; Wang, W. Influence of Multi-Pass Rolling and Subsequent Annealing on the Interface Microstructure and Mechanical Properties of the Explosive Welding Mg/Al Composite Plates. *Mater. Sci. Eng. A* **2018**, *723*, 97–108. [CrossRef]
28. Gondcharton, P.; Imbert, B.; Benaissa, L.; Verdier, M. Voiding Phenomena in Copper-Copper Bonded Structures: Role of Creep. *ECS J. Solid State Sci. Technol.* **2015**, *4*, P77–P82. [CrossRef]
29. Lin, J.; Li, X.; Wang, C.; Xu, R.; Zhang, X.; Lu, F.; Lin, P.; Mei, H.; Liu, Y.; Zhuang, Y.; et al. Interfacial Behaviors and Mechanism of ZrC-SiC Composite and Ti System under Pulsed Electric Current. *Compos. Part B Eng.* **2023**, *260*, 110771. [CrossRef]
30. Ran, M.; Bian, G.; Zhang, H.; Yan, J.; Wang, W. Electropulsing-Enhanced Atomic Diffusion and Recrystallization to Optimize Mechanical Properties of Al/Cu Laminated Metal Composites. *J. Manuf. Process.* **2024**, *119*, 224–234. [CrossRef]
31. Tian, N.; Ji, X.; Zhang, C.; Lv, P.; Guan, J.; Cai, J.; Guan, Q. Influence of High-Current Pulsed Electron Beam Irradiation on Elemental Diffusion and Mechanical Properties of Copper/316L Stainless-Steel Bonded Joints. *Nucl. Instrum. Methods Phys. Res. Sect. B Beam Interact. Mater. At.* **2022**, *531*, 115–122. [CrossRef]
32. Song, H.; Hao, W.; Mu, X.; Han, T.; Che, C.; Geng, G. Effect of Pulse Current-Assisted Rolling on the Interface Bonding Strength and Microstructure of Cu/Al Laminated Composite. *Metals* **2020**, *10*, 1555. [CrossRef]
33. Wang, K.; Tan, T.; Fu, Z.; Zhang, J.; Wang, Y.; Wang, W.; Zhang, Q. Study on Atom Diffusion under the Treatment by Pulse Current Heating. *Mater. Sci. Eng. B* **2006**, *135*, 154–161. [CrossRef]

34. Ji, R.; Wang, H.; Wang, B.; Jin, H.; Liu, Y.; Cheng, W.; Cai, B.; Li, X. Removing Loose Oxide Layer and Producing Dense α-Phase Layer Simultaneously to Improve Corrosion Resistance of Ti-6Al-4V Titanium Alloy by Coupling Electrical Pulse and Ultrasonic Treatment. *Surf. Coat. Technol.* **2020**, *384*, 125329. [CrossRef]
35. Huang, T.; Xing, B.; Song, K.; Xiang, N.; Xu, L.; Huang, L.; Guo, J.; Yang, X. Dislocation Motion Induced by Pulse Current in Ti/Al Bimetal Composite Observed by in-Situ TEM. *Mater. Charact.* **2024**, *214*, 114096. [CrossRef]
36. Wu, Y.; Wang, T.; Ren, Z.; Liu, Y.; Huang, Q. Evolution Mechanism of Microstructure and Bond Strength Based on Interface Diffusion and IMCs of Ti/Steel Clad Plates Fabricated by Double-Layered Hot Rolling. *J. Mater. Process. Technol.* **2022**, *310*, 117780. [CrossRef]
37. Cao, J.; Zhang, J.; Tang, H.; Shen, X.; Song, K.; Zhou, Y.; Cui, C. Investigation on the Microstructure Evolution and Strengthening Behavior of Rolled Bonding Cu Strip. *J. Sci. Adv. Mater. Devices* **2024**, 100835. [CrossRef]
38. Hedayati, A.; Najafizadeh, A.; Kermanpur, A.; Forouzan, F. The Effect of Cold Rolling Regime on Microstructure and Mechanical Properties of AISI 304L Stainless Steel. *J. Mater. Process. Technol.* **2010**, *210*, 1017–1022. [CrossRef]
39. Wang, T.; Wei, X.; Zhang, H.; Ren, Z.; Gao, B.; Han, J.; Bian, L. Plastic Deformation Mechanism Transition with Solute Segregation and Precipitation of 304 Stainless Steel Foil Induced by Pulse Current. *Mater. Sci. Eng. A* **2022**, *840*, 142899. [CrossRef]
40. Gu, S.; Liu, C.; Kimura, Y.; Yoon, S.; Cui, Y.; Yan, X.; Ju, Y.; Toku, Y. Realizing Strength–Ductility Synergy in a Lean Duplex Stainless Steel through Enhanced TRIP Effect via Pulsed Electric Current Treatment. *Mater. Sci. Eng. A* **2023**, *883*, 145534. [CrossRef]
41. Chen, X.; Jiang, F.; Jiang, J.; Xu, P.; Tong, M.; Tang, Z. Precipitation, Recrystallization, and Evolution of Annealing Twins in a Cu-Cr-Zr Alloy. *Metals* **2018**, *8*, 227. [CrossRef]

metals

MDPI

Article

Multi-Physical Field Coupling Analysis of Electro-Controlled Permanent Magnet Blank Holder Processes Considering Thermal Magnetic Losses

Zhanshan Wang [1], Linyuan Meng [2,*], Gaochao Yu [2] and Xiaoyu Ji [3]

1 Intelligent Equipment Department, Suzhou Vocational Institute of Industrial Technology, Suzhou 215104, China; 00759@siit.edu.cn
2 School of Mechanical Engineering, Yanshan University, Qinhuangdao 066004, China; ygc@ysu.edu.cn
3 CCCC Second Harbor Engineering Company Ltd., Wuhan 430040, China; xycccc2024@163.com
* Correspondence: mlyysu@126.com; Tel.: +86-180-3359-0906

Abstract: Electro-permanent magnet (EPM) technology is characterized by high integration, strong modularity, and stable magnetic force, making it a current research focus when combined with sheet metal deep drawing processes to develop EPM blank holder deep drawing technology. In this study, we investigated the issue of thermal magnetic quantitative magnetic loss after the prolonged use of the EPMBH process, analyzing the variation in magnetic force with the temperature increase to provide necessary data support for the application of the EPMBH. First, a thermal network model for the four-magnetic pole unit EPM magnetic device was established, and through calculations on this model, the thermal equilibrium temperatures for the permanent magnet (PM)-NdFeB and reversible magnet (RM)-AlNiCo were found to be 72.13 °C and 72.41 °C, respectively. Second, the magnetic performance of PM and RM at different temperature points was measured to analyze the variation in their magnetic characteristics with the temperature increase. Third, a magnetic force model of the EPM magnetic device was established, and finite element analysis was conducted using the measured magnetic characteristics data of RM and PM. The results indicated that an increase in temperature leads to a reduction in magnetic force, with a maximum reduction of 18.57% observed after thermal equilibrium. An experimental testing platform was designed and built to validate the calculation and simulation results. Finally, a sheet metal deep drawing experiment using the EPMBH process was conducted, taking into account thermal magnetic loss factors. The results showed that magnetic force loss due to temperature rise affects the forming quality of the sheet metal. Therefore, in practical applications, it is necessary to establish a real-time temperature monitoring system and develop a temperature-based magnetic force compensation module.

Keywords: electro-permanent magnet blank holder; deep drawing; temperature-dependent magnetic loss; thermal filed; coupled magnetic–stress field

1. Introduction

Deep drawing forming is one of the primary methods of sheet metal forming and is widely used in industrial production. During the deep drawing process, if the blank holder force is too low, tangential stress can accumulate in the flange area of the blank, leading to instability and causing the blank to wrinkle [1]; if the blank holder force is too high, it can cause excessive thinning or even fracture at the dangerous edge of the blank.

The application of an appropriate blank holder force is an important means to ensure the quality of the formation [2–4]. Du Bing [5,6] analyzed the loading path and energy flow direction to establish a critical determination criterion for wrinkling in box-shaped parts. Won [7] analyzed the forming process of box-shaped parts, and the results indicated that the force and deformation distribution in the flange area of the formed parts are uneven. The unreasonable application of blank holder force can easily lead to wrinkling and instability in the flange area, thus affecting product quality and mold life. Susila et al. [8] conducted research on the maximum blank holder force for cup-shaped parts and performed finite element analysis experiments for validation.

Over the past few decades, researchers have conducted in-depth studies on the loading and control modes of blank holder force. Senior [9] and Hill [10] have studied the issue of the critical blank holder force for wrinkling using the energy method and bifurcation theory, respectively. Hauptmann [11] optimized the structure of stretched cardboard by adjusting the relationship between the blank holder force and the stroke in deep drawing. Sim [12], based on the concept of closed-loop control of blank holder force, obtained the curve of blank holder force against stroke for the deep drawing process of cylindrical parts, which can be controlled in real time, using numerical simulation methods. Kergen [13] obtained the ideal blank holder force trajectory curve based on the wrinkle-free experiment that measures the gap between the mold and the blank holder ring. Wang [14] used theoretical calculations and finite element simulation methods to derive the "V" type blank holder force setting mode, which is conducive to reducing the thinning rate of formed parts.

Generally, BHF is applied by hydraulic pressure or other external forces in deep drawing. But, due to high energy consumption, long transmission chains, and complicated control processes during BHF by hydraulic or mechanical transmission, there are some disadvantages in realizing the real-time control of BHF. In order to solve the problems of traditional blank holding, numerous scholars have used auxiliary blank holder devices to load and control the blank holder force, achieving good forming results [15–17]. Seo [18] first proposed the electromagnetic blank holding method. Li [19] developed a new type of electromagnetic blank holder force system suitable for conventional deep drawing processes and verified the effectiveness of the electromagnetic blank holder system. Huang [20] designed a kind of pulsed electromagnetic blank holding system. This method uses the electromagnetic attraction or repulsion generated between coils as the blank holding force acting on the blank holder ring to achieve blank holding. Due to the need for continuous power supply to maintain the magnetic field, there are some difficulties in overcoming defects, such as high energy consumption, coil temperature rise and heating, and safety hazards like demagnetization upon power failure, which limit its further application in actual production.

In the late 20th century, the electro-controlled permanent magnetic chuck was invented by Tecnomagnetes S.P.A. (Lainate, Italy). Afterwards, this technology has been continuously improved and gradually expanded. The electro-controlled permanent magnet technology was originally applied in the fields of lifting, rapid mold changing, and fixing during machining processes [21,22]. The electro-controlled permanent magnet chuck constructed based on this technology has advantages such as independent loading, a short transmission chain, ease of control, and energy efficiency. Qin [23,24] combined the electro-controlled permanent magnet technology with the sheet metal deep drawing process to propose an electro-controlled permanent magnet blank holding method. Tooling and molds were designed based on the magnetic force of electro-controlled permanent magnets for blank holding, and the finite element analysis and experimental verification of the magnetic and stress field were conducted. Qin and Zhang [25,26] have analyzed the temperature rise effect of the EPM in the electro-controlled permanent magnet blank holder (EPMBH) deep drawing process, as well as the thermal field and the magnetic–mechanical field, but they did not analyze the impact of temperature rise on the magnetic properties of magnetic materials and the magnetic force.

In this paper, we analyze the issue of heat effects generated by the control current passing through the excitation coil in the EPMBH, adopt the thermal network analysis method to establish the thermal transfer network of the magnetic force device of FMPU, and calculate the thermal equilibrium temperature of each component. We also analyze the impact of temperature rise on the magnetic materials in the model, conduct finite element analysis on the coupled fields of temperature, magnetic, and stress fields for FMPUs, and, finally, determine the trend of how temperature rise affects the magnetic force. This provides a basis for force control in the EPMBH deep drawing process to ensure effective and continuous operation.

2. Materials and Methods

2.1. Principle of EPMBH

As shown in Figure 1a, the EPM and the suction plate are the essential components of the EPMBH, together creating a magnetic attraction force. This force serves as the blank holder force necessary for deep drawing operations. A single magnetic pole unit can decompose into three parts: reversible magnet (RM), permanent magnet (PM), and copper coils. Based on the magnetic properties, NdFeB is characterized by high remanence and high coercivity, which allows it to provide strong magnetic force and excellent magnetic stability. AlNiCo is characterized by high remanence and lower coercivity, enabling it to provide strong magnetic force while allowing its magnetic polarity to be changed by an external magnetic field. AlNiCo is selected as the RM, while NdFeB serves as the PM.

The working principle of the EPMBH is highly dependent on the hysteresis property of the AlNiCo. As shown in Figure 1b, AlNiCo demonstrates variable magnetic characteristics under distinct loading currents, manifesting as diverse hysteresis loops. Adjusting the intensity of the loading current allows for the control of the blank holder force, and I_s is the saturation magnetizing current, corresponding to the saturation hysteresis loop of AlNiCo, which produces the maximum blank holder force (BHF) in this state. In the control process, the magnetization direction of NdFeB is fixed; as shown Figure 1b,c, a positive current that induces a magnetic field in the same direction as that of the NdFeB magnet is applied. The state in which the magnetization of the AlNiCo follows the poles of the NdFeB is called the forward state (state (3)). In contrast, the state where the poles of the AlNiCo are the opposite of those of the NdFeB is called a reverse state (state (1)). Figure 1c depicts the full cycle of the EPMBH working principle divided into four steps as follows:

(i) **[Unloading state]**: I (working current) = 0, AlNiCo is in state (1). The magnetic flux lines form a loop within the EPM and do not exhibit magnetic attraction externally.
(ii) **[Forward magnetization state]**: I > 0, loading time is 20 ms, AlNiCo transitions from state (1) through state (2) to state (3)
(iii) **[Loading state]**: I = 0, AlNiCo is in state (3), the magnetic induction lines of the EPM extend outward, exhibiting magnetic attraction, resulting in BHF.
(iv) **[Reverse magnetization state]**: I < 0, loading time is 20 ms, AlNiCo transitions from state (3) through state (4) to state (1).

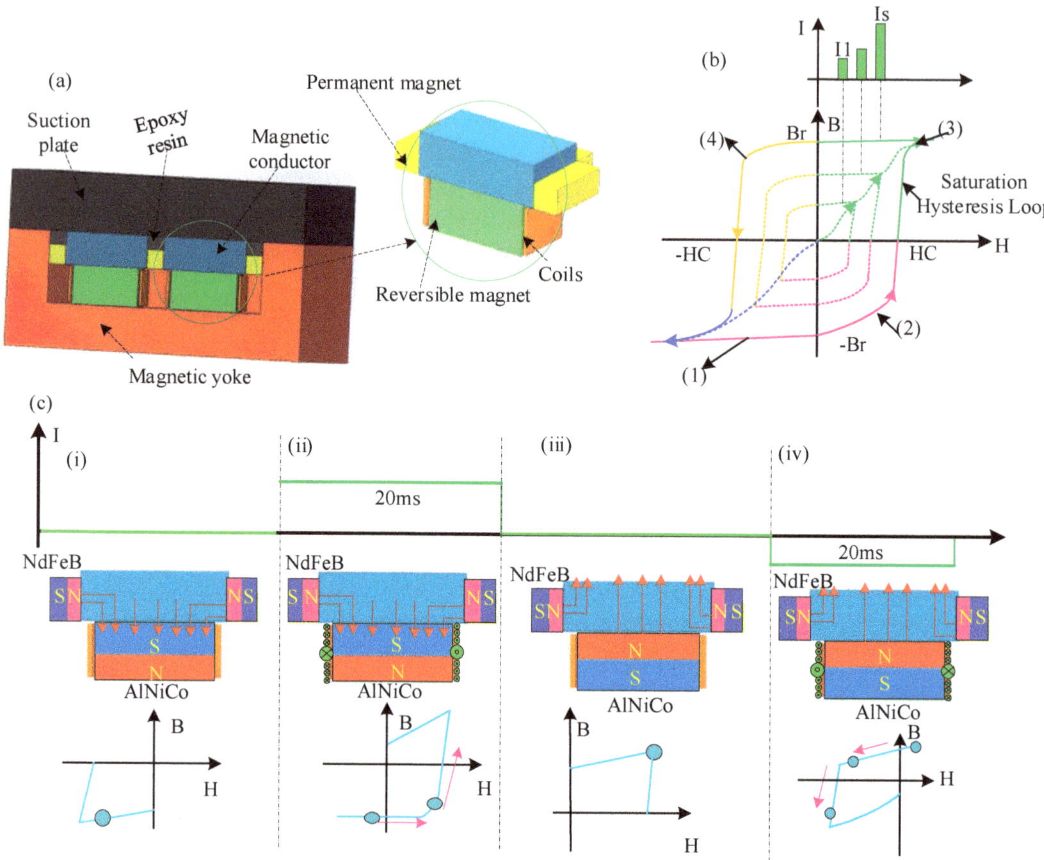

Figure 1. Principle of the EMPBH: (**a**) structure of the EPMBH; (**b**) hysteresis curve of the Al-Ni-Co; (**c**) schematic of the full-cycle fundamental principle of the proposed EPMH; the red arrows represent the magnetic field direction induced inside the core. The blue dots show the estimated field of the EPMBH in the state with an applied current measured at a certain distance from the core tip.

2.2. Setup Tools Using EPMBH

Designing the EPMBH tools, the structure of the EPM magnetic pad is as depicted in Figure 2a, comprising 36 magnet pole units. As shown in Figure 2b, the EPM magnetic pad is integrated with a moveable beam through connecting rods. The sheet metal is positioned between the EPM magnetic pad and the suction plate, which together create a magnetic force; this force is distributed across the slab by a flange ring as BHF to facilitate the deep drawing process. Upon the completion of the deep drawing, the magnet pad is reversed to a demagnetized state, entering an unloading state with no magnetic force between the pad and the suction plate; this allows for the easy removal of the formed part.

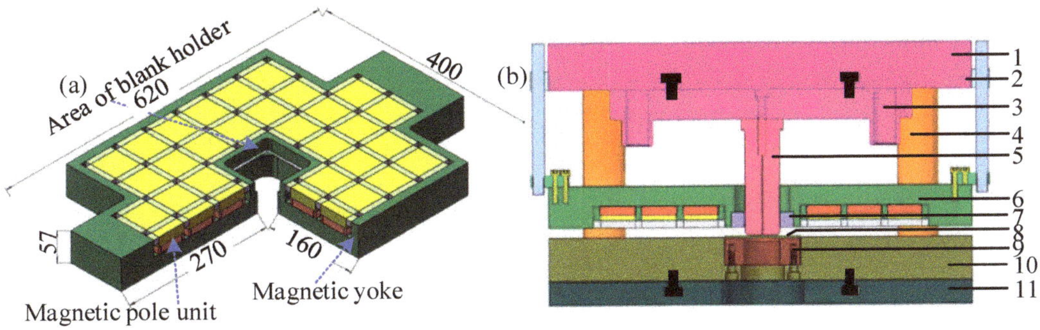

Figure 2. Mold for the EPMBH: (**a**) structure of the EPMBH; (**b**) EPMBH deep drawing tools and 1. movable beam, 2. connecting rod, 3. upper base, 4. guide pillar, 5. punch, 6. EPM, 7. blank holder, 8. sheet metal, 9. die, 10. suction plate, 11. lower base.

2.3. *Analyses of Thermal Field of FMPU*

2.3.1. Models of FMPU

In EPM technology, the magnetic pole units are used in pairs, and the thermal fields of four magnetic pole units include all the modes of heat conduction in the EPM magnetic pad, so FMPUs are taken as an example for description. As shown in Figure 3a, the dimensions of FMPUs, RMs, and PMs are 150 × 150 × 50 mm, 45 × 45 × 20 mm, and 43 × 43 × 12 mm, respectively. As shown in Figure 3b, resistance temperature detectors (RTDs) are positioned inside the 4-EPM. RTD-1 is located within the coil to assess its temperature, RTD-2 is mounted on the NdFeB surface for tracking its thermal state, and RTD-3 is placed atop the AlNiCo surface to gauge its temperature.

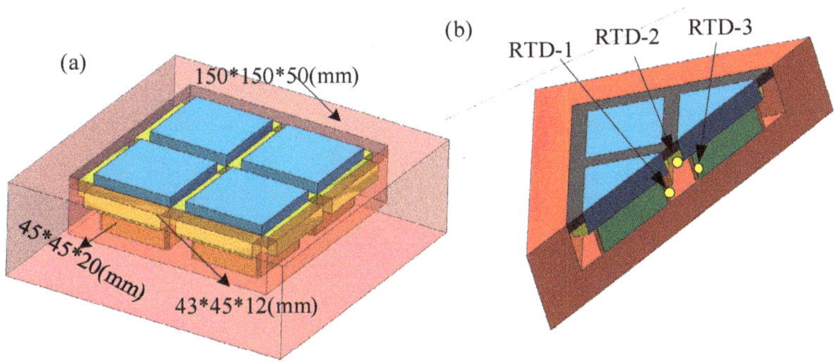

Figure 3. Mold for FMPUs: (**a**) 3D diagram; (**b**) sectional view.

2.3.2. Thermal Network Model for FMPUs

The thermal network model based on thermal resistance and capacitance for FMPUs was established, and the integrated nodes in the thermal network model were numbered. As shown in Figure 4, the numbering situation was as follows: epoxy resin (5, 9, 13, 16), PM (1, 2, 3, 4, 6, 7, 8, 10, 11, 12, 14, 15), RM (18, 20, 22, 24), coil (19, 21, 23, 25), magnetic yoke (17), and air (26).

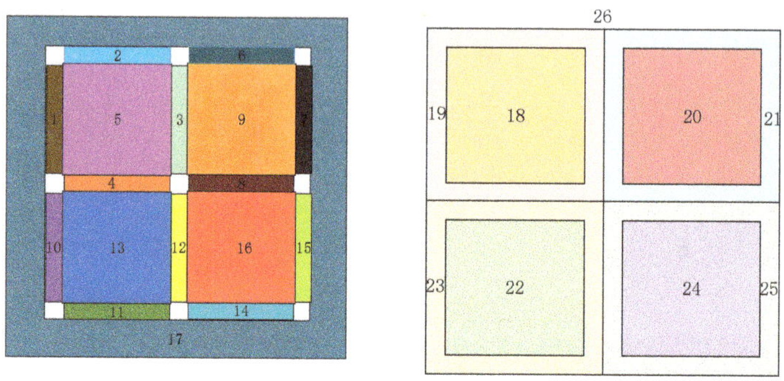

(**a**) (**b**)

Figure 4. Node number for FMPUs: (**a**) the numbering situation of the surface; (**b**) the numbering situation of the interior.

The thermal network model method was based on thermal resistance, wherein there are mainly three forms of thermal resistance, namely conduction thermal resistance, convection thermal resistance, and radiation thermal resistance, while in the FMPUs, there are mainly conduction thermal resistance and convection thermal resistance. The thermal resistance R*ij* between the parts in the heat transfer network represents the thermal resistance of the number *i* and the number *j*, as shown in Table 1. And the schematic diagram of the thermal network model as shown in Figure 5.

Table 1. Thermal resistance form.

Thermal Resistance Form	Number
conduction thermal resistance	R5.1, R5.2, R5.3, R5.4, R9.6, R9.7, R9.3, R9.8, R13.4, R13.10, R13.12, R13.11, R16.8, R16.12, R16.14, R16.15, R18.5, R20.9, R24.25, R22.13, R24.16
contact thermal resistance	R22.23, R17.1, R17.7, R17.11, R17.20, R17.19, R17.25, R17.2, R17.15, R17.10, R17.22, R17.21, R20.21, R18.19, R17.6, R17.14, R17.18, R17.24, R17.23,
convection thermal resistance	R26.others

According to heat transfer theory, the conductive thermal resistance can be represented in Equation (1).

$$R_{i,j} = \frac{L_i}{2\lambda_i A_{i,j}} + \frac{L_j}{2\lambda_j A_{i,j}} \tag{1}$$

where the $R_{i,j}$ is the thermal resistance of conduction between node *i* and *j* (K/W); L_i is the length of the conduction direction at node *i* (mm); L_j is the length of the conduction direction at node *i* (mm); λ_i is the thermal conductivity of material *i* (W/(m·K)); λ_j is the thermal conductivity of material *j* (W/(m·K)); and $A_{i,j}$ is the conductive area between node *i* and *j* (mm^2).

parameters has been simulated and calculated, with the results shown in Figure 7e. The magnetic force of FMPUs on the suction plate is 16.524 KN at 25 °C. When the temperature rises to 50 °C, the magnetic attractive force decreases to 15.6195 KN, a drop of 0.9045 KN or 5.474%. When the temperature rises further to 75 °C, the magnetic attractive force drops further to 13.455 KN, a drop of 3.069 KN or 18.57%.

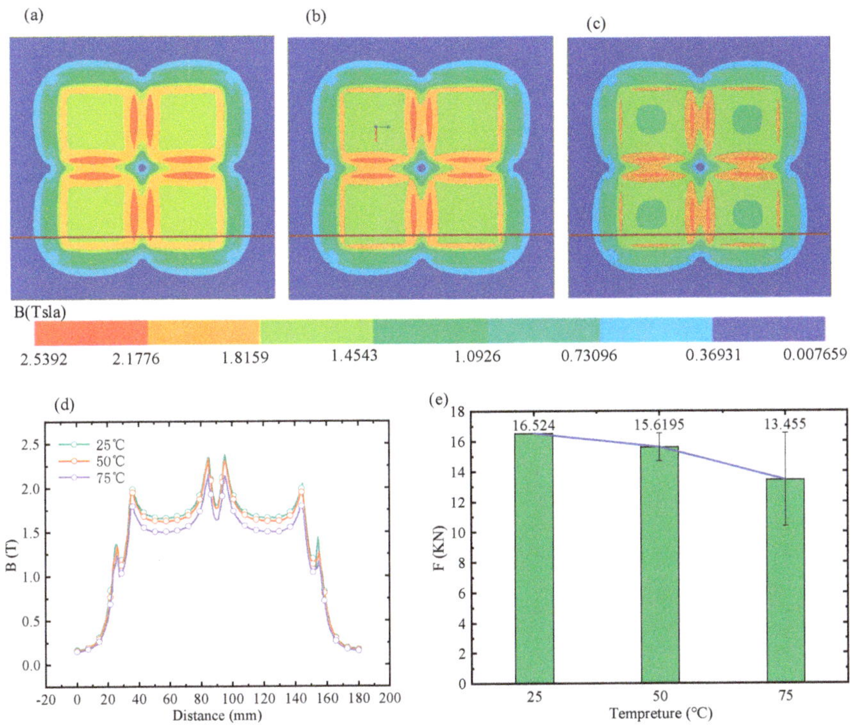

Figure 7. The analysis results of coupling thermal, magnetic, and stress fields under loading conditions: magnetic induction intensity contour maps of the attracted plate surface at different temperatures ((**a**) 25 °C, (**b**) 50 °C, (**c**) 75 °C); (**d**) magnetic induction intensity curve recorded by the marking line; (**e**) magnetic force variation curve graph at different temperatures.

Using the same method for the finite element analysis of the unloaded state of FMPUs, as shown in Figure 8a–c. the distribution of magnetic induction lines at 25 °C, 50 °C, and 75 °C under the condition of magnetic unloading, As shown in Figure 8d, the magnetic force changes at different temperatures. At 25 °C, the residual magnetic attraction force of the attracted plate is 102.3 N, with a corresponding unload ratio of 0.6%. At 50 °C, the residual magnetic attraction force increases to 110.6 N, and the unload ratio slightly rises to 0.7%. At 75 °C, the residual magnetic attraction force further increases to 125.4 N, with an unload ratio of 0.93%. This indicates that as the temperature rises, the residual magnetic attraction force does indeed increase, but the unload ratio consistently remains below 1%, suggesting that the temperature increase has a minimal effect on the unloading of the magnetic device.

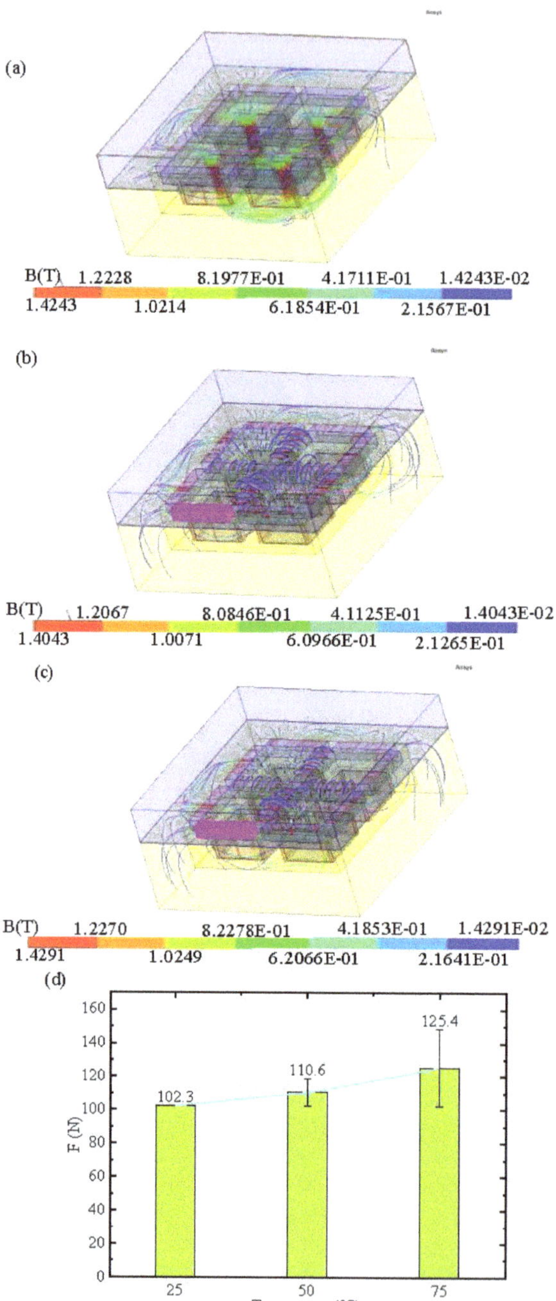

Figure 8. The analysis results of coupling thermal, magnetic, and stress fields under unloading conditions: distribution of magnetic induction lines at different temperatures ((**a**) 25 °C, (**b**) 50 °C, (**c**) 75 °C); (**d**) residual magnetic force at different temperatures.

3. Results

3.1. Experimental Verification

As shown in Figure 9a, the threaded force sensor is fixed to the back of the suction plate using a bolt, a through-hole is set in the middle of the suction plate, and the force-transmitting copper pillar passes through the hole to make contact with the FMPUs. A positive current is applied to the EPM by the EMP controller, generating a magnetic attraction force from the suction cup. This magnetic force is transferred to the force sensor through the force-transmitting copper pillar. During the experiment, the magnetizing and demagnetizing currents as well as their frequencies are set according to the designed operating parameters of the suction cup. The experiment is conducted, and during the process, signals from the temperature sensor and force sensor are conditioned by signal conditioners. The measurement and control system collects sensor signals through an acquisition card and carries out data storage and display. The experimental apparatus is shown in Figure 9b.

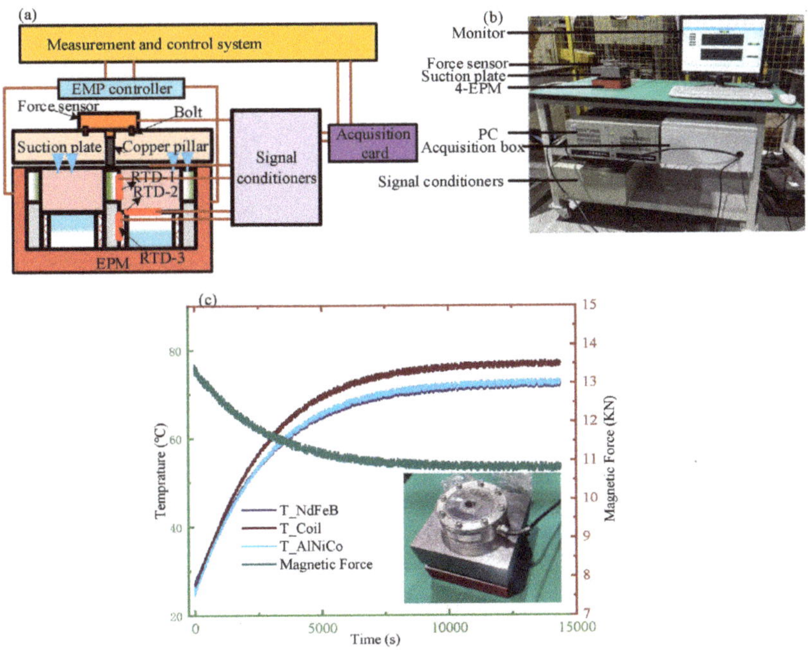

Figure 9. Temperature–magnetic force test apparatus: (**a**) the schematic of the device; (**b**) photo of experimental apparatus; (**c**) results of experiment.

The error between the simulated data and the experimental data is represented by %E, and its calculation formula is shown in Equation (9); in Equation (9), $\hat{y}_i$ represents the simulated value and y_i represents the measured value.

$$\%E = \frac{\left|y_i - \hat{y}_i\right|}{y_i} * 100\% \tag{9}$$

As shown in Figure 9c, after 4.17 h, each component within the FMPUs magnetic device reached a state of thermal equilibrium. The equilibrium temperature for the PM (NdFeB) was 71.92 °C, and for the RM (AlNiCo), it was 72.82 °C. The temperature error of the PM is 1.09%, and the temperature error of the RM is 0.93%. These temperatures are in close agreement with the theoretical values listed in Table 2, confirming the accuracy of the thermal network model for calculating the temperatures of the components within the magnetic device.

As the temperature increased, the magnetic attraction force gradually weakened, decreasing from an initial 13.22 KN to 10.18 KN, a decline of 22.99%. Compared to the simulated values, the simulation errors for the initial and final values of magnetic force are 22.81% and 25.76%, respectively. This is due to a certain magnetic gap during the experimental measurements, which caused some loss of magnetic force. The magnitude of magnetic force attenuation is approximately similar, with a difference of 4.425%. This consistency validates the precision of the finite element analysis of the coupled thermal–magnetic force field in the EPM magnetic pad.

3.2. Deep Drawing Process Based on EPMBH

The deep drawing equipment is shown in Figure 10. To assess the impact of magnetic force reduction due to temperature rise on the forming effect, this study conducted stretching experiments on 08AL (60 mm in radius and 0.6 mm thick) steel plates under four different edge pressing force conditions, the initial edge pressing forces were set at 55 KN and 42 KN, and the corresponding forces after an 18% reduction were 45 KN and 34 KN.

Figure 10. Photograph of experimental setup.

The experimental results, shown in Figure 11, indicate that with an initial edge pressing force of 55 KN, the forming effect on the steel plate was good; even when the force was decreased to 45 KN, the forming quality remained satisfactory. However, with an initial force of 42 KN, while the forming effect appeared to be good at first, wrinkling occurred in the flange area of the plate when the force was reduced to 32 KN, indicating that the edge pressing force was insufficient to complete the deep drawing forming. Therefore, during the EPMBH deep drawing process, it is crucial to pay attention to the reduction in magnetic force caused by temperature rise and to select an appropriate edge pressing force to ensure the effective progression of the forming process.

Figure 11. Drawn cups of 08Al sheet with diameter of 60 mm: (**a**) forming effect with BHF of 55 KN; (**b**) forming effect with BHF of 45 KN; (**c**) forming effect with BHF of 42 KN; (**d**) forming effect with BHF of 34 KN.

4. Comparative Analysis of Energy Consumption

The EPMBH process uses the magnetic force of permanent magnets as the blank holder force, significantly reducing energy consumption. To demonstrate the energy-saving effect of this process, an analysis of the process energy consumption was conducted with the target blank holder forces set at 42 kN and 153 kN, respectively.

The energy consumption of the EPMBH process is primarily due to the heat generated by the excitation current passing through the excitation coil. The energy consumption Q for a complete deep drawing process is shown in Equation (10).

$$Q = \left(I_m^2 + I_d^2\right) * R * T_{ct} \tag{10}$$

I_m and I_d are the loading and unloading currents, respectively. R is the resistance of the control coil, 180 Ω. T_{ct} is the working time of the loading current and unloading current, 0.02 s., with the target BHF being 42 kN and 153 kN. In the EPM blank holder process, the loading current I_{m42} is 8 A and I_{m153} is 15 A; the unloading current under different loading currents is the same as 15 A.

According to the previous study [25], in the traditional BHF deep drawing process, the energy consumptions of 42 kN and 153 kN BHF in a deep drawing cycle are 1.89 kJ and 6.89 kJ, respectively.

Figure 12 presents the energy consumption comparison using different blank holder techniques. In comparison to a traditional deep drawing process, the EPMBH process is more energy-efficient than the conventional hydraulic blank holder deep drawing process. When the target blank holder force is 42 kN, it achieves a 44.97% energy saving compared to the traditional hydraulic process. At a target blank holder force of 153 kN, the energy savings increase to 76.48%. This indicates that the greater the target blank holder force, the more significant the energy-saving effect.

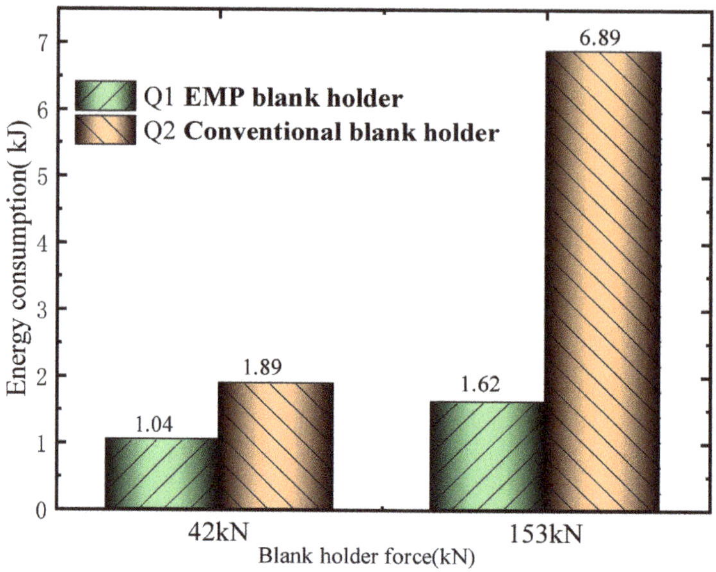

Figure 12. Comparison of energy consumption.

5. Discussion

The electric control permanent magnet technology converts magnetic force into edge pressing force, offering significant energy-saving benefits. Its widespread and long-term application can greatly reduce energy consumption in industrial production, playing a crucial role in promoting carbon neutrality. This paper provides a quantitative analysis of the thermo-magnetic losses in the EPMBH process under conventional conditions, offering data support for its industrial application. According to the experimental results, firstly, a real-time temperature monitoring system for the EPM magnetic device should be established. Secondly, necessary magnetic force compensation should be made based on the temperature–magnetic force variation curve. For scenarios with high performance requirements, high-temperature NdFeB series magnets can be selected, although they are more expensive. Staff can choose suitable permanent magnets based on their specific needs. Future research will focus on reducing thermo-magnetic losses, including analyzing hysteresis losses in high-temperature series permanent magnets, increasing forced convection to lower temperature rise, optimizing load current to reduce heat accumulation, and adding high permeability materials in the working gap to decrease magnetic losses, thereby reducing the operational current and further minimizing heat buildup.

6. Conclusions

Considering the properties of magnetic materials, a finite element analysis of the coupled temperature field–magnetic field–stress field in the EPMBH process was carried out and experimentally verified. The trend of BHF variation with temperature rise in the EPMBH process was deduced and validated through deep drawing tests. Taken together, we can come to the following conclusions:

(1) A thermal network model of the FMPU was constructed using the thermal network analysis method, and calculations were conducted to obtain the thermal equilibrium state of each component. The results indicate that the thermal equilibrium temperature of Alnico (AlNiCo) is 72.12 °C, while that of NdFeB is 72.41 °C; this temperature has not exceeded its curie point, but is close to this critical temperature limit.

(2) The coupling effects of the thermal field, magnetic field, and stress field were analyzed. The results show that as the temperature rises, the magnetic parameters of Alnico (AlNiCo) remain largely unchanged, whereas those of NdFeB exhibit significant changes, with a maximum magnetic energy product reduction of 17.78%. This reduction leads to a weakened magnetization intensity on the surface of the attracted plate, which in turn reduces the magnetic attraction force on the plate, with a maximum decrease of 18.82%. Therefore, in the application of the EPMBH process, staff need to closely monitor the temperature of the chuck to prevent excessive thermo-magnetic losses.

(3) The deep drawing experiments conducted under the consideration of the temperature rise effect show that the increase in temperature has an impact on the deep drawing process. To successfully complete the deep drawing, it is essential to select the appropriate blank holder force.

Author Contributions: Conceptualization, Z.W. and L.M.; Methodology, L.M.; Software, X.J.; Validation, Z.W.; Formal analysis, L.M.; Investigation, L.M., G.Y. and X.J.; Data curation, Z.W.; Writing—original draft, L.M.; Writing—review and editing, Z.W. and G.Y. All authors have read and agreed to the published version of the manuscript.

Funding: This research received no external funding.

Data Availability Statement: The original contributions presented in the study are included in the article, further inquiries can be directed to the corresponding author.

Conflicts of Interest: Author Xiaoyu Ji was employed by the CCCC Second Harbor Engineering Company Ltd. The remaining authors declare that the research was conducted in the absence of any commercial or financial relationships that could be construed as a potential conflict of interest.

References

1. Tang, H.; Wen, T.; Hong, J.; Zhou, Y.; Zhang, L. Analysis of shear stress wrinkling of asymmetric sheet specimen under offset loading. *J. Mech. Sci. Technol.* **2022**, *36*, 1451–1457. [CrossRef]
2. Siegert, K.; Doegf, E. CNC Hydraulic Multipoint Blank-holder System for Sheet Metal Forming Presses. *CIRP Ann.* **1993**, *42*, 319–322. [CrossRef]
3. Kitayama, S.; Natsume, S.; Yamazaki, K.; Han, J.; Uchida, H. Numerical Investigation and Optimization of Pulsating and Variable Blank Holder Force for Identification of Formability Window for Deep Drawing of Cylindrical Cup. *Int. J. Adv. Manuf. Technol.* **2016**, *82*, 583–593. [CrossRef]
4. Sun, C.Z.; Chen, G.L.; Lin, Z.Q. Improvement of the Formability of Box Deep Drawing Using Variable Force. *J. Shanghai Jiao Tong Univ.* **2003**, *37*, 1883–1886.
5. Du, B.; Zhao, C.; Xie, J.; Li, H.; Zhao, C.; Du, Z. Influence of stress loading path on the limit of plastic wrinkling and instability of plates and shells. *J. Mech. Eng.* **2021**, *57*, 83–91.
6. Bing, D.; Pengfei, S.; Jun, X.; Changcai, Z.; Fenglong, G. Prediction of critical wrinkle instability of thin plates by combining energy method theory with numerical simulation. *J. Mech. Eng.* **2020**, *56*, 57–64. [CrossRef]
7. Won, C.; Kim, H.G.; Lee, S.; Kim, D.; Park, S.; Yoon, J. Wrinkling prediction for GPa-grade steels in sheet metal forming process. *Int. J. Adv. Manuf. Technol.* **2019**, *102*, 3849–3863. [CrossRef]
8. Candra, S.; Batan, I.M.L.; Berata, W.; Pramono, A.S. Analytical study and FEM simulation of the maximum varying blank holder force to prevent cracking on cylindrical cup deep drawing. *Procedia CIRP* **2015**, *26*, 548–553. [CrossRef]
9. Senior, B.W. Flange wrinkling in deep-drawing operations. *J. Mech. Phys. Solids* **1956**, *4*, 235–246. [CrossRef]
10. Hill, R. A theory of the yielding and plastic flow of anisotropic metals. *Proc. R. Soc. London Ser. A Math. Phys. Sci.* **1948**, *193*, 281–297.
11. Hauptmann, M.; Weyhe, J.; Majschak, J.-P. Optimisation of deep drawn paperboard structures by adaptation of the blank holder force trajectory. *J. Mater. Process. Technol.* **2016**, *232*, 142–152. [CrossRef]
12. Sim, H.B.; Boyce, M.C. Finite element analyses of real-time stability control in sheet forming processes. *J. Eng. Mater. Technol.* **1992**, *114*, 180–188. [CrossRef]
13. Kergen, R.; Jodogne, P. *Computerized Control of the Blank Holder Pressure on Deep Drawing Process*; SAE Technical Paper: Warrendale, PA, USA, 1992.
14. Wang, D.Z.; Lou, Z.L.; Zhang, Y.Q. Numerical simulation of variable blank holder force in box deep drawing. *J. Shanghai Jiaotong Univ.* **2001**, *35*, 1543–1546.

15. Cui, X.; Li, J.; Mo, J.; Fang, J.; Zhou, B.; Xiao, X.; Feng, F. Incremental electromagnetic-assisted stamping (IEMAS) with radial magnetic pressure: A novel deep drawing method for forming aluminum alloy sheets. *J. Mater. Process. Technol.* **2016**, *233*, 79–88. [CrossRef]
16. Siopis, M.S.; Kinsey, B.L.; Kota, N.; Ozdoganlar, O.B. Effect of severe prior deformation on electrical-assisted compression of copper specimens. *J. Manuf. Sci. Eng.* **2010**, 731–737. [CrossRef]
17. Fang, J.; Mo, J.; Cui, X.; Li, J.; Zhou, B. Electromagnetic pulse-assisted incremental drawing of aluminum cylindrical cup. *J. Mater. Process. Technol.* **2016**, *238*, 395–408. [CrossRef]
18. Seo, Y.R. Electromagnetic blank restrainer in sheet metal forming processes. *Int. J. Mech. Sci.* **2008**, *50*, 743–751. [CrossRef]
19. Li, H.; Wang, Q.; He, F.; Zheng, Y.; Sun, Y. Design, numerical simulation, and experimental validation of a novel electromagnetic blank holding system for conventional drawing process. *Int. J. Adv. Manuf. Technol.* **2019**, *102*, 2183–2193. [CrossRef]
20. Huang, Y.; Lai, Z.; Cao, Q.; Han, X.; Liu, N.; Li, X.; Chen, M.; Li, L. Controllable pulsed electromagnetic blank holder method for electromagnetic sheet metal forming. *Int. J. Adv. Manuf. Technol.* **2019**, *103*, 4507–4517. [CrossRef]
21. Huang, C.D. Engine with Permanent Magnetic Chucks. US. WO2015021887(A1), 18 February 2015.
22. Cheng, F.; Qin, S.; Lin, Q.; Kong, X. The Electronically Controlled Permanent Magnet Sucker End Pickup for the Rapid Die Changing System of Multi-Station Press: China. CN201020682973.5, 14 December 2010.
23. Qin, S.J.; Zhang, H.S.; Mao, Y.B.; Yang, L.; Li, X.; Hu, Z.; Cheng, X. Electro-permanent magnet blank holder technique in sheet metal deep drawing. *Int. J. Adv. Manuf. Technol.* **2020**, *106*, 5497–5507.D. [CrossRef]
24. Qin, S.; Kong, X.; Ma, Y.; Yang, L. The Invention Relates to a Drawing Die with Variable Blank Holding Force with Memory Characteristics and a Control Method: China. Patent 201610606036.3, 14 December 2016.
25. Zhang, H.; Qin, S.; Cao, L.; Meng, L. Research on Deep Drawing Process Using Radial Segmental Blank Holder based on Electro-permanent Magnet Technology. *J. Manuf. Process.* **2020**, *59*, 636–648. [CrossRef]
26. Qin, S.; Cheng, X.; Zhang, H.; Lu, T.; Gu, T.; Meng, L. Analyses of thermal field and coupled magnetic-mechanical field in electro-permanent magnet blank holder technique. *Int. J. Adv. Manuf. Technol.* **2020**, *110*, 499–510. [CrossRef]
27. Li, Y.; Li, H.; Geng, H.; Gong, X.; Yang, F. Measurement and Analysis of Hysteresis Loss of Nd-Fe-B Permanent Magnet under Superheated Loss of Magnetism. *Electr. Power* **2020**, *50*, 50–57.

metals

MDPI

Article

Study on Near-Net Shape Forging of Large Marine Crank Throws

Longjiang Niu [1], Qingliang Zhang [1], Yongwan Zhang [1], Jingyu Wang [1], Weiping Luo [1], Donghang Liu [1], Tengfei Ma [1] and Xavier Velay [2,*]

1 School of Mechanical Engineering, Shanghai Dianji University, Shanghai 201306, China; niulj@sdju.edu.cn (L.N.); 236000020601 20@st.sdju.edu.cn (Q.Z.); chuyuan0805@163.com (Y.Z.); bielin329480@163.com (J.W.); luog1152569551@163.com (W.L.); ldh20000815@163.com (D.L.); matfei1997@163.com (T.M.)

2 Faculty of Engineering and Design, Atlantic Technological University, F91 YW50 Sligo, Ireland

* Correspondence: xavier.velay@atu.ie; Tel.: +353-87-318-5887

Abstract: The crankshaft is a critical component in large marine ships, often regarded as the "heart" of the vessel due to its role in transmitting power and motion. This article addresses the technological challenges in the forging of marine crank throws, a key segment of the crankshaft. The study employed finite element simulations to evaluate three Near-Net-Shape (NNS) forming methods: One-Step Extrusion (OSE), Upsetting/Backward Extrusion (U/BE), and Grooving–upsetting/Backward Extrusion (G–U/BE). The results show that the G–U/BE method requires the lowest load. The grooving–upsetting step in the G–U/BE process forms a rigid journal end web shape that influences the subsequent backward extrusion, with the relative groove depth (the ratio of groove depth to width) playing a crucial role in the final forging quality. Optimal crank throw formation occurs when the ratio is 1.5; deeper grooves increase the load required, diminishing the effectiveness of the grooving–upsetting step. Scaled-down experiments validate G–U/BE as a practical and feasible method for producing large marine crank throw forgings, ensuring both the desired shape and microstructural properties.

Keywords: forging simulation; marine crankshaft; near-net shape; grooving–upsetting/backward extrusion

1. Introduction

Marine crankshafts are critical components in ship propulsion systems and are subjected to extreme mechanical stresses and fatigue during operation [1]. The manufacturing process of crankshaft throws, particularly through forging, plays a crucial role in determining the quality and performance of the final product. Simulation and experimental testing have become indispensable tools for optimizing these forging processes, enabling engineers to predict and refine the microstructural and mechanical properties of the finished components.

Large marine engine crankshafts, such as the 23-m-long S90 semi-built crankshaft shown in Figure 1, can weigh up to 460 tons and are challenging to manufacture as a single piece. Consequently, engine manufacturers have categorized crankshafts into the following four types:

Figure 1. S90 semi-built crankshaft.

Solid-Built Crankshaft. The entire crankshaft is made from a single piece. This design provides excellent grain flow characteristics compared to other types, resulting in significantly better fatigue resistance. However, main engines on ships are too large to use this type of crankshaft, so it is typically employed for smaller engines. Additionally, due to its high rigidity, the solid-built crankshaft cannot accommodate small misalignments.

Fully-Built Crankshaft. All parts of the crankshaft are manufactured separately through casting or forging and then machined before being assembled using shrink fitting [2]. These crankshafts exhibit good build quality and surface finish, however, their fatigue strength is low due to uneven grain flow.

Welded Crankshaft. This type is gradually becoming the preferred choice for large marine engines. There are two manufacturing methods for producing welded crankshafts: (i) welding crank arms (consisting of half the main journal, half the crank pin, and one crank web) at the pin and the middle of the bearing journal, and (ii) welding the main journal to a single forged crank throw piece. Welded crankshafts provide an optimal solution in terms of cost, strength, and weight.

Semi-Built Crankshaft. This is currently the most popular type for large marine engines. It consists of two main components: the journal and the crank throw [3,4]. The forged journal is shrink-fitted into the crank throw, which is a single piece comprising two webs and a pin, forged as one unit. This design improves grain flow. Furthermore, the assembly offers additional flexibility, allowing it to sustain some degree of misalignment.

The crank throw, which includes two webs and a crank pin (see Figure 2), is particularly challenging to produce due to its complex shape, substantial weight, and stringent performance requirements arising from demanding operating conditions [5].

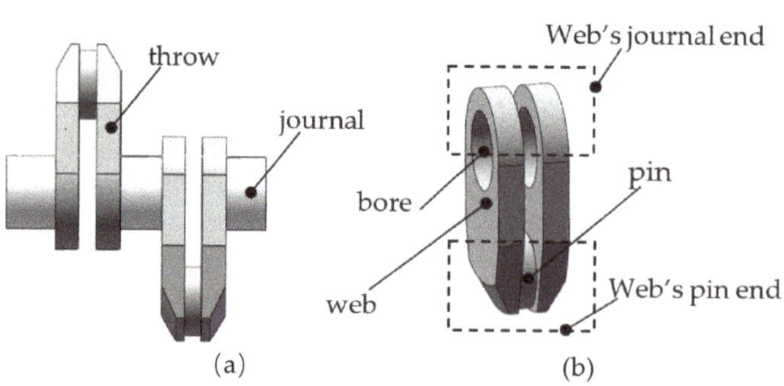

Figure 2. (**a**) Section of the S90 crankshaft, and (**b**) description of the crank throw and pin.

Traditionally, manufacturers produced crank throws directly from a forged block using the Block method. Later, the so-called Ring method was developed, which begins with a hollow ingot or a punched billet [6]. By expanding the hole and flattening the ring, two throws can be obtained by cutting it in half. The Block method is clearly machining-intensive, cost-ineffective, and results in throws with discontinuous grain flow. While the Ring method achieves continuous grain flow and a comparatively high material utilization rate, it is too complicated to implement [7].

Currently, the two primary methods for forging crank throws are Bend Forging [8] and Die Forging [3,9], as illustrated in Figure 3. In the Bend Forging method, a preform with a specific design is bent into a V-shape and then flattened to create a crank throw forging. The Die Forging process, developed by Kobe Steel in Japan, involves inserting a round bar into a die and forming the crank throw through backward extrusion.

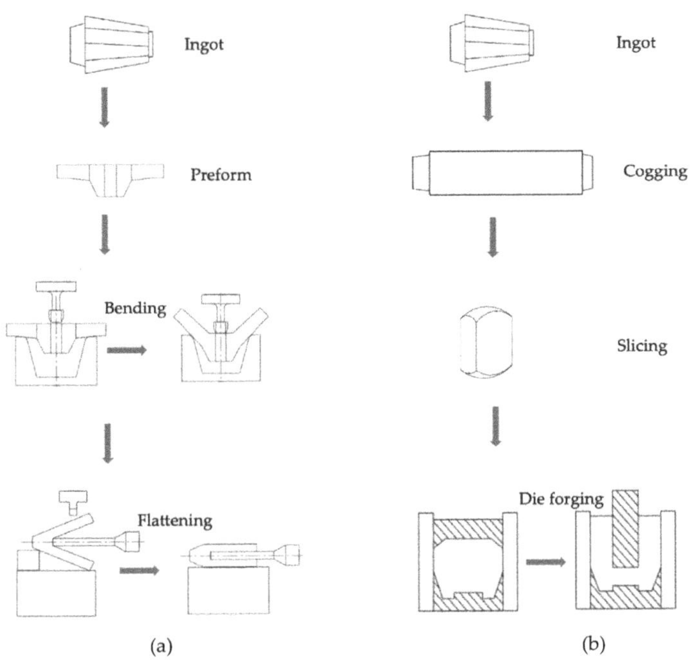

Figure 3. Processes for (**a**) Bend Forging, and (**b**) Die Forging [4].

While both methods produce crank throw forgings that meet technical requirements, each has its limitations. The bend forging method results in large material allowances and requires extensive subsequent machining. Its efficiency is notably low, and the quality of the products is highly dependent on the operator's skill, making consistent near-net shape production a significant challenge [9]. On the other hand, Kobe Steel's die forging method faces difficulties in centering the block within the die and requires high press capacity. The high load requirements inherent to this method limit its application, particularly for large parts [10–12]. However, Kobe Steel's method is a Near-Net Shape (NNS) forging process that aims to produce components closely resembling the final shape, thereby reducing material waste and machining time.

Crankshafts are subjected to continuous cyclic loads during operation and static loads when at rest. The demanding service environment is carefully considered when designing crankshafts and selecting their materials. The choice of material depends on factors such as crankshaft design, geometry, and engine type. In any case, crankshafts must possess high strength. Fully-built and semi-built crankshafts are typically made from normalized unalloyed carbon steel. For welded crankshafts, the preferred materials are hardened and tempered low-alloy chrome–molybdenum steel or normalized low-carbon manganese steel. In this study, S34MnV steel is used for both the simulations and the experiments.

S34MnV steel is a low-alloy steel that has been extensively studied [13–17]. Due to its excellent comprehensive mechanical properties achieved through quenching and tempering, it is widely used in the manufacturing of large marine crankshafts, including both journals and throws [18]. Its mechanical properties are presented in Table 1, and its composition is provided in Table 2 [19].

Table 1. Mechanical properties of S34MnV steel.

Item Tested	Temp. °C	Min. Tensile Strength (MPa)	Min. Yield Strength (MPa)	Min. Elongation (%)	Reduction of Area (%)	Charpy V-Notch (J)	Hardness (HB)	
				Longitudinal	Longitudinal	Longitudinal	Min.	Max.
Specifications	20	610	350	18	40	18	180	220

Table 2. Chemical composition of S34MnV steel (in weight percent).

Component	C	Si	Mn	P	S	Cr	Ni	Mo	V
Measured	0.35	0.02	1.13	0.006	0.002	0.27	0.26	0.11	0.10

Recent advancements in numerical modeling and simulation techniques have significantly improved our ability to analyze and optimize forging processes for crankshaft throws. These simulations accurately predict forging loads and key microstructural data, such as grain characteristics, which are directly influenced by the forging process. Experimental testing complements these simulations by providing real-world data to validate and refine computational models. These findings highlight the importance of integrating simulation and experimental approaches to optimize forging processes.

The finite element method (FEM) is a powerful and advanced tool in scientific research. Many scholars have used FEM to study metal-forming processes. Jayanthi et al. utilized FEM to optimize forging process sequences for compressor discs, analyzing force, temperature, strain, and material properties [20]. Raja et al. employed Deform-3D and 3D processing map to study microstructural and mechanical characteristics of hot worked homogenized AA7068 [21]. Zeng et al. simulated the hot forging of high-Mn steel turnout cores, obtaining optimal parameters through systematic analysis [22]. Zhang et al. applied repeated continuous extrusion forming to Al–Mg–Si–Cu alloys, investigating deformation behavior, microstructural evolution, and material properties. Their results revealed enhanced tensile strength and elongation with uniform grain size [23]. The numerical simulations in these studies were consistent with physical experiments, demonstrating that simulating forging processes can significantly reduce the need for extensive physical trial and error, thereby lowering development costs.

The global demand for large marine crankshafts is expected to grow steadily in the coming years, driven by several factors: the expanding marine engine market, increasing maritime trade, a focus on fuel efficiency, stricter environmental regulations, and the growth of low-speed engines. Semi-built crankshafts offer a good balance between strength and ease of manufacture for larger engines, making them a cost-effective choice for large marine applications.

The cost of the forging process for large maritime crankshaft throws is influenced by several factors: material costs, equipment investment, energy consumption, labor costs, quality control and certification, and research and development. Forging is a capital-intensive process, however, the resulting near-net-shape forgings provide benefits such as reduced material waste, improved strength, and potential weight savings, which can offset the initial manufacturing costs over the component's lifecycle. This research uses an S90 marine crank throw as a case study to identify the optimal forging process.

2. Objective of the NNS Forging of a Large Marine Crank Throw

As shown in Figure 2, a U-shaped marine crank throw comprises two webs and a pin. A main journal is shrink-fitted into the web bore. For convenience, the boxed upper side of the throw in Figure 2b is referred to as the journal end of the web, as this is where the main journal will be shrink-fitted. The crank throw's operating conditions and assembly requirements demand that this end have a semicircular shape. The lower side, termed the pin end, is so named due to its proximity to the crank pin. To reduce the mass of the rotating part, the pin end is designed with a conical surface. The middle section of the web has a rectangular cross-section to transmit high torques.

The gap between the two inner faces of the webs is very narrow, typically narrower than the thickness of the webs themselves to save space. Additionally, this gap is wide and deep, posing significant challenges for forging. Another obstacle is the lack of rolled billets suitable for forging large, heavy crank throws. As a result, the complete workflow for manufacturing crank throws involves the following steps: smelting → ingot casting → heating → open-die forging billets → heating → surface cleaning → NNS forging of crank throws → heat treatment → machining [24].

From Figure 2, it is evident that if web bores could be produced directly during the NNS forging process, significant material savings and machining hours could be achieved. However, due to the limitations of conventional presses, it is currently very difficult to form the bores directly through forging, necessitating machining instead. Consequently, the NNS forged crank throw design should resemble that shown in Figure 4b. The billet shape should closely approximate the final forged throw to streamline the process. A rectangular parallelepiped billet, as shown in Figure 4a, is ideal for this purpose, as it is easy to forge and facilitates surface cleaning.

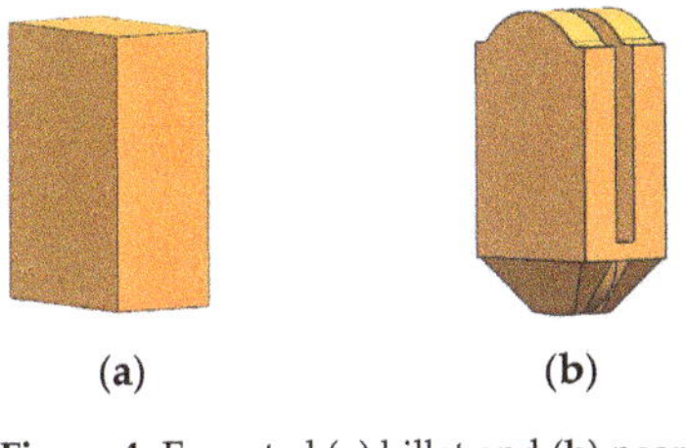

Figure 4. Expected (**a**) billet and (**b**) near-net forged throw.

3. Analysis of NNS Forging Methods of Crank Throw

As described in Sections 1 and 2, the shape characteristics of crank throws make extrusion the most suitable method for producing forged throws. In this section, three NNS extrusion methods are designed and analyzed using numerical simulation, followed by a comparison to identify the optimal process.

The leading metal forming software, Forge® (version3.1, Transvalor S.A., Biot, France), was used to simulate the various NNS forging processes of the crank throws. Figure 5 illustrates the finite element models, which include the billet, the upper die, and the lower die. Both dies are assumed to be 'rigid' (i.e., non-deformable), while the billet is considered deformable. At the start of the simulation, the billet is meshed with 30,000 tetrahedron elements. To maintain accuracy and optimize computational time, the mesh box technique was employed. This technique controls mesh refinement in highly deformed zones, as indicated by boxes 1 and 2 in Figure 5.

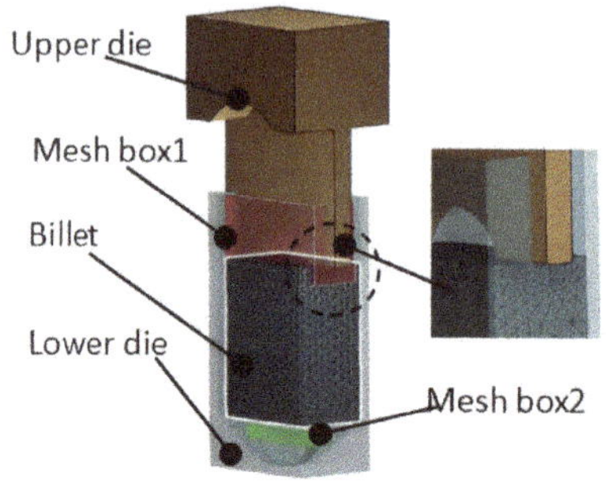

Figure 5. Finite element model of crank throw extrusion.

An Arrhenius equation model (see Equation (1)) was used to accurately predict the rheological stresses generated during deformation [6]. The model for S34MnV steel was implemented in the software code through a subroutine.

$$\dot{\varepsilon} = 3.842 \times 10^{11}[\sinh(0.012\sigma)]^{4.346} exp\left(-\frac{321943}{RT}\right) \tag{1}$$

where $\dot{\varepsilon}$ is the Strain Rate, σ is the Flow Stress, R is the Universal Gas Constant, and T is the Temperature. The Activation Energy for S34MnV steel is 321,943 kJ/mol.

Other process parameters for the simulations are listed in Table 3.

Table 3. Process parameters.

Parameters	Value
Billet's initial temperature	1200 °C
Die's initial temperature	50 °C
Friction coefficient between billet and dies	0.15 (water + graphite)
Heat transfer coefficient between billet and dies	2000 W/m^2·K
Heat transfer coefficient between billet and air	10 W/m^2·K
Upper die speed	60 mm/s

3.1. One-Step Extrusion (OSE)

3.1.1. Numerical Simulation and Analysis of OSE

Figure 6 shows a simulation of the OSE process for a crank throw. Extrusion begins immediately when the punch contacts the billet, as the billet's cross-section closely matches that of the die cavity. This process involves combined extrusion, with both ends of the billet deforming simultaneously. Figure 6b shows the backward extrusion at the upper end and the forward extrusion at the lower end. When the punch stroke reaches 95% (Figure 6d), the pin-end die cavity is fully filled, marking the end of the combined extrusion phase and the beginning of backward extrusion at the upper end. Finally, the material flows upward, completely filling the die cavity to form the journal end (Figure 6e).

(a) (b) (c) (d) (e)

Figure 6. One-step extrusion: (**a**) 0% stroke, (**b**) 20% stroke, (**c**) 80% stroke, (**d**) 0% stroke, and (**e**) end stroke.

3.1.2. Influence of Asymmetrically-Placed Billets

In real production, to facilitate the billet's entry into the die cavity, its cross-section must be slightly smaller than the die cavity. For large billets, the gap between them can be as wide as 50 mm or more. In most cases, the billet is not perfectly centered within the die cavity. Figure 7 illustrates the OSE process for both a centered billet and an off-centered billet.

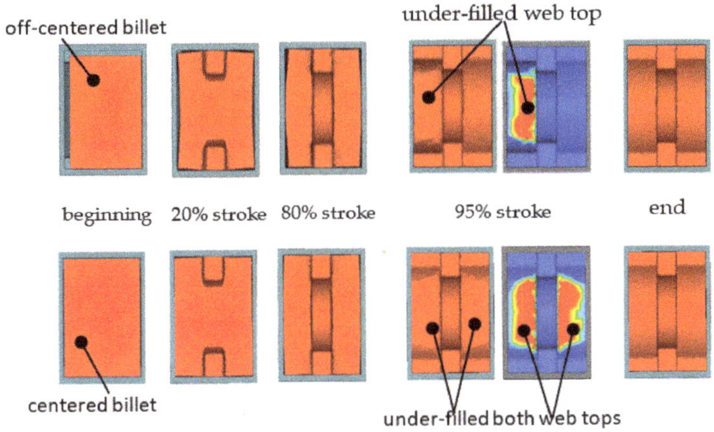

Figure 7. OSEs with off-centered and centered billets.

At the end of forging, both cases produce good crank throw forgings. However, when the billet remains centered throughout the process, its deformation is symmetric. In the case of an off-centered billet, the right web forms better than the left during most of the stroke. At 95% stroke, the right web is already fully formed (represented in blue), while the left remains under-filled (area represented in red). This asymmetry leads to differences in the required loads.

Figure 8 shows the load-time curves for both cases. The load curves are nearly identical except at the end of the forging process. In the off-centered billet case, additional force is required at 95% stroke to push the material from the right side to the left, ensuring the left web fully fills the die cavity. The maximum load for a centered billet is 41,000 tons, whereas for an off-centered billet, it reaches 49,000 tons.

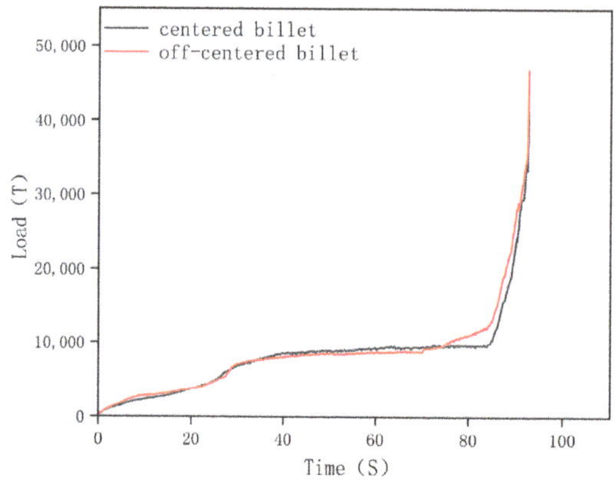

Figure 8. Load-time curves for extrusion with off-centered billet and centered billet.

This indicates that to reduce the load and achieve high-quality crank throw forgings, it is crucial to ensure the billet is centered at the start of the process. If the billet begins off-centered, implementing an automatic method to reposition it to the center is necessary.

3.2. Upsetting/Backward Extrusion (U/BE)

Figure 9 illustrates the U/BE process for a crank throw, where an upsetting step is incorporated to ensure the billet is centered in the die. In this method, during the upsetting stage, an upsetting punch with an end face matching the shape of the webs is used. The billet undergoes closed-die upsetting at this stage, followed by backward extrusion using an extrusion punch.

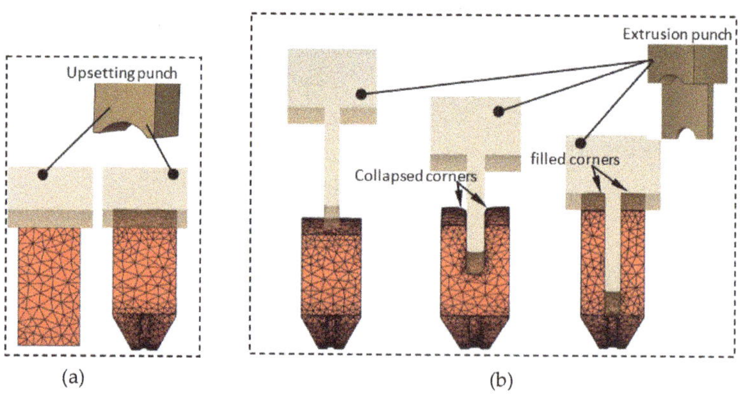

Figure 9. Upsetting/backward extrusion of the crank throw. (**a**) Upsetting and (**b**) Backward extrusion.

During the upsetting stage, the billet is not only aligned to the die center but also shaped at both ends of the throw under high temperatures. This approach effectively reduces the load required during the subsequent backward extrusion phase.

Figure 10 shows the load-time curves for the upsetting/backward extrusion process. During the upsetting step, the load increases at an approximately constant rate, except for a sharp rise at the end of the stage when both ends of the throw are fully formed (see Figure 9b). In the subsequent backward extrusion step, the load initially rises rapidly, then stabilizes for most of the extrusion process. However, toward the end, the load increases steeply.

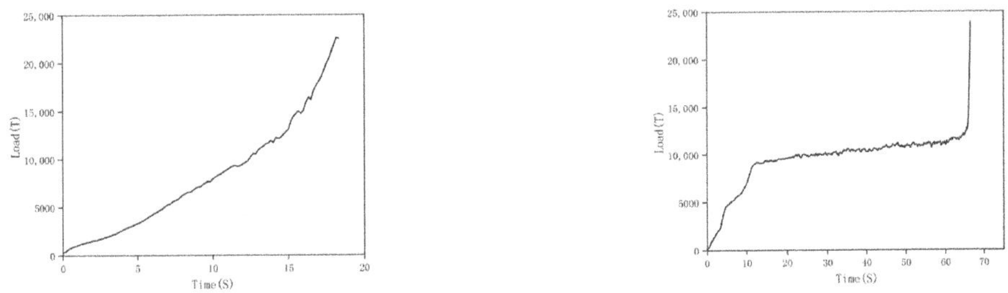

(a) (b)

Figure 10. Load-time curves for the upsetting/backward extrusion. (**a**) Upsetting and (**b**) Backward extrusion.

This sharp rise occurs because a very high load is required to eliminate the collapsed corners on the web tops (see Figure 9b), which are caused by friction between the extrusion punch and the inner sides of the web tops. Additionally, to accurately form the top end of the web, the extrusion punch must match the shape of the corresponding part of the web. These curved surfaces are complex to manufacture, significantly increasing production costs.

Furthermore, due to the backward extrusion punch's length being much greater than its thickness, deflection can occur at the beginning of the extrusion process, leading to unequal web thicknesses. To address these challenges and ensure better outcomes, an improved process must be developed.

3.3. Grooving–Upsetting/Backward Extrusion (G–U/BE)

Based on the U/BE process, a groove (actually obtained through backward extrusion) is added during its upsetting step. Grooving–upsetting is a combined extrusion process, as shown in Figure 11. The principle is that after the billet is placed into the die cavity, it is first pressed by a punch with a "tongue" extending from its end face. The deformed billet is shown in Figure 11b at the end of grooving–upsetting. This process retains the advantage of ensuring the billet remains centered, as in the U/BE process. It not only forms the two web ends and the crank pin end but also produces a shallow guiding groove that serves to correctly position the extrusion punch for the subsequent backward extrusion, which helps control the web thickness variation.

The load-time curves for the G–U/BE process are shown in Figure 12. It can be seen that the curves for the grooving–upsetting step (Figure 12a) and the upsetting step (Figure 10a) are similar, except that the grooving–upsetting step requires a lower maximum load, indicating that the groove helps reduce the load. The load-time curves for both processes at the backward-extrusion step (Figures 10b and 12b) are also similar, as they both increase rapidly initially and level off at around 10,000 tons. The notable difference is that the load in the U/BE process increases steeply towards the end, while in the G–U/BE process, there is only a slight increase in load at the end. This is because, with an appropriate groove depth, the subsequent backward extrusion has little effect on the shape of the web ends produced in the grooving–upsetting step. Hence, unlike U/BE, there is no need for closed-die forming to eliminate collapsed web corners, and no very high load is required. Additionally, the extrusion punch for the G–U/BE process can be much simpler than that used in U/BE, since the web ends are already completed in the preceding grooving–upsetting step.

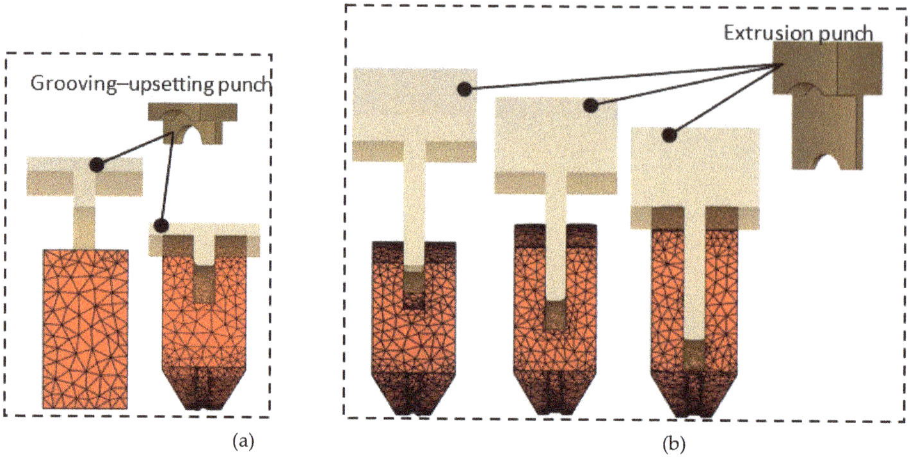

Figure 11. Grooving–upsetting/backward extrusion of the crank throw. (**a**) Grooving–upsetting and (**b**) Backward extrusion.

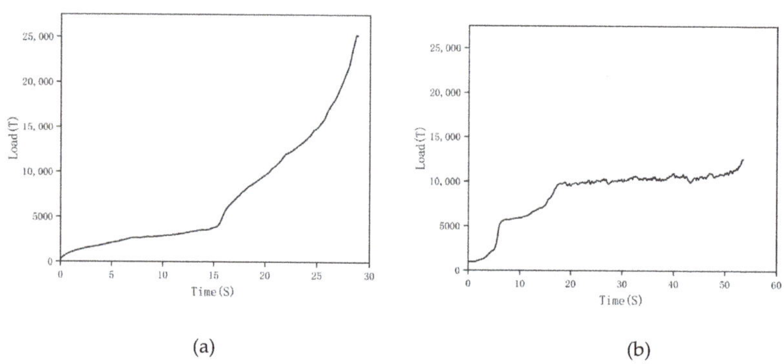

Figure 12. Load-time curves for the grooving–upsetting/backward extrusion. (**a**) Grooving–upsetting and (**b**) Backward extrusion.

3.4. Determination of the Optimal Method

3.4.1. Forging Load

Forging load is usually an important indicator for evaluating a forging process, and it directly impacts the cost of the press, energy consumption, and tool life. The maximum loads for each step of these three methods are listed in Table 4. As shown in Table 4, G–U/BE results in the lowest load.

Table 4. Loads of each operation in different methods for the S34MnV steel.

Method	Load (tons)		
	Upsetting	**Grooving–Upsetting**	**Backward Extrusion**
OSE	-	-	49,000
U/BE	22,500	-	25,000
G–U/BE	-	24,700	12,500

3.4.2. Comparison of Forging Forming Quality

At the end of a forging process, the product's temperature and its equivalent strain are two key factors affecting the forging's microstructure. A high final forging temperature tends to cause grain growth. Although deformation can refine the grains during the forging process, if the forging temperature is too high, the previously refined grains tend to coarsen, resulting in lower properties of the forging [11]. Figures 13 and 14 show the temperature fields and equivalent strain fields of the forged throw at the end of the three methods, respectively. It is clear that they are essentially the same.

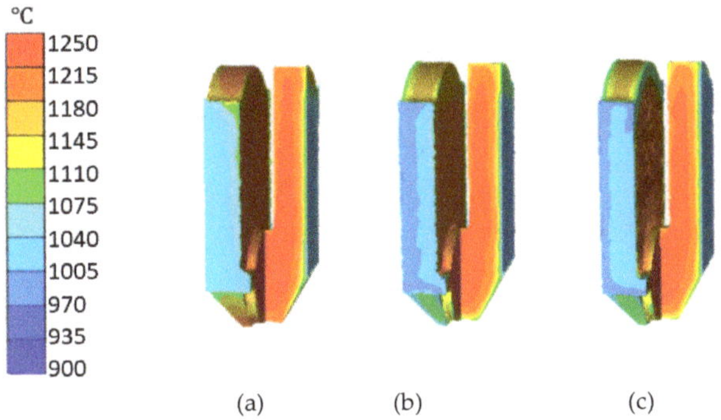

Figure 13. Final forging temperatures. (**a**) OSE, (**b**) U/BE, and (**c**) G–U/BE.

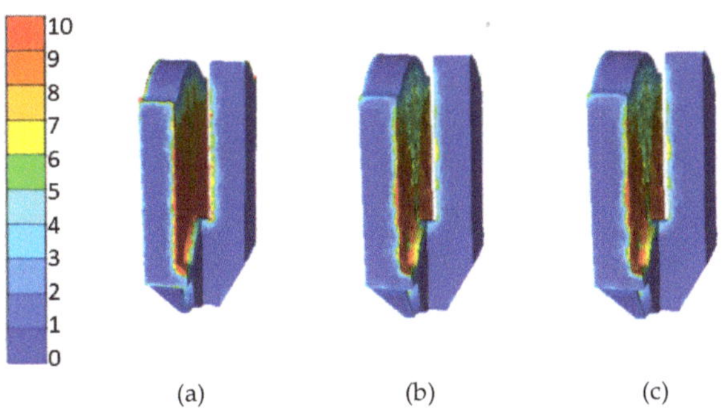

Figure 14. Equivalent strains (unitless). (**a**) OSE, (**b**) U/BE, and (**c**) G–U/BE.

Numerous studies have indicated that the billet's temperature and equivalent strain are key factors influencing the forging's microstructure [25–28]. Therefore, it can be concluded that the microstructures of the forgings produced by the three methods are also similar.

3.4.3. Comparison of the Temperature Rise of the Lower Die

The die's temperature is the most important factor influencing its life. Elevated die temperatures can seriously affect its hardness and mechanical properties, resulting in a decrease in its ability to resist deformation and wear [7]. Among the three methods, the lower die has the longest contact time with the billet, and thus, it reaches the highest temperature at the end of the process. Figure 15 shows the lower die's temperature fields at the end of the three processes, and their highest temperatures are listed in Table 5. It can be seen that the temperature of the lower die in OSE is the highest, while those in U/BE and G–U/BE are basically the same.

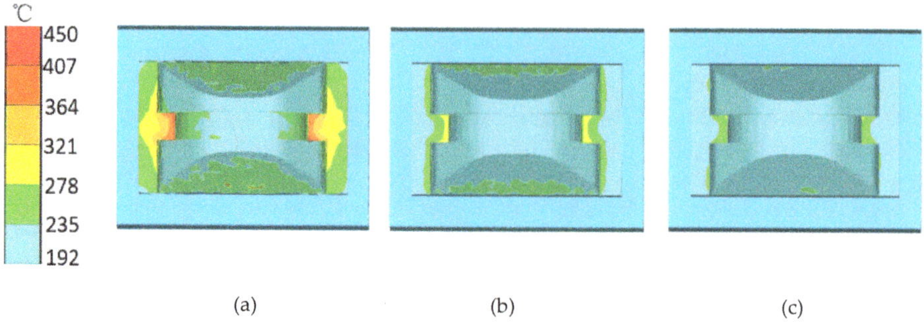

Figure 15. Lower die temperature at the end of the three processes. (**a**) OSE, (**b**) U/BE, and (**c**) G–U/BE.

Table 5. Highest temperatures of the lower die at the end of the processes.

Method	OSE	U/BE	G–U/BE
Temperature (°C)	408	280	246

4. Study on the Optimal Groove Shape

Based on the above discussion, it is safe to say that G–U/BE is the best method for near-net forging of large marine crank throws. It has four advantages: first, it solves the billet's initial off-center problem; second, during the subsequent backward extrusion, the groove serves to guide the extrusion punch; third, it improves the shape and size accuracy of the journal ends; and fourth, it lowers the maximum forging load. However, these benefits can only be achieved if the optimal groove shape is selected.

4.1. Selection of the Optimal Groove Shape

The width of the groove is limited by the gap between the webs, leaving only the depth of the groove as a variable. The goal of finding the optimal groove depth is, first, to obtain the required shapes of the journal ends and pin ends at the end of the grooving–upsetting step, and then to ensure that the journal ends remain unchanged as rigid zones throughout the backward extrusion. Obviously, if the groove is too shallow, the rigid zone cannot be formed, and as a result, the subsequent backward extrusion deformation will alter the web end shape. If the groove is too deep, it becomes difficult to prevent the unequal web thickness caused by the off-centered billet. Therefore, there must be an optimal groove depth.

As is known from plastic mechanics, the groove forming can be approximated as a plane strain problem, where the main deformation zone is located beneath the punch. During backward extrusion, under the action of the punch, the metal flows into the two webs. This flow is restricted by the size and shape of the deformation zone, and the characteristics of the deformation zone depend on the web gap width (the punch width) and the thickness of the web. These two dimensions vary with crank throws of different specifications. For convenience, the following two parameters—relative punch width (κ) and relative groove depth (χ)—are introduced, expressed by Equations (2) and (3):

$$\kappa = \frac{s}{t} \tag{2}$$

$$\chi = \frac{h}{s} \tag{3}$$

where meanings of $h,\ s,\ t$ are demonstrated in Figure 16.

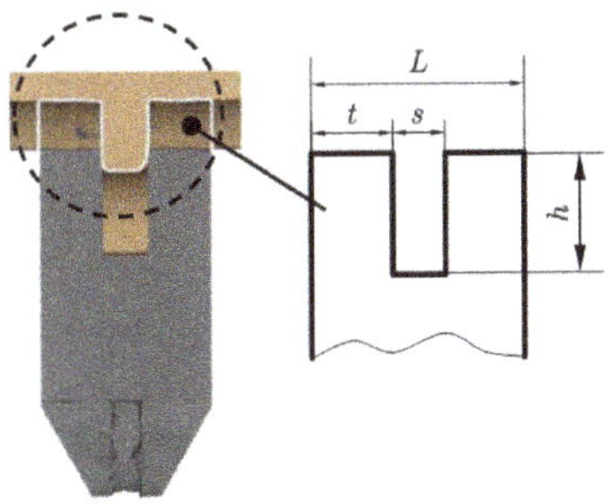

Figure 16. Billet's journal end after grooving–upsetting.

4.2. Influence of the Groove Depth (h) on the Shape of the Journal End

According to data from classification societies, the relative width (κ) of marine crank throws ranges from 0.5 to 0.8. Figure 17 shows the journal end shape of the web after backward extrusion. Shape parameters (λ) and (μ) are introduced and expressed by Equations (4) and (5):

$$\lambda = \frac{a}{t} \tag{4}$$

$$\mu = \frac{b}{t} \tag{5}$$

where meanings of a and b are demonstrated in Figure 17.

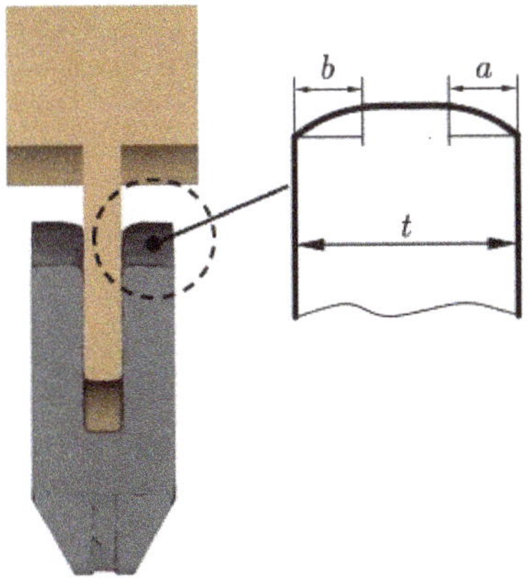

Figure 17. Billet's journal end during backward extrusion.

Finite element simulation is employed to find the best combination of χ and κ. As shown in Table 6, since data indicate that the relative width of marine crank throws ranges from 0.5 to 0.8, three values (0.5, 0.65, 0.8) are selected for χ, and four values (0, 0.5, 1.0, 1.5) are selected for κ. Simulations are carried out for combinations of these two parameters. The calculated results for λ and μ are also shown in Table 6.

It can be seen from Table 6 that when the relative groove depth (χ) $\geq$ 1.5, the journal end of the web formed during grooving–upsetting remains unaffected during the subsequent backward extrusion. Figure 18 shows a side-by-side view of the journal end shape at the end of grooving–upsetting and at the end of the subsequent backward extrusion with relative groove depths of 0.5, 1.0, and 1.5, respectively. It is clear that with χ equal to or greater than 1.5, there are no obvious collapsed corners at the web's journal ends, and the well-formed journal end shape remains unaffected during the following backward extrusion.

Table 6. The influence of the groove depth on the webs' journal ends' shape.

χ \ κ	0.5		0.65		0.8	
0	λ	0.37	λ	0.29	λ	0.25
	μ	0.35	μ	0.31	μ	0.29
0.5	λ	0.097	λ	0.089	λ	0.083
	μ	0.084	μ	0.081	μ	0.077
1.0	λ	0.029	λ	0.021	λ	0.018
	μ	0.026	μ	0.019	μ	0.016
1.5	λ	0.006	λ	0.005	λ	0.003
	μ	0.005	μ	0.003	μ	0.002
2.0	λ	0.004	λ	0.003	λ	0.002
	μ	0.005	μ	0.003	μ	0.002

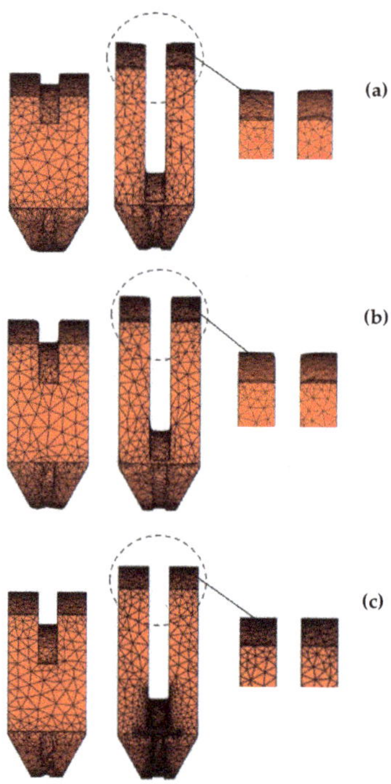

Figure 18. Grooved and upset billet and final billet with different χ: (**a**) $\chi = 0.5$, (**b**) $\chi = 1$, (**c**) $\chi = 1.5$.

As discussed in Section 3.1.2, the initial billet before grooving–upsetting is not centered. This asymmetry leads to uneven web forming, and a very high load is required at the end of the process to complete the underfilled web (see Figures 7 and 8). Similarly, the deeper the groove, the higher the load required at the grooving–upsetting step. It would be impractical to require an unreasonably high forging load just to maintain the web's journal end shape. For this reason, it is necessary to study the influence of groove depth on the load. For convenience, a load coefficient (z) is introduced, expressed by Equation (6):

$$z = \frac{P_\chi}{P_0} \tag{6}$$

where, P_χ is the maximum load at the grooving–upsetting step when $\chi > 0$ while P_0, the maximum load when $\chi = 0$ (i.e., the upsetting step in the U/BE).

Table 7 shows the calculated values of z for different combinations of k and χ. It can be seen that the load does not increase significantly, and the maximum value of z is 1.08. In fact, an appropriate increase in groove depth does not cause a significant change in the temperature, deformation zone, or outer surface area of the billet, and therefore, will not substantially increase the forging load.

Table 7. Effect of the groove depth on load.

z / k / χ	**0.5**	**0.65**	**0.8**
0.0	1.00	1.00	1.00
0.5	1.03	1.02	1.02
1.0	1.06	1.04	1.03
1.5	1.08	1.05	1.04

5. Experiment

The main purposes of a forging process are to achieve the part's required shape and improve its properties [29]. Shape is the primary requirement; in addition, the performance of the forging should be enhanced as much as possible.

5.1. *Near-Net Forged Crank Throw Experiment*

An S90 crank throw weighs 19.7 tons, and its forging weighs 32.50 tons. Therefore, scaled-down experiments are commonly used for scientific investigations. In this study, a scale of 1:5 is selected for the experiment, and the initial billet weighs 260.4 kg.

The press used in the experiments is a 12,000-ton press at the Precision Forging Company of China MCC22 Group Corporation Ltd. (Tangshan, China). Figure 19 shows the press and the tooling used in the experiments.

(**a**) (**b**)

Figure 19. (**a**) Press and (**b**) tools used for experiments.

The procedure is as follows: billet cutting → heating → high-pressure water de-scaling → G–U/BE. Figure 20 shows the billet at different stages: (a) initial billet, (b) after grooving–upsetting, (c) and (d) as the final forging. It is clear that the near-net forged crank throw using grooving–upsetting/backward extrusion meets the required shape specifications.

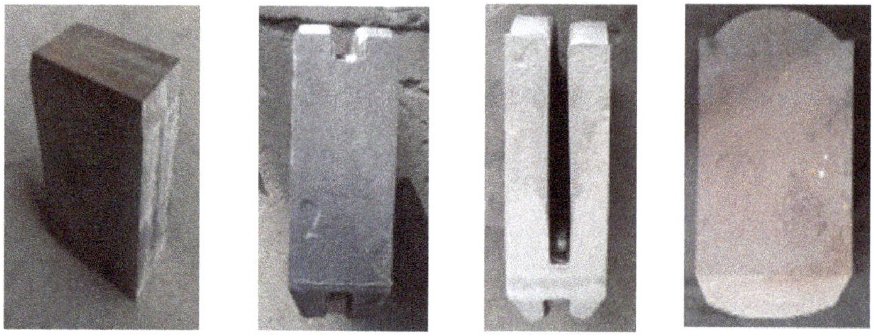

(a) (b) (c) (d)

Figure 20. Experiment of a near-net forged crank throw: (**a**) initial billet, (**b**) after grooving–upsetting, (**c**,**d**) as the final forging.

5.2. Microstructure and Performance Testing

Crankshafts' high-temperature and high-pressure working conditions impose extremely high requirements on the throws' microstructure and mechanical properties [30]. Microstructure and property tests were carried out on a near-net forged crank throw according to the forged crank throw acceptance criteria [31]. Figure 21 shows the specimens for tensile and impact tests, as well as the microstructure analysis. The results are listed in Tables 8 and 9. Figure 22 shows the equipment that was used for the various tests.

(a) (b)

Figure 21. Test specimens: (**a**) tensile test, and (**b**) impact test.

Table 8. Test results for the mechanical properties (S34MnV steel).

Item	R_m(MPa)	$R_{0.2}$(MPa)	A_5(%)	Z(%)	A_{KV}(J)
Required	610	350	18	40	18
Measured	658	390	23.7	52.3	29

Table 9. Microstructure results (S34MnV steel).

Specimen No.	Grain Size Number (G)	Microstructure
1	6.5	Ferrite + Pearlite
2	7.5	Ferrite + Pearlite

(**a**) (**b**) (**c**)

Figure 22. Experimental equipment: (**a**) material fatigue testing system; (**b**) pendulum impact testing machine; (**c**) metallographic microscope.

The ASTM grain size number, also referred to as G, was determined by measuring the average grain size using the intercept procedure outlined in the ASTM E112-13(2021) [32] standard. This method provides a precision better than ±0.25 grain size units. The macrostructure analysis was performed using the ZEISS Axio Imager (a light microscope for material sciences), as shown in Figure 22c, in conjunction with the ZEISS ZEN core analysis software and its GxP module for the intercept procedure.

Figure 23 shows that the forged crank throw obtained a homogeneous microstructure with a grain size number of 7. The test results indicate that all measured indexes are well above the required values.

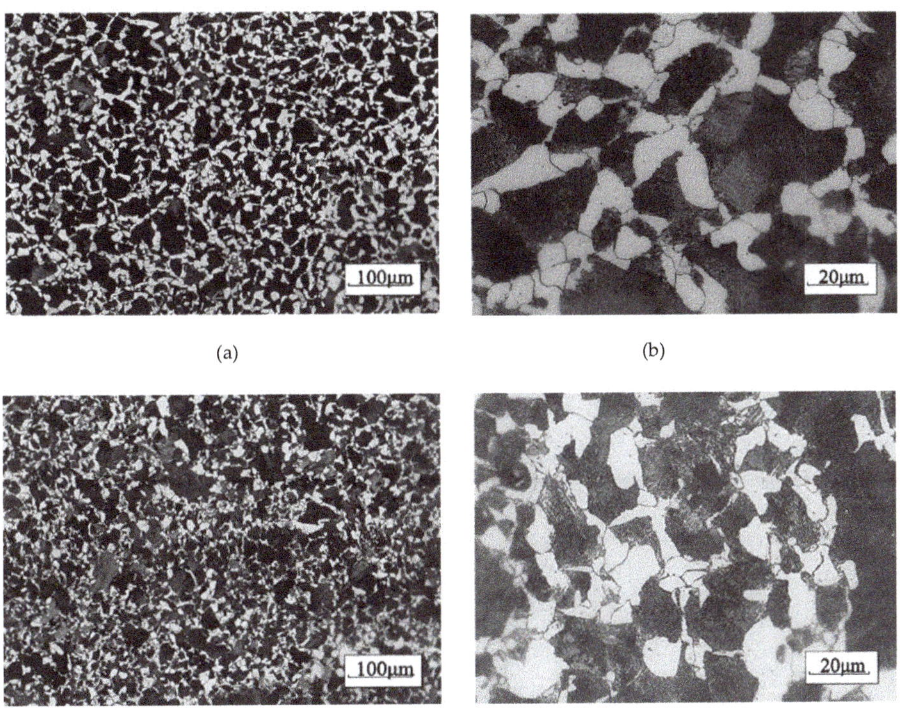

(a) (b) (c) (d)

Figure 23. Microstructures of forged throws: (**a**) specimen #1 100 μm scale, (**b**) specimen #1 20 μm scale, (**c**) specimen #2 100 μm scale, and (**d**) specimen #2 20 μm scale.

6. Conclusions

1. Finite element (FE) software was used to simulate three near-net-shape (NNS) forming methods: OSE, U/BE, and G–U/BE. The results indicate that G–U/BE requires the lowest load.
2. The journal end web shapes formed at the end of the grooving–upsetting step in the G–U/BE process create a rigid zone that remains intact during the subsequent backward extrusion. The relative groove depth (χ) significantly influences the final forging. Deeper grooves are more favorable for the final crank throw formation but require a higher load at the grooving–upsetting stage.
3. When χ is greater than or equal to 1.5, the web's journal end shape is optimal. However, if the groove depth exceeds this value, the required load increases to levels comparable to one-step extrusion, rendering the grooving–upsetting step ineffective. Therefore, the optimal value of χ is 1.5.
4. Scaled-down experiment results confirm that G–U/BE is a practical and feasible NNS forming method for producing large marine crank throw forgings, achieving both the desired shape and microstructure.

Author Contributions: Conceptualization, L.N. and Q.Z.; methodology, L.N., Q.Z., J.W. and X.V.; software, Q.Z. and Y.Z.; validation, Y.Z., J.W., W.L., D.L. and T.M.; formal analysis, L.N. and W.L.; investigation, L.N., J.W. and W.L.; resources, L.N. and X.V.; data curation, Q.Z., D.L. and T.M.; writing—original draft preparation, L.N., Q.Z. and Y.Z.; writing—review and editing, X.V.; visualization, Q.Z., Y.Z., D.L. and T.M.; supervision, L.N. and X.V.; project administration, L.N. and X.V.; funding acquisition. All authors have read and agreed to the published version of the manuscript.

Funding: The authors wish to express their sincere gratitude for the support received from the Industry-University-Research Cooperation: Project of Jiangsu Province (Project No. BY20230258), the Shanghai Engineering Technology Research Center of Multi-directional Die Forging (Project No. 20DZ2253200), as well as the Key Scientific Research Platform and Projects of the Guangdong Provincial Department of Education (Project No. 2024ZDZX3065), which made this research project possible. The funding has not only provided the necessary resources but also fostered an environment conducive to innovative research and scholarly exploration.

Data Availability Statement: The original contributions presented in this study are included in the article Further inquiries can be directed to the corresponding author.

Conflicts of Interest: The authors declare no conflicts of interest.

References

1. Gomes, J.; Gaivota, N.; Martins, R.F.; Silva, P.P. Failure analysis of crankshafts used in maritime V12 diesel engines. *Eng. Fail. Anal.* **2018**, *92*, 466–479. [CrossRef]
2. Meier-Peter, H.; Bernhard, F. *Compendium Marine Engineering*; Seehafen Verlag: Hamburg, Germany, 2009.
3. Kubo, H.; Mori, H. Trends in Manufacturing and Technological Development of Crankshaft Material. *Mar. Eng.* **2006**, *41*, 672–676. [CrossRef] [PubMed]
4. Hanawa, Y.; Kajihara, S.; Kagawa, Y.; Mori, H.; Hamada, T. Development of High Strength Cast Steel for Semi-built up Type Crankshaft of Low Speed Diesel Engine, and Stress Measurement and Evaluation of Crankshaft. *Mar. Eng.* **2005**, *40*, 254–259. [CrossRef] [PubMed]
5. Fonte, M.; Duarte, P.; Anes, V.; Freitas, M.; Reis, L. On the assessment of fatigue life of marine diesel engine crankshafts. *Eng. Fail. Anal.* **2015**, *56*, 51–57. [CrossRef]
6. Instructions on the Group Standard of General Technical Specifications for Die Forging Marine Crankshaft Forgings. 2022, Confederation of Chinese Metalforming Industry. Available online: https://max.book118.com/html/2023/1222/5032211321011030.shtm (accessed on 25 December 2024). (In Chinese)
7. Liu, K. *Study on Die Forging Process of Large-Sized Crankthrow by Simulation*; Yanshan University: Qinhuangdao, China, 2012.
8. Song, M.C.; Lee, Y.U.; VanTyne, C.; Moon, Y.H. Symmetric bending technology using a floating die to forge crank throws for marine engines. *J. Mater. Process. Technol.* **2016**, *237*, 197–207. [CrossRef]

9. Fujitsuna, N. Development of Steel Castings and Forgings for Vessels. *Kobelco Technol. Rev.* **2017**, *35*, 1–6.
10. Altan, T.; Fiorentino, R.J. Prediction of Loads and Stresses in Closed-Die Forging. *J. Eng. Ind.* **1971**, *93*, 477–484. [CrossRef]
11. Tanishq Jaiswal, V.I.; Kakde, A. A Review on closed die forging. *Int. J. Adv. Eng. Manag.* **2022**, *4*, 5.
12. Sheth, D.; Das, S.; Chatterjee, A.; Bhattacharya, A. Modeling of Closed-Die Forging for Estimating Forging Load. *J. Inst. Eng. Ser. C* **2017**, *98*, 53–61. [CrossRef]
13. Li, C.; Li, M.V.; Li, S.; Li, D.; Peng, X. Effect of stresses on martensite transformation kinetics and transformation plasticity of S34MnV steel. *Mater. Res. Express* **2019**, *6*, 076531. [CrossRef]
14. Zhang, Z.; Li, H.; Zhou, Y.; Guo, W.; Jiang, R.; Zhu, Y. Research on Thermal Deformation Behavior of Marine Crankshaft S34MnV Steel. *Steel Res. Int.* **2021**, *92*, 2100140. [CrossRef]
15. Yan, Y.; Li, M.V.; Bu, H.; Zheng, S. Continuous Cooling Transformation Behavior and Transformation Kinetics of S34MnV Steel. *Cailiao Daobao/Mater. Rep.* **2021**, *35*, 20129–20136. [CrossRef]
16. Hu, Z.; Wang, K.; Yang, Y. A comparative study on the activation energy for hot deformation of 5CrNiMoV and S34MnV steel. *Curr. Mater. Sci.* **2021**, *14*, 70–79. [CrossRef]
17. Chen, Z.; Nash, P. Hot Deformation Behavior and Processing Maps for a Large Marine Crankshaft S34MnV Steel. *Steel Res. Int.* **2018**, *89*, 1700321. [CrossRef]
18. Hu, Z.; Wang, K.; Yang, Y. Modelling and simulation of a bending process for S34MnV steel. *Int. J. Microstruct. Mater. Prop.* **2019**, *14*, 432–447. [CrossRef]
19. Chen, Z.; Nash, P.; Zhang, Y. Correlation of Cooling Rate, Microstructure and Hardness of S34MnV Steel. *Metall. Mater. Trans. B* **2019**, *50*, 1718–1728. [CrossRef]
20. Jayanthi, A.; Anilkumar, M.; Ravisankar, B. Selection of forging process for compressor disc for aero engine using finite element analysis. *Mater. Today Proc.* **2022**, *60*, 2111–2116. [CrossRef]
21. Raja, N.; Daniel, B.S.S. Microstructural and mechanical characteristics of hot worked homogenized AA7068 using 3D processing map and DEFORM-3D. *Mater. Today Commun.* **2023**, *36*, 106574. [CrossRef]
22. Zeng, Y.; Ji, H.; Song, C.; Wang, M.; Li, J. Numerical simulation and experiment on hot forging of high-Mn steel turnout core. *Mater. Today Commun.* **2024**, *40*, 109588. [CrossRef]
23. Zhang, L.; Lu, R.; Tang, J.; Jiang, F.; Fu, D.; Zhang, H.; Teng, J. Microstructural Evolution and Mechanical Properties of a Continuously Cast Al–Mg–Si–Cu Alloy Processed by Repetitive Continuous Extrusion Forming. *Met. Mater. Int.* **2023**, *29*, 2028–2039. [CrossRef]
24. Xu, Z.; Wang, S.; Gao, L.; Qiao, X.; Cui, Y. Fatigue life analysis model of crankshaft under uncertain working conditions based on physical-data collaboration. *J. Eng. Res.* **2023**, *in press*. [CrossRef]
25. Derazkola, H.A.; Garcia, E.; Murillo-Marrodán, A.; Hardell, J. The effect of temperature and strain rate on the mechanical properties and microstructure of super Cr13 martensitic stainless steel. *J. Mater. Res. Technol.* **2023**, *24*, 3464–3476. [CrossRef]
26. Derazkola, H.A.; García Gil, E.; Murillo-Marrodán, A.; Méresse, D. Review on dynamic recrystallization of martensitic stainless steels during hot deformation: Part I—Experimental Study. *Metals* **2021**, *11*, 572. [CrossRef]
27. Momeni, A.; Dehghani, K. Prediction of dynamic recrystallization kinetics and grain size for 410 martensitic stainless steel during hot deformation. *Met. Mater. Int.* **2010**, *16*, 843–849. [CrossRef]
28. Sakai, T.; Belyakov, A.; Kaibyshev, R.; Miura, H.; Jonas, J.J. Dynamic and post-dynamic recrystallization under hot, cold and severe plastic deformation conditions. *Prog. Mater. Sci.* **2014**, *60*, 130–207. [CrossRef]
29. Chen, Z. Study on Numerical Simulation of Metal Flow and Microstructure Evolution of a Crankshaft Forging Process. 2013. Available online: https://xueshu.baidu.com/usercenter/paper/show?paperid=af5310c3647d0b4a20fb10c916c9fce2&site=xueshu_se (accessed on 25 December 2024).
30. Taylor, D.A. *Introduction to Marine Engineering*; Elsevier: Amsterdam, The Netherlands, 1996.
31. Society, C. Section 4 Forgings for Crankshafts. Available online: https://www.imorules.com/LRMAT_CH5_4.html (accessed on 28 November 2024).
32. *ASTM E112-13*; Standard Test Methods for Determining Average Grain Size. ASTM International: West Conshohocken, PA, USA, 2021.

metals

MDPI

Article

Theoretical Study of Asymmetric Bending Force on Metal Deformation in Cold Rolling

Zhuwen Yan, Shuaizhen Pan *, Yingxin Tang and Wenjun Cao

Jiangsu Provincial Engineering Laboratory of Intelligent Manufacturing Equipment, Industrial Technology Research Institute of Intelligent Equipment, Nanjing Institute of Technology, Nanjing 211167, China; yan-zhuwen@njit.edu.cn (Z.Y.); njtangyingxin@outlook.com (Y.T.); cwj7192@163.com (W.C.)
* Correspondence: panshuaizhen1101@163.com

Abstract: A three-dimensional elastic–plastic finite element model of a six-roll cold rolling mill has been developed using the finite element software ABAQUS. The actual parameters of the rolling mill have been incorporated into the finite element model, with the working conditions applied as boundary constraints and load conditions. Subsequently, a non-symmetrical bending force is introduced to the finite element model. Through simulation calculations, this study analyzes the patterns of change in the transverse pressure of the rolling mill and roller pressure during non-symmetrical bending, as well as the variations in strip thickness, crown, edge drop, and flatness. Additionally, the regulating function of the bending force is examined. Each adjustment of 5 t in the asymmetric bending force results in an increase of approximately 0.01 mm in the thickness of the positive bending side of the strip while causing a decrease of about 0.01 mm in the thickness of the negative bending side. Therefore, the application of asymmetric bending forces proves to be effective in controlling the shape of lateral wave defects on the edges of steel strips.

Keywords: asymmetrical bending force; flatness; strip; finite element

1. Introduction

High precision in controlling board shape is a common objective for workers in the rolling process and is crucial for enhancing the quality of strip rolling technology. Modern cold rolling machines often employ various plate-shape control techniques, including roll tilting [1], cross-rolling [2,3], segmented cooling control [4], and bending rolls [5,6].

To investigate the impact of these controls on shape, an effective and precise calculation method for rolling is essential. Since the inception of rolling technology, a range of analytical and numerical methods have been utilized for rolling calculations. Traditional computational methods include the elastic beam method [7], influence function method [8], plate method [9], and boundary element method [10], among others. In comparison to these methods, the finite element method [11–16] stands out as a practical and powerful tool for computation.

In recent years, an increasing number of scholars have employed the finite element method to develop rolling models. Wang et al. [17] established a two-dimensional finite element model to examine the effects of various factors, including the width of the steel strip, rolling force, bending force, roll convexity, and roller diameter, on the convexity of the steel strip. However, models created using two-dimensional finite element software typically represent flat rolls, which differ significantly from actual rollers, leading to reduced accuracy. Li et al. [18] further advanced this research by developing a half-cylindrical roller model based on a three-dimensional finite element framework, investigating the impact of edge cooling on the shape and flatness of the steel strip. The use of a one-half model can enhance computational efficiency; however, it significantly reduces data reliability and accuracy. Consequently, some researchers have started to develop finite element models based on dynamic principles. When employing the implicit method for computation, each iteration necessitates solving a substantial number of linear equations, which results in decreased computational efficiency and a higher likelihood of divergence.

Therefore, most contemporary researchers employ explicit dynamic methods to develop rolling models [19–22]. Wang et al. [23] utilized the explicit dynamics method to create a finite element model, investigating the impact of horizontal shift control of work rolls on the edge drop in six-roll cold rolling mills. They analyzed the modeling process, highlighting the advantages of the explicit dynamics method, including excellent convergence, high stability, accuracy, and efficiency. Yu et al. [24] and Pan et al. [25] applied the explicit dynamics finite element software LS-DYNA 970 to simulate the 3-pass and 16-pass hot-rolling processes, respectively, and innovatively developed geometric modeling techniques. Wang et al. [26] created a hot-rolled strip flatness analysis model that incorporates lateral metal flow and established a three-dimensional finite element model using the explicit dynamics method, confirming the model's reliability. Utilizing the finite element method (FEM), Kapil S. et al. [27] formulated the equation governing the motion of the working roll in a four-high rolling mill setup. This model facilitates the prediction of the final strip's profile shape and the variation in exit stress, which is crucial for preventing common rolling defects, such as edge and center buckling. Dasari SK et al. [28] employed numerical simulation through finite element analysis (FEA) to accurately predict the softening phenomena occurring during the hot rolling process. By integrating this methodology, they significantly advanced the understanding and control of material behavior under high-temperature and deformation conditions. Sabar SK et al. [29] focused on applying finite element method (FEM) software strategies to forecast the rolling force (RF) in hot rolling processes, emphasizing the integration of nano-lubrication conditions. The aforementioned studies demonstrate that the finite element models developed using the explicit dynamics method exhibit high accuracy and reliability. Consequently, this paper adopts the explicit dynamics module of the ABAQUS 2023 simulation software for rolling simulations.

The common types of roll bending technology include support roll bending, working roll bending [30], and intermediate roll bending. The traditional control methods for these rolls primarily involve symmetric roll bending controls [31–34]. Shi et al. [35] applied the finite element software MARC 2005 to simulate the four-roll milling process of steel strips and found that the symmetric bending force significantly impacts board convexity. As the positive bending force increases, the thickness of the central region of the strip gradually increases, while there is minimal change in the edge reduction zone, and a decrease is observed in the abrupt reduction zone. Building on this, Ma et al. [36] utilized the finite element software ANSYS 7.0 to couple the relationship between the rolled piece and the roller, establishing a rolling model. The results indicated that while the bending force can enhance the symmetry of bilateral edge waves, excessive bending force may lead to increased machine power consumption and roller wear, with only marginal improvements in board shape. However, symmetric bending control is limited to regulating symmetric second and fourth board shape defects and cannot address non-symmetric board shape defects. To tackle the issue of asymmetric strip shapes, various researchers have developed methods for asymmetric bending roll control. Liu et al. [37] employed the influence function model to analyze the strip exit thickness, roll force distribution, and tension distribution following asymmetric bending control. Their findings revealed that asymmetric bending rolls can alleviate the unbalanced distribution of roll forces and, in certain cases, may even reduce the need for some roll tilt control. Hu et al. [38] used ANSYS software to simulate and analyze the force dynamics of the roll system under both positive and negative bending rolls. Additionally, Liu et al. [39] established a rolling model using ANSYS to determine the shape of the work roll and the bearing roll gap. Their results indicated that a four-roll mill equipped with asymmetric bending rolls could effectively address the challenge of weak control over the bearing roll gap's opening degree at various points along the full width of the board, thereby enhancing the mill's ability to control the board's flatness. While the aforementioned studies analyzed the impact of asymmetric bending rolls on strip thickness, pressure distribution between rolls, and the shape of the bearing roll gap [40,41], they did not further investigate the effects of asymmetric bending rolls on critical shape parameters such as crown, edge drop, and flatness.

This article primarily investigates the optimal conditions for strip steel rolling. A higher friction coefficient between the rolls indicates an increased degree of roll wear. In this study, roll wear is addressed by establishing an appropriate friction coefficient. To ensure the numerical analysis has broad applicability, a 1580 mm conventional six-high rolling mill from a specific steel rolling plant is utilized as a model, which is widely employed across various sizes of steel rolling mills. C40 steel (DIN EN ISO 683-1:2018) [42] is selected as the strip material due to its excellent plasticity and toughness, making it widely used in machinery manufacturing, construction, and the aviation industry. Given the selection of the most commonly used rolling mill and strip material, the numerical results and patterns derived can provide a comprehensive theoretical foundation for subsequent rolling experiments and manufacturing processes.

This paper utilizes ABAQUS simulation software to develop a model of asymmetrical bending rolls and analyze key shape parameters, including strip transverse thickness, roller pressure, rolling force, crown, and flatness based on the results obtained. Furthermore, it evaluates the regulatory effectiveness of bending forces to assess their capability in controlling strip shape.

2. Establishing Finite Element Simulation

2.1. Scenario Selection

To accurately determine the deformation behavior of steel strips, a high-precision finite element model is essential. Consequently, ABAQUS software is employed to develop the simulation model. ABAQUS offers two solvers: the implicit dynamic method [43] (ABAQUS/Standard) and the explicit dynamic method [44] (ABAQUS/Explicit). The rolling process of steel strips presents a nonlinear quasistatic challenge characterized by complex contact conditions and substantial deformations. Utilizing the implicit method necessitates extensive computational resources and the resolution of numerous linear equations at each iteration, which can lead to low computational efficiency and potential divergence. Therefore, the explicit dynamic method is adopted to effectively simulate the rolling process of steel strips.

2.2. Parts and Materials

The model is divided into seven components, consisting of six rolls and one strip of steel. The roll bodies and necks are designed as integrated models to more accurately simulate the integrated casting of rolls. The geometric parameters of the rolls and strips are presented in Table 1. The foundation for investigating the impact of varying bending forces on the shape change in the strip lies in studying the variations in strip thickness and roll gap. Since the rolls exhibit elastic behavior during the rolling process, they cannot be treated as rigid bodies. Therefore, the six rolls are modeled as elastic bodies, while the strips, which undergo plastic deformation during rolling, are modeled as elastic-plastic bodies. Table 1 details the parameters for the various components of a six-high rolling mill.

The densities and elastic properties of the rolls [45] and strips [46] are identical, with a density of 7.85 g/cm^3, Young's modulus of 210,000 MPa, and a Poisson's ratio of 0.3. Additionally, the plasticity characteristics of the strips are described by the Johnson–Cook model, which consists of three primary components that represent strain hardening, strain rate strengthening, and thermal softening of the material. This model comprehensively accounts for the relationships among flow stress, strain, strain rate, and temperature, effectively addressing the requirements for simulating materials under various conditions.

The mathematical expression of the Johnson–Cook plasticity model [47] is as follows:

$$\sigma = (A + B\varepsilon^n)(1 + C\ln\frac{\dot{\varepsilon}}{\dot{\varepsilon_0}})(1 - [\frac{T - T_r}{T_m - T_r}]^m) \quad (1)$$

In the equation, A is the initial yield stress, in units of pressure. B is the hardening constant, also in units of pressure. n is the coefficient of strain rate sensitivity. The value of n determines the direction of plastic flow and the material model:

1. When $n = 1$, the material behaves as an ideal linear elastic material;
2. When $n = 0$, the material behaves as a nonlinear elastic material;
3. When $0 < n < 1$, the material behaves as a plasticity-dominant material.

Table 1. Geometry of parts of the model.

Component	Size
Rolled product cross-sectional dimension	38 mm × 1200 mm
Work roll diameter	760 mm
Work roll neck diameter	510 mm
Intermediate roll body diameter	840 mm
Intermediate roll neck diameter	740 mm
Supporting roll body diameter	1520 mm
Supporting roll neck diameter	1000 mm
Roll body length	1580 mm
Roll neck length	100 mm
Steel strip biting thickness	27.5 mm
Piece length	500 mm

c and m are dimensionless model parameters related to the strain rate and thermal softening effects. $T* = (T - T_r)/(T_m - T_r)$ is a dimensionless temperature, where T_r and T_m are reference temperatures, and T is the current temperature, while ε is the strain rate. Strip materials utilize C40 steel (DIN EN ISO 683-1:2018), and the five primary parameters of the Johnson-Cook model for C40 steel are presented in Table 2.

Table 2. Five parameters of the Johnson–Cook model of C40 steel (Adapted from Refs. [48,49]).

Parameter	Numeric Value
A	10.487
B	178.63
C	0.08139
n	0.25644
m	0.68196

2.3. Solution to Improve Computational Efficiency

The rolling direction, width direction, and thickness direction of the strip steel establish the spatial coordinates X, Y, and Z, respectively. Unlike scenarios where symmetric control shapes are employed, this article also examines the effects of asymmetric bending rolls on shape. Consequently, it is not feasible to utilize a half model based on symmetry about the XY plane to enhance computational efficiency.

Since an explicit central difference method is employed to solve dynamic equations, the discrete mass matrix significantly influences both computational efficiency and accuracy. When the mass scaling method is applied appropriately, it is possible to maintain computational accuracy while substantially enhancing computational efficiency. In slow-speed rolling, the rolling process of strip steel is typically regarded as a quasi-static process. Given that the stiffness and mass of all components in the model are uniform, the mass scaling method for static analysis can be applied to the entire model. Under any circumstances, there is no need to reduce the actual mass of the model, and arbitrarily increasing the mass will generally compromise computational accuracy. This article utilizes semi-automatic mass scaling, adjusting the time increment in ABAQUS/Explicit to 1×10^{-7} s, thereby reducing computation time and improving computational efficiency.

2.4. Rolling Conditions

The roller body and neck are flexible, altering in shape and size during motion. Therefore, directly driving the flexible body necessitates careful consideration of the forces and torques resulting from deformation and transformation, which adds complexity to the process. Additionally, in practical applications, the bearing drives the neck to transmit the motor's torque to the roller. To facilitate this, twelve rigid small cylinders are evenly distributed along each neck. The twelve rigid small cylinders are configured as rigid bodies, simulating fixed rollers and restricting their rotation. The rotational speed around the Z-axis for these rigid small cylinders is set to 5 revolutions per second, while the other five degrees of freedom are constrained. To ensure the strip is smoothly fed into the rolls, the initial speed in the X-direction is set to 1900 mm/s, matching the linear speed of the work rolls. In the explicit dynamic analysis, the penalty function method is employed for contact calculations, utilizing the "face-to-surface" interaction feature. The Coulomb friction coefficient between the strip and the rolls is set to 0.3.After the strip is bitten by the rolls, it advances in the direction of the rolling force due to the action of friction. Therefore, the strip is allowed to move freely in the X, Y, and Z directions, while its rotational freedoms are restricted to zero. To achieve a better shape in actual production, a tensile stress of 0.1 MPa is applied to the front surface of the strip, and a compressive stress of 0.08 MPa is applied to the rear surface.

2.5. Mesh Division

The accuracy and computational efficiency of a finite element model are significantly influenced by the mesh division. The types of grid elements include first-order tetrahedra, second-order tetrahedra, first-order hexahedra, and second-order hexahedra. The number of nodes for each type of element is 4, 8, 10, and 20, respectively. Generally, a higher number of nodes leads to more accurate results; however, it also decreases computational efficiency. Consequently, first-order tetrahedral and second-order hexahedral grids are typically not employed in standard calculations.

First-order hexahedral grids feature fewer elements and greater computational efficiency; however, obtaining rational grids for cylindrical models is more challenging, often necessitating complex model partitioning to achieve satisfactory grids. In contrast, second-order tetrahedral grids contain more elements, which increases computational time but also improves computational accuracy and ensures a more uniform distribution of the grid.

This paper employs a second-order tetrahedral element division while treating the rigid small circle as a solid with no deformation, which is represented as a hexahedral element. To balance accuracy and efficiency, the mesh utilizes a manual local division method. The mesh density is highest around the steel strip, followed by the surface of the roller, with the edges of the roller exhibiting the coarsest mesh. The total number of elements after division is 1,616,274. Figure 1 is the Roller edge mesh gradation schematic.

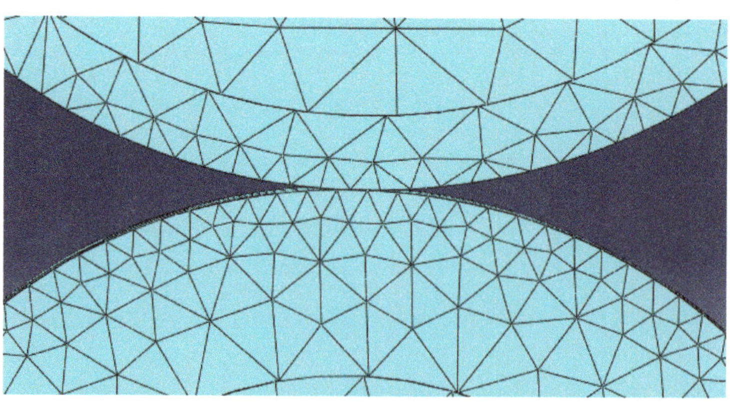

Figure 1. Roller edge mesh gradation schematic.

3. Simulation Results

The width of the simulation board for the rolling of strip steel is 1200 mm, and the explicit dynamics module of ABAQUS is utilized. Figure 2 is the stress diagram of the model. The control effect on the plate shape is most significant when applying bending forces to the working rolls; therefore, non-symmetric bending forces are applied at both ends of the working rolls. The bending force on the operational side is opposite to that on the transmission side, while the upper and lower work rolls experience the same force. The specific distribution of the roll bending force is illustrated in Figure 3. The bending force applied to the neck surface of the working roller is typically expressed in kilonewtons (kN), whereas in finite element analysis, it is represented as surface pressure, measured in megapascals (MPa). According to the mechanical formula, an increase of 1 MPa in surface pressure corresponds to a change of 10.2 kN in bending force. To minimize errors caused by unit conversion and to facilitate subsequent calculations, the bending force in this paper is expressed in MPa. After completing the rolling simulation with various roll bending forces, 61 nodes are selected on both the top and bottom surfaces of the strip. The thickness distribution along the horizontal direction of the strip is determined by subtracting the coordinates of the bottom nodes from those of the top nodes. Subsequently, the flatness, crown, and other shape assessment criteria of the strip are analyzed, and the regulatory effects of different roll bending forces are further investigated. For clarity in all illustrations, the left side represents the operating side, the right side represents the transmission side, and "left-right" refers to the horizontal distance between the operating and transmission sides of the strip.

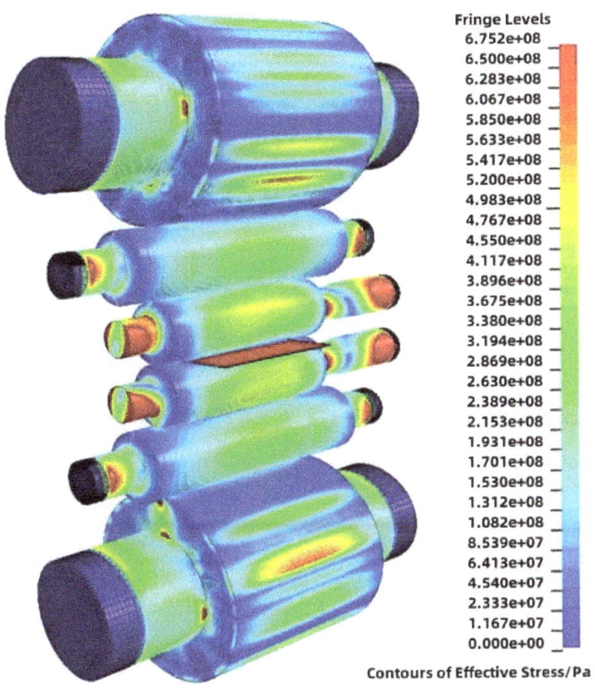

Figure 2. Contours of effective stress (maximum stress: 675 MPa, minimum stress: 12 MPa).

Figure 3. Asymmetric roll bending force schematic.

3.1. The Impact of Asymmetric Roll Forces on Equalizing Forces

The equivalent force diagrams for various conditions are presented in Figures 4–6. By analyzing these diagrams, it can be concluded that the concentrated region of equivalent force is situated 180 mm from the edge of the strip and exhibits left–right symmetry. Following the application of non-symmetric bending rolls, the concentrated area of equivalent force on the positive bending roll side decreases while the area on the negative bending roll side increases. This observation corresponds with the distribution pattern of rolling pressure discussed in the subsequent section.

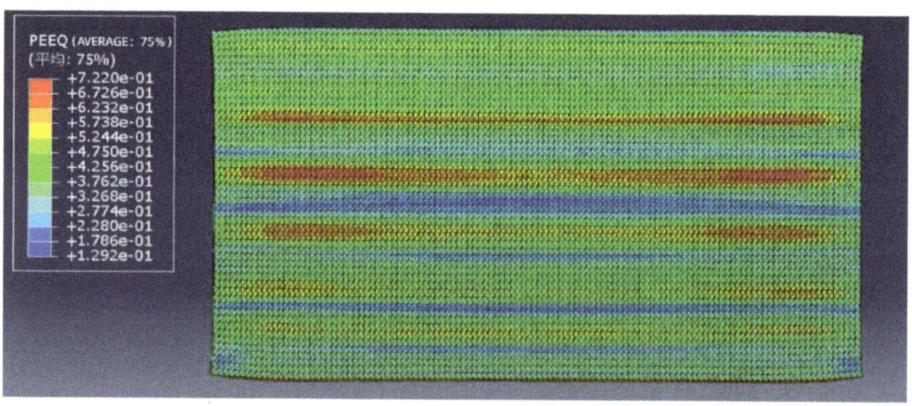

Figure 4. The equalizing force diagram without bending roller force.

3.2. The Impact of Asymmetric Bending Force on Rolling Pressure

Since the data and conclusions presented in this article are based on finite element simulations, we conducted experiments on rolling force under conditions identical to those in the simulations (i.e., without any bending force) to enhance the reliability of our findings. Figure 7 displays both the experimental rolling force curve and the simulated rolling force curve. The experimental results indicate that the simulated rolling force curve closely aligns with the experimental curve, with a maximum error of approximately 3%. Therefore, the precision of the finite element method described in this study meets the required standards.

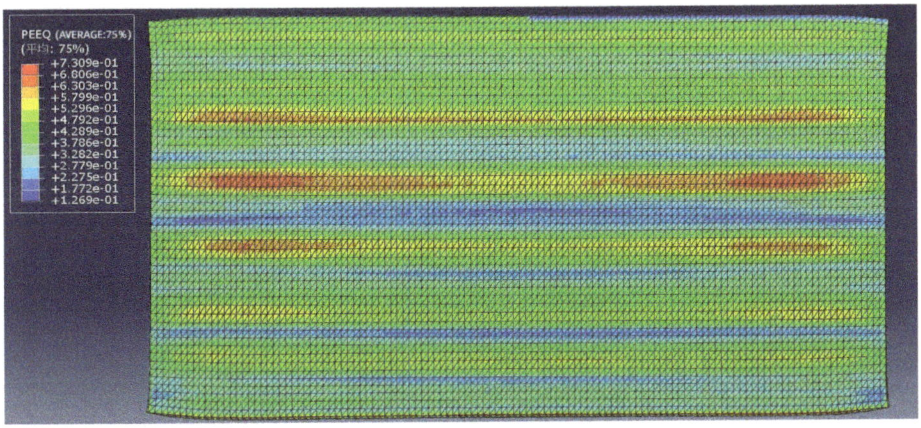

Figure 5. The equalizing force diagram with left negative bending roller force and right positive bending roller force.

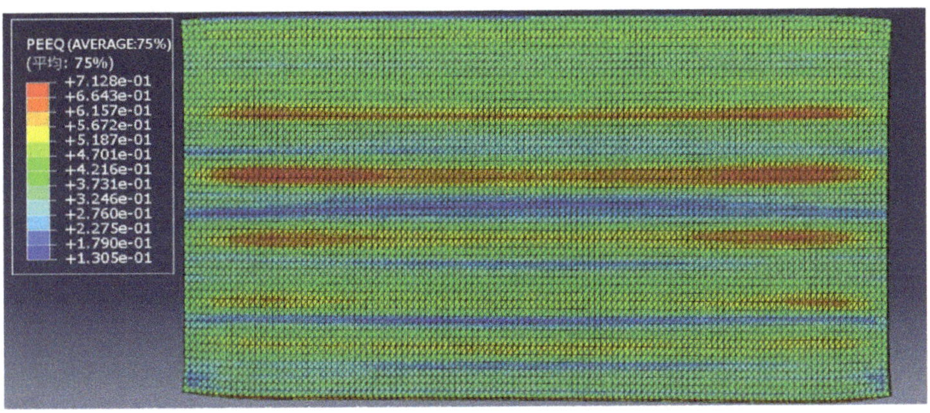

Figure 6. The equalizing force diagram with left positive bending roller force and right negative bending roller force.

Figures 8 and 9 illustrate the distribution curves of rolling pressure in the horizontal direction for cold-rolled strips subjected to various non-symmetrical roller forces. An analysis of Figure 8 indicates that within approximately 400 mm from the center of the strip, the distribution curve of the rolling pressure exhibits a parabolic shape, with a minimum value of about 180 MPa at the center and a maximum value of approximately 225 MPa at 400 mm from the center. In the range of 200 mm from the edge of the strip, the rolling pressure decreases linearly, dropping rapidly to around 115 MPa. By combining the analyses of Figures 8 and 9, it is evident that the rolling force undergoes asymmetric changes when subjected to non-symmetrical roller pressure. The rolling pressure on the side experiencing negative roller pressure increases slightly; however, this change is relatively minor, particularly within the 200 mm range from the edge, where the rolling pressure remains nearly constant. In contrast, the variation in rolling pressure on the side of the positive bending roller is significant. As the positive bending force increases, a clear trend of decreasing rolling pressure is observed. It is apparent that adjusting the non-symmetrical bending force is akin to modifying the rolling pressure at both ends of the mill, resulting in alterations to the thickness and shape of the steel strip.

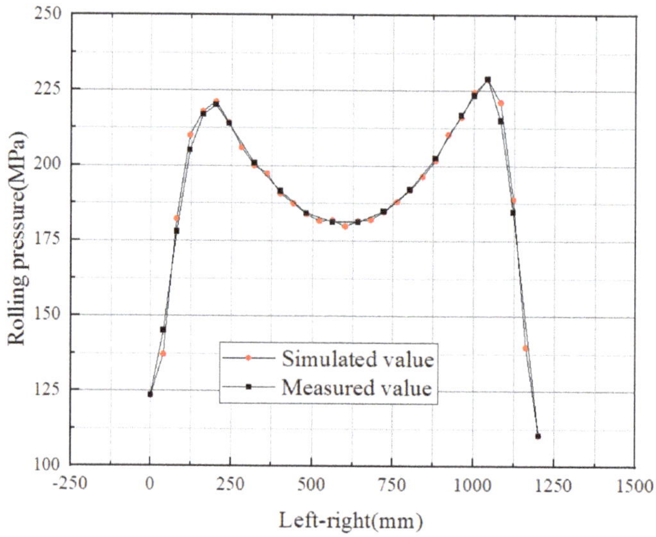

Figure 7. Comparison of measured values and actual values.

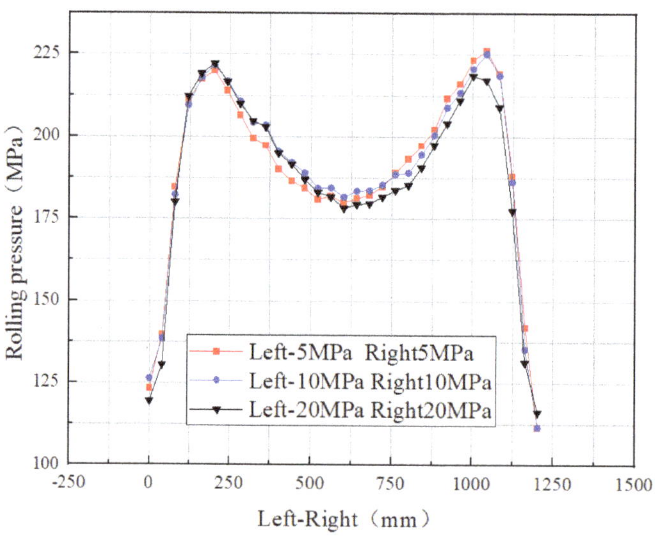

Figure 8. Diagram of the transverse distribution of rolling pressure with negative bending roll on the operating side and positive bending roll on the drive side.

3.3. The Impact of Asymmetric Roll Force on Inter-Roll Pressure

The distribution of inter-roll pressure across the working rolls and intermediate rolls at various levels of bending force is illustrated in Figure 10. In the absence of a bending force, the maximum inter-roll pressure reaches approximately 475 MPa at the center of the rolling mill and gradually decreases to about 60 MPa as one moves away from the center. When a non-symmetrical bending force of 30 MPa is applied to both sides of the working rolls, the change in inter-roll pressure at the center of the rolling mill is relatively minor. The pressure between the work rolls varies significantly within a 300 mm range from the edge of the roller, specifically increasing on the side where the positive bending force is applied and decreasing on the side where the negative bending force is exerted, resulting in asymmetric changes in roll gap pressure. As the non-symmetrical bending force continues to increase to 60 MPa, the behavior of the working roll resembles that of tilted rollers, with the pressure between the rolls in the middle section decreasing by approximately 50 MPa. The working and intermediate rolls on the positive bending force side compress each other, leading to an increase in roll gap pressure. The pressure between the rolls gradually flattens as it approaches the center of the roll at a distance of 700 mm. In contrast, there is a significant drop in pressure between the rolls in the area near the edge of the roll, approximately 100 mm from the center. Consequently, the pressure between the rolls on the negative bending force side decreases, with the pressure at the very edge of the roll dropping from 60 MPa to 0 MPa.

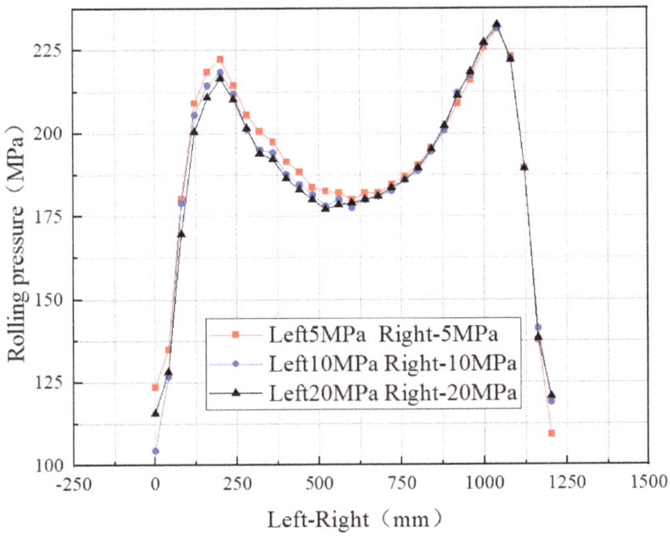

Figure 9. Diagram of the transverse distribution of rolling pressure with positive bending roll on the operating side and negative bending roll on the drive side.

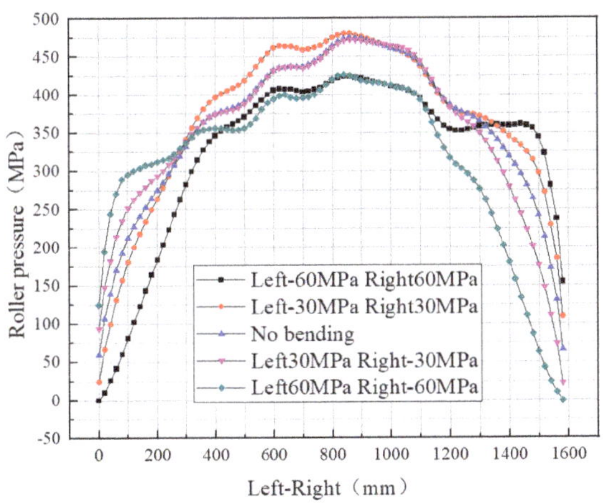

Figure 10. Horizontal distribution chart of working and intermediate roller pressures.

Figure 11 illustrates the distribution of pressure between the working and intermediate rolls under varying bending forces. In the absence of bending forces, the rolling pressure fluctuates continuously, with the supporting and intermediate rolls adjusting in real time to balance the overall interaction force between the rolls. This results in an unbalanced roll gap, where the operating side experiences higher pressure than the transmission side. As depicted in Figure 11, the application of negative and positive bending forces on the operating and transmission sides, respectively, alleviates the imbalance in roller pressure. The region between 0 and 200 mm on the operating side shows a slight reduction in roller pressure, while the area between 200 and 1580 mm on the transmission side exhibits a significant increase in roller pressure, averaging 25 MPa at a non-symmetric bending force of 30 MPa. The maximum roller pressure occurs near the center of the rollers, and the area where roller pressure is zero on the transmission side decreases. When positive and negative bending forces are applied to the operating and transmission sides, respectively, the imbalance in roller pressure is exacerbated. The transition zone between the operating and transmission sides is defined by the center of the rolls. On the operating side, the roller pressure increases rapidly, averaging 25 MPa under a non-symmetric bending force of 30 MPa. Conversely, on the transmission side, there is a slight decrease in roller pressure, and the number of areas where the roller pressure is zero increases. From the analysis above, it can be concluded that applying asymmetric bending forces significantly impacts changes in roller pressure. In practical engineering applications, excessive bending forces should be avoided to prevent unbalanced roller pressure, which may damage the rolls.

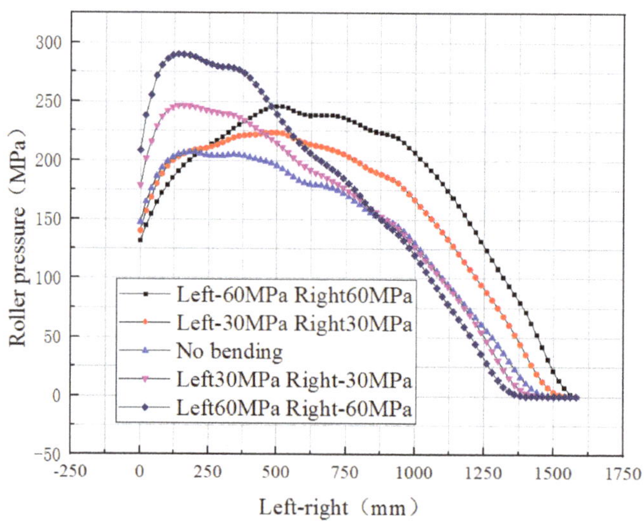

Figure 11. Horizontal distribution chart of inter-roller and support-roller pressures.

3.4. The Impact of Asymmetric Bending Force on the Thickness of the Steel Strip

An analysis of Figure 12 indicates that, in the absence of bending rolls, fluctuations in rolling forces at both ends of the mill result in a steel strip that is thinner on the left side compared to the right, with the center serving as the dividing line. This leads to a phenomenon where the thickness of the steel strip is greater on the right than on the left. As the non-symmetric bending force gradually increases, the change in thickness within 100 mm of the center remains relatively small, while significant changes occur on either side. Specifically, the thickness of the steel strip on the transmission side, influenced by positive bending rolls, increases, whereas the thickness on the operating side, affected by negative bending rolls, decreases. This results in a growing disparity in thickness between the two sides.

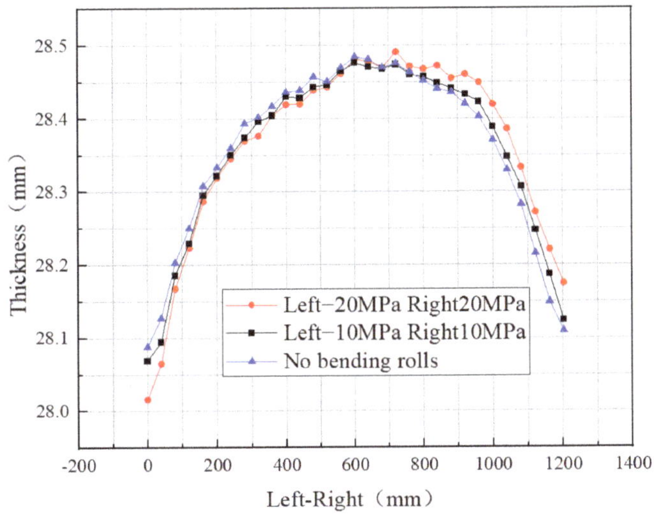

Figure 12. Strip transverse thickness distribution diagram with negative bending roll on the operating side and positive bending roll on the drive side.

This paper presents a set of simulation results that contrast with those depicted in Figure 12, where positive bending rolls are applied on the operating side, and negative bending rolls are applied on the transmission side. An analysis of Figure 13 reveals that when a positive bending roll of 10 MPa is applied on the operating side and a negative bending roll of 10 MPa is applied on the transmission side, the steel strip transitions from a left-thick, right-thin state to a relatively balanced thickness on both sides. However, as the non-symmetric bending force increases to 20 MPa, the steel strip once again exhibits a left-thick, right-thin trend. Therefore, when the phenomenon of unequal thickness on both sides of the steel strip occurs during the rolling process, a negative bending force can be applied to the thicker side, while a positive bending force of the same absolute value can be applied to the thinner side to address the issue of unbalanced shape.

3.5. The Impact of Asymmetric Bending Forces on the Crown and Edge Drop of the Steel Strip

As illustrated in Figure 12, the asymmetry of the bending force affecting the thickness of the steel strip results in significant differences in crown and edge drop between the operating and transmission sides of the strip. The calculation of crown and edge drop using the method of summing and averaging values from both sides does not accurately reflect the results. Therefore, it is essential to calculate the crown and edge drop of the steel strip on each side separately. For instance, the variation in thickness within 200 mm from the center of the steel strip on the operational side is relatively minor. However, beyond 300 mm from the center, the thickness of the metal strip decreases significantly, resulting in the formation of the edge thinning zone. Consequently, the difference between the thickness at the midpoint of the steel strip and the thickness 200 mm away from the center is defined as the steel strip's crown (C), while the difference between the thicknesses at 300 mm and 580 mm from the center is referred to as the steel strip's edge drop (*E*). The specific formulas for calculating the crown and edge drop of the steel strip are as follows:

$$C = h_i - h_j \tag{2}$$

In the formula, h_i is the thickness of the steel strip at its center, and h_j is the thickness of the metal strip 200 mm away from its center.

$$E = h_a - h_b \tag{3}$$

In the formula, h_a is the thickness of the metal strip 300 mm away from its center, and h_b is the thickness of the metal strip 580 mm away from its center.

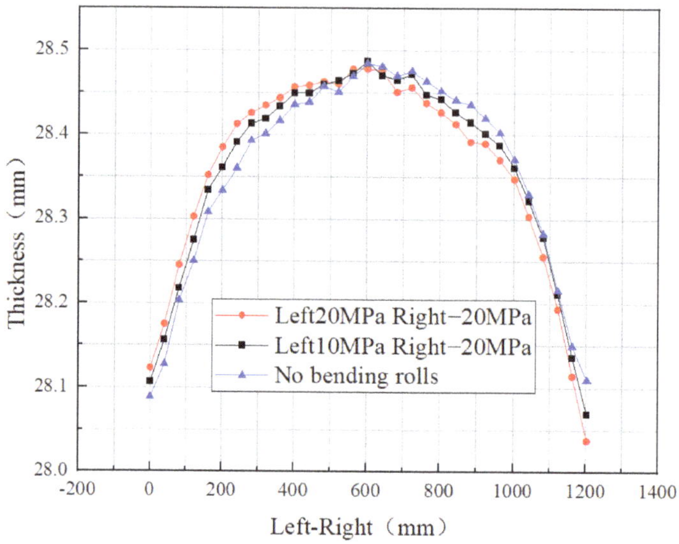

Figure 13. Strip transverse thickness distribution diagram with positive bending roll on the operating side and negative bending roll on the drive side.

As illustrated in Figure 14, both on the operational and transmission sides, the crown decreases with an increase in positive bending force and increases with an increase in negative bending force. Furthermore, there is a generally linear relationship between bending force and crown; adjusting the bending force by 1 MPa results in a change of 0.0009 mm in the crown of the metal strip. This text explains that when using asymmetric bending rolls to control the shape, applying force from the positive bending roll side helps reduce the crown of the metal strip and achieve better flatness. In contrast, using the negative bending roll side results in an increased crown and negatively impacts the flatness on one side of the metal strip. Analyzing Figure 15 reveals that the edge drop pattern on one side of the metal strip closely mirrors its crown change pattern; specifically, applying a positive bending force to one side alleviates the edge drop phenomenon while applying a negative bending force exacerbates it. Furthermore, the relationship between bending force and edge drop is linear; for every 1 MPa increase in bending force, there is a corresponding 0.001 mm change in edge drop. Therefore, when the edge drop phenomenon on one side of the metal strip is significant, the asymmetric bending force from a unilateral positive bending roll can be employed to regulate the shape.

3.6. The Impact of Asymmetric Bending Rolls on the Flatness of the Strip

The flatness of metal strips, also referred to as planarity, indicates the degree of arching before and after the rolling process. To analyze the impact of asymmetric bending rolls on the flatness of metal strips, this paper establishes the spatial coordinates along the width of the metal strips post-rolling. It translates all curve midpoints to a common point for a clearer comparison of the influence of non-symmetrical bending forces on metal strip flatness. In Figure 16, the variable X represents the coordinate of the metal strip along the width, while Y denotes the coordinate of the metal strip in the thickness direction, both measured in millimeters. Figure 16 illustrates the varying degrees of arching of the metal strip in the width direction under different conditions of non-symmetrical bending. Analyzing Figure 16 reveals that as the force of the asymmetric bending roll increases from 5 MPa to 20 MPa, the left end of the metal strip bends downward by approximately 0.0729 mm, while the right end bends upward by about 0.06076 mm. The nature of the shape defects in the metal strip gradually transitions from a near-sine wave to an edge wave. Consequently, the asymmetric bending role exerts a non-symmetrical control function over the shape. It can be inferred that when unilateral edge waves manifest in the metal strip, appropriate asymmetric bending forces can be employed to manage the transformation of the metal strip's shape from edge waves to sinusoidal waves. This shape can then be further adjusted through symmetric bending forces or other methods to correct the sinusoidal waves.

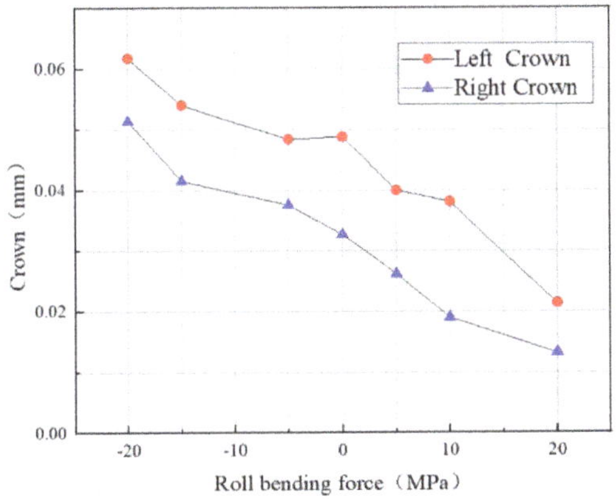

Figure 14. Bending force-crown diagram.

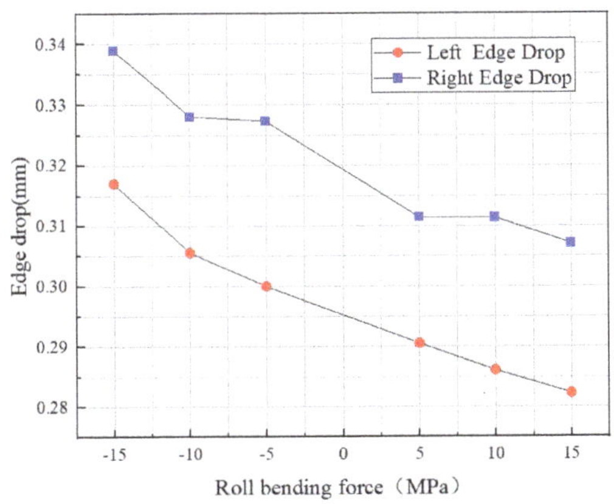

Figure 15. Roll bending force-edge drop diagram.

3.7. The Impact of Asymmetric Bending Forces on Their Controlling Effect

The coefficient of control effectiveness evaluates the ability of asymmetric bending forces to correct shape defects. The formula for the control effectiveness coefficient is as follows:

$$M = \frac{\Delta Y}{\Delta X} \tag{4}$$

In the formula, M represents the coefficient of control effectiveness, with units of mm/MPa; ΔY refers to the change in shape due to bending force adjustment; and ΔX refers to the adjustment quantity of bending force.

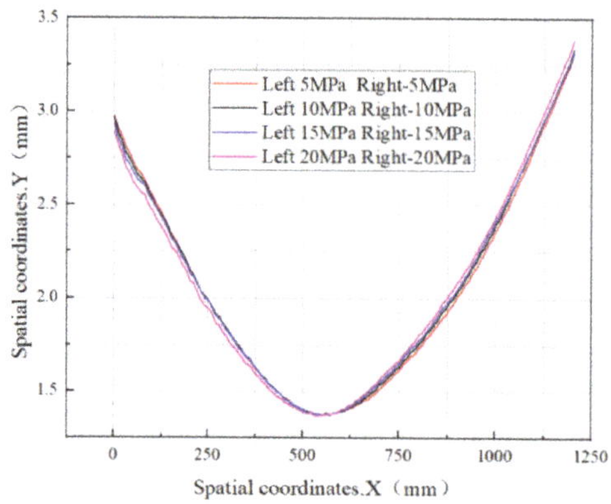

Figure 16. Metal strip flatness graph.

This article employs this formula as its foundation, selecting 121 points along the width of the steel strip. It calculates the coefficient of control effectiveness for non-symmetric bending at each point and analyzes the capacity of non-symmetric bending to regulate shape.

The function of bending roll adjustment is illustrated in Figure 17, where a negative bending roll force of 10 MPa is applied on the operating side, and a positive bending roll force of 10 MPa is applied on the transmission side. An analysis of Figure 16 reveals that the control effectiveness of bending rolls is significantly asymmetrical when non-symmetric bending forces are applied. The control effect on the edges of the strip is most pronounced, gradually decreasing as it moves toward the center of the strip, ultimately becoming zero at the horizontal axis of the strip. This indicates that asymmetric bending rolls can effectively control edge wave defects in strips without impacting their thickness.

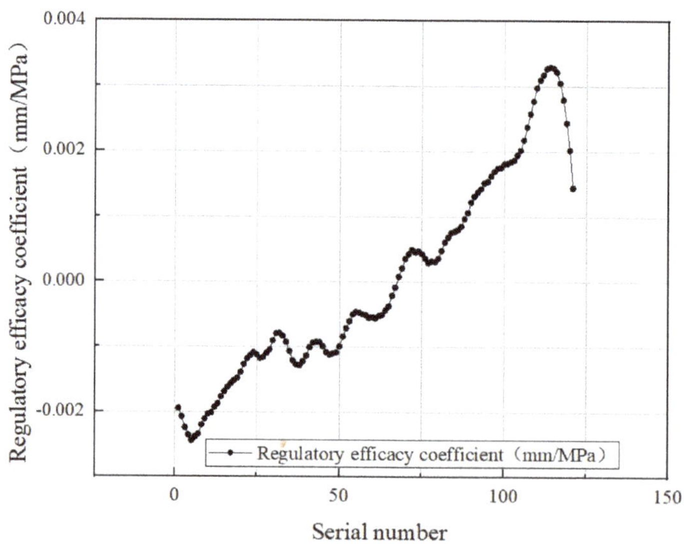

Figure 17. Diagram of regulatory efficacy of asymmetrical bending rolls.

To analyze the impact of the magnitude of asymmetric bending force on the control coefficient, this paper presents curves depicting the control coefficient at various magnitudes of asymmetric bending force. However, due to the instability of the rolling process, the curves of the control coefficient exhibit fluctuations of varying degrees. When these fluctuations are removed, the curves appear to be approximately linear. Consequently, this paper conducts linear fitting on the control coefficient curves. As illustrated in Figure 18, these are the fitted curves of the control coefficient at different non-symmetric bending forces. Analyzing Figure 18 reveals that the fitted curves of the control coefficient for different non-symmetric bending forces overlap significantly. The edge control efficiency coefficient for hot-rolled steel is approximately 0.002 mm/MPa, while the center control efficiency coefficient is roughly 0 mm/MPa. The greater the curvature slope, the larger the difference in shape control between the center and the edges, resulting in a higher effectiveness of bending roll force regulation. When the non-symmetric bending force is ±5 MPa, the slope of the curve is −0.000032; when the non-symmetric bending force is ±10 MPa, the slope of the curve is −0.000036; and when the non-symmetric bending force is ±20 MPa, the slope of the curve is −0.000038. This indicates that an appropriate increase in the non-symmetric bending force can enhance the control coefficient; however, the enhancement is minimal, and the control coefficients for different non-symmetric bending forces are quite similar.

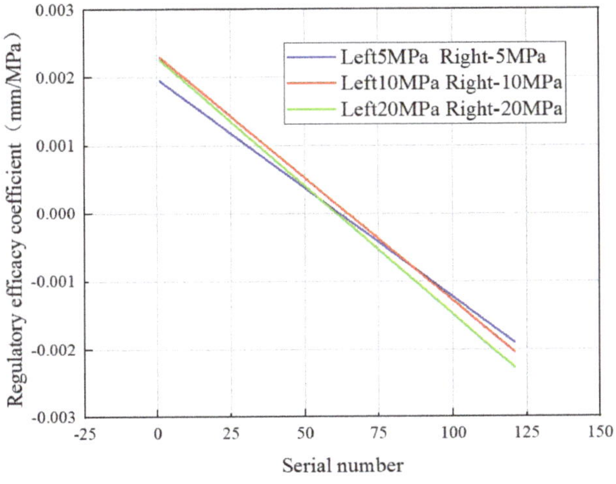

Figure 18. Fitting diagram of regulatory efficacy.

4. Conclusions

1. When steel strips are rolled using asymmetric bending rolls, the rolling pressure on the positive bending side is significantly reduced, while the rolling pressure on the negative bending side is slightly increased. This leads to non-uniform changes in strip thickness, with the thickness on the positive bending side increasing and the thickness on the negative bending side decreasing.
2. The shape of the rolled steel strip gradually transitions from a convex defect to a concave defect as the non-symmetrical bending force increases. Therefore, it can be concluded that when a unilateral concave shape defect occurs, an appropriate non-symmetrical bending force can be employed to correct the shape defect.
3. The inter-roller pressure in response to the non-symmetrical bending force exhibits an asymmetric change; specifically, the inter-roller pressure on the positive bending side increases while the inter-roller pressure on the negative bending side decreases.
4. During the rolling of steel strips using asymmetric bending rolls, the crown of the strips is influenced by the respective bending rolls, resulting in a linear relationship between the change in the crown and the change in bending force. The crown on the positive bending side flattens, while the crown on the negative bending side becomes more pronounced. The patterns of edge drop and crown variation in strips during asymmetric bending roll processing are similar. Additionally, edge drop changes and

bending forces are also linearly related. The occurrence of edge drop on the positive bending side is diminished, whereas it is intensified on the negative bending side.

5. The regulatory effect of asymmetric bending rolls on strip thickness varies linearly across the width of the strip, and the regulatory coefficients for different asymmetric bending rolls are generally consistent.

Author Contributions: Conceptualization, Z.Y.; methodology, Z.Y., S.P., Y.T. and W.C.; software, Z.Y., S.P., Y.T. and W.C.; validation, Z.Y., S.P., Y.T. and W.C.; formal analysis, Z.Y., S.P., Y.T. and W.C.; investigation, Z.Y., S.P., Y.T. and W.C.; resources, Z.Y.; data curation, Z.Y., S.P., Y.T. and W.C.; writing—original draft preparation, Z.Y., S.P., Y.T. and W.C.; writing—review and editing, Z.Y., S.P., Y.T. and W.C.; visualization, Z.Y., S.P., Y.T. and W.C.; supervision, Z.Y.; project administration, Z.Y.; funding acquisition, Z.Y. All authors have read and agreed to the published version of the manuscript.

Funding: This study is financially supported by the Natural Science Foundation General Program in Jiangsu Provincial of China (No.: BK20241965) and the Innovation Fund General Project of Nanjing Institute of Technology (No.: CKJB202209).

Data Availability Statement: The original contributions presented in the study are included in the article, further inquiries can be directed to the corresponding author.

Conflicts of Interest: The authors declare no conflict of interest.

References

1. Liu, Y.; Lin, D.; Zhao, X. Study on mechanical parameters and strip steering of aluminium alloy JP1235 under the influence of mill tilt. *Mod. Manuf. Eng.* **2008**, *12*, 62–65. [CrossRef]
2. Benke, M.; Schweitzer, B.; Hlavacs, A.; Mertinger, V. Prediction of Earing of Cross-Rolled Al Sheets from {h00} Pole Figures. *Metals* **2020**, *10*, 192. [CrossRef]
3. Li, W. Roll wear model and effect of work roll shifting on roll wear in hot srip mill. *J. Wuhan Inst. Technol.* **2013**, *36*, 98–103.
4. Zhang, J.S. The application status of aluminum strip and sheet cold rolling multi-stage cooling board shape control. *Technol. Sci. Technol. Wind* **2020**, *21*, 6+15. [CrossRef]
5. Sheng, Q.; Ren, P.J.; Fu, Q.K.; Dong, Y.Y.; Qu, X.D.; Wang, J. Research on the optimization of high-strength steel bending roller control process. *Metall. Equip.* **2023**, *S2*, 1–5+57.
6. Byon, S.M.; Roh, Y.H.; Yang, Z.R.; Lee, Y.S. A roll-bending approach to suppress the edge cracking of silicon steel in the cold rolling process. *Proc. Inst. Mech. Eng. Part B J. Eng. Manuf.* **2020**, *235*, 112–124. [CrossRef]
7. Stone, M.D.; Gray, R. Theory and practical aspects in crown control. *Iron Steel Eng.* **1965**, *8*, 73–90.
8. Shohet, K.N.; Townsend, N.A. Roll bending methods of crown control in four-high plate mills. *J. Iron Steel Inst.* **1968**, *11*, 1088–1098.
9. Fleck, N.; Johnson, K.; Mear, M.; Zhang, L.C. Cold rolling of foil. *Proc. Inst. Mech. Eng. Part B J. Eng. Manuf.* **1992**, *206*, 119–131. [CrossRef]
10. Kihara, J.; Peng, M.X. Application of BEM to Calculation of the Work Roll Deformation and Residual Stress in the Rolled Sheet. In *Boundary Elements VIII*; Tanaka, M., Brebbia, C.A., Eds.; Springer: Berlin/Heidelberg, Germany, 1968; Volume 8. [CrossRef]
11. Wang, Q.L.; Li, X.; Hu, Y.J.; Sun, J. Numerical analysis of intermediate roll shifting-induced rigidity characteristics of UCM cold rolling mill. *Steel Res. Int.* **2018**, *89*, 1700454. [CrossRef]
12. Montemayor-de la Garza, K.; Zambrano-Robledo, P.d.C.; Zapata-Hernandez, O.J.; Leduc-Lezama, L.A. Finite Element Modeling of Hot Rolling of 1075 Carbon Steel Process with Variable Cross Section. *Materials* **2023**, *16*, 2. [CrossRef]
13. Pondaven, C.; Erzar, B.; Spadaccini, A.; Grion, M. Finite element modeling evaluation of a void closure criterion using a multi-scale approach during hot rolling. *Metall. Ital.* **2023**, *5*, 36–41. [CrossRef]
14. Tian, B.; Kleber, S.; Turk, C.; Tolliner, S.; Schneller, S.; Markiewicz., P. Quantitative evaluation of relative sliding between billets and rolls in hot rolling. *Metall. Ital.* **2023**, *5*, 24–28. [CrossRef]
15. Linghu, K.Z.; Jiang, Z.Y.; Zhao, J.W.; Li, F. 3D FEM analysis of strip shape during multi-pass rolling in a 6-high CVC cold rolling mill. *Int. J. Adv. Manuf. Technol.* **2014**, *74*, 1733–1745. [CrossRef]
16. Shahani, A.R.; Setayeshi, S.; Nodamaie, S.A.; Asadi, M.A.; Rezaie, S. Prediction of influence parameters on the hot rolling process using finite element method and neural network. *J. Mater. Process Technol.* **2009**, *209*, 1920–1935. [CrossRef]
17. Wang, R.; Yang, Q.; He, A.; Shao, J.; Bian, H.T. Strip shape control capability of hot wide strip rolling mills. *J. Univ. Sci. Technol. Beijing Miner. Metall. Mater.* **2008**, *15*, 91–95. [CrossRef]
18. Li, Y.L.; Cao, J.G.; Qiu, L.; Kong, N.; He, A.; Zhou, Y.Z. Effect of strip edge temperature drop of electrical steel on profile and flatness during hot rolling process. *Adv. Mech. Eng.* **2019**, *11*, 1687814019840471. [CrossRef]

19. Yan, Z.W.; Bu, H.N.; Li, H.; Hong, L. Numerical simulation analysis of the rolling process based on the particle swarm hybrid algorithm. *Ironmak. Steelmak.* **2023**, *50*, 1321–1330. [CrossRef]
20. Sun, W.; Chen, L.; He, A.; Liu, C.; Yuan, T.H.; Qiang, Y. Study on quarter-wave control of DP980 steel based on a bending force linear combination strategy. *Int. J. Adv. Manuf. Technol.* **2023**, *127*, 2881–2892. [CrossRef]
21. Li, X.; Wang, Q.L.; Zhang, F.Y.; Zhang, Y.F. Present status and future prospects of strip flatness control based on elastic-plastic finite element. *Steel Roll.* **2020**, *37*, 1–11. [CrossRef]
22. Xie, H.B.; Xiao, H.; Zhang, G.M.; Liu, J.C. Analysison rolling pressure distribution of strip with different reductions by rxplicit dynamic FEM. *Gangtie Yanjiu Xuebao (J. Iron Steel Res.)* **2002**, *14*, 33–35.
23. Wang, P.; Yan, Z.; Li, X.; Zhang, D.H.; Duan, S.W. Edge drop control of cold rolled silicon steel strip based on model predictive control. *J. Manuf. Process.* **2022**, *82*, 88–95. [CrossRef]
24. Yu, H.L.; Liu, X.H.; Zhao, X.M.; Kusaba, Y. FEM analysis for V–H rolling process by updating geometric method. *J. Mater. Process Technol.* **2006**, *180*, 323–327. [CrossRef]
25. Pan, C.G.; Zhao, C.X.; Chang, Q.M.; Zhou, J.L.; Wu, Q. Three-dimensional metal particle flow simulation during the whole rolling process for 60 kg/m heavy rail. *Adv. Mech. Eng.* **2017**, *9*, 1–19. [CrossRef]
26. Wang, Q.L.; Sun, J.; Li, X.; Wang, Z.H.; Wang, P.F.; Zhang, D.H. Analysis of lateral metal flow induced flatness deviations of rolled steel strip: Mathematical modeling and simulation experiments. *Appl. Math. Model.* **2020**, *77*, 289–308. [CrossRef]
27. Kapil, S.; Eberhard, P.; Dwivedy, S.K. Dynamic Analysis of Cold-Rolling Process Using the Finite-Element Method. *J. Manuf. Sci. Eng.-Trans. Asme* **2016**, *138*, 041002. [CrossRef]
28. Dasari, S.K.; Ganguly, S. Implementation of Experimental Static Recrystallization of High Strength Steel into Computational Simulation of Multi-pass Slab Hot Rolling. *Met. Mater. Int.* **2023**, *29*, 3340–3355. [CrossRef]
29. Sabar, S.K.; Patel, R.K.; Ghosh, S.K. Roll force prediction by combined FEM and ANN in the hot rolling process under nano-lubrication condition. *Int. J. Adv. Manuf. Technol.* **2024**, *134*, 3893–3904. [CrossRef]
30. Ji, Z.M.; Sun, K. Analysis and application of the work roll bending control system. *Shanxi Metall.* **2022**, *45*, 139–141. [CrossRef]
31. Jiang, X.Y.; Kang, Z.Q.; Li, Z.F.; Ma, Y.L. Analysis about the influence of bending roll force on plate shape of cold rolled sheet. *Inn. Mong. Sci. Technol. Univ. J.* **2013**, *32*, 148–151. [CrossRef]
32. Peng, W.J.; Peng, S.B.; Li, M.G.; Xu, H.; Liu, D. Effect of bending force and roll-shift on strip shape. *Wuhan Inst. Eng. J.* **2020**, *42*, 351–354. [CrossRef]
33. Zhang, Z.Q.; Li, H.J.; Huang, Q.X.; Jia, Z.H. The finite element analysis on the impact of bending force on the flatness of strips. *Shanxi Metall.* **2012**, *35*, 8–10+53. [CrossRef]
34. Zhang, G.Q. *The Simulation Study on the Influence of Cold Rolling Hydraulic Bending Force on the Board Shape*; Liaoning Technical University: Fuxin, China, 2008.
35. Shi, X.; Liu, X.H.; Wang, G.D.; Li, Q.S.; Xu, J.Y. FEM Analysis of Effect of Bending Force on the Crown of Strip. *Steel Roll.* **2006**, *3*, 10–13. [CrossRef]
36. Ma, C.; Zhang, G.Q.; Zhao, D.H.; He, T.Q.; Shang, R. Studies on Numerical Simulation of the Inflections of Bending Force for Strip Profile in Cold Rolling. *Angang Technol.* **2009**, *5*, 36–40.
37. Liu, B.Q.; Zhang, H.; Wang, Z.D.; Wang, J.S.; Zhang, Y. Theoretical research and application of the asymmetrical bending of work rolls for shape control in a cold rolling mill. *J. Beijing Technol. Bus. Univ.* **2012**, *34*, 184–189. [CrossRef]
38. Hu, D.Z.; Han, W.; Guo, R.; Li, Y.J. The influence of the bending roller mechanism of the heavy plate leveller on the stress of the rollers. *Metall. Equip.* **2024**, *2*, 53–56+41.
39. Liu, J.W.; Wen, J.G.; Wang, Y.; Zhang, L.; Sun, X.L. FEM analysis for asymmetric bending roll of roll process in hour-high mill. In Proceedings of the Ninth Chinese Metallurgical Society Young Academic Conference, Beijing, China, 15–17 October 2018; The Chinese Society for Metals: Beijing, China, 2018; pp. 378–380. [CrossRef]
40. Liu, S.L.; Li, T.T.; Li, R.F.; Qi, K.; Liu, Z.G. A comparative study of microstructure and corrosion resistance in DP980 steel joints under different laser welding method. *J. Mater. Res. Technol.* **2023**, *27*, 3870–3880. [CrossRef]
41. Duan, T.T. *Special Properties Analysis of Shape Control for HC Mill Based on Asymmetrical Shifting and Bending Force*; Yanshan University: Qinhuangdao, China, 2010.
42. *DIN EN ISO 683-1:2018*; Heat-Treatable Steels, Alloy Steels and Free-Cutting Steels. European Committee for Standardization: Brussels, Belgium, 2018.
43. Plessier, A.; Del Pino, S.; Després, B. Implicit discretization of Lagrangian gas dynamics. *Esaim-Math. Model. Numer. Anal.* **2023**, *57*, 717–743. [CrossRef]
44. Namadchi, A.H.; Alamatian, J. Explicit dynamic analysis using Dynamic Relaxation method. *Comput. Struct.* **2016**, *175*, 91–99. [CrossRef]
45. Liu, J.X.; Han, J.T.; Zhang, Y.J. Research status of high speed steel for rolls. *Mater. Rep.* **2009**, *23*, 74–77.
46. Xian, D.X.; Zheng, X.Z.; Xu, H.Q.; Zhang, A.M.; Song, R.G.; Tang, L.D.; Wang, F.X.; Cheng, Y. The development of Q345B hot-rolled steel plates with improved performance. *Shandong Metall.* **2004**, *1*, 189–191. [CrossRef]
47. Shu, C.; Cheng, L.; Xu, Y. Parameter estimation of Johnson-Cook constitutive model. *Chin. J. Nonferrous Met.* **2020**, *30*, 1073–1083.

48. Singh, G.; Singh, P.K. Hot profiled rolling of C40 steel: Production variable's effect on rolling performance. *Mater. Manuf. Process.* **2023**, *39*, 871–891. [CrossRef]
49. Dong, F.; Germain, G. Determining the Johnson-Cook Constitutive Equation Material Parameters via Finite Element Analysis Method. *J. Shanghai Jiao Tong Univ.* **2011**, *45*, 1657–1660+1667. [CrossRef]

MDPI AG
Grosspeteranlage 5
4052 Basel
Switzerland
Tel.: +41 61 683 77 34

Metals Editorial Office
E-mail: metals@mdpi.com
www.mdpi.com/journal/metals

www.ingramcontent.com/pod-product-compliance
Lightning Source LLC
Chambersburg PA
CBHW040809250926
51850CB00007BA/1119
* 9 7 8 3 7 2 5 8 6 9 4 8 0 *